Jesuit Studies

Contributions to the arts and sciences

by members of the Society of Jesus

Jesuit Studies

The Churches and the Schools
FRANCIS X. CURRAN

Deception in Elizabethan Comedy
JOHN V. CURRY

Bishop Lancelot Andrewes
MAURICE F. REIDY

Master Alcuin, Liturgist
GERALD ELLARD

Theodore Dwight Woolsey
GEORGE A. KING

The Praise of Wisdom
EDWARD L. SURTZ

The Wagner Housing Act
TIMOTHY L. McDONNELL

The Honor of Being a Man
EDWARD GANNON

The Presidential Election of 1880
HERBERT J. CLANCY

Work and Education
JOHN W. DONOHUE

JESUIT STUDIES

Northern Parish

A SOCIOLOGICAL AND PASTORAL STUDY

Joseph B. Schuyler, s.j.

LOYOLA UNIVERSITY PRESS

Chicago, 1960   4074

IMPRIMI POTEST: Thomas E. Henneberry
Provincial of the New York Province
October 28, 1959

IMPRIMATUR: ✠ Albert Cardinal Meyer
Archbishop of Chicago
December 21, 1959

Dedicated

WITH GRATEFUL ESTEEM TO

MY MOTHER AND FATHER

Toward the end of his *Ars poetica* Horace advises a writer to hide his work in a drawer for nine years before publication. However, the timeliness of a parish study in this embryonic era of its development convinces me that nine years from now this study of NORTHERN PARISH no longer may serve the purpose for which it was intended. In the decision to publish now I am encouraged by one of the wise paradoxes of the late G. K. Chesterton: "Anything worth doing well is worth doing half well."

Development of a new field of science, whether it be physical or social, requires the collation of much data before even limited hypotheses can be tested and confirmed as trustworthy theories. Parish sociology has been developing in recent years, though our pace in America has been slower than that of our European confreres. In this country we have already welcomed the works of Brother Gerald Schnepp, S.M., Brother Augustine McCaffrey, F.S.C., Father George Kelly of New York, Professor Joseph Nuesse and Father Thomas Harte, C.SS.R., of the Catholic University of America, and especially the very noteworthy work of Father Joseph Fichter, S.J., of New Orleans. The latter's *Southern Parish* and *Social Relations in the Urban Parish* have perhaps been most responsible in recent years for arousing both scientific and pastoral interest in systematic parish study. The present study, NORTHERN PARISH, is intended as a contribution to this same field.

One of the serious difficulties in this field is the necessity of appealing to, and satisfying, two very different groups of readers—the academic sociologist, who is frequently a novice in pastoral matters, and those active in the apostolate, both clergy and laity, who are not usually very patient with social science's approach to and method of communicating knowledge. In many instances what will interest one group holds no charm for the other. One solution to the problem would be to write two different books. I am hopeful, however, that the social scientists will find in NORTHERN PARISH some insight into the functioning of one type of social system, the Catholic parish; and that priests and laymen who are interested in a parish apostolate will find in this study some helpful suggestions toward achieving a more adequate knowledge of parochial society and an increasingly effective pastoral policy.

Both the academic sociologist and the zealous priest or laymen concerned more with what is happening than with the reasons for the fact that it does happen will be interested in such problems as those described by Canon Boulard in his recent studies of religious practice in France. The interest of those belonging to one or the other of these two groups may be prompted by somewhat different reasons, or by different aspects of the same reason, yet in both cases the interest may be equally great.

A very summary account of the studies of Canon Boulard will be found in footnote 8, pages 3-4. The results of numerous other studies are presented in Appendix I. The cumulative effect of all these investigations is to focus attention upon the existence of problems—perhaps of unsuspected and startling problems—that urgently call for solution.

Why is it that within the same geographical area the same Christianity under the leadership of the same priests is practiced in different degrees by different occupational groups? Why is it that French vocations to the priesthood, for example, are consistently more numerous in some geographical and social milieu than in others? Perhaps it is true that religious life is partially caused and therefore partially explained by natural social factors. To that extent religious institutions, as well as their impact upon society and the impact of society upon them, can be studied by sociologists with the same scientific methods that they use to study other aspects of social life.

The present sociological study of a Catholic parish does not aim to do more than suggest possible reasons for various uniformities and divergencies in religious practice. There is at the present time a dearth of the knowledge that would be necessary were one to seek to do more than ascertain what does exist and offer tentative reasons for the fact of its existence. Final answers to numerous questions must await further research. If this work, however, provides the sociologist with a deeper insight into the little-analyzed field of the Catholic parish, and if the priest and the interested layman derive from the study some appreciation of the value of visualizing the Catholic parish scientifically as a social unit, our purpose in undertaking the study will have been achieved.

Another problem of presentation is that of length. Readers will remember that Father Fichter's study of *Southern Parish* was projected on a four-volume basis. However, since the chief objective of NORTHERN PARISH is to explore the benefits to be achieved from a parish study and the proper methodological approach, the subject matter has been limited, as far as feasible, to relevant essentials. In the interest of conciseness and readability much of the original text of Chapters 1-6 has been dropped to footnotes. Since a great amount of that material is very pertinent to our study, it is my hope that the more serious and interested readers will not overlook it.

One further aspect of NORTHERN PARISH should be explained. It is my conviction that, both scientifically and pastorally, we must first be concerned with what actually exists before we can do much about what should exist. In other words, a parish study should first concern itself with persons associated with the parish before being critical of the percentage of persons not associated with the parish. If 70 per cent of the parish are faithful to religious observance, it seems that both social scientist and pastor must recognize this as a more obvious characteristic of the parish than the fact that 30 per cent of the parish members do not practice their religion. The emphasis in NORTH-ERN PARISH is on the positive side—on what the parish is rather than what it is not. The positive and the negative are of course two sides of the same coin. But attention to the negative can come later, for many good reasons: scientific, psychological, and pedagogical.

Thanks are due to the *American Catholic Sociological Review, Apostolate,* and the *Catholic Management Journal* for permission to use in this book selections of articles which I first published in their pages. For help in the completion of this study of NORTHERN PARISH I acknowledge my gratitude above all to the Right Reverend Monsignor Patrick A. O'Leary, pastor of Our Lady of Mercy Parish in the Bronx in New York City. He not only graciously permitted, aided, and encouraged the study, but also contributed a grant of almost three thousand dollars to finance its execution. A deep debt of gratitude is due also to his reverend assistants, Fathers John Conlon, William Brady, Thomas McNulty, James Griffin, and Brian Kelly, the priests of OLM, for their help and guidance in the parish census; to the lay staff and members of the parish for consistent cooperation; to the members of the Legion of Mary of OLM; to the author's Jesuit superiors, to Loyola Seminary, and to Fordham University for making available the necessary time and funds; to his colleagues in the Fordham University Sociological Research Laboratory, particularly Doctor Frank Santopolo and Father Joseph Scheuer, C.PP.S., and several laboratory assistants; to Professors Nicholas Timasheff, Thomas O'Dea,

William Frasca, and fellow Jesuits Joseph Fitzpatrick and J. Franklin Ewing for their guidance and criticism; to Father Joseph Fichter, S.J., for fraternally given and professionally competent criticism; to Brother Edward Moran, S.J., Brother James Kenny, S.J., and his staff, and to several of the author's students for their help in various technical matters and the making of charts and maps; to Mr. Edwin B. Simmons for typing and constructive assistance; to Mr. Charles Benda for typing the final draft; and in a special way to my parents, Mr. and Mrs. Joseph B. Schuyler, for their untiring assistance in sorting and recording research data and typing several drafts of the manuscript while the work was in progress.

J. B. S.

COLLEGE OF PHILOSOPHY AND LETTERS
    FORDHAM UNIVERSITY
LOYOLA SEMINARY
Shrub Oak, New York
August 9, 1959
Feast of Saint John Mary Vianney,
    Parish Priest of Ars

CONTENTS

---

xvii

xix

CHAPTER I

Sociology
and the Parish

Recently at a dinner a highly respected colleague praised the work being done in the university's Sociological Research Laboratory. "But," he insisted, "you'll never get anywhere by applying statistics to religion. Religion involves a supernatural relationship between man and his God; modern science can't understand it and can't help to improve it." In a similar vein an influential French writer, Father Rouquette, after asking whether certain sociologists were not trying to construct a new scientific type of pastoral, said:

> Doesn't such a pastoral run the risk of forgetting the absolutely essential primacy of grace in conversion, the initiative of the Holy Spirit, the incomparable importance of supernatural means such as intercessory prayer, sacraments, and so on? St. Paul, that peerless master of spreading the gospel, does not seem to have given up his clever way of discoursing at Lystra and Athens in preaching "in season and out of season" Jesus Christ and Jesus Christ crucified.[1]

This attitude is shared widely by many who are convinced that religion and science belong to two mutually exclusive categories, and can have little to do with each other.

---

[1] Quoted by Simon Ligier in *L'adulte des milieux ouvriers. Volume 2, Essai de psychologie pastorale*, p. 27. Paris: Editions Ouvrières, 1951.

And yet Cardinal Feltin of Paris wrote very clearly to the author of a study on French vocations: "But above all you have proved, with a multitude of facts to support it, that the number of vocations [to the priesthood] depends directly on the sociological milieu."[2] Other renowned members of the hierarchy have given enthusiastic approval to sociological studies of religious realities: Cardinal Liénart, the late Cardinal Suhard, Cardinal Lercaro.[3] Pope Pius XII on several occasions, and most clearly in his 1955 address to the pastors and lenten preachers of Rome, emphasized the value and need of a scientific collation and interpretation of pastoral data.[4] In the French Canadian Semaines Sociales of 1953, Father Archambault cited both the pope and a series of articles in the *Osservatore Romano* on the importance of statistical analysis of religious activity, and he himself explained the need of seeking and recognizing social uniformities connected with religious practice.[5]

The fact is that there are many responsible persons, in both scientific and religious fields, who remain oblivious to the theo-

---

[2] In his prefatory letter to Fernand Boulard's *Essor ou declin du clergé français?* p. 6. Paris: Editions du Cerf, 1950.

[3] For Cardinal Liénart see *Structures sociales et pastorale paroissiale* (proceedings of the National Congress of Lille for 1948), p. 2 (Paris: Union des Oeuvres Catholiques de France, 1948). For Cardinal Suhard see his prefatory letter to Fernand Boulard's *Problèmes missionaires de la France rurale*, Vol. 1, pp. 1-3 (Paris: Editions du Cerf, 1945). For Cardinal Lercaro see his remarks at the First Italian Congress of Religious Sociology, Milan, March 10-11, 1954, partially quoted in *Actualité religieuse dans le monde*, no. 32, July 15, 1954, pp. 15-16. Cardinal Delay also made favorable remarks in his preface in Lucien Gros's *La pratique religieuse dans le diocèse de Marseille*, pp. 7-9 (Paris: Editions Ouvrières, 1954).

[4] See the NCWC News Service translation under date of March 18, 1955. In one of his most pertinent remarks, just after he had demanded that pastors diligently and accurately learn the facts of religious practice, his holiness said: "Having determined the figures, it is necessary to study their significance, in order to understand the causes of some defections or some returns. Merely to discover an evil is not enough for the diagnosis, without which one cannot speak of a right prognosis and even less of adequate treatment."

[5] *La paroisse: cellule sociale*, p. 20. Montreal: Institut Social Populaire, 1953.

retical and practical implications of studying religious phenomena scientifically,[6] and that nevertheless there have been in
recent years a spreading growth of such study and a deepening
appreciation of its value. Our next chapter will review the origin, background, and achievements of these studies in religious
sociology. These developments have been by no means limited
to Catholic circles, though our own study here will not include
the fine researches carried out by other religious bodies.

Two types of readers have been kept in mind in these pages:
the academic sociologist and the religious leader, both priest
and layman. Each would be interested, for different aspects of
the same reason, in such problems as those described by Canon
Boulard in his recent researches in religious practice in France.[7]
Why is it that within the same geographical area the same Christianity under the leadership of the same priests is practiced in
different degrees by different occupational groups? Why is it
that French vocations to the priesthood are consistently more
numerous in certain geographical and social milieu than in others? Perhaps there is some value to Cardinal Feltin's observation. Perhaps it is true that religious life is partially caused and
therefore partially explained by natural social factors. To that
extent religious institutions, as well as their impact on society
and society's on them, can be studied in sociology with the same
scientific methods which it uses to study other aspects of social
life.[8] The present sociological study of a Catholic parish does
not aim to explain the reasons for different uniformities in reli-

---

[6] See the introductory chapter, "Religion and Social Science," in Father Joseph H.
    Fichter's *Social Relations in the Urban Parish* (Chicago: The University of
    Chicago Press, 1954).

[7] Two of the most prominent and significant are those already cited in footnotes
    2 and 3 above. Further discussion on this matter is found in Chapter 2.

[8] Fichter, *Urban Parish*, p. 1. It seems well to discuss further here the question
    whether a sociology of religious manifestation, so obviously connected with
    divine inspiration and grace, is at all possible. It is difficult enough, certainly,
    to deal with merely free human acts in the social sciences. But what of free

gious practice. That would be pretentious indeed, for there is still a great dearth of necessary knowledge. If these chapters, however, provide the sociologist with a deeper entree into the little-analyzed field of the Catholic parish,[9] and if the priest and interested layman derive from them some appreciation of the value of visualizing the Catholic parish scientifically as a social unit, our purpose will have been achieved.

What is sociology? And what is religious sociology?[10] Man's life in society is the object of several human sciences: politics,

----

acts influenced by divine grace? How can human science ever measure and describe the extent of divine influence? The answer is very simple: it can't. But the difficulty is not limited to religious manifestation. That is no less apart from God's interest than any other human act—an act of crime, a choice of vocation, an act of public service. Therefore the objection is no more or less valid against religious sociology than against any other social science. God is author of the natural as well as the supernatural order! On the other hand, Cardinal Feltin spoke of vocations as "depending directly on the sociological laws of the milieu." Father Fernand Boulard states in a very striking passage, several times quoted, that a man walking across France from Brest to Strasbourg could find in the first part of his trip, to Angers, that every inhabitant makes his Easter duty, on the second part, from Angers to Nancy, that hardly any inhabitant does make it, and on the last part, from Nancy to Strasbourg, that almost everyone does make it (*Premiers itinéraires en sociologie religieuse*, pp. 29-30. Paris: Editions Ouvrières—Economie et Humanisme, 1954). Perhaps God's grace is the sole cause of such differentiation, but more probably God waits for Apollo and Paul to plant and water before He Himself grants the grace and increase. We must also remember the lesson taught in the Parable of the Sower who sowed seed that fell on different types of ground. All receive the opportunity, some lose it, some have it taken away, and some make use of it. Not everything depends on environment and social pressures. Whenever we try to explain the religiously nonobservant, we have also to keep in mind that many in the same circumstances are observant. This recalls the critical issue in all sciences of free human beings. Nature and nurture, or heredity and environment: how much do they contribute to character and personality? How much comes from the individual's free development, from divine grace? All sociology can do is establish relationships between conduct and social factors of influence.

[9] Chapter 2 discusses studies that have been conducted in this field.

[10] Sometimes a distinction is attempted between religious sociology and the sociology of religion. There need not be any, though some consider that the adjectival form implies a particular pragmatic motive or a particularistic orientation. The French seem to use both terms equivalently.

economics, anthropology, ethnology, and many others. Sociology is the science which studies the social relationship, of whatever kind (political, economic, domestic, and so forth), in itself. How has the particular social relationship originated? What type is it? What causes its development or dissolution? What are the purposes for which it exists? What are its functions, and those of its members? What are its general and particular characteristics? What draws its members closer together in cooperative interaction; what drives them apart into mutual unconcern or opposition? To what extent is one social relationship like or unlike another? Science, whether social or physical, seeks to recognize likenesses, or uniformities, or classes, so that conclusions reached about one unit in the class can be applied, *mutatis mutandis*, to other units in the same class. The pull of gravity affects all units of weight; self-government is restricted in all dictatorial regimes; every social organization has a common standard of (at least some) values.

Some social organizations have a religious purpose—a synagogue, a church society, a religious order, a sect. And just as social organizations with political, or economic, or recreational purposes are studied by the sociologist in political sociology, economic sociology, and so forth, so can the religious organizations be studied sociologically insofar as they are social. We might understand religious sociology as the study of social phenomena within or connected with religion.[11] Since the Catholic

---

[11] See G. Mensching, *Sociologie religieuse: Le rôle de la religion dans les relations communautaires des humains,* pp. 7-18, a French translation by Pierre Jundt (Paris: Payot, 1951). See also the contributions of Thomas O'Dea, "The Sociology of Religion," *American Catholic Sociological Review* 15:73-103, June 1954 and John Donovan, "American Catholic Sociologists and the Sociology of Religion," *ibid.* 15:104-14, June 1954. The earliest sociologists of religion, such as Durkheim, Frazer, and Kautsky, were rather historians of comparative religion, usually with a deterministic bias. Their respective schools have little significance in the current development of religious sociology, as Mensching points out.

parish is a functioning, widespread form of religious social life, it provides us with an important object of study: important to the sociologist because it is another kind of society on which to test his sociological theories, and to the priest and lay leader because adequate knowledge is an essential precondition to effective policy. That phase of religious sociology which is concerned with the parish we designate simply as parish sociology.

The significance of religious sociology for understanding human life and society should be clear. Joachim Wach, who has delineated the developments in religious sociology so succinctly,[12] has pointed to the importance of religion as an integrating factor of human society. Philosophies of life, value systems, national and international unities, wars and revolutions, have flowed from religious sources. Many public institutions and customs—holidays, symbols, edifices and monuments, international conventions and local bus schedules, educational systems and neighborhood fiestas—derive from religion. On the other hand, the origin of many religious sects has been motivated by social conditions, and all religions, great or small, true or not true, have been affected more or less by them.[13]

Father Fichter has written two superb essays on the mutual worth of social science and religion.[14] Fundamentally his point is that both need each other: religion, in its quest to win and

---

[12] See Joachim Wach's chapter on "Sociology of Religion" in Georges Gurvitch and Wilbert Moore, editors, *Twentieth Century Sociology* (New York: The Philosophical Library, 1945).

[13] See Joachim Wach's *Sociology of Religion* (Chicago: The University of Chicago Press, 1944) and J. Milton Yinger's *Religion in the Struggle for Power: A Study in the Sociology of Religion* (Durham: The Duke University Press, 1946). Yinger's attempt to prove a thesis sometimes leads him to say more than can be substantiated and to omit contrary evidence, but his analysis of the impact of society on religious thought and conduct is very helpful. His newest book, *Religion, Society and the Individual* (New York: The Macmillan Company, 1957) is a superb contribution.

[14] Fichter, *Urban Parish*, the introductory chapter on "Religion and Social Science" and "Utility of Social Science for Religion" in the Appendix.

hold man's acceptance, must make use of social knowledge, just as the Church has so often adapted, sooner or later, to local culture and conditions; and social science, in its search for truth, needs the help of religion because so much of social reality is so closely interwoven with religion. Over 45,000,000 Americans are Catholics,[15] almost one fourth of the entire nation. Aside from religion's being the national asset which it is,[16] it must be impossible to understand the American social structure without weighing the impact of those 45,000,000 religious adherents on American customs, morals, and values.[17]

---

[15] This is a somewhat arbitrary figure. The *Official Catholic Directory* for 1958 gives a total Catholic population of 36,023,977. Yet the Bureau of Census of the Department of Commerce estimated, from a survey conducted in March of 1957, that Catholics number nearly 44,000,000. This number applies only to those who profess themselves to be Catholic, not to the uncounted millions who no longer profess the faith. The higher figure is confirmed by two diocese-wide censuses conducted recently. In March 1958 the Archdiocese of Washington found that it had 281,000 professed Catholics, about 50,000 more than had been officially recorded; in the fall of 1957 the dioceses comprising the state of Wisconsin conducted their own census, which showed their Catholic population to number nearly 40 per cent of the state's population instead of the officially recorded 32 per cent. Furthermore, a comparison of Catholic infant baptisms with total United States live births over the last twenty years shows that over 25 per cent of all American babies born over the past two decades have been baptized Catholics. (See Bernard Mulvaney, "Catholic Population Revealed in Catholic Baptisms," *American Ecclesiastical Review* 133:183-93, September 1955.) In 1954, 29 per cent (1,161,304) of all babies born in the United States (4,021,000) were baptized Catholics. By 1957 the proportion rose to just over 30 per cent (1,284,534 out of 4,254,000). The baptismal figures may be considered accurate, for pastors are strictly bound to keep and transmit baptismal records. For further comment see Chapter 4, footnote 9.

[16] See a statement issued on November 15, 1952 by the American Catholic Hierarchy, "Religion: Our Most Vital National Asset," *Catholic Mind* 51:56-64, January 1953.

[17] Note that most of those 45,000,000 Catholics live in cities, areas of more or less dense population concentration. Religious leaders, whether priests or lay apostles, cannot hope to understand their people, their difficulties, their needs, their aspirations, the competition for their loyalty, without recognizing the influence of the urban milieu in which they live. As a matter of fact, several of the recent initial French studies in parish sociology simply add an analysis of the parish religious life to a sociological survey of the parish neighborhood.

Despite the indifference of the many which is always with us and the rear-guard action of some who remain convinced that religion and science should have little in common except mutual forbearance, there has developed in recent years a promising infancy of Catholic interest in religious sociology. But the journey from infancy to man's estate is a long one indeed. The more quickly we can concern ourselves with knowing the facts and the more surely we adopt a scientific approach to that knowledge, the sooner will maturity arrive.[18]

France and other European countries have taken the lead in sociological research of religious life because their religious situation cried desperately for such an instrument.[19] As a result

---

[18] See Joseph P. Fitzpatrick, "Catholics and Scientific Knowledge of Society," *American Catholic Sociological Review* 15:2-8, March 1954; also his "Catholic Responsibilities in Sociology," *Thought* 26:384-96, Autumn 1951.

[19] See R. Mols, "Croissance et limites de la sociologie religieuse," *Nouvelle revue théologique* 77:144-62, 263-81, February, March 1955. This is as fine a summary of the history of practical religious sociology and of the objections which still beset it as can be found in brief form.

Hindsight, always easier than foresight, shows the extent to which lack of clear-sighted awareness of social conditions can result in tragedy. The absence of Catholic life in parts of France, as contrasted with other French regions where the faith runs deep and is devoutly practiced, is a fact both clear and tragic. Though the Belgian Adolphe Quételet (1796-1874) was showing for the first time in the last century how useful a tool statistics could be in the observance and assessment of social phenomena, precisely when migration to industrial centers was depopulating thousands of rural parishes and overcrowding urban ones, little attention was paid to this growing process of unbalance, and nothing was done about it. Because of this lack of enlightened adaptation a situation arose and remained wherein devitalized "rotten parishes," to adapt a phrase from England's "rotten boroughs," had the use of many priests, the greater part of whose flocks had wandered to city dwellings where the shepherds were not enough to care for them. Cardinal Suhard, archbishop of Paris during the early 1940's, was shocked to sleeplessness on reading a report of France's dechristianization and instituted many attempts to meet the situation. He believed strongly that his people should know the facts of their own diocesan and parish life—facts ascertained through careful study. See *The Church Today: The Collected Writings of Emmanuel Cardinal Suhard*, p. 17 (Chicago: Fides Publishers, 1953). In a foreword by Sally Whelan Cassidy mention is made of his eminence's shocked reaction to Abbé Godin's *La France, pays de mission?*

new institutions have been formed, such as Mission de France, which recently, after a period of trial, received official approval and standing through the promulgation on August 15, 1954 of the apostolic constitution *Omnium ecclesiarum.*[20] Our own situation is certainly not desperate; on the contrary it appears to be strong, vital, and growing. But there are weak spots, some of them serious. Nor do we know how extensive they are.[21] Since any society's policy must depend largely on its knowledge of itself, certainly the Church in America can make use of social science in knowing itself better.

The first area of research must certainly be the parish. It is the unit of the Church's organization, the member of the body. It is limited enough to be studied conveniently and universal enough to be everywhere available. Its importance is such that on its vitality depend the health and vigor of the diocese and the whole Church. Knowledge of a diocese presumes knowledge of the parish. And it is on the parish level that the flock is in closest touch with its shepherd and, for the most part, manifests its religious life. Through the parish, too, the Catholic is related in so many ways with the universal Church. As Cardinal Suhard put it:

> Do you realize, my friends, what a great appreciation a bishop or archbishop has for the life of his parishes? First because his diocese is as good as the parishes which comprise it, and also because he knows . . . that it is on the hierarchical level of the parish that the essential part of the work is accomplished. . . . It is in the parish that memberships of souls in the Church occur, it is there that people receive their spiritual life, there that they are formed as Christians, there that the Church is really built.[22]

---

[20] For full text and commentary see *Actualité religieuse dans le monde*, no. 38, October 15, 1954, pp. 13-23.

[21] If we can err by 25 per cent in estimates of our Catholic population, any assessment of religious observance must be uncertain.

[22] *Structures sociales*, p. 88.

Two qualifications should be interposed here, particularly for the benefit of the reader less acquainted with Catholic and parish life. First, despite the great uniformity in basic structure which characterizes all Catholic parishes—priest and people, church and territory, a cycle of feasts, the administration of the sacraments, and so on—there are many different kinds of parishes. The relationship between priest and people, between the people themselves, and between parish and neighborhood community is different in urban and rural parishes.[23] A small university town will present to the parish one type of people to be served, a rail terminal another, and a newly founded community of young families a third. The point is, one must treat with extreme caution the term "typical parish," unless the "type" being discussed is clearly understood.

The second qualification is the fact that the parish, though primary, is not the only organ of Catholic vitality. The directory of almost any city-concentrated diocese contains several columns of organizations that meet the problems of, and supply services for, the whole diocese. Some operate on a nationwide basis. One thinks readily of such organs of apostolate as the supraparochial school systems—high schools, colleges, and universities; various diocesan organizations, Newman clubs on non-Catholic campuses, hospitals, labor schools, Catholic Charities, Cana and Pre-Cana conferences, the various divisions of the National

---

[23] A rural parish in an area where most people are Catholic, have a Catholic tradition, and practice the faith devotedly is different from one in which Catholics find themselves in a small minority; and both are different from a third rural parish in an area where, though Catholics are the largest group, the faith is kept as a vague tradition and hardly practiced at all. Likewise in the city, a parish situated in a downtown residential section presents a quite different picture from the business-district parish, and both are easily distinguishable from the more suburban parish. As stated, these parishes do not vary in basic structure, but many of the services asked of them, the problems they have to face, and their social relationships differ according to the type of society surrounding them.

Catholic Welfare Conference, the Catholic press, and such phases of Catholic action as the Christian Family Movement, the Young Christian Workers, the Young Christian Farmers, the Young Christian Students, the interracial councils, and many others. Yet none of these can take the place of the parish. They are auxiliary to the parish and, indeed, presuppose it.

For with relatively few exceptions Catholics live in parishes. Aside from other types of jurisdiction, mostly in mission territory or for special circumstances, the Church's world is divided into dioceses, and by church law dioceses are divided into parishes.[24] Thus almost every Catholic lives in a territory served by an appointed pastor and an assigned church. There we have the four elements of the parish as listed by church law: territorial division of a diocese, the people living in it, the church assigned to it, and the pastor placed in charge over it. We shall be studying the nature of the parish in more detail later, but beyond the words of Cardinal Suhard cited above we might consider the hypothesis of Father Fichter that the "sociological roots of Catholicism are in the parish" and that "a vigorous parochial system not only bespeaks an internally strong Catholic social structure but also promises solidarity for the larger community and the nation in which it exists."[25] Thus parish study is a direct way to the humanly attainable knowledge of Catholic achievement, weakness and strength, constancy and adaptation, actual and potential value to the general community.

Here are two further thoughts on the significance of the parish to Catholic life. As the "Church in miniature,"[26] the parish

---

[24] *Codex iuris canonici,* Canon 216, 1, 3.

[25] Joseph H. Fichter, *Southern Parish. Volume I: Dynamics of a City Church,* p. 8. Chicago: The University of Chicago Press, 1951.

[26] This key phrase for expressing the nature of the parish, often quoted, was used by Cardinal Cushing in an address to the Third Regional Congress of the Confraternity of Christian Doctrine, Biloxi, Mississippi, November 4, 1947. The address is carried in full in *The Call of the Popes to the Laity,* pp. 13-18 (Paterson: Confraternity Publications, 1948).

manifests that same element of continuity, with or without change, that characterizes the Church as a whole through the centuries. Personalities come and go, the turn of the decades and centuries brings changes and adaptations, yet the same basic structure and function pattern remain, the same value system (doctrine), the same social form of divine worship, the same hierarchy of social control. This is evident to anyone who reads parish histories, whether the thousand-year-old history of a French parish, the hundred-year-old record of a parish that began on the American frontier, or the ten-year-old account of a newly established suburban parish. And deriving from those characteristics of sameness and continuity is the direct and confident link the individual Catholic can possess through his parish with the Church universal. As Abbot Gasquet expressed it, though with misgivings about the modern world:

> . . . in the Middle Ages the conscious sharing in a world-wide tradition bound the local to the universal life, and through art and ritual the minds of the poor were familiarized with the facts of the Christian faith. By our own poor I fear these facts are very dimly realized.[27]

The approach to parish study and analysis followed in this book is positive rather than negative; that is, we are more interested in what actually is than in what is not. Every social organization manifests a certain degree of conformity with its ideal and a certain degree of failure or deficiency. The negative approach studies the latter, which indeed is an important aspect of truth and reality. But when sight is lost of the positive, the whole truth can be badly obscured. To describe a man, a school, or a parish by describing only its vices is producing but half-truths. It seems better and more scientific to observe first what the parish is and to what extent it is actually functioning in accordance

---

[27] Aidan Gasquet, *Parish Life in Mediaeval England*, p. 273. London: Methuen, 1906.

with its purposes. Any deficiencies can be deduced from whatever discordance exists between purpose and functioning, and they can be studied against the background of the total picture. Aside from the advantage of being scientifically objective, this positive approach prevents loss of the baby with the bath—a frequent calamity when only the negative is considered.[28]

And what does it mean to be scientific? Comment on this apparently elementary question is not superfluous, for unfortunately only an ill-concealed hostility exists between many religionists and many social scientists. This is because many of the religionists direct their suspicion toward something that science is not, having a very hazy if not inaccurate idea of what social science is; and because many a reputed social scientist uses his professional standing to publicize personal theories and convictions which have nothing to do with his science or scientific objectivity. Some religionists have the false notion that social science is antireligious, materialistic, and therefore hostile toward all their values.[29] Fortunately religious and scientific

---

[28] This positive approach is followed by the widely read and effective French pastor Père Georges Michonneau. See his *The Missionary Spirit in Parish Life*, p. 47 (Westminster: Newman Press, 1950). The same can be noted in such recent important conferences on the parish as the French Canadian Semaines Sociales of 1953 and the more recent Bologna Conference. A good report of this conference, which occurred in September of 1954, can be found in *Documentation catholique*, Vol. 52, no. 1194, 1955, cols. 327-34. Paris' Professor Le Bras, who has provided excellent leadership in socioreligious analyses, summarized the aims of the positive approach a decade ago when he said: "what interests both scientist and Christian is the organization, the mentality, the religious vitality of the group, of the various social classes, of each individual. Statistical data on Pascal Communion, assistance at Mass, solemn religious acts; lists of pastoral activities, institutions and achievements; the study of relations between (Catholic and non-Catholic) religious groups, or between the two (Church and State) powers: these are the ascertainable elements of an accurate science." See Le Bras's prefatory letter in Jacques de Font-Reaulx's *L'église de Crest: Sa construction, cent ans d'histoire paroissiale, 1846-1946*, p. 5 (Crest: Imprimèrie Veziant, 1947).

[29] When Kingsley Davis refers in *Human Society*, an otherwise excellent work, to the nonexistence of beings in the spiritual world—a most unscientific observa-

leaders in constantly increasing numbers are coming to reject
such mutual distrust.

This is as it should be. Knowledge is the first objective of
the scientist and the necessary tool of the religionist. The latter's
is often of the "common-sense" variety, whose limits and in-
accuracies can be corrected by properly applied scientific
techniques. Science, or scientific knowledge, is simply a more
refined and trustworthy tool of human intelligence for knowing
facts and their interrelationships, particularly those which the
ordinary, or common-sense, or untrained variety of intelligence
finds it difficult to attain. Both science and common sense succeed often enough in achieving knowledge, and both fail not a
few times.[30] False judgment simply means error in using the

---

tion for a social scientist to make—he cannot hope to influence religionists
favorably, win their confidence, or dispel their suspicion. Professor Hobbs of
Pennsylvania concludes from a study of more than fifty textbooks in sociology
that over thirty of them advise religious organizations to become more secular-
ist and less doctrinal. He points out with sharp irony that it is none of social
science's business to recommend more or less secularization to religious organizations. Obviously these textbooks would hardly allay the fears of the religionists—and just as obviously they fail to stay within the bounds of their
science and they fail with regard to scientific objectivity. See Gordon George,
"Some Sociologists out of Bounds," *America* 92:397-98, January 15, 1955.

Another defect on the part of many leading social scientists has been
pointed out by Father Fichter (see *Southern Parish*, p. 8). In the various
community studies which have become so standard in sociological literature
surprisingly inadequate attention has been paid to the role of religious life. In
Middletown, Elmtown, Yankee City, Plainville, Black Metropolis, and other
sociologically analyzed communities, the influence of religious life and its
contribution to social values and morality receive remarkably superficial treatment. It is at least clear that many prominent social scientists are either deficient in their understanding of the actual role in society played by religion,
or wrong in their understanding of what religion is, or both.

[30] Science, which considers the discovery of past error opening the door to truth,
has made its mistakes, as constantly changing theories in medicine and
physics, psychology and industrial sociology, economics and history, readily
attest. But our concern here is rather with the common-sense approach to
knowledge, since it is the currently ordinary equipment of most busy religionists. And common sense has its share of errors, too. For example, a very important study, *The American Soldier* (Princeton: Princeton University Press,

tool of intelligence, whether science or common sense. As Father Furfey points out, "the two types of knowledge differ, not essentially but in degree."[31]

Examples of the inadequacy of common-sense "knowledge" of the parish are legion. One experienced and knowledgeable pastor gave the number 800 as his official estimate of the families in his parish; investigation showed that there were closer to 2,000. That might help to explain why the reported number of American Catholics was about 34,500,000 in 1957, whereas inferences from statistics suggested that there were more than 45,000,000. It is understandable that Cardinal Lercaro in urging the development of statistical studies was willing to tolerate a margin of error as high as 20 per cent,[32] so great are we beginning to suspect is the difference between our common-sense assumptions and the actual facts.[33]

1949), by Samuel A. Stouffer and others, included a test of three common-sense attitudes: "Soldiers from white collar jobs were less adjusted, since they had sacrificed more than lower class men," "Negro soldiers, knowing barriers against promotion were rigid, did not work for promotion as hard as white men," and "Soldiers in units with high promotion rates had a more optimistic view of promotion chances and were more satisfied with promotion policies than were soldiers in units with low promotion rates." Each of these attitudes was shown to be unfounded. Again, interracial housing need not increase interracial tension, as is widely assumed, but can promote interracial amity: see Morton Deutsch and Mary Collins in their *Interracial Housing* (Minneapolis: The University of Minnesota Press, 1951).

[31] Paul Hanly Furfey, *The Scope and Method of Sociology*, p. 55 and Chapter 3, "The Nature of Scientific Knowledge," *passim* (New York: Harper and Brothers, 1953). This chapter contains a remarkably clear discussion of scientific and common-sense knowledge. See also James Conant's *Science and Common Sense* (New Haven: Yale University Press, 1951).

[32] Reported, together with his establishment of the Diocesan Statistical Office, in *Actualité religieuse dans le monde*, no. 25, April 1, 1954, p. 23. In the same article are recorded Pope Pius XII's words to the Central Institute of Italian Statistics: "And if statistics are used especially in the study of material development, in the social, economic and moral life of the nation, they can be used likewise in the study of a religious situation."

[33] Another parish energetically sponsored Saturday-night summer dances for its people, which was a very fine idea. The assumption that Irish people predom-

The present writer recalls another clear example of the same. In discussing with the pastor and curates of a parish in a small Allegheny city the results of Father Fichter's investigations in *Southern Parish*, he was assured that such a situation certainly could not exist in the local parish. The zealous priests knew their 3,000 parishioners well enough to be certain that only a few were remiss in their practice. Yet the parish church had a capacity of somewhat more than 350 and the parish had five Masses on Sunday, the first two of which were attended by half-capacity congregations. Evidently the crowds at the late Masses and the fact that the priests were constantly busy led to a false assumption which an organized investigation would have rectified.

It works the other way too. Sometimes investigation shows the situation to be better than was assumed. As a result of studies of French religious practice it was becoming accepted that the working classes were lost to the Church. Yet Swoboda refers to several examples of working communities completely loyal and regular in their practice—a condition very frequently found in the Church in America. It is one of the purposes of science, both static and dynamic, to check up on conclusions based only on common sense and to push back the frontier of knowledge available to common sense.[34]

---

inated in the parish led to the enthusiastic and almost exclusive playing of Irish songs. Unfortunately, the majority (three fifths) of the parish were Italians who came to watch for a while with interest—but not to stay. The project failed. Another pastor refused to increase the facilities of his school, on the assumption that there were too few children because the young people moved away after marriage instead of staying in the parish. An organized check would have shown that the housing facilities in his parish were too costly for families of two, but did attract growing families after the first few years of marriage. A check did show that in one square block (the parish comprised about sixty blocks) there were 78 children within two years of school age.

[34] We should add, by way of further clarification and in view of the two classes of readers intended in this book, that science can be understood in different ways:

To neglect the practical potentialities of a scientific approach to religion is something we cannot afford. Father Bier's psychological testing program indicates the possibility of alleviating both heartache and economic loss through more helpful screening of young candidates for priestly training.[35] Professor Culver has indicated in *Negro Segregation in the Methodist Church* that "although integrationist policies are being adopted by more and more Christians each year, the churches remain among the most segregated institutions in America."[36] It might be asked whether divine inspiration has prompted this slowness on the part of churches, or whether it has been caused by a crass unawareness of social reality within which religion should be functioning and which it should help form. Again, if investigations of religious practice should show certain uniformities—for

the static, or knowledge itself; the dynamic, or the quest for new knowledge with the help of effective, tested, and organized methods. (See Conant, *Science and Common Sense*, pp. 25-27.) There is also practical science and theoretical science. The practical aims at organized knowledge for the direct help of the practitioner, the man of affairs, the artist; theoretical science strives to build upon organized knowledge of facts and their relationships a growing series of concepts and propositions, validated hypotheses and theories, which will comprise a system of principles and laws or generalizations governing the activity of the subjects studied in the particular science. The priest and the lay apostle will be concerned with the practical aspect of parish sociology; the academic sociologist will be more interested in the theoretical phase. The former centers in the organized presentation of the facts and relationships of parish life; the latter in the application of the sociological concept to the parish. In this book we make use of the sociological concept "social system" to be explained later in Chapter 3.

[35] For an exposition of Father William C. Bier's work, see his *Comparative Study of a Seminary Group and Four Other Groups on the Minnesota Multiphasic Personality Inventory* (Washington: The Catholic University of America Press, 1948) and articles on "Psychological Testing of Candidates and the Theology of Vocations," *Review for Religious* 12:291-304, November 1953 and "Practical Requirements of a Program for Psychological Screening of Candidates," *ibid.* 13:13-27, January 1954. There is an account of his methods in the *National Catholic Educational Association Bulletin* 51:128-35, August 1954.

[36] Dwight W. Culver, *Negro Segregation in the Methodist Church*, p. 9. New Haven: Yale University Press, 1953.

example, that there is a real decline in observance at a certain age, or by a certain age group; or that one sex is more constant in practice than the other; or that residents of a certain area in the parish, or of a certain occupational group or educational background, show more or less attachment to parish life—it would seem that awareness of such uniformities should prompt certain orientations of parochial and pastoral policy.

Certain cautions, however, must be observed. The readiness to "break into print" as soon as someone notices a social constant or apparent uniformity can do real harm (and deepen the impression that many sociologists tend to be superficial!). For instance, the fact that only 3 per cent of the working class in a certain French city practice their religion, as contrasted with 20 per cent of the white-collar class, might warrant the observation that the former should be the special object of the Church's apostolate. But with 80 per cent of the white-collar class staying away from church, it is folly (an obvious violation of common sense) to exclude them from intense consideration too. Again, an American study showed, as our own study shows, that Catholics in their thirties tend to be less observant than any other age group, presumably because of certain worldly considerations and carelessness. Yet it is the thirty-year-olds who are responsible for the Catholic education and church attendance of their children. Again, everyone knows that statistics can be used for deceptive purposes. This is clearly an abuse of ordinary scientific methods, but it should not dissuade anyone from making an honest use of scientific and statistical methods, since there is so much good to be gained from them. In decrying the petty attitudes of extremists who would either belittle science or claim for it special privilege, President DuBridge of California Institute of Technology calls science man's "tool in his eternal struggle to achieve his highest . . . spiritual ends."[37] His thought is

---

[37] Quoted in *Time* 65:79, May 16, 1955.

particularly pertinent in relation to the attitude that should be taken toward the science of parish sociology.

We have discussed the meaning of a sociological study of religion and the value of a scientific approach. We might also consider its *urgency*, recalling the late Cardinal Suhard's shock on learning of the tragic religious conditions in France, as well as the incredulity and shock of Cardinal Ganglbauer of Vienna when he learned in 1888 how grossly inadequate was the seating capacity of all his churches in numerical proportion to Vienna's Catholics.[38] Bishop Wright tells the tragic story of the Parisian lad who died in battle in his native Catholic city during the recent war—died with a question on his lips, who God might be?[39] Has the society which could have given him that knowledge failed? If so, how, when, where? How can it learn to function for others of its members so dispossessed? As Bishop Wright mentions further, the problem is not in France alone. In several countries maps of religious practice show the Church strongest among the numerically weakest levels of the population. The problem in France grew—partially at least—because the Church's leaders did not keep abreast of the social change induced by industrial migration. Over 10,000,000 refugees moved into Germany after World War II, many of them Catholics, and many of them into areas already short of priests because nazism had not encouraged priestly vocations. How provide pastors for such dispersed flocks—the diaspora?

Our own day sees the continuing development of a social phenomenon in which the Church is deeply involved, particularly in its parish life. More and more our culture is becoming an urban one, our social relationships more secondary, and the public demand for all kinds of services (including religious) more concentrated and impersonal. It might seem strange to call

[38] Heinrich Swoboda, *Grossstadtseelsorge*, p. 135. Regensburg: Pustet, 1911.
[39] Suhard, *The Church Today*, pp. xiii-xiv.

the problem of the city parish unique, since in industrial countries there are so many of them. Yet from the viewpoint of almost 2,000 years of history, and in comparison with parishes all over the world in nonurban areas, the city parish does indeed possess characteristics and problems hitherto seldom faced in parish life. Insofar as that is true, the great increase in number of city parishes invests sociological study of the urban parish with great importance. About 80 per cent of American Catholics, according to current estimates, live in cities.[40] Many European urban parishes have been called on to serve populations well over 50,000.[41] It makes no sense to think that such concentrations of people can be adequately served in their religious needs by a single parish. Evidence shows they are not.[42]

Apparently we do not consider that the difficulties placed in the way of this ideal relationship are of relatively recent origin in the history of the parish. This is probably the reason for the general slowness to realize that the ideal can be achieved, or made possible of achievement, only through changes adapted to social developments. As Swoboda pointed out in 1911, within a century Germany changed from having only one city with more than 100,000 inhabitants to a land having forty-one such cities in 1905, so that one German out of every five lived in a large city.[43] The proportion has continued to grow rapidly since then, not only in Germany of course, but in every country with an urban culture. From 1850 to 1950 the number of cities with a

---

[40] Luigi G. Ligutti, *A Survey of Catholic Weakness*, p. 11. Des Moines: National Catholic Rural Life Conference, 1948.

[41] Swoboda, *Grossstadtseelsorge, passim.*

[42] For just as the assembly line and modern industry's multiple-thousand-man work force destroyed the familiar relationship between employer and employee, so the huge parish makes impossible the "I-know-mine-and-mine-know-me" relationship between flock and shepherd which the Good Shepherd exemplified.

[43] *Ibid.*, pp. 6-7. Swoboda refers also—almost fifty years ago—to the difficulties of anomy, lack of contact, anonymity, atomism, and nomadism that characterize urban life.

population of 100,000 increased from 94 to 750.[44] It must be clear that, if such urban concentrations brought with them changes in parish society, then there must be changes from the parish policies followed before those social changes occurred.[45]

One particular type of in-city migration can and does impose new problems. Not too much different in most respects from earlier foreign-born immigrants to this country, the Puerto Ricans have been swarming into some American cities. Actually one sixteenth of New York City's total population—500,000 out of 8,000,000—is now Puerto Rican—for the most part a staggering development of less than twenty years. Since very many of them come from rural or urban areas in Puerto Rico where the numerical insufficiency of the priests is extremely serious, they frequently practice their religion poorly and have little

---

[44] Clarence B. Odell, "The Distribution and Age of the World's Largest Cities," *Annals of the Association of American Geographers* 40:139-40, June 1950. Cited by Francis Houtart in *Social Order* 5:170, April 1955.

[45] That the parish society has been seriously affected is clear from the remarks of Father Gariépy at the French Canadian Semaines Sociales in the summer of 1953. The Catholic countryside of French Canada has been experiencing more recently than most countries large cityward migration. They have become quickly conscious of the problems imported by the new social structure, particularly in the metropolis of Montreal. After describing his own parish and the varieties in urban parish structure, he clearly pointed out some of the problems of the city parish: first, the pastor does not know his parishioners well enough, nor can the parishioners know their pastor; second, through the absorption by various types of public-welfare agencies the pastor's sphere of influence and points of contact with his flock have been reduced; third, the very fact that urban concentrations have necessitated development of institutions on a supraparochial, diocesan basis meant that the role of the parish in the Catholic's life became—whether it should have or not—less important; fourth, a materialistic standard of values, apparently deriving from urban life, deters the people from embracing the spiritual standards for which the Church (and the parish) stands; money has become king of many people's hearts, thanks to materialism and a couple of war derangements; and finally, and not least important, priests are simply not numerous enough for the task. (See *La paroisse: cellule sociale*, pp. 76-97.) More will be said on this later; but meanwhile it is pertinent to remark that, if the difficulties mentioned by Father Gariépy exist in a parish of 20,000 persons, just imagine what they must be in the even more mammoth parishes of Paris and Vienna!

training in their faith despite their attachment to it. Impeded by language difficulties, uncertain and unsettled, they often impose another serious burden on already overburdened parishes.

In view of the foregoing we can have no doubt about the necessity of studies in parish sociology. It is a necessity that is now pressing. Though we have not done much yet in this country, we should not have the idea that parish sociology is entirely new. We can note that Swoboda's *Grossstadtseelsorge* appeared in 1911, and Boulard's remark: "Twenty years later [after the appearance in 1931 of Le Bras's initiatory work on the history of the Church in France] the projects of research and practical interpretations deriving from this initiative have expanded so much that one is almost incapable of merely describing their major trends."[46] We believe that a service can be done the Church in America, as well as to social science, by adding American studies to what the Europeans have already done.[47]

Parish sociology aims at gaining certain knowledge which would be standard equipment in pastoral life and which could be applied according to circumstances to direct policy for the better achievement of the parish's purpose. It is a great advantage to know oneself realistically, one's strength as well as one's weakness, thus to exploit the one and correct the other. To achieve improvement diagnosis must precede prognosis, as Pope Pius XII pointed out to the pastors of Rome in 1955.[48] In the

---

[46] Boulard, *Sociologie religieuse*, p. 13.

[47] We should not suppose, however, that a scientific approach is completely new to American Catholicism. Much that is called scientific elsewhere is taken for granted as common sense by American standards. For example, the planning of sites for new churches, hospitals, and schools is now attended in several European centers with a good deal of scientific preparation. Yet the American bishop simply takes it for granted that diversified planning and advice, based on professional knowledge, must precede the laying of a brick. Despite some omissions and mistakes, this is standard procedure which recalls to mind what was said a few pages above: that one aim of science is to push back the frontiers of common-sense knowledge.

[48] NCWC News Service translation under date of March 18, 1955.

same vein Cardinal Lercaro has cited our Lord's parable about
the king who would go to war but stops to consider whether his
army of 10,000 can match his enemy's 20,000; and the one
about the builder who first calculates all expenses before building.[49] As a result of such calculations the French have been ex-
perimenting with intensively prepared popular missions which
are conducted, not for a single parish but simultaneously for
many adjacent parishes.[50]

We also expect parish sociology to aid in testing the value
of certain proposed solutions to problems of religious practice.
For example, Boulard was able to show that many too easily
suggested remedies are often quite without value; for instance,
increasing the number of Masses in the country at the expense
of those in the city because of the great number of pastorless
parishes in France's countryside. Then again, we hear more and
more that modern conditions require an institutional rather than
a personal apostolate. It is doubtful whether anyone at the present time could explain how to implement an institutional apostolate. It may well be the answer, but a scientific study of the
parish would seem to be a precondition for arriving at it.

There are many different approaches to parish study, as to
the study of almost any society.[51] The more obvious are introductory: the demographic—simply getting the facts about a
parish's membership, their age and sex breakdown, national origin, education, economic status, regularity of religious practice,
and so on; or the ecological, wherein the parish is studied in
terms of its physical structure and environment, such as natural
or man-made helps or obstacles to parish life—hills, arteries of

---

[49] Remarks at First Italian Congress of Religious Sociology. See footnote 3 above.

[50] See *Actualité religieuse dans le monde*, no. 50, April 15, 1955, p. 6. See also
P. Virton, *Enquêtes de sociologie paroissiale* (Paris: Editions Spes, 1953).

[51] See C. Joseph Nuesse and Thomas J. Harte, editors, *Sociology of the Parish*,
pp. 209-29 (Milwaukee: Bruce Publishing Company, 1951) and Fichter,
Urban Parish, "Major Issues in the Sociology of the Parish," pp. 195 ff.

traffic, the effects of the weather, the area of the city, and the like. Simple studies of observance of religious obligations and participation in parish life can be very revealing, as can the determination and analysis of the mutual impact of parish and neighborhood. Sociologists would want to examine the different roles played by priest and layman, their respective statuses resulting from those roles, and their interrelationships. To what extent are members of a parish integrated with one another? What effect on social conduct is exercised by the religious doctrine and moral code which they profess, and by the liturgy, their participation in divine worship? How does life about them (the values and conduct of their neighbors and their interaction with them) affect their own lives in terms of the parish and religious ideal? Does the parish attract its married couples to participate in group activity more than they would do so ordinarily? How much contact exists between the parish and its members of various types? What laymen would have the most to contribute (not in terms of money) to parish vitality? What kind does contribute the most? How attract the others to contribute their talent and interest?

The present study does not seek to answer or even discuss all these questions. Each would require a study in itself. Our aim is more limited: to bring the reader up to date on what has been done in parish sociology (Chapter 2); to offer an introductory understanding of the parish conceived as a social system (Chapter 3); to explain our choice of Our Lady of Mercy Parish as "Northern Parish" and the techniques utilized in our study (Chapter 4); to describe the structure and functioning of this parochial religiosocial system. Every parish has its own physiognomy, its own characteristics. Those of Our Lady of Mercy Parish (hereafter called OLM) will appear from the analysis. Our search is for any key to further understanding the parish, for any hints of significant constants—and the accent is on the positive.

It may be asked whether the identity of OLM should not have been concealed. Actually there are strong reason *pro* and *con,* but the decision lay strongly against concealment.[52]

From the viewpoint of the pastor and the religious practitioner, parish sociology is but a guide helping the pastor to lead his flock or find the wanderers and the lost. It has the role of facilitating for the Church its task of transmitting its treasure, thanks to a more precise knowledge of the social condition of its children and of the social pressures which help or hinder them.

---

[52] Against concealment it may be argued that one is faced with the dilemma of losing the sharpness of accuracy and reality through disguise or risking exposure—both of which usually happen anyway! On this point see Fichter, *Urban Parish,* pp. 218-24. The present study makes no attempt to conceal the parish's identity. This was the decision of the pastor, the curates, and the author, for it was agreed that no purpose would be served by concealment— at least in this particular study. As mentioned above, a positive rather than negative analysis of the parish was intended, and it was conducted with the help of the parish staff and personnel. A more independent survey could have been attempted, perhaps with praise and/or criticism in view. But the risk of error would have been very great indeed. This has been evident to the author through the great amount of information and insight gained through his association with the pastor and priests of OLM. He could not possibly have gained it without them. And the lack of such information must have made any other type of study of OLM that much less accurate and complete. On the other hand, this report is not intended to be an encomium. OLM has its weaknesses, and its priests know them and await the opportunity to improve. There is no human society without weakness. As will be seen, OLM has much to teach others. But if some of its exceptional advantages are made apparent through this report, the purpose will not be to praise OLM especially, but to provide examples of OLM's functioning as a certain type of social system. In view of the circumstances and intention, and with the approval of OLM, the author has thought it completely unnecessary in this report to retain anonymity.

CHAPTER II

Origin and Current Status
of Parish Sociology

Necessity mothers many inventions—in day-to-day living, in the natural sciences, and also in the social sciences. Science is interested in knowledge, in the ordered knowledge of facts and the relationships between them; social science centers on the facts of social phenomena, on human interrelationships. The parish, a form of several types of social relationship, is quite obviously a legitimate object of social science.[1] However, it was only from a pressing need to know the not-too-obvious facts of parish functioning and to understand what caused them and what might modify them that parish sociology was born. The present chapter reviews briefly the history of that birth and its subsequent infancy up to the present time. Appendix I gives details of substantive developments in various countries.

When the Catholic Church was hastening its reform from within during the sixteenth century, motivated not a little by the

---

[1] Not seldom has it happened to Catholic graduate students at non-Catholic universities famed for social research that, on their request for counsel (and sometimes without such request), they were advised to study the Catholic parish. For it is, they were assured, a social and potentially sociological object both important, widespread, varied, and familiar to them; besides it was at least to some extent available to them and not to others, others would be interested in the results of parish study, and it would serve as another testing and development ground for sociological theories.

unfortunate developments of the Protestant Revolt, its organ of reform (the Council of Trent) ordered that parish boundaries be clearly established and parish records accurately kept.[2] For a while, particularly through the last part of the sixteenth and the first half of the seventeenth centuries, records kept by church officials were quite complete and have merited the praise and gratitude of modern demographers and population experts. Often the records included data far beyond merely religious facts, partly because civil records in those days were often rather inadequate. But though statistical techniques and uses were soon to advance on many fronts, religious statistics began to recede in both accuracy and coverage. Even more disheartening is the fact that they were hardly ever analyzed or interpreted in terms of the human or social situation to which they pertained. This lack was to cost dearly. Cityward migrations of the industrial era left pastors out of control of their flocks; they lost touch with them, could not know them, could not serve them in the disrupting changes of a population revolution. As has been said with truth, the masses did not become dechristianized, nor did they desert the Church, nor did the Church lose them; rather they were formed outside the Church, beyond the known confines of the flock, out of view of the shepherds.

It has been only within the past two decades that a concerted effort was being made, born of necessity, to ascertain the facts scientifically and to study both causes and possible means for rectification. There were some earlier studies, but apparently they were like lost straws in the wind.[3]

---

[2] Council of Trent, Session 24. See Mols, pp. 149-60, cited in Chapter 1, footnote 19, for other sources and further developments.

[3] Mols cites Bertolotti's *Statistica ecclesiastica d'Italia*, published in 1885, as the forerunner of national religious statistical yearbooks. Dr. Swoboda's *Grossstadtseelsorge*, published in 1911, presents a survey of parishes and people in about thirty large cities; in Paris alone each of five parishes contained 85,000 persons (one had over 96,000), another ten had more than 50,000 each. Despite some controversy concerning the accuracy of these figures, they were

Between the two world wars two expanding movements helped to open people's eyes to the tragic situation: the development of the foreign missions and the very vaguely designated social migrations. The first joined an awareness of apostolic conquests for the faith with an interest in statistical records of religious matters; the second caused people to wonder if religious life also were not in some way affected by social conditions. France, the mother of so many missionaries, began to realize that many of her own children were so out of touch with the Church as to constitute a real mission objective. Realization led to scientific investigation which, in turn, developed extensive speculation on how to interpret the facts and do something about them.

Professor Gabriel Le Bras, who has been in the very forefront of the development of parish sociology, published in 1942 the first of his two small volumes on religious practice in France, nine years after he had begun his researches. The first volume analyzes the history of practice in France, and the second, published in 1945, adds a sociological interpretation.[4] Variations in practice are correlated with age and sex, professions and socioeconomic classes, political parties and geographic areas. This was the real beginning of the scientific development of parish sociology. Others joined Le Bras, organs of study were created, and Le Bras himself used his position at the University of Paris and other schools to create interest and secure participation in the project.

-----

generally true, and one can readily see the impossibility of such parishes' functioning adequately for all their members. Sheerly in terms of hours available for services and room in the church a large portion of the people could not crowd into Mass or other religious functions even if they wanted to.

[4] Gabriel Le Bras, *Introduction à l'histoire de la pratique religieuse en France,* 2 vols. (Paris: Presses Universitaires de France, 1942, 1945). Le Bras has more recently published a collection of his articles *Collection de sociologie contemporaine,* 2 vols. (same publisher, 1954). He and Canon Boulard are the most significant figures in French religious sociology.

Meanwhile the publication of two important books contributed to both public awakening and scientific interest. Father Godin's *La France, pays de mission?* published in 1943 and the cause of Cardinal Suhard's shock mentioned previously, was "more a cry of alarm than a sociological research study," but perhaps for that very reason it created interest and willingness for research.[5] It was a stinging revelation of some of the more drastic aspects of the loss of so many children to Catholic France, the Church's "eldest daughter," and played its part in the cardinal's decision to institute the Mission de Paris, the widely discussed temporary priest-worker experiment, and to sponsor several research projects.

One of the men on whom he called was Father Fernand Boulard, long active in the rural pastorate, whose two-volume *Problèmes missionaires de la France rurale*[6] was a thoroughly competent answer to the question, "Is rural France, at least, which comprises 45 per cent of the nation, solid in its traditional Christianity?" The answer: in some places yes; in others no.[7] As

---

[5] Henri Godin, *La France, pays de mission?* (Paris: Editions du Cerf, 1943). See Simon Delacroix, "Parish Inquiries in France," *American Catholic Sociological Review* 13:169-73, October 1952.

[6] Boulard has also authored *Premiers itinéraires en sociologie religieuse,* already cited in Chapter 1, footnote 8, a brief summary of the aims, methods, and achievements of positive research in religious sociology, and *Paroisses urbaines, paroisses rurales* (Tournai: Casterman, 1957). He has been the driving force behind the lively magazine *Ami du clergé rural,* which offers results of socio-religious research of interest to rural religionists. Recently he has conducted similar research in the West Indies, particularly in Haiti.

[7] It might be pertinent to recall an experience of the author, no doubt shared by many. While he was staying briefly at a rural parish in the Dordogne valley, just southwest of the middle of France, out of 1,000 adult parishioners just two men attended Sunday Mass, from twenty to thirty women, and the children under 12. The parish was typical of the area, as the intelligent pastor assured me and as the religious observance maps confirmed. Yet not many miles further to the southwest, in the Diocese of Bayonne near the Basque country, religious practice was general and devout. The two experiences emphasized the lesson that the constancy of varying patterns makes unquestionable the influence of the social milieu on participation in religious society.

a result of this study Boulard and Le Bras collaborated on a map of religious practice in rural France which graphically represented the sobering facts.[8] Holland and Belgium soon followed with religious observation maps of their own.[9]

More and more research projects got under way. Boulard, at Cardinal Suhard's bidding, completed an almost exhaustive study of the vocation problem.[10] Studies of religious practice were conducted in parishes and whole dioceses, in rural areas and in cities. Such organizations as Le Centre Catholique de Sociologie, the Dominicans' Economie et Humanisme, the Jesuits' Action Populaire, the Union des Oeuvres in their biennial conferences, Le Bras's Centre d'Etudes Sociologiques, as well as some schools, directed their energy to such projects as correlating religious practice with allegiance to political parties with type of neighborhood, type of occupation, heritage of historical tradition, and so on.[11] A spirit of study and observation has developed a willingness to face the facts, and a conviction that solution of the problem requires a humble and zealous dedication no matter how discouraging the odds. The establishment of priest teams and the adoption of an institutional more than a personal pastoral have resulted from these studies.

The French example and leadership have inspired similar awareness, work, and investigatory studies in several other coun-

---

[8] Originally published in *Cahiers du clergé rural*, no. 92, November 1947 and published separately in larger size by the same publisher in 1952. Various hatchings show those parts of France, exclusive of cities, which are (1) practicing —at least 45 per cent of all adults consistently observe their religious duties; (2) indifferent—only a minority of the adults practice, though there is fairly general use of baptism, church marriage, and religious funeral; (3) real mission territory—at least 20 per cent of the children are not baptized or have been taught no catechism; (4) areas of Protestant concentration.

[9] For the Belgian see *Lumen vitae*, Vol. 7, no. 4, October-December 1952, pp. 624-30; for the Dutch see *ibid.*, Vol. 6, nos. 1-2, January-June 1951, p. 48.

[10] Boulard, *Clergé français*.

[11] Boulard, *Sociologie religieuse*, p. 145, describes several research organizations and gives addresses of their respective headquarters.

tries. Belgium, Holland, and several dioceses in Italy and Spain
have instituted offices of religious statistics.[12] Germany has had
a superb religious statistical center since before World War I,
though it has lagged in analyzing and interpreting its data.
Starts have been made in Latin America and Canada. The
United States has already produced a few excellent studies. Before reviewing what researches have revealed, we shall glance
briefly at the works produced in the countries that have been
active in the movement. The French are unquestionably in the
lead in both quantity and variety of researches. Mols, in his
already cited article in *Nouvelle revue théologique*, though not
limiting his observation to the predominant French productions,
makes the remark:

> Impossible to analyze everything. Impossible even to cite every-
> thing. Merely naming works that have been done would exceed the
> scope of this (quite lengthy) article. From the parish monograph
> to mammoth researches embracing a whole diocese, all methods
> have been tried. They have studied numerically the problems of
> religious convictions, of the impact of modern objections against
> religion, of mixed marriages, divorces, priestly and religious voca-
> tions, of other topics besides. Above all they have studied reli-
> gious practice.

The bulk of positive research efforts has been in the nature
of parish, diocesan, and area or regional studies.[13] The diocesan

---

[12] Mols, p. 161, as cited in Chapter 1, footnote 19, gives the following information
for these offices: Germany: Official Church Statistics Bureau for Catholic Ger-
many, 1915, Cologne; Holland: Catholic Social-Ecclesiastical Institute, 1946,
The Hague; Belgium: Belgian Center of Religious Sociology, 1951, Brussels;
Spain: General Office for Church Information and Statistics, 1952, Madrid;
France: Catholic Center for Sociology, 1954, Paris.

[13] Among others not quite so extensive, diocesan researches have been conducted
in Paris and Versailles, Marseilles, Lyons, Rennes, and Lille. For Paris see
Yvan Daniel, *Aspects de la pratique religieuse à Paris* (Paris: Editions
Ouvrières, 1952); for Marseilles see Gros, *La pratique religieuse dans le diocèse de Marseille*; for Lyons see Jean Labbens, *Les 99 autres . . . ou l'église
aussi recensé* (Lyons: Vitte, 1954); for Versailles see *Semaine religieuse du
diocèse de Versailles* (May 2, 1954); for Rennes see Fernand Boulard, "La

and parish studies are for the most part rather simple records of religious practice analyzed according to such more obvious factors as age and sex, occupation and neighborhood. The area and regional studies tend to be broader and more professional.[14] They have used sociological area analysis as practiced by American sociologists, have included a socioreligious analysis, and have capably applied graphic, photographic, and cartographic techniques. The Grenoble and Lyons studies include clear photographs of the city, and both the Grenoble and the Rouen studies append some twenty-five transparent overlay maps representing different social realities, which can be viewed in terms of each other.[15]

pratique religieuse dans le diocèse de Rennes," in *Connaître une population,* special issue of *Economie et humanisme,* nos. 2-3; others, such as Lille, Nancy, Rheims, and Saint-Etienne, are reported in various periodicals.

Data from more particularly parochial studies can be found in Louis Brochard's *Saint-Gervais: histoire de la paroisse* (Paris: Firmin-Didot, 1950); Marcel Brongniart's *La paroisse Saint-Médard au Faubourg Saint-Marceau* (Paris: Editions Picard, 1951); J. Chelini's *Génèse et évolution d'une paroisse suburbaine marseillaise* (Marseille: Saint-Léon, 1953); De Font-Reaulx's *L'église de Crest, 1846-1946;* Emile Pin's *Pratique religieuse et classes sociales dans une paroisse urbaine Saint-Pothin à Lyon* (Paris: Editions Spes, 1956).

Area and diocesan studies include, aside from some already mentioned, Michel Quoist's study of Rouen, *La ville et l'homme* (Paris: Editions Ouvrières, 1952); Virton's *Enquêtes de sociologie paroissiale;* Mme. Jean Perrot's *Grenoble: essai de sociologie religieuse,* seconde édition augmentée (Grenoble: Centre d'Etudes des Complexes Sociaux, 1954).

See also two books of George Michonneau, *Revolution in a City Parish* and *The Missionary Spirit in Parish Life,* published in English translation by the Newman Press in 1952 and 1950, respectively.

[14] Such areas as the Seine-Marne departments, Grenoble, Rouen, and the Jura region have been the objects of rather extensive analysis—demographic, ecological, economic, recreational, cultural, educational, and religious. See Simon Ligier's *Recherches sociologiques sur la pratique religieuse du Jura,* 4 mimeographed vols. (Lons-le-Saulnier: Jules-Ferry, 1951), which studies one urban and one adjacent rural area; and V.-L. Chairneau's *Documentation préalable a l'étude sociologique de la pratique du culte catholique dans le départment de Seine et Marne, 1944-1949* (Meaux, 1950).

[15] To illustrate, one could take a transparent overlay map showing Rouen's occupational distribution, or age-sex distribution, or neighborhood units, or housing

Other writings, not so much in the field of parish life and practice, have contributed to the general and scientific interest. Cardinal Suhard's scholarly, paternal, and earnest pastorals on the condition of the Church, the parish community, the priest, and other subjects have been translated and have won acclaim in several countries.[16] A few studies have tried to capture the psychology of working classes and rural people in the process of dechristianization in their respective milieu.[17] Additional researches have analyzed political allegiance and election results to search for any correlation with religious practice.[18]

Another prolific source of information on the French religious situation and the results of research on it is to be found in several periodicals.[19] And in view of the widespread interest and growing research, together with the activity of vigorous

---

quality, and superimpose it on any other or on the map of religious observance. Seeing one aspect in terms of others makes readily visible any probable correlation or interaction. Are the poor or the wealthy, the professionals or the workers, the Catholic-school or public-school educated, the well-housed or the ill-housed groups the more regular in their religious observance? A glance at overlay maps provides a quick answer.

16 Suhard, *The Church Today.*

17 See Ligier, *L'adulte des milieux ouvriers* and Paul Schmitt-Eglin, *Le mécanisme de la déchristianisation* (Paris: Editions Alsatia, 1952).

18 See François Goguel, *Géographie des élections françaises de 1870 à 1951.* Paris: La Fondation des Sciences Politiques, 1951.

19 Some of the better ones are: *Actualité religieuse dans le monde,* later changed (June 1955) to *Informations catholiques internationales,* which contains a great deal of information, publishes pertinent documentation, and reports all researches in religious sociology—a sort of religious *Time* in format, not without occasional errors; Father Boulard's *Cahiers du clergé rural,* which reports rural developments, and his *Masses ouvrières,* which deals more with urban conditions; *Economie et humanisme,* published by Dominicans near Lyons; *Action populaire,* edited by Jesuits near Paris, and *Chronique sociale,* all of which include much discussion of idea and theory along with reporting recent developments. The addresses of these periodicals are: *Actualité* (now *Informations*), 31, boulevard de Latour-Maubourg, Paris (7e); *Cahiers,* 13, rue du Docteur Reux, Paris (15); *Masses,* 23, rue Jean de Beauvais, Paris (5e); *Economie,* La Tourette, L'Arbresle (Rhone); *Action,* 15, rue Marcheron, Vanves (Seine); *Chronique,* 16, rue du Plat, Lyon (2e).

French apostolic groups, it is natural that France should have had several conventions dedicated to this theme.[20] Conceivably this growing diligence and competence in socioreligious research will help France stem the tide of dechristianization and achieve once more a foremost rank in Catholic life.

In smaller Belgium, across the French border, the problem of religious observance has grown similarly without being so extensive or complex. On the other hand, differences are both apparent and great between Fleming and Walloon, farmer and factory worker, devout, conservative rural Flanders and radical, largely dechristianized Charleroi and Mons. Belgium, too, has produced some studies of significance for parish sociology. Several organizations have sponsored and/or published positive studies in religious sociology.[21] The Belgian priest, Father Fran-

---

[20] For example, the fourth convention of the International Conference of Religious Sociology was held in L'Arbresle, La Tourette, near Lyons, in October 1953, its proceedings having been since published in *Evangeliser;* the proceedings of the National Congress of Lille in 1948 were published in *Structures sociales et pastorale paroissiale.* A summary of developments in religious sociology since the third convention in Breda was given by Jean Labbens at the L'Arbresle convention, and was published in *Documentation catholique,* Vol. 50, no. 1161, 1953, cols. 1493-1524. The conference had been founded in Louvain, Belgium, in 1948, met there again the following year, moved to southern Holland's Breda in 1951, and held its next meeting in October 1953 in L'Arbresle near Lyons, France. The fifth conference was held at Louvain, Belgium, in August 1956, and was reported in *Informations catholiques internationales,* no. 31, September 1, 1956, pp. 15-23. These conventions and conferences add to the interest in sociological research in socioreligious matters, and inspire further study.

[21] Thus the bilingual International Center for Studies in Religious Education at 27, rue de Spa, Brussels, publishes *Lumen vitae,* which has frequently carried articles on religious sociology, particularly in Vol. 3, no. 1, January-March 1948; Vol. 6, nos. 1-2, January-June 1951 (proceedings of the Third International Conference of Religious Sociology) ; and Vol. 7, no. 4, October-December 1952, containing the Belgian religious-practice map. Le Centre Belge de Sociologie Religieuse, a private organization, sponsored research required for the construction of that map. Le Centre d'Etudes Sociales Godefroid Kurth, another private organization, undertook research for and publication of *La déchristianisation des masses proletariennes* (Tournai: Casterman, 1948). L'Institut des Recherches Economiques et Sociales de l'Université de Louvain

çois Houtart, whose study of the parishes of Chicago will be cited later, has engineered some helpful research, particularly his study on the parishes of Brussels for the last 150 years.[22] The impact of the social milieu on the religious practice of young people about to be married is studied by Claire Leplae in *Pratique religieuse et milieux sociaux.*[23] A very significant book is *Godsdienstpraktijk en sociaal Milieu,* by Father J. Kerkhofs,[24] who helped to construct the religious-observance map for

published its own bulletin under the directorship of Jacques Leclercq (see his "Les problèmes de la sociologie religieuse," 13:683-93, June 1948). The latter aided in Claire Leplae's *Pratique religieuse et milieux sociaux* (Louvain: Institut des Recherches Economiques et Sociales de l'Université de Louvain, 1949). Finally, some journals have published studies in religious sociology. For example, *Nouvelle revue théologique* published in 1955 Mols's "Croissance et limites de la sociologie religieuse" and Léon de Coninck's series in 1947-1948 on "Problèmes de l'adaptation en apostolat."

[22] François Houtart, *Les paroisses de Bruxelles, 1803-1951* (Louvain: Institut des Recherches Economiques et Sociales de l'Université de Louvain, 1955). It is unfortunate that Father Houtart, despite his careful scholarship in some areas, lacked such care in some reports about the United States. As suggested in our first chapter, we need badly to ascertain the truth about ourselves, and it could be advantageous if an outside observer could help us do so. But by citing only the less favorable studies, omitting the others, and relying on guess-work estimates of a pessimistic character in rather unsettled conditions, Father Houtart has failed to present an objective picture of American Catholic religious practice. It is doubtful if the article in *Actualité religieuse dans le monde* (February 1, 1955) does more good than harm. His article "Faut-il abandonner la paroisse dans la ville moderne?" (*Nouvelle revue théologique* 77:602-13, June 1955) is worth considering seriously.

[23] Louvain: Institut des Recherches Economiques et Sociales de l'Université de Louvain, 1949. The research covers one medium-sized, well-conducted parish, but its value is limited by the fact that it reports only percentages rather than numbers. The reader cannot ascertain the size of the sample or population.

[24] Published as Cahier V of *Lumen vitae* (Brussels, 1953). The book is written in Flemish, but contains summaries in French and English. Sociologically speaking, it will be important to observe whether dechristianization, if it continues, will develop from south to north, for Limburg's southern neighbor has been most affected already by this process, while its northern neighbor has been thus far less affected by it. *Actualité religieuse dans le monde*, which had recorded Kerkhofs' study in its no. 28 issue (May 15, 1954), gives a brief report of a Liege survey (Limburg's southern neighbor) in its no. 47 issue (March 1, 1955). Kerkhofs includes several transparent overlay maps.

Belgium. The particular value of his study is that it takes part of a thoroughly Catholic island (Belgian Limburg, the Dutch provinces of northern Brabant and Limburg, adjacent German districts on the Rhine, and some contiguous parishes from other Flemish dioceses) in a sea of completed or developing dechristianization and examines the impact of the sea on the island. The social changes which have developed in Belgian Limburg through the pressure of socioeconomic revolution, plus the influence of ideas and attitudes from neighboring areas, are eroding the Catholic island shore. Aside from the scientific task of analyzing social facts and developments, Father Kerkhofs hopes that such study can bring to light practical answers to the problem of how to stem the areligious tide.

Belgium's northern neighbor, Holland, whose strong southern Catholics are closely bound in many ways with the Flemings, likewise boasts a Catholic Institute of Socio-Ecclesiastical Research.[25] Its works, directed by Professors Zeegers, Oldendorff, and Dellepoort, have been rather more sociographic than sociological, and much of Zeegers' own effort has been expended in the German diaspora, where millions of refugees lack even minimal religious ministration. In both the Dutch and the German diaspora, the emphasis has been on establishing and representing the facts, the better to ascertain existing needs and supplies, whether of priests, doctors, other professional people, churches, schools, or hospitals, or of anything else with an influence on religious life.[26]

------

[25] Katholick Sociaal-Kerkelijk Institut, Paul Gabrielstraat 28-30, The Hague. More recently the institute expanded its scope and established international headquarters, first in Geneva, Switzerland and then in Austria. Much of its work would strike the American reader as merely enlightened common sense, except that it does unearth unsuspected facts and correlations between them, and the Dutch have to reckon with a historical situation seemingly averse to either physical or social mobility which we cannot well appreciate in this country.

[26] At least two of the institute's brochures have been concerned with the strictly pastoral—an analysis of Catholic Amsterdam, its history and growth, its city-

Crossing the Rhine to Germany, we find that, despite the havoc and disruption of war, German Catholicism has the finest and most complete statistical record of its religious practice. As long ago as 1904 the Jesuit Father Krose was campaigning for the institution of an office for Catholic statistics. The campaign found success in the first publication, 1908, of the *Kirchliches Handbuch für das Katholische Deutschland*, together with the erection in Cologne, a few years later, of the desired office, Die Amtliche Zentralstelle für Kirchliche Statistik des Katholischen Deutschlands. The first postwar volume (No. 23) of the directory covered the years 1944 to 1951, and supplied the data for Germany's Catholic religious-affiliation and observation map.[27]

wide social structure, and the pastoral implications of that structure; and a breakdown, by maps, of current and projected parishes in Rotterdam. The institute has also edited a map of religious observance in Holland (see *Lumen vitae*, Vol. 6, nos. 1-2, January-June, 1951, pp. 46, 48) and has prepared maps showing other aspects of Dutch life suitable for correlation measurements with the preceding. A statistical study of vocations in Holland, similar in scope to those prepared in Belgium, France, and Germany, has been provided by Professor Dellepoort. See, for example, the following publications of the institute: *Sociografische Aspecten van de Emigratie*, by Zeegers and Oldendorff; *Demographie en Gezinspolitiek*, by Zeegers and Godefroy; *Artsenbehoefte en Artsenvoorziening, 1950-52*, by Zeegers, Oldendorff, Heere, and Godefroy; *De Toekomst van de Academisch Gegradueerden Opnieuw Beschouwd*, by Godefroy; *Katholiek Amsterdam: Schets van zijn Kerkelijke en sociale Ontwikkeling*, a report by the Institute, 1954; *Rapport over de binnenstad Rotterdam*, The Institute, n. d.

27 Its information is based on the replies to forty-two questions on the familiar official questionnaire which is filled out by all pastors and checked by respective deans before being collected by dioceses and analyzed by the Central Office (Marzellen Strasse 32, Köln, Germany). Until recently no religious-observance map had been constructed for Germany similar to those in use in France, Belgium, and Holland; but the January 1955 issue of *Herder-Korrespondenz* included such a map according to practice in the twenty-three German dioceses and their divisions. Again, taking a leaf from the studies of other countries, the May issue included two maps showing the number of priests and seminarians in proportion to the number of Catholics in each diocese. Many more analyses and interpretations could be derived from the religious data compiled in the directory, but it would seem that little attempt has thus far been made to correlate them with other facts of the social milieu. This is understandable in a Germany busy with postwar reconstruction. As a matter of fact, plans

Catholic Austria, which includes about 90 per cent of the Austrian people,[28] is waging a battle no less serious than that of the Church in France.[29] Some progress is being made in Austria by such apostolic groups as the Young Christian Workers, but there has not been much development of scientific investigation of the type in progress in the countries already named.[30]

Below the Alps, Italian researches have already been considerable, though not so connected as the French.[31] Since the

---

have been introduced for conducting sociographical studies on a parochial basis. See Neundorfer, in *Lumen vitae*, Vol. 6, nos. 1-2, January-June 1951, pp. 238-40. See also *Herder-Korrespondenz*, Freiburg i. B., Vol. 9, no. 4, January 1955 and no. 8, May 1955 for inserts at pp. 168-69 and 360-61.

[28] See *Oesterreichs Bevölkerung in Bild und Zahl*, p. 32 (Vienna: Oesterreichischen Statistischen Zentralamt, 1953).

[29] See *Informations catholiques internationales* (formerly *Actualité religieuse dans le monde*), no. 2, June 15, 1955, pp. 15-22 for a good report on the Catholic situation in Austria. The author was told by several Austrians in 1953 in Vienna and Innsbruck that three elements require consideration: first, the Austrians lack the varied ferment of revitalization that one finds among the French; second, the indifference of the stable country folk is a serious disadvantage, for they resist the appeal of new developments toward religious revitalization; and fortunately many young people in the city have begun to dedicate themselves to a national religious revival.

[30] Some fifty years ago Dr. Swoboda produced his pioneering work, *Grossstadtseelsorge*, and recently Father Linus Grond and several collaborators have produced a series of reports on the parishes of Vienna. Annual pastoral conferences generate enthusiasm and interest but not much actual research. *Informations catholiques internationales*, no. 60, November 15, 1957 reports a study of Monsignor Otto Mauer which shows the proportion between priests and people in Austria to be one for 1,500 in general, one for 3,000 in Vienna, and one for 5,500 in other cities having a population of 20,000 or more. See also *Die Pfarre: Gestalt und Sendung* (Wien: Herder, 1953), the proceedings of the Vienna Pastoral Conference, January 1953. See also, as cited by Leopold Rosenmayr in *American Catholic Sociological Review* 15:158-59, June 1954, Linus Grond and collaborators, *Bericht 1, Die Wiener Pfarren von 1932-1952; Bericht 3, Einige vorläufige Ziffern bezüglich der Situation der Weltpriester in einigen oesterreichischen Diözesen;* and *Bericht 10, Zur Wiener Stadt und Kirchenplanung* (Vienna, 1952).

[31] For a good account see Paul Droulers and Antoine Rimaldi in *Lumen vitae*, Vol. 6, nos. 1-2, January-June 1951, pp. 75-91; for further references see Mols as cited in Chapter 1, footnote 19. Even before World War I an Italian priest, appointed to an allegedly hostile district in Rome, began his apostolate by

awakening after World War II parts of the study weeks for the clergy in 1947 and 1948 were used to publicize existing statistics on religious vitality or the lack of it, and to stimulate cooperation in further fact-finding enterprises.[32] Various regional surveys have showed, as in France, great differences among many areas.[33] Including a wealth of data, some of the studies have not stopped at external observance but have inquired also into religious attitudes and convictions. The increasingly serious attempts of many Italians to understand their religious situation should be productive of helpful information, particularly in the matter of practice differentials, which in some areas seem to cut across the usually divisive urban-rural areas.

In the Mediterranean's other Latin Catholic peninsula Spaniards, too, show signs of trying to cope with the results of generations of nonpractice in many areas. A few studies during the past twenty-five years reflect confusion and discouragement in Spanish Catholicism.[34] Accompanying its new religious revival,

---

investigating the facts, which turned out to be not so bad as reputed, and reported them in "Cio che possono dire i dati statistici di una parrocchia" by G. de Rossi (Milan: Vita e Pensiero, 1914-1915). Some twenty years later two Milanese priests tried to awaken their countrymen from lethargy by citing extensive statistics of Italian apostasy and religious nonpractice in two books: *Ut vitam habeant* (Rome: A. V. E., 1935) and *Vivere in Christo* (Milan: Treviso, 1940).

[32] Serious attempts to inaugurate an extensive statistical coverage of the whole Church seem to have won some attention, but nothing further has as yet resulted. Several private researches have been conducted, however. Droulers and Rimaldi (see footnote 31 above) cite articles on Italian vocations, Professor D'Agato's *Statistica religiosa* (Milan: Giffre, 1943) and Pier Giovanni Grasso's *Elementi di sociologia religiosa* (Turin: Gili, 1953) explain methods used elsewhere to compile and interpret religious data as a help for other Italian researchers. For an up-to-date bibliography on Italian and other studies see *Aggiornamenti sociali*, anno 6, no. 12, December 1957, pp. 697-702.

[33] For example, the well-executed study of the Diocese of Mantua by Aldo Leoni, *Sociologia e geografia di una diocesi* (Rome: Gregorian University, 1952). See also R. Perenna, *Innovazione e rinnovamento della Parrochia* (Como, 1950) concerning conditions in the area of Milan.

[34] See Leo Delaa, Florentino del Valle, and Jose J. Piquer y Jover in "The Changes in Religious Life in Spain during the Last Twenty Years" (*Lumen*

as in other countries, has been an interest in scientifically ascertaining socioreligious facts and analyzing them.[35] Although this Spanish interest is not as yet comparable in depth or results to the French or Italian, the establishment in 1952 of the General Office of Church Information and Statistics has already contributed to our knowledge of Spanish religious life and should be productive of further studies.[36]

Leaving continental Europe for the British Isles, we find that little has been done till quite recently. In 1954 the Newman Association Demographic Survey undertook to study the Catholic community of England and Wales according to age and sex, education and economic situation, size of family, size of school population, and number of conversions and reclamations. While this does not pertain directly to parish study, its results should provide a demographic framework within which parish study can be more meaningful. The most recent publication on English Catholic practice comes from the Young Christian

---

vitae, Vol. 6, nos. 1-2, January-June 1951, pp. 104-18), in which are reported the studies of Father Francisco Peiro: *El apostolado seglar* (Seville, 1933) and *El problema religioso-social en España* (Madrid: Razon y Fe, 1936) and of Father Raymond Sarabia, *España . . . ; es catolica?* (Madrid: El Pepetuo Socorro, 1939).

[35] *The Spanish Ecclesiastical Yearbook* has been published since 1915, but for a long time was seldom utilized. More recently Professor Aznar studied religious vocations by year since 1930, and in proportion to people and parishes in different parts of Spain. See Severino Aznar, *La revolucion española y las vocaciones eclesiasticas* (Madrid: Instituto de Estudios Politicos, 1949).

[36] Recent statistical studies of Spanish religious life include two surveys on observance in rural areas, others on the city and outlying districts of Barcelona, and others on the following dioceses: Ciudad Rodrigo, Bilbao, Madrid, Vigo. Similar to Father Houtart's historical survey of parishes in Brussels, Jose Maria Diaz Mozaz published in *Ecclesia,* a Spanish journal of Catholic action, a study of the growth of the Spanish population since 1769 (from 9,400,000 to nearly 30,000,000) as contrasted with the practically stable number of Spanish parishes during that time (18,169 two centuries ago and 19,194 in 1956). See *Actualité religieuse dans le monde,* no. 23, March 1, 1954 and no. 26, April 15, 1954, and *Informations catholiques internationales,* no. 36, November 15, 1956 and no. 66, February 15, 1958.

Workers, who conducted a survey of the practice of Catholic youth (ages 15 to 24) in English cities.[37] The representative sample of 8,196 persons studied in this survey showed 76 per cent regular Sunday attendance at Mass, which may be compared with a British Broadcasting Company discovery in 1955 that 68 per cent of adult Roman Catholics attend church at least every other Sunday.

Coming across the Atlantic Ocean to generally Catholic Latin America, we find a whole continent whose religious situation is generally more tragic than any land which we have thus far encountered. With a population of about 175,000,000, its rate of increase is at present the world's greatest (about 2 per cent annually), and it numbers roughly 150,000,000 claimed Catholics.[38] Yet not more than 15 per cent of these Catholics practice the faith with any regularity. All these Catholics have only 30,000 priests to minister to them on terrain that is for the most part rural and difficult to travel. Thus there is but one priest for every 5,000 Catholics in Latin America, in contrast to the worldwide ratio of one for every 1,200 (with no thought of non-Catholics to be reached).[39] There has gradually developed a

---

[37] See A. E. C. W. Spencer, E. Mellon, and W. N. T. Roberts, *Youth and Religion* (London: Young Catholic Workers, 1958). Concerning England it might be observed that a fine source for parish study—rather the totality of parish life than records of current religious observance—can be found in Gasquet's *Parish Life in Mediaeval England.*

[38] See *Basic Ecclesiastical Statistics for Latin America—1954,* compiled by Thomas Burch and Donald Burton and edited by William Gibbons (Maryknoll: World Horizons Press, 1955). Latin America is considered to include not only South America and its outlying islands but also Central America, Mexico, and the Caribbean Islands. Dr. Milton Eisenhower referred to the high rate of population increase in the report on his official trip to Latin America in 1953.

[39] In addition to the foregoing reference see Richard Blow, "The Sociology of Religion in Latin America," *American Catholic Sociological Review* 15:161-75, June 1954. The author concludes his article with the not-too-encouraging disclaimer: "Certainly it will be some time before Catholic Sociologists in any Latin American republic will be able to construct national religious maps as those of Prof. Gabriel Le Bras and Rev. Fr. Boulard in France."

sense of urgency concerning this mighty problem, though as yet
few significant studies on it are available.[40]

Here in the United States, and in Canada, there have also
been beginnings, though not comparable with what has been
done in France. That is understandable, for the problem of religious disaffection and lack of practice has not been nearly so
pressing here, except in some areas. Besides, a great portion of
American Catholic effort is expended in trying to keep pace with
migrant movements (of Puerto Ricans in the Northeast, of Mex-
icans in the Southwest) and continued heavy population expansion. As to the latter, the United States now has over 130
dioceses and archdioceses (as contrasted with 23 in Germany,
5 in Holland, 6 in Belgium, 8 in Austria, under 90 in France,
almost all being long-established). In addition there has been
an increase of well over 1,000 parishes in the last ten years. On
the other hand, many American dioceses and parishes have long
since become mature, and one might expect some scientific evaluation of their respective positions. Actually not much has been
accomplished, although, as elsewhere, a start has been made.

Universities, particularly the Catholic University of America, have sponsored several studies centering on the parish. The
most valuable of these are Brother Gerald J. Schnepp's *Leakage
from a Catholic Parish*, Brother Augustine McCaffrey's *Youth*

---

[40] *Informations catholiques internationales* has carried several informative articles
on Latin America: nos. 5-6, August 1955, pp. 13-24, on Brazil; no. 15, January 1, 1956, pp. 24-27, on Latin America in general; no. 60, November 15,
1957, pp. 13-24, on Chile. See also Thales de Azevedo's thoughtful evaluation
"Catholicism in Brazil" in *Thought* 28:253-74, Summer 1953 and Alberto Hurtado's *Es Chile un pais catolico?* (Santiago: Editorial Splendor, n. d.), the
Chilean counterpart to the French bombshell *La France, pays de mission?*
The Chilean study showed less than 10 per cent regular religious observance
in nearly 25 per cent of the nation's parishes. The Brazilian study showed a
record hardly any better. It might be timely to emphasize that our concern
here is not only the negative one that not all is well with Catholic life and
practice, but also the positive one that there be continuing study of the facts
as a prerequisite for progressive pastoral policy.

in a Catholic Parish, and the twin studies of Catholicism in Florida, *Catholics and Practice of the Faith* and *Catholic Fertility in Florida,* by Fathers George A. Kelly and Thomas F. Coogan, respectively.[41] These last two researches were based on the census returns of the Diocese of St. Augustine, and (of direct pertinence to the present study) the census schedule constructed by the authors was used in a few Fordham University Sociological Research Laboratory studies, including the present one. The Kelly study correlates religious practice with a wide variety of factors: marital status, parents' religion, education, place of birth and residence, economic status; the Coogan project correlates fertility with religion of the partners' parents, religious practice, socioeconomic levels, education, place of birth and residence, and the size of the families of the wives' parents. It can be seen quite readily that a diocesewide survey including the above information must give a good idea of the composition of the Catholic population, of interesting and indicative social influences on Catholic practice and of the influence of the latter on society, and greatly facilitate parish analyses.

The *Sociology of the Parish,* edited by two professors at the Catholic University of America, is a fine introduction to parish

---

[41] Brother Gerald J. Schnepp's study, published in 1942, is of a parish "located in an urban area on the Atlantic seaboard." He found 80 per cent regular practice, 16 per cent irregular observance, and 4 per cent dormancy. It is significant that Father Houtart makes no reference to this study, the data of which are far more encouraging than those which he does cite, and that reference to it in European bibliographies emphasizes the negative aspect: "Remarquable étude sur l'abandon de la pratique en milieu urbain" (Boulard, *Sociologie religieuse,* p. 151). Brother Augustine McCaffrey's youth are members in an "outlying urban parish" between the ages of 16 and 24; his study was published in 1941. See also Father David Fesselman's *Transitions in the Development of a Downtown Parish* (Washington: The Catholic University of America Press, 1952). Among the university's other publications on the parish are Maria Cristina Salazar's *A Socio-Religious Survey of the Parish of Cristo Rey in Manizales, Colombia* (1957), Joseph E. Ciesluk's *National Parishes in the United States* (1944), and Thomas Clarke's *Parish Societies* (1943). The Kelly and Coogan studies were published in 1946.

study. As Father Fichter suggests, most of its chapters contain little sociology,[42] but its delineation of the history of the parish, of the various types of parishes, of the need and desired scope of parish research, and of suggested methods for that research make it a helpful beginning for the would-be parish sociologist.

The most significant contribution to parish sociology in this country is found in the writings of Father Joseph Fichter, S.J., notably *Southern Parish*[43] and a series of articles expanded and published in book form under the title *Social Relations in the Urban Parish.*[44] The first investigates, describes, and analyzes religious practice in a fairly large, prominent parish in a southern metropolis, and includes a chapter on the extent of the "Catholic mind" among certain parish leaders. The second, far more sophisticated and professionally sociological, constructs certain criteria according to which parishioners might be typed and thus better studied in terms of the parish life. Then it correlates religious practice with age and sex, mobility, and social status, and discusses various social relationships within the parish. Two fine chapters explore the relationship between religion and science, and three others give thoughtful consideration to several problem areas in parish research, such as ethical limitations in reporting the research findings, clarifying parish concepts, and studying unexplored areas in parish life.

The Belgian Father François Houtart, who has contributed to parish sociology in his own country, has also made a study of

---

[42] See Fichter, *Urban Parish,* p. 195. To Nuesse and Harte, editors of *Sociology of the Parish,* goes the credit of encouraging, stimulating, and producing studies in religious sociology in the Catholic University of America.

[43] Fichter, *Southern Parish.*

[44] Fichter, *Urban Parish.* Between the publication of the two volumes on southern parishes, Father Fichter spent considerable time studying the parish in Germany. One fruit of that study is his *Soziologie der Pfarrgruppen: Untersuchungen zur Struktur und Dynamik der Gruppen einer Deutschen Pfarrei* (Münster: Aschendorff, 1958). His most recent work is *Parochial School: A Sociological Study* (Notre Dame: University of Notre Dame Press, 1958).

Chicago's parishes in terms of historical development, clergy, and current characteristics—size, geographical situation, and membership by number and territory or national origin.[45] As another manifestation of Catholic interest in religious sociology, the June 1954 special issue of the *American Catholic Sociological Review* was given over entirely to that subject,[46] and several of the society's parent conventions have included sessions on parish sociology.

The noted studies of Father John Thomas, S.J., on the Catholic family and marriage have a direct bearing on parish sociology, for, as he points out, information on the number of mixed and invalid marriages in a parish can be an index of parish religious vitality, "since mixed marriages and invalid marriages appear as both effects and causes of religious indifference."[47] The Thomas studies are based on an examination of almost 50,000 households in forty-four parishes. Another study, of which further mention is made in Appendix I, is the *Catholic Digest* survey of religion in the United States.[48]

Since the parish has been for so long the heart of French Canadian life, its vital records have always been important to

---

[45] François Houtart, *The Parishes of Chicago*, mimeographed, 1953. This work was done at the University of Chicago. Its sociology department, under Professor Everett Hughes, has made studies of some aspects of Catholic parish life.

[46] Other articles pertinent to parish sociology in the *American Catholic Sociological Review* include: "Nationality and Leakage" derived from Brother Schnepp's study (3:154-63, October 1942); Eva Ross, "The Sociology of Religion in France Today" (11:12-14, March 1950); Bertha Mugrauer, "Variations in the Pastoral Role in France" (11:15-24, March 1950); John Donovan, "The Sociologist Looks at the Parish" (11:66-73, June 1950); Joseph Fichter, "Urban Mobility and Religious Observance" (11:130-39, October 1950); Simon Delacroix, "Parish Inquiries in France" (13:169-73, October 1952); and Joseph B. Schuyler, "The Parish Studied as a Social System" (17:320-37, December 1956) and "Elements of Organization and Disorganization in Northern Parish" (18:98-112, June 1957).

[47] John F. Thomas, "Family and the Parish." *Social Order*, new series, 1:293, September 1951.

[48] A series of thirty articles in the *Catholic Digest*, beginning with November 1952 and concluding with May 1954.

French Canadian leaders. But little has been published. Professor Falardeau contributed articles on parish sociology in Canada to both *Lumen vitae* and *Sociology of the Parish,* and he has both written other small articles and reviews[49] and required parish researches on the part of his students. Three significant contributions have been Everett C. Hughes' *French Canada in Transition,* which shows the impact on parish life caused by socioindustrial changes;[50] Archbishop Maurice Roy's published address on *The Parish and Democracy in French Canada,* first delivered at the University of Toronto, which shows some aspects of French Canadian parish structure quite unknown to American Catholics;[51] and Horace Miner's more or less anthropological study of a French Canadian rural parish.[52] In 1953 the French Canadian Semaines Sociales were given over to discussions of the parish. The report of the proceedings contains an excellent appreciation of the parish in Canada's past and present, and the growing crisis it is now undergoing as a result of cityward migration and the spread of urban culture to the country.[53] Both the convention itself and the publication of its proceedings have served as a stimulus to popular and scientific interest. Meanwhile, for the last few years the English Canadians have had in operation their National Catholic Social Life

---

[49] See *American Journal of Sociology* 60:308-10, November 1954 for Falardeau's reviews of Fichter's *Southern Parish* and Nuesse and Harte's *Sociology of the Parish.* See also *La paroisse: cellule sociale,* pp. 136-47.

[50] Chicago: The University of Chicago Press, 1943.

[51] Toronto: University of Toronto Press, 1950. The laity's voice in financial matters and even in some matters of parish policy is particularly foreign to the American way of viewing parish responsibility. A recent news item to the effect that the Sacristans' Union negotiated an agreement with about 100 Montreal parishes covering salary, vacation, disputes, union membership, and other issues would strike many an American priest and layman as fantastic. But see Fichter's treatment of the Kirchenvorstand (board of directors) of a German parish in *Pfarrgruppen.*

[52] Horace Miner, *Saint-Denis, a French Canadian Parish.* Chicago: The University of Chicago Press, 1938.

[53] *La paroisse: cellule sociale.*

Conference, which has urged upon the diocese and the parish the responsibility of using its already existing structure to meet such problems as those arising from new emigration.

After this cursory view of developments in Catholic religious sociology in various countries, we might well ask what these developments have indicated. It would be helpful if we could construct a chart showing, for example, the results of all surveys thus far made: place, date, population, percentage of religious observance, the sex, age, and occupational ratios, and so on. Such a chart would make uniformities and variations quickly evident. But we would have to make so many qualifications in the various categories that the plan is not too feasible; for some surveys make allowance for those legitimately excused and others do not, there is much variation in the information which is sought, and age limits for youth vary. Boulard constructed a simple type in his *Premiers itinéraires en sociologie religieuse* but it would not suit our purpose.

Instead, in Appendix I of this book we cite the findings of numerous surveys of religious observance, paying particular attention to degree of observance, the predominance of women and the young in religious practice, and the observance rates of persons active in different occupations.[54] In summation of those surveys we can say that, with very few exceptions (such as surveys in Bilbao and Antwerp, a couple in northern Italy, and apparently several in Holland and Germany), large cities studied in continental Europe and Latin America show a Sunday religious observance of about 15 per cent, ranging from 10 per cent

---

[54] Just about all the information used in Appendix I has been taken from studies cited in this present chapter. In addition summary material and a few more recent tabulations can be found in two excellent articles in the short-lived *Actualité religieuse dans le monde*, no. 32, July 15, 1954 and no. 52, May 15, 1955. This last issue ended the periodical's life, and it yielded to *Informations catholiques internationales*, whose no. 31 (September 1, 1956, pp. 15-23) issue contains another fine summary in "Trois ans de sociologie religieuse en France."

to 30 per cent. It is somewhat better in smaller cities, and better still in rural areas, observance in rural France being just under 40 per cent. Though the urban-rural pattern admits of exceptions, the pattern of women's higher rating is almost completely consistent. Their ratio of superiority ranges between 3 to 2 and 2 to 1. Invariably, too, children are far more faithful than adults, and children of the bourgeoisie surpass those of working-class families. The working class is far less observant than the bourgeoisie, though the latter's record is itself quite poor. Since the working class usually has lower income, poorer housing, and less education, we cannot pronounce any of these factors decisive in determining poor practice.

Our few American studies have indicated a generally different situation in the United States. In the first place, though our statistics are far from adequate, some 60 to 70 per cent of American Catholics seem to be attending Mass regularly on Sunday. Secondly, though men still yield to women in faithfulness of observance, the women's lead is closer to an 8 to 7 ratio as contrasted with the European 3 to 2 or 2 to 1. Little difference in observance has been recorded for different occupations, and the urban situation compares not unfavorably with the rural. Observance records in England seem to be closer to the American than to the Continental. On the other hand, when our statistics are so inadequate as to leave uncounted over 10,000,000 born Catholics, and when from 30 to 40 per cent of our known Catholics miss Sunday Mass more or less regularly, we might well recognize the need for self-examination.

The Church in the United States is flourishing; yet it has weaknesses. We cannot afford to allow those weaknesses to grow to European or Latin-American proportions, and we must work for their arrest and correction. Improvement presupposes self-knowledge. This is easiest to achieve on the parish level, which explains our interest in developing sound parish analyses.

CHAPTER III

What Is the Catholic Parish?

Definition, it has been said, is both the beginning and the end of scientific knowledge. To study something we must first have delimited it from other objects, and then we can proceed to sharpen our understanding of its characteristics. Thus we come to a more perfect knowledge of the thing itself. The title of this chapter was not chosen to create the impression that an ultimate definition of the Catholic parish would be offered. Actually such a task is quite difficult, and at any rate it could not be assayed before the completion of a parish study. Even then only the definition of one parish, the object of our study, could be offered with any certainty.

However, since this book reports a parish study, we should have some notion, even if only a working definition, of what it is or what we can expect to find it to be. Later chapters report on the composition, structure, and activity of one northern urban parish, Our Lady of Mercy Parish in New York City's Bronx County. The present chapter first seeks to give some general understanding of the Catholic parish, its history, and its importance to Catholic life; then it offers a logically consistent and sociologically sound conceptual framework within which a parish, as well as any social organization, can be effectively studied. Our own study will be conducted within that sociological framework, that of the social system.

It has been mentioned previously that the Council of Trent ordered that dioceses, under the rule of a bishop, should be divided into parishes so that, territorially speaking, every person might have recourse to and benefit from the ministry of an available pastor. This represented the culmination of a historical development in irregular stages from the earliest centuries of Christianity. In the first centuries the word *paroikein* had nothing to do with a church administrative district. It meant dwelling in a foreign land, having references to the Christian minority living in a transient pagan world. Of course such Christians lived usually in the city, and under the pastorship of a bishop. With the victory of Christianity, however, the social achievement of its permanent status, and the spread of the Church into pagan, nonurbanized mission lands, the word came to mean more dwelling in the country under the pastorship of a simple priest, by which is meant a priest not raised to the rank of the episcopacy. Thus the word parish *paroikia* came to mean a division of a diocese subordinate to the head of the diocese.

By definition of canon law[1] the parish has these four characteristics: *territory*, which is a distinct part of the diocese; *its own church*, the visible center of parochial unity, the place for the people to join in divine worship, the house of God and God's people; *its own people*, including everyone in the parish who has not been exempted from the pastor's care;[2] *its own assigned pastor*, who receives his appointment from and is subordinate to the bishop of the diocese.

We have spoken of the high regard of the bishops for the work done by their parishes. Cardinal Cushing once said:

> The Catholic parish, with its pastor and priests, its altar and confessionals, its pulpit and its schools, its good works, its sinners and saints—the Catholic parish so constituted is a microcosm, it

---

[1] *Codex iuris canonici*, Canon 216, 1.
[2] *Ibid.*, Canon 464.

is the whole Church in miniature; and through the parish Christ does for a limited group what He founded the Universal Church to do for all the world. Through the parish, on the other hand, a group of the faithful, in a corner of the world, do for Christ what all the total Church in heaven, in purgatory and on earth does for Him throughout creation. Christ is adored in the parish Liturgy; Christ is preached in the parish pulpit; Christ is praised by the parish choirs; Christ is meditated in the parish convent; Christ is imitated, reproduced, in all the mysteries of His life, by the hidden lives of unknown parish saints, by the public zeal of parish workers, by the sufferings of the parish sick, the privations of the parish poor.[3]

The aim of the Church in the whole world, of the parish in its own territory, is to spread and safeguard Christ's religion—its creed, code, cult, and communion. This means that it seeks to adopt those measures calculated to help in the sanctification of its individual members and so to influence social institutions that they will at least not be detrimental to the Christian living of its members. To appreciate how effectively the parish continues, at least in some areas, to exercise its functions, one has only to investigate cursorily certain large parishes in Negro neighborhoods in New York, Philadelphia, and Chicago, where successful evangelization has completely transformed the attitudes, ways of thinking, religious practices, and even social evaluations of tens of thousands of persons who previously had had no connection with the Church.

We might cite at length the picture of an urban parish in Montreal presented by Father Gariépy, after ten years as pastor, to the French Canadian Semaines Sociales:

Urban parishes are most varied in their structure. Though identical in their essential formation, they each have their own physiognomy proper to the neighborhood where they are located. One parish, situated in a commercial environment, will have problems

[3] Richard Cardinal Cushing, "Address to Third Regional Congress," in *The Call of the Popes to the Laity*, pp. 13-18.

unknown to the almost exclusively residential parish. Another will have in large part a working-class population. Another will have the middle class. Further on a parish will be made up of professional, industrial, and commercial people. Here you find a Jewish zone, a Protestant area, one of Irish Catholics, Italians, Germans. Yonder the parish territory is featured by a factory, a hotel, rooming houses, a section openly recognized for the prostitution which is practiced there. Certain parishes number up to 20,000 souls. Others don't reach the number of 3,000. Some have the honor of a long and noble history, and will know no further development. They have been split more than once. The invasion of business has transformed them. A stable and thriving population is found in them more rarely. Others have been founded only yesterday. Blooming projects are many. The population is not so dense in them; but soon homes are built, businesses are set up, and you can foresee the day when there will no longer be room for one desiring to live there. There is a constant migration of our people who are leaving the country for the city; then, if their fortune permits it, they leave the crowded business districts to establish themselves in a district where they can find lodgings, fresh air, and room to live better and to raise their children better.

I could not pause, obviously, at each type of urban parish. Having had the privilege of being pastor of the parish of the Immaculate Conception at Montreal for ten years, I believe I have met the majority of problems which the urban parish presents. Founded in 1884, Immaculate Conception, mother of a half-score large parishes carved from her original territory, numbered up to last year more than 20,000 souls grouped around her church steeple within a radius which one might cover by foot in some twelve minutes. A very dense population, mostly working and middle class, living in houses of two or three stories. Lafontaine Park, the only unoccupied space, allows the people who go there some fresh air and recreation. Commerce constantly encroaches upon districts used for residences. Stores are being opened on the principal thoroughfare, which is becoming a little St.-Catherine Street. Grocers, butchers, restaurants, are springing up on every corner of the street. Some industrialists have there the headquarters of their firms. Nevertheless the neighborhood remains residential to a very large degree, counting several families resident in the parish for half a century and more. To this stable group has been added a considerable number who have left downtown to settle in a better part of the city, while several have been leaving Immaculate for roomier neighborhoods with nicer homes. The increasing number of boarding houses has created a serious annoyance in the ministry. Two high schools for boys and girls, six elementary schools, of which two are conducted by private institutions, and a convent provide education for the young. The Sisters of Providence have built there the headquarters of homes for old men and women and an orphanage for girls. The normal school Jacques-Cartier has been raising its magnificent structure there.

There is the external physiognomy of Immaculate Conception, an urban parish more or less similar to all city parishes. Considered, and justly so, as one of the finest parishes because of the social and religious quality of its people, because of the devotion of its faithful to their pastors, the parish of the Immaculate Conception is nevertheless no longer what it was only lately. She has experienced the touch of the scourges of the city. Consequently she can guide, with her wealth and imperfections, a study of the urban parish.[4]

The speaker went on to detail some of the problems of his parish, but one point for us to notice is the impact of a changing urban environment on this church society and its members functioning as something real and continuous in a definite territory for almost seventy years. This prompts us to ask the questions: what is the parish, what does it come from, what does it do?

Archbishop (now Cardinal) Montini, writing at a time when he was papal prosecretary of state, said:

Just what is the parish? It is the smallest part of the one and universal flock entrusted to Peter by the Lord. Under the authority of a responsible priest who has received from his bishop the care of souls it is, in the Church of Jesus Christ, the primary community of Christian life, a community of such human size that the shepherd can know his sheep, and the sheep their shepherd. A delimited territory usually traces its contours within the heart of the diocese, and so the parish is bound to an area, intimately linked with local

traditions and definite points of view. In the heart of this area, surmounted by its belfry, stands the parish church, with its baptistry,
its confessional, its altar, and its tabernacle; the church, symbol of
unity, center of the community life.

It is important to keep this in mind, that the parish is above all
the hearth of religious life and of missionary expansion. . . . Now,
it is precisely such a parish, a really living and active cell of the
body of Christ, which is called, by its very fidelity to its proper
religious mission, to play a role of first rank in the regeneration of
modern society.[5]

Can we then find a definition of a parish less juridical than
the one implicit in canon law, yet in conformity with ecclesiastical norms, reflective of observable social reality, and meaningful to both ecclesiologist and sociologist? The sociologist is
reluctant to accept a theological definition if it is not realized in
the actual order. The ecclesiologist has to set down the criteria
according to which realization can be tested. Without such criteria the sociologist cannot judge whether an existing parochial
structure is what it is supposed to be.

Our question has invited difference of opinion, even confusion. Father Francis B. Donnelly, both a pastor and a student of
the parish, calls the parish "a community of Christian souls under the spiritual care of a pastor."[6] Yet Father Fichter rather
denies the concept of community as applied to the parish, as
also the notion even of group, and even rejects the expression
cited previously, that of the "Church in miniature," the *ecclesi-
ola in ecclesia.*[7] In *Sociology of the Parish* Nuesse and Harte

---

[5] J. B. Montini, letter to Cardinal Paul-Emile Leger of Montreal on occasion of the
thirtieth session of Semaines Sociales (French section), in *La paroisse:
cellule sociale,* pp. 7-11.

[6] Francis B. Donnelly, "The Pastoral Ministry in Transition," in Nuesse and Harte,
Sociology of the Parish, p. 289.

[7] Fichter, *Urban Parish,* p. 143. See also pp. 18-19, 42, 51, 55, and 68. Father
Fichter shifted his position on this point. In his earlier book, *Southern Parish,*
pp. 14-15, he accepts this expression as indicative of the nature of the parish;
in *Urban Parish* he denies that the definition applies in the real order.

define the parish as "a formally organized group of association, since it is a distinctive and organized plan of relations by designated persons participating in the pursuit of some one or several implicit or explicit values."[8] Conceivably the difference in opinion comes from variation in concepts. That is why we offer in this chapter a conceptual scheme within which our own and other parish studies might be conducted with some degree of consistency, mutual relevance, and comparability.

An attempt to make a study of the Catholic parish scientifically and sociologically deeper than, let us say, demographic analysis requires the use of the same scientific tool needed in any scientific study: a conceptual scheme, a frame of reference, a mental and lingual instrument for better understanding, analyzing, comparing, and generalizing about facts in social or physical reality. The suggestion is here offered, in expectation of further parish study, that our thinking and speaking about the parish society can profitably revolve around the concept "social system."[9] Our purpose here is twofold: to clarify the observed data by organizing and classifying them within an adequate conceptual scheme; and to study the parish in the same way, within the same frame of reference, in which any other social organization can be studied. Thus the parish can be brought more readily within the scope of sociological analysis, and sociological principles can be applied more readily to the parish.[10]

-----

[8] See Nuesse and Harte, *Sociology of the Parish*, p. 6. John Donovan, quoted by Father Fichter in *Southern Parish*, p. 14, seems to be of the same mind: "The Catholic parish must be conceived of as a real social group composed of the Catholic Clergy, religious and laity within certain territorial boundaries who share a unity founded on common religious beliefs and who participate in socioreligious relationships institutionally defined by the parent organization of the Church."

[9] The author is happy to acknowledge that many of the ideas in this chapter concerning the articulation of the concept "social system" derive from the lectures and writing of Professor Nicholas S. Timasheff of Fordham University.

[10] Sociologists have trouble finding agreement even in their particular terminology. If words like "democracy" and "socialism" or "conservatism" and "liberalism"

What, then, is a "social system" and how is it applicable to the Catholic parish? Sociologists have represented meaningful union between human beings by such expressions as society, community, association, social system, social group, social order, social organization, social class, and so on. All these expressions are proper enough. But for more precision, writers have tried to differentiate one from the other. Their differentiation did not always contribute to clarity. Of all the expressions just named, only two remain which are sufficiently general and unlimited by an opposing term to be freely applicable to all types of social unions. These two are social system and social group. Of the two, social group tends to be rather amorphous, not necessarily indicative of much more than people simply being assembled together in some way. Social system seems to add more clearly the notion of parts forming a whole, of interdependence aiming at achievement of a common goal.[11]

---

have several, sometimes contradictory, meanings in popular usage, so sociologists disagree on such key sociological expressions as "society," "community," "race," "institution," and others. Most confusion in sociological thinking and literature can be traced to misleading conceptual schemes on the universal level and lack of agreement on particular terminology. Hence the importance in parish study of adopting a frame of reference or conceptual scheme which is both clear and compatible with other sociological study.

In his enlightening book *Science and Common Sense*, James Conant, president and formerly a professor of Harvard University, defines science as "an interconnected series of concepts and conceptual schemes that have developed as a result of experimentation and observation and are fruitful of further experimentation and observation." He cites the words of William James, "The intellectual life of man consists almost wholly in his substitution of a conceptual order for the perceptual order in which his experience originally comes," and he himself refers to science as "an activity which increases the adequacy of concepts and conceptual schemes which are related to certain types of perception and which lead to certain types of activities; it is one extension of common sense" (Conant, *Science and Common Sense*, pp. 25, 32).

[11] Logan Wilson and William Kolb distinguish in *Sociological Analysis*, p. 843 (New York: Harcourt, Brace and Company, 1949) between social system and social group. For them social system adds the elements of emotional solidarity, common purpose, a role-defining culture, and means of differentiation from nonmembers. They likewise speak on p. 344 of communities and societies con-

As a matter of fact, in recent years sociological writers have been using this concept more extensively.[12] It has many advantages. It is a key concept in every scientific field: in philosophy we speak of Platonic, Aristotelian, and Thomistic systems; we have the reproductive, respiratory, and digestive systems in biology; the atomic system in physics, and the solar system in astronomy; the Christian system of theology, the Keynesian system in economics, the democratic system of government. We can refer to whole sciences as systems: the system of economic principles, of theology, of law, of medicine, and so on. Thus sociological terminology could conform more helpfully with other scientific terminologies. The point is that various parts of reality or knowledge so fit together that they give to the totality of parts a significance and effectiveness far in excess of the meaning of the sum of the individual parts in themselves. A man dressed in leather helmet and moleskin pants and wearing shoes with heavy cleats might well appear to be a mere oddity; in unison with ten teammates on a football field his significance transcends his own separate appearance.

taining and being comprised of social systems and relations. We would say that such systems are subsystems, while the societies and communities are themselves systems. Nicholas Timasheff, "The Basic Concepts of Sociology," *American Journal of Sociology* 58:176-86, September 1952, gives several leading sociologists' definitions of the social group, social system, society, and other fundamental sociological terms.

[12] A. N. Whitehead, quoted in George Homans' *The Human Group*, p. 87 (New York: Harcourt, Brace and Company, 1950) speaks of "the idea of an organized whole, or system, existing in an environment is 'a fundamental concept which is essential to scientific theory.'"

For a more complete development of the meaning, history, importance, and applicability of the concept social system see Joseph B. Schuyler, "The Parish Studied as a Social System," *American Catholic Sociological Review* 17:320-37, December 1956 and "Elements of Organization and Disorganization in Northern Parish," *ibid.* 18:98-112, June 1957. In the first of these articles, from which material has been drawn for this chapter, an account is given of the contributions of Vilfredo Pareto, Lawrence Henderson, George Homans, Talcott Parsons, Lloyd Warner, Logan Wilson, William Kolb, Wilbert Moore, Nicholas Timasheff, Charles Loomis, and Allan Beegle.

The same with social phenomena. A store has no meaning without clerks, merchandise, and customers; nor does a teacher without students, nor a marriage law without people of marriageable age. But when we have a plurality of people mutually dependent, interacting in a particular set of circumstances and cooperating to achieve a certain goal, obviously we have an organization of parts comprising a totality with properties far in excess of the sum of the properties of the parts.

A system is a plurality of parts so interrelated as to form a distinctive whole. A *social system* is a plurality of persons and/or groups of persons so interrelated through interaction and shared attitudes as to form a distinctive social whole with properties superior to those of its members. The latter retain their identity, however, and might well participate in other systems. For example, the same person can be and often is a family man, a parishioner, a lawyer, and a member of an athletic club. Our concern here is to discuss the applicability of the concept social system to the Catholic parish, and accordingly to consider the characteristics of the parish social system.

The explanation of a social system found in Loomis and Beegle's *Rural Social Systems* is excellent:

> [We] believe that such an organization [around social systems] supplies an approach more adequate than others in meeting the demands of science, especially in regard to prediction, understanding and control. Furthermore we feel that the social system approach is superior to many frames of reference which employ abstract terms pertaining to less functional entities. This approach, authors feel, is particularly applicable to administrators who have specific roles in concrete social systems and to those engaged in modern group work.

In their definition of social system they add another aspect of its importance:

> Social systems are organizations composed of persons who interact more with members than with non-members when operating

to attain the system's objectives. All social systems, whether small silo-filling rings or large farmers' organizations such as the Farm Bureau, have elements in common which the social scientist, educator and administrator must consider if he is to understand them. The elements of both social structure and value orientation (ends, objectives, norms), of course, are so inextricably interrelated that any classification that separates them will be somewhat unrealistic.[13]

Practically the same words might be used to indicate the value to the priest administrator or parochial leader of studying the parish as a social system. He could compare strong and weak factors in his own system with similar factors in other systems and probably find some practical indications.

We are now ready to consider more substantively the social system and to seek to understand in detail its application to the parish. Without dwelling upon the abstract definition of a social system as stated above,[14] let us look at a simple ex-

---

[13] Charles P. Loomis and J. Allan Beegle, *Rural Social Systems*, pp. 3, 33, and *passim* (New York: Prentice-Hall, 1950). As does Homans, so Loomis and Beegle develop a series of comparisons between different social systems: a religious farm family, a labor group, and a government bureau. The norms of comparison, particularly valuable tools for sociological analysis, are those elements of social structure and value orientation which all social systems must have, and variations which differentiate one type of system from another. Loomis and Beegle do not separate these variations into classes, but rather place them on the extremes of a continuum, thus enabling us to compare juxtaposed systems more readily and accurately. An example is seen in the contrast between the community and associational types (Sorokin's familistic and Tönnies' Gessellschaft types). Thus the familistic-Gemeinschaft-community type of system would be expected to manifest such characteristics of nonrationality and nonaccessibility, functional diffuseness in roles, authority patterns, norms and ends, shared reactions to most events, and a required integration of roles both within and out of the system. On the other extreme the contractual-Gessellschaft-associational type would be rather rational, functionally specific, and so on. See pp. 10-29. By such comparative analysis the sociologist can evaluate one system's weakness in terms of the other system's strength, and in both diagnosis and prognosis act accordingly.

[14] For most of the ideas pertaining to the structure of the social system the author is indebted to the authors thus far cited, and particularly to the authors of *Rural Social Systems* and *The Human Group* (see footnotes 12 and 13 above) and Professor Timasheff.

ample of human beings joining in common action. A man approaches a newsstand, places a nickel in the hand of the custodian, receives in return a copy of the morning newspaper, perhaps exchanges a greeting, and departs. The same event occurs each day, with the same persons as the actors. If we analyze this recurring event, we see that each of the actors, in performing his own action, is interacting with the other. This interaction is carried on for a purpose: the exchange of an object of worth for a coin in accordance with the needs of each person. This constant interaction implies a relationship between them in which each expects the other to act in accustomed fashion—in other words, to play his role; each accepts the other's position, whether as customer or vendor. Each realizes that he is protected, let us say, from any fraudulence of the other by social rules to which both are subject. In addition to the attitude of cooperation in the exchange of goods there might be the attitude of friendliness expressed in greeting or passing conversation. Bound together by this relationship, there can be a reluctance on the part of the customer to buy his paper from anyone else and a willingness of the vendor to save a paper for the customer although he might sell it more quickly to another buyer. Perhaps the location of the newsstand was the reason why the vendor started his business and why the customer first bought his paper there. At any rate, it is the place where their daily interaction occurs.

Or take a school. Teachers teach, administrators govern, and students listen, study, and learn. Their respective actions involve them in recurrent interaction for the purpose of imparting or gaining knowledge. Certain personal and social needs are being satisfied by the functioning of this relationship. Each member of this relationship, whether teacher, student, or administrator, has a certain position or status with definite rights and duties deriving therefrom; each has a certain role to play, an expected way of acting in accordance with established norms whether officially or otherwise imposed.

So it is with any social system, large or small—including the parish. It consists of a plurality of human beings, purposeful by nature, acting or disposed to act jointly, therefore interacting, in a common aim. Their unity is reality which transcends even the additive totality of all of them as parts, for outside of the mutual meaningful dependence and functional interdependence which form their collective unity, their respective individual personalities, talents, and actions are incapable of the functioning which is possible in concert. This is as true of a government, or factory, or ball team, or parish, as it is of a television set or a railroad network. The distinctive feature of a social system, as distinct from any other kind of system, is that it is comprised of human beings. The human being is not completely absorbed in any social system: he retains his identity and individuality, he can enter into relationships in at least some other social systems simultaneously.[15] A parishioner, for example, is usually also a member of a family, a citizen, related with an economic association, and so on.

What are the bonds of these relationships of union? They might result from selective affinity, utilitarian choice, or even coercion. Common action implies not only mutual purposes or values but also a norm of conduct to be observed in achieving those purposes. Naturally there must be a place, a *locus*, in which the system functions, with the limitations or advantages of which—space requirements, for example—the system must be compatible.

In the social system, then, there must always be:

1. Plurality of human beings,
2. repeatedly performing certain actions, or being disposed to perform them,

---

[15] See Robert M. MacIver and Charles H. Page, *Society: An Introductory Analysis*, p. 49 (New York: Rinehart and Company, 1949); also John F. Cox, *A Thomistic Analysis of the Social Order*, pp. 107-08 (Washington: The Catholic University of America Press, 1943).

3. in concert, thus engaging in interaction,
4. with such frequency as implies continuity,
5. for a purpose, the *raison d'être* of the interaction,
6. implying certain values, whether of the individual persons or the collectivity,
7. achieved through functioning for the satisfaction of needs,
8. thus involving norms of conduct;
9. a relationship as the static phase of this functioning interaction,
10. including roles and statuses,
11. also attitudes, and especially attitudes of attraction or repulsion;
12. and not least: place.

These elements of the social system are graphically illustrated in Figure 1.[16]

A valuable feature of the social system, thus analyzed into its component parts, is that it and its elements can be readily studied, even measured and compared, although comparison in social matters must usually be qualified more broadly than in physical studies. The expression *ceteris paribus* has a particular relevance to social science. Nevertheless the closeness, or effectiveness, or exclusiveness of a system's interaction and relationships can be measured; the purposes for which the system exists can be tested for their meaningfulness and validity in the minds of its members; and the distribution of roles in one social system can be compared with that in another similar one. Incidentally, such analysis of the social system and its elements can be of inestimable value for the leaders themselves in the face of social change, as Homans has explained so pointedly.[17]

---

[16] Figures 1-15 will be found inserted between pages 106 and 107, and Figures 16-26 between pages 202 and 203.
[17] Homans, *The Human Group*, Chapter 16.

The first element of a social system, a plurality of people, is obviously present in the parish. That there is frequent action and interaction follows from the centuries-long continuity in religious evangelization and administration. The parish's standard of values, no less than the Church's, derives from the conviction that God created the world out of love and saved it through Christ's blood out of love, that men might achieve eternally happy union with Him. From this conviction and the facts upon which it rests there follows the purpose of Church and parish, of helping men know God's truth, live according to the moral code consonant with it, and so far as possible achieve union with God (holiness) in this life through the divinely bestowed and Church-embellished cult of divine worship, especially Mass and the sacraments. This primary purpose of missionary endeavor and sanctification implies a secondary one: adopting such measures so to affect the secular institutions and values with which men's lives must also be concerned that they not only will not conflict with men's sacred interests but will be a help thereunto.

Since these secular institutions and values are constantly shifting, at least in accidental form, with social change—for example, urbanization, suburbanization, educational democratization, and so forth—the parish must itself be ready to modify its own secondary measures accordingly. Cardinal Suhard once expressed it by saying that the Church knows how to give up; namely, to give up secondary outmoded measures in place of new more suitable ones. We might recall recent changes in Eucharistic-fast legislation and the mixed marriage ceremony. A major question in a dynamic society is whether the parish's system of interaction and relationships is so organized that it can withstand changing pressures, meet new obstacles, and exploit new opportunities.[18] The perfectly organized social system is

---

[18] Undertaking modern phases of the social and educational apostolates could be cited as other prime examples. In such moves, too, does the Church, and with

one in which all coordinated parts are so constructed and so function as to lead to the most effective achievement of its aims and purposes.

The use of the concept social system in parish study should profit sociological theory and encourage its use as a tool of sociological analysis, both generally and in particular for parish study. The sociologist should be able to see the Catholic parish as a social system, an organization of parts comprising a whole which far transcends those parts. For the parish is more than a few men who are priests, and many people who are laity, and a building which is a church, and rites, and norms and values, and interactive functioning, and a geographical area. It is all these and more: it is the functioning totality which gives its own value to the operations of its parts. One man's placing a wheaten wafer on another person's tongue can be merely a social oddity. When an ordained priest places the consecrated host on the parishioner's tongue, one of the parish's most sacred values is realized. Each aspect of this social-system concept can be sought and found in the parish by the sociologist. He can make a study of the roles and statuses of its individual members and subgroupings. He can investigate its system of values, and analyze the connection between functions, norms, and values. He can study

---

it the parish, play its role of witnessing to Christ and leavening the social mass. Urbanization is a typical major social change requiring the Church and parish to react accordingly for the preservation and continued expansion of their own values. For urbanization has apparently accelerated and facilitated the attractiveness of conflictive secular values such as uninhibited material gain, unrestrained pleasures of the flesh, and freedom from religious norms and practices. The prevalence of secondary associations has meant the decline in importance of the primary social relationships which ordinarily would curb a revolt against traditional moral values. Hence the urban parish's need of recognizing its mission in the market place. A major portion of this study is spent in inquiring to what extent the social system which is Our Lady of Mercy Parish has been effective in functioning for and with its members. Not least important will be our concern with the response of the parishioners to value questions in the various questionnaires.

the impact of place on the parish's functioning, noting the variations among parishes because of their location and the variations of social participation within the parish for the same reason. He can observe the individual member freely participating in other systems without detriment to the parish system, thus verifying the principle that, although the total system transcends its parts, it does not completely absorb them. In short, the sociologist can number the parish among the social forms which can be included in the conceptualization of social system; and, using parish data, he can test hypotheses drawn from the study of other social systems.

The parish analyst too can find this conceptualization a handy tool. His parish is a system, comprised of parts organized to fit the system's purposes. To improve the system there is usually required an improvement either in the parts themselves or their organization. How consonant with his parish's aims, personnel, and facilities are the parish boundaries? How helpful are other ecological factors? Is there an occupational, educational, or other cultural milieu to which the parishioners are attached and which obstructs or favors communication of parish values? Can spiritual interaction be fostered by auxiliary services? If so, by which ones, in view of the parishioners' social orientations? Is the priest playing a businessman's role—for example, in financing and building a parish school—so vigorously that his roles of father, mediator, counselor, and friend are overshadowed? That happens not seldom. If status and role are essential for social participation, what system of statuses and roles can be constructed which the parish laity can utilize to achieve parish purposes? Are the parish functions themselves such that the auxiliary are taking precedence over the primary?

Parishes in different situations—urban or rural, business or residential, territorial or national, young or long-established— can be expected to manifest different expressions of the relationships to be found in any parish. All parishes have priest, people, church, and territory, and all serve the primary aim of administering to the spiritual needs of their members. This ministration includes certain functions and services: sometimes more, sometimes less, sometimes exclusively spiritual, sometimes including many of a material or mixed nature. The priests and people are related to each other, but their relationship can range from the purely formal, passing, and functional to the primary, constant, and communal. Given the existing facts of these functionings and relationships, their extent and characteristics, the pastor and those sharing with him the responsibility for the parish system's effective functioning are faced with this question: in view of the parish aims, are these elements of the system as they should be? In view of the situation within which the parish is, what change, if needed, can be effectuated? Is the communal type of parish the ideal? Even if it is the ideal (which might be questioned from some aspects), can it be achieved in a populous, religiously mixed, urban environment? Might the answer lie in an attempt to introduce more communal-like elements to a structure which must remain, at least to a large extent, associational? Answers to all of these questions can well be sought within the conceptual framework of the social system. The following outline for making a study of the parish may prove helpful to one interested in such a study.

AN OUTLINE FOR THE STUDY OF A PARISH

I. Plurality of human beings (the demographic element)
  A. Vital statistics
    1. Population
      a. Of all within the parish boundaries
      b. Of all Catholics
      c. Of all registered parishioners
    2. Proportion of priests to people
      a. Within the parish boundaries
      b. Catholics only
      c. Registered parishioners
    3. Age and sex composition (its significance)

      4. Birth, marriage, and death rates
      5. Implication of priests' time spent
        a. In baptisms
        b. In marriage preparations and weddings
        c. In funerals
        d. In other services rendered to individual persons
  B. Backgrounds and qualities (their significance)
      1. National and/or racial origin
      2. Education
        a. Catholic
        b. Non-Catholic
      3. Occupation
        a. In or out of parish
        b. Economic status
  C. Level of religious practice
      1. The Fichter categories: nuclear, modal, marginal, dor
        mant
      2. The Schnepp categories: ideal, average, lax, lapsed
      3. Correlation of each of the above categories and charac
        teristics with one another
II. Place and physical environment (the ecological element)
  A. The parish boundaries
      1. Natural
      2. Artificial
  B. As a help or hindrance to administration
  C. As a help or hindrance to community solidarity
      1. Border crossings
      2. Neighbors belonging to different parishes
  D. Too much territory or too little
  E. Climate
  F. Topography
      1. Hills
      2. Parks
      3. Other natural assets
      4. Other natural obstacles
  G. Land use
      1. Main thoroughfares
      2. Other channels of communication
      3. Traffic barriers
      4. Transportation facilities

H. Types of housing
   1. Geographical patterns thereof
   2. Walk-ups
   3. Apartments
   4. Private dwellings
   5. Slums
I. Industry and commerce
   1. Shopping centers (influence on religious services)
   2. Type and quantity of traffic (impact on youth recreation)
J. Educational and other cultural establishments
   1. Opportunity for mutual cooperation
   2. Availability of respective facilities and services
   3. Movies, various recreational facilities, seen as assets or liabilities
K. Hospitals, prisons, other public services
   1. Drains on parish priests' time and energy in nonparochial work
   2. Opportunity for lay help, apostolic contribution
L. The parish plant: church, school, rectory, and so forth
   1. Adequate for number of communicants
   2. Adequate for those practicing
   3. Adequate for those who should be practicing
   4. Qualitatively satisfying and helpful (architecture, paintings, and so forth)
III. Repeated action and interaction
   A. Provision of parish services
      1. Mass
      2. Sacraments
      3. Instructions
      4. Spiritual and corporal works of mercy
   B. Use of parish services
      1. Directly religious
      2. Parish absorption and integration of natural community functions (for example, recreation)
   C. Frequency of interaction
   D. Quality of interaction
      1. Degree of internal conviction
      2. Conformity between external comportment and norms
   E. Specific analysis of each of above in terms of parish's purpose (see IV)

IV. Purpose of such interaction (the reasons for the parish's existence)
- A. The system of parish values
  1. Implicated ends, norms, institutions
  2. Living the two great commandments (note pertinence to, perhaps inadequacy of, categories of religious practice, as listed in I, C)
- B. Living the faith and religion
  1. Knowledge and acceptance of the creed
  2. Observance of the code, the commandments, canons, and so forth (note items in social morality, for example, *re* race, industrial relations, Sunday observance, courtship and marriage patterns)
  3. Practice of cult (Mass, sacraments, other liturgy)
  4. Realization of communion (love and solidarity of Christian community)
  5. Growth in Christian perfection (knowledge and practice)
  6. Personal holiness and community christianization
  7. Community happiness and holiness
  8. Apostolic interest in, impact on, civic community and its institutions
  9. Estimate of extent to which such values are being realized in the parish

V. Relationships defined and/or connoted by such interaction
- A. Roles and statuses
  1. Recognition of psychological need for having same
  2. Recognition of sociological need for having same
- B. Priests and people
  1. Primary and secondary roles of priest
  2. Fichter's list of sixteen observed modern roles
  3. Exercise of such roles by the priest
     a. Proper coordination and subordination of roles according to parish values
     b. Definition by authority
     c. Attitude of domination or cooperation
  4. Primary and secondary roles of the people
     a. Mere passivity, or active social cooperation
     b. Played by the consistent few, or by the widespread many

       5. Roles of priests with one another
       6. Roles of people with one another
    C. Parish societies
       1. Adequate for parish purposes in type
       2. Adequate for parish purposes in number and membership
       3. Wedded to antiquated formalism, or aware of modern circumstances
       4. Opportunity for lay initiative and responsibility
       5. Utilization of the better trained (what of the college graduate?)
  VI. In view of an estimate made of the achievement of these purposes, is there need to reform the system of roles and statuses prevailing in a particular parish, or to conserve and strengthen it?

Obviously this list is capable of almost indefinite extension. From what has been included, however, it should be obvious how pertinent and potentially useful the tools of sociological analysis, and particularly when organized around the social-system concept, are for parish study, on both the academic or theoretical and also the empirical and practical level.

We might ask a further question, whether there is any ideal type of parish, parish practice, and parishioner? One might ask in reply, *"Whose ideal type?"* Would the ideal imply perfection? Then, conceivably, each parishioner would be a saint, and the ideal parish would have no room for sinners. Yet the parish exists, in part, to help the sinner return to peace with God. Does the ideal parishioner only assist at Mass, receive daily Communion, and participate in several parish activities? If so, does that mean that the busy Catholic mother of a young family and the family's devotedly Catholic breadwinner fail to meet the ideal because their sacramentally blessed family obligations prevent them from such extended participation? Sociologically speaking, would one base the ideal on the primary, closely knit community, or on the more complex associational pattern, on the concept of family group or on the concept of service organization?

One writer has well expressed his idea of the good and ideal parish as follows:

> A "good parish" is generally described as a parish which exhibits such signs of parochial health as a large attendance at Mass, general frequentation of the Sacraments, adequate financial support, active parish societies and a good annual crop of converts. An *ideal* parish might be described as one which exhibits in addition to all these undeniable blessings a real participation on the part of the people in the total life of the parish. An ideal parish might be one in which the sanctifying and unifying influence of the Church penetrates beyond the walls of the church and school and rectory into the family and working lives of all the people. It might be described as a parish in which the parishioners play an active and vital part, have a deep sense of "belonging," and more than that, a realization of their obligation towards the parish as a whole and towards each other as members of the parish. Such a parish would be one of which the people think with pride and affection as *their parish;* it would be a parish in which the priests know the people and the people know the priests, a parish in which priests and people work together on a spiritual and apostolic level. *In a word, the ideal parish might be described as a parish in which the Church is the very heart and center of a community, a parish which is itself a community.*[19]

The foregoing beautifully expressed ideal is very attractive though one is left with many unanswered questions induced by realities of time, space, and number in an urban setting.

We propose the following as a sort of norm which might be used in appraising any given parish. We might say that:

> The perfectly organized parish, in the most complete sense, is a
>   functioning social system:
> of such size and physical equipment;
> of such numerical proportion among priests, staff, lay leaders, and
>   other members;

---

[19] Gerard P. Weber, *Chaplain's Manual: Christian Family Movement*, pp. 3-4. Chicago: Chicago Federation of the Christian Family Movement, 1952.

of such a network of cooperating and mutually appreciated relationships and societies;

so consciously possessed in its members of the knowledge of Christian doctrine and moral;

so dedicated to the achievement of communal and personal holiness
through use of Mass and the sacraments and pursuit of the two
great laws of divine and fraternal love;

so constant in its maintenance of the primacy of its spiritual values
and apostolic commission over coordinated subsidiary temporal values;

so welded by the communal concern of its members

that

there exists the practical and exploited opportunity for the spiritual
and derivatively temporal richness of the faith to be brought to
its every actual and potential member and to every institution
of its coextensive civic community.

Admittedly this "definition" is cumbersome. But it is submitted that any parish priest or apostolic layman will find in it
just about all the criteria according to which his own parish
might be appraised. For example, do the parish boundaries
make sense? Many do, many do not. Is the physical plant adequate? The churches of some large European parishes are simply not large enough to accommodate all parishioners should
they all decide to live up to their Sunday obligation. Nor need
we go to Europe to find that! What of the still large percentage
of Catholic school children who cannot find room in the Catholic
school? What is to be done about it? Do priests and people know
one another, or are the former known by just a relatively small
circle of the latter while the majority of parishioners are simply
the unknown and unknowing mass? What should be done about
it? What *can* be done about it? Might the parish staff be enlarged, perhaps through having the laity assume, with or without pay, some less priestly functions? Do the people know one
another? If not, how might it be brought about?

How well and maturely do the parishioners know the faith?
We do not refer to recollection of catechism answers from gram-

mar school, but to a knowledge that is satisfying to and sufficient for mature adults. This is of course one of our greatest weaknesses, and few parishes would score a satisfactory mark on that question. How might the situation be improved? How pertinent to parish needs and the flock's interests are the Sunday sermons? Do we know the answer to that question, or do we just assume or guess?

Are the parish's social and business enterprises (financing and building) adequate? Are they perhaps more successful than the parish's spiritual enterprises? What is to be done about it? Do the laity actually consider themselves part of the parish, or merely persons to be administered to? How much nonmonetary contribution is there room for them to make? How much opportunity is available to them for participating in the parish's apostolate? Do the laity look for ways to participate? Do the clergy, following the Church's urging, accept them or look for ways to direct them toward participation?

How much true, fraternal, Christian love is evident in the parish, toward fellow Catholics, toward non-Catholic members of the parish? (Or has it been forgotten that *all* persons living within the parish are considered by the Church to be part of the parish and objects of the parish's apostolic concern?) To what extent does the parish school contribute to parish solidarity, not merely in the sense of rallying around the old school team and banner, but in the sense of forming in young students the sense of gratitude and loyalty to their spiritual home?

Perhaps some of the foregoing questions imply a certain idealism. They do, for we are considering an ideal parish as a norm for appraisal. With such an ideal in mind, obviously none of us can rest with what we have.

The first step is to find out the facts, and some of the questions above will suggest what facts are to be looked for—not that there are not hundreds of other pertinent questions. The study of Our Lady of Mercy Parish in the following chapters provides only some of the facts, tries to answer only some of the questions. It is published, however, in the hope that it will serve as a case study in parish analysis, as an indication of the positive elements present in a functioning parish social system, and as a stimulus to future parish studies of somewhat similar nature.

Perhaps if we had more studies of the parish, not all parishes would have to ask all the questions suggested above. We might build up a core of socioparochial knowledge on which all might draw. For parish sociology is but a guide helping the pastor to lead his faithful flock or find the wanderers and the lost. It has the role of facilitating for the Church its task of transmitting its treasures, thanks to a more precise knowledge of the social situation of its children, of the social pressures which help or hinder them.

CHAPTER IV

Scope and Method
of This Study

As background for our own study previous chapters explained the scope of parish sociology, coursed through its development, and offered a conceptual framework within which to understand and analyze a parish. In which direction is our study headed? A broad choice was available. An addition to any previous study would be a contribution: a historical survey of parish birth and growth; a simple demographic exposition in charts and tables of parish facts and parishioner characteristics; a mere record of religious practice on the part of the 14,000 Catholics within Our Lady of Mercy Parish borders or of the 11,000 not enrolled in the local national parish and adjacent territorial parishes or of the 8,570 parishioners who were fully recorded in the OLM census; a description of OLM's ecological situation and the influence it has on OLM's religious life; a comparison of OLM's records with the published reports of other parish surveys; or an inquiry into the social relations of OLM parishioners among themselves or with neighborhood nonparishioners. Each of these approaches would have value, and something of each of them is included in the following pages.

Actually, we aim to examine an urban Catholic parish as a social system, as one kind of functioning social structure. Having noted in Chapter 3 what the builders of this type of society intended, we want to evaluate its structure and functioning in terms of that purpose. In so doing we shall utilize the conceptual scheme explained previously, that of the social system.[1]

In our study we are not interested in offering criticism or congratulation. We are concerned with careful observation and analysis of sufficient factual data in the everyday life of OLM Parish to show the validity and profitability of the social-system concept. What methods we used, how we obtained and analyzed our data, and how these methods can be helpful in other parish studies concern us in the present chapter. But first, why was OLM chosen?

In the first though least important place, OLM was in close geographical proximity to the author's residence and Fordham University's Sociological Research Laboratory. In terms of convenience and efficiency, this advantage turned out to be far greater than even originally expected. Second, though the expressions good parish and typical parish are extremely vague and sometimes almost meaningless, according to several rule-of-thumb criteria OLM had an excellent reputation in the judgment of lay parishioners and nonparishioners, as also of several priest associates of the author. Besides, viewed according to apparent ecological and socioeconomic conditions, OLM seemed to be in a social milieu typical of that shared by many other parishes in its own neighborhood and in similar neighborhoods in

---

[1] Consequently we are not so much interested in other conceptualizations of the parish, such as those outlined by Father Fichter; for example, those of the legal corporation, the superimposed association, the institutionalized association, the communal group, the cluster of subgroupings, the series of statistical categories, or any others. (See Fichter, *Urban Parish*, pp. 182 ff.) Each of these conceptualizations might well be used with profit, but they do not fit in with the convenience of the social-system concept. It should not be thought that this frame of reference can be taken for granted. After all, Father Fichter, whose sociological acumen concerning the parish is evident in his own analyses, denies that the parish is a social group, a concept very comparable to that of social system. (See *ibid.*, pp. 18-19, 42, 51, 55, 68.)

its own and in other cities. This does not mean that OLM is typical of all city parishes: in some ways of course it is, in others it is not. For example, OLM church is right off a main thoroughfare and a shopping center. Many parish churches are not. This occasions a difference in confession service on Saturdays and before First Fridays. Again, OLM, though it has very few colored people, has received a sizable quota of Latin-American immigrants. This quota is not comparable to that of some downtown residential parishes where Latin Americans have settled in large numbers; nor is it comparable to other city parishes in higher-class residential areas where Latin Americans have not yet arrived. In OLM Parish live many Catholics who belong to a nearby national parish. While this is not a unique situation, it is not usual. On the other hand, some features of OLM are rather unique: responsibility for two hospitals within its territory and sponsorship of such social services as a very successful credit union, an employment bureau, and a social-welfare bureau. Despite these characteristics, OLM appeared to be sufficiently representative for our kind of study.

Besides its typicalness and good reputation, another favorable characteristic, one of really essential importance, attracted the author to OLM: the strong interest and sincere cooperation of the pastor and clergy. Without such interest and cooperation no adequate parish survey can be a success. Not only does accessibility to parish records depend on them, but much insight into parish life and conditions is impossible without them. After a period of participant observation in some parish activity, performance of some priestly work in the parish, and frequent discussions with each and all of the parish staff, the author was satisfied that OLM would be most acceptable for the purposes of a sociological survey.

Most European parish surveys were limited to ascertaining anonymously the number, age, sex, family status (married, single, and so forth), occupation, and number of children or adults attending Sunday Mass. Usually the inquiry was conducted on a "typical" Sunday of fall or spring in all the Masses of the parish church and auxiliary chapels. Several diocesan inquiries included all the parishes of the diocese simultaneously. The inquiry did not take the place of the parish census (usually lacking), for the respondent was not asked to write his name on the inquiry blank.[2]

No matter what the method, those types of survey have a rather limited scope and value. They enable the bishop or pastor to have a more precise, but still very general, idea of his flock's practice, as described in the last chapter. He can further specify this knowledge through comparison with the population statistics recorded by the local civic jurisdiction, whether nation, province, county, city, or ward. But a great number of things, religious as well as secular, are very important for adequate

---

[2] Ordinarily, printed forms were distributed at each Mass, and the congregation was instructed to fill them out either during the usual sermon time or immediately after Mass. Apparently the former method was more effective, since many persons were not willing to wait till after Mass. Supplying a few thousand pencils for each Mass created a problem; but for the most part, depending on proper execution, the inquiries proved to be over 90 per cent effective. In one method, used in Belgium, the congregation was supplied with cards consisting of detachable stubs for the various categories. The advantage of the method was that it made pencils unnecessary and facilitated analysis, as did our McBee cards described in Appendix II. The disadvantage was that mistakes (detaching the wrong stub) were irremediable. A particular advantage of this type of survey is that it permitted knowledge of the extent of Mass attendance by people from other than parish territory. Our own survey at OLM did not include this advantage, though it would have been desirable, because it was felt that the parishioners had already been bothered enough for their cooperation.

A couple of surveys were even less well controlled. Mass attendance in one Belgian survey was estimated by counting the number of holy pictures distributed by parish boys to every member of the congregation who left the church after Mass. Anyone who knows anything about crowds pouring out of churches after services (or about young lads in such a situation) would have reservations about the accuracy of this method. (See A. Ryckmans, "Qu'est-ce qu'un catholique pratiquant?" *Nouvelle revue théologique* 76:965-72, November 1954.)

knowledge of a parish or diocese; for example, reception of sacraments, validity of marriage, residential mobility, amount and quality of education, and so on. To be at all fruitful parish sociology must include at least such elements.

One particular difficulty to be faced in inquiries about religious practice is the meaning and importance ascribed to practice. Practice of the Catholic religion is not limited to assisting at Sunday Mass, or even to receiving all the sacraments in due time, and frequently if they can and should be received frequently. The founder of the Christian religion made it quite clear that there are two great commandments binding His followers, love of neighbor as well as love of God. Boulard tried somewhat successfully to include this element in his rural surveys. It would even have to be established that the parishioner who is regular in his religious exercises is prompted by the proper motives before it could be certain that such practice manifested love of God. Conversely, some persons who do not attend divine worship live "good" lives motivated by Christian principles in dealing with their neighbors: they are not irreligious, but their religious practice is deficient. It is also true that participation in some religious functions need not imply full communion with the Church or parish. For example, someone who attends Mass regularly but does not receive Holy Communion at least at Easter time is seriously remiss in his religious practice. However, despite the truth of these qualifications, observance of religious obligations remains an important sign of the value of religion in the life of a person or community. Since in the Catholic religion certain practices are required by church law and since, as external, they are somewhat observable and to that extent scientifically measurable, calculation of a parish's practice must be the religious sociologist's first step in assessing the effectiveness of the functioning of the parochial society.

Beyond the relatively simple method of the single Sunday Mass survey, other procedures have been utilized. One of the

Marseilles studies retested a half year later and compared results. They were fairly close. Le Bras and Boulard compared rises and dips in religious practice and number of vocations with developments in secular history, as well as with prevalence of attitudes peculiar to particular parts of the country. Le Bret's extensive questionnaire in *Guide pratique de l'enquête sociale*[3] aims at as complete a knowledge of a person's or community's active and passive role in social life, within which the religious aspect is to be examined, as could be planned. The use of photographs, especially aerial photographs, has proved valuable for giving clearer understanding of parish divisions, the locale of certain socioreligious uniformities, and the composition of the total parish. Probably of even more practical value is the construction of several transparent parish maps on which are indicated, either through dots, shadings, or hatchings, the degree of concentration of various phenomena. By simply superimposing the map showing area distribution of one characteristic—for example, good housing—upon another showing a different characteristic, let us say years and quality of education, or perhaps religious practice, one can immediately see to what extent relationships are present.[4]

None of the European studies which the author has been able to find utilized a census, properly speaking, to gather the data which it analyzed, though it would seem that some of the rural

---

[3] L.-J. Le Bret, *Guide pratique de l'enquête sociale.* 2 vols. Paris: Presses Universitaires de France, 1951-1952.

[4] Just as the urban sociologists have used this technique to show relationships between poor housing and ill health, broken homes, delinquency, and so on, so too European religious sociologists have shown, in some areas, similar relationships between lack of religious practice and minimal or non-Catholic education, blue-collar occupations, crowded housing, and similar characteristics. The lesson is quickly evident to the pastor, charged with exercising the shepherd's role toward every member of the flock in his territory, that in precisely those areas where the weaknesses of his parish are greatest there is the greatest need of his presence.

studies might have done so. The American studies, on the contrary, based most of their analyses on data acquired in the census. Both have made use of pertinent civic data available for the zones within which their respective parishes were situated. This technique is an important part of our own procedure.

Each of the American religious-practice studies—those by Schnepp, McCaffrey, Kelly, Coogan, Fichter—began after a preliminary examination of the parish's geographical situation and, in some instances, of population data provided by United States Census Bureau publications and other public and civic files, with as complete a religious census as possible. This has been thought desirable, even necessary, for several reasons. First, the pastor is to some extent responsible for everyone living within his parish, for even though the Catholics are his primary charge, all others are potentially members of his flock, and thus he must know and act toward them accordingly insofar as that is possible;[5] second, particularly among mobile Americans in crowded cities, the presence of many resident Catholics, practicing or lapsed, is unknown to their respective pastors. Only an adequate census can provide a complete register of parish members and the information pertaining to them. There are other practical pastoral reasons, not directly pertinent to scientific research, such as the advantage of some personal contact between parishioner and pastor (or his representative).[6]

---

[5] *Codex iuris canonici*, Canon 1350, 1.

[6] Father Kelly, in his contribution on "The Parish Census" in Nuesse and Harte, *Sociology of the Parish*, pp. 234-60, would include these reasons under what he calls the therapeutic census as opposed to statistical and research censuses. In the McCaffrey, Schnepp, and Fichter studies a good deal of interviewing complemented census data and enabled the respective investigators to bring to bear much personal experience and insight while they analyzed their data. The Kelly-Coogan survey involved the tabulation and analysis of over 40,000 extensive schedules, practically the same as that used in our OLM study, and apparently there was neither much opportunity nor place for personal participation by way of interviewing. At least no mention is made of it in their respective reports.

Despite the remissness of very many parishes, for whatever reason, in this matter of keeping adequate census files, the importance of the census cannot be disputed. Later chapters explain the multiple relationships binding pastor and people, and his effective management of those relationships very often depends on the information contained in his census records. Church law requires that each parish have, among the parish books, one for recording the *status animarum*, which might be freely translated as "the spiritual condition of the members of the parish."[7] While many parishes have a fine record in this respect, and others a poor one, it would seem that the Archdiocese of Philadelphia (perhaps there are others) is most exemplary. There each parish is required to take up a block census annually, and the archdiocese is in the process, already in its eighth year, of collecting, filing, and keeping up-to-date census records for the entire archdiocese.[8]

A further very important reason for the parish census is that diocesan and national statistics depend for their completion and accuracy on local reports. That figures are far from accurate is readily admitted—not least readily, the author has been assured, by P. J. Kenedy and Sons, publishers of the annual *Official Catholic Directory*.[9]

---

[7] *Codex iuris canonici*, Canon 470, 1.

[8] Briefly described in a gracious letter to the author from the Most Reverend John F. O'Hara, C.S.C., archbishop of Philadelphia.

[9] See Thomas B. Kenedy's editorial discussion of the divergence between his own reports and United States Bureau of the Census estimates in *Official Catholic Directory for the Year of Our Lord 1958*, p. i. See also Chapter 1, footnote 15. There is additional evidence that the Catholic population is higher than officially claimed. The *Catholic Digest* survey concluded statistically that in 1952 there were 23,700,000 Catholics over 18 years of age, some 23 per cent of the population, although the official claim amounted to less than 20 per cent at that time. The Catholic population below 18 years should have at least a proportion equal to that of adult Catholics, which would indicate a national Catholic population of about 38,000,000. A survey prepared for the Health Insurance Plan of Greater New York City reported that nearly half of New York's

Of course much depends, in this matter of numbering Catholics, on what is meant by the term Catholic. One who has been baptized in the Catholic faith remains a member of the Church until separated from it by heresy, schism, or excommunication. But many who are actually members, so far as can be known, never attend Catholic services and are no longer in conscious contact with the Church. The sociologist, without denying that these persons are or may be members in the theological sense, would not consider them members in the sociological sense, for there is no manifestation of a social relationship existing between them and the Church as members and society.[10]

---

population (47.6 per cent) is Catholic, as compared with 26 per cent Jewish and 23 per cent Protestant. (See *New York Times*, March 21, 1955.) In Connecticut in 1954 of all babies born, 61 per cent were baptized in the Catholic religion (see NCWC News Service, May 31, 1955), and in Rochester, New York, a city reputedly only 50 per cent Catholic, the infant baptism rate was 70 per cent of all Rochester births. It would seem that either the Catholic population has been underestimated, or that the Catholic birth rate is much higher than the national rate, or that possibly both are true. Finally, though the author has been assured by the Military Ordinariate that no exact statistics are available concerning the number of Catholics in the armed forces during the last war, one cannot help wondering if the estimates of military chaplains were without foundation. Almost invariably they claimed that Catholics constituted over 30 per cent of the armed forces. We can be sure only by getting the facts—with the help of the census. It should be unnecessary to mention that this attempt to add to the reported number of Catholics derives from no desire to boast. In fact, almost the contrary; for if Catholics are far more numerous than is officially known, then the question whether our parishes are functioning effectively becomes seriously compounded.

[10] As Father Joseph H. Fichter pointed out several years ago (see "Catholics in the United States," *America* 82:523-24, February 4, 1950), the baptism of many children is simply a social event in the lives of their parents, who recognize little religious significance in it. On the other hand, we might tend to presume too much remissness. The *Catholic Digest* survey concluded that, whereas 82 per cent of adult Catholics attended church at least sometime within the previous twelve-week period, 62 per cent claimed to have attended every Sunday out of the twelve. Certainly the 62 per cent and even the 82 per cent would have to be listed as Catholic, not only theologically but also sociologically. What of the other 18 per cent? Apparently they are, if not quite dormant, at least very lax. Even so, they admit to being Catholic, even profess it. Perhaps the sociological bond of membership between the lax or

A final observation concerning the problem of religious-affiliation statistics is pertinent here. An easy, relatively painless, and quite professional solution would be the inclusion of one simple question on the national decennial census. Warmly debated in the recent past, the plan was enthusiastically endorsed by a preponderance of scientific, civic, and church groups, and it proved to be both acceptable and fruitful in a midwestern trial run. However, in the interests of public peace and to avoid the opposition of a contentious minority, the plan was shelved as far as the 1960 census is concerned.[11]

---

dormant Catholic and his Church is weak, but one cannot deny that it is there. Incidentally, by dropping 18 per cent from the calculated 38,000,000 of 1952 (see footnote 9 above), we arrive at a figure fairly close to the 32,500,000 reported in the *Official Catholic Directory*. As Father Fichter suggests, this might indicate a high degree of accuracy in the annual reports.

[11] The reader is invited to consider the editorials on "The Census Debate" (*America* 97:498, August 17, 1957) and "Religion in the Census" (*Commonweal* 66:438, August 2, 1957) as well as the present author's letter concerning the latter and *Commonweal's* response in the subsequent issue of September 13, pp. 591-92.

There had been planned a fifth national religious census for 1956, the first four having been conducted decennially from 1906 to 1936. The intended 1946 census had been dropped owing to post-World War II difficulties. Unfortunately all these religious censuses depended on the reports of the several religious denominations rather than on complete personal pollings. When plans for the 1956 census were scuttled the aim was conceived of including a question on religious affiliation in the 1960 federal population census. This would have the twin benefits of eliminating the inaccurate information of the past and of coordinating American religious data with all other American social data collected in the census. Some opposition was expected, particularly from persons who have the notion that a religious question in the census tends to endanger the separation between church and state. Yet democratic states in Europe include the question of religious affiliation in their government census schedules. Besides, the very reasons given by the Census Bureau for conducting the coming census in 1956 would be more valid if the data were more accurate. These reasons, as expressed in the *New York Times* of May 7, 1955 by the census director, Robert W. Burgess, are: (1) It would show the world that the United States democracy has a strong spiritual base. (2) It could be used commercially by manufacturers of religious items in marketing their products. (3) It would be a guide for the various denominations in determining how large a following they have and in what areas.

Our study of Our Lady of Mercy Parish began with a census, though only after lengthy preparation.[12] In order to set up a control we first mapped the parish in terms of United States Census tracts. As appears on the map (see Figure 2), the heart of OLM Parish (and actually quite a good cross section of the parish) is Bronx Census Tract 399, within which the parish church and school are located. OLM includes also most of Tract 401 and part of Tract 237 to the west of Tract 399, most of Tract 397, and parts of Tracts 383, 385, and 387 to the east of Tract 399. Our interest in collecting Census Bureau data on

---

It is difficult to see why the question could not be asked, with the respondent having the option of not replying. Any religious-affiliation information gathered in the census would amount to sheer gain. Incidentally (and this is subordinate to more important considerations) inclusion of the religious-affiliation question on the national census schedule would save religious leaders the large expense which parish censuses often involve. In an answering letter to the author, who inquired about the methods to be used in the forthcoming 1956 religious census, Census Director Burgess wrote: "There has also been a feeling in the past that a direct question on religious affiliation in the decennial census might prove sufficiently controversial to seriously impair the quality of the information collected. At the present time, however, we are giving serious consideration to this problem, and certainly the possibility of asking a question on religious affiliation will be carefully examined when the time comes to determine the content of the schedule for the 1960 Census." Unfortunately, the shelving of this plan means the loss for at least a decade of a tremendous amount of valuable information. We might hope and *strive earnestly* that it be realized at least in the 1970 national census.

[12] Since the completion of this report on OLM, the author wrote a series of short articles on parish sociology for *Catholic Management Journal*. One of these articles (Spring 1958) was on "Parish Census" and provided an explanation of the steps to be followed in compiling a "numerically complete, informationally extensive, and administratively maneuverable" census. The first step is to compile, preferably in a loose-leaf folder with pertinent block maps, an address and religious-affiliation file of every home in the parish; the next, to make two sets of alphabetical indexes, on simple 3 by 5-inch or other cards, of all Catholic families, one to be retained in absolute alphabetical order, the other to be broken down according to parish sections in alphabetical order; the next, to gather census information from all Catholic families; finally, to arrange that information on readily accessible and maneuverable research cards. See the description and explanation of the OLM census card in Appendix II.

these several parish tracts was threefold. First, we wanted to know as much as we could about the milieu within which and part of which OLM was; second, we wanted to be able to compare OLM data with the data of its neighborhood; third, we wanted to have a norm and also a control check for our census work. For example, we would know from the United States Census that some particular block had so many households, so many individuals, so many renters and owners, so many single, married, divorced, separated, or widowed persons, so many people with such-and-such educational and economic achievements. These data, particularly with regard to residence, provided a backdrop and norm for our OLM address file and census assignments. Incidentally, United States Census reports and maps, including census-tract and block statistics, are available in most large libraries and at the United States Government Printing Office. Census-tract information is contained in the population bulletins, and census-block data are found in the housing bulletins.

Since the national census is taken only every ten years, not all parishes could hope to get exact information about their population in the later years of the decade. Census data remain pertinent throughout the decade in many already established urban areas in which there has been little change since the decennial census. This was fortunately true in OLM. In many cities which have undertaken urban renewal projects or in which areas have been affected by residential and industrial mobility, and in the many burgeoning suburban areas, census data may no longer give an accurate picture of the existing situation. They are still valuable, however, as bases for comparison and indicators of likely enumeration districts in the parish. Furthermore, several cities and counties undertake mid-decade censuses.

Having made maps of each census tract in the parish, as also of each block in each tract, our next step was to draw up a file of every address and apartment number in the parish. This was done with the competent and energetic assistance of the priest moderator and members of the OLM Legion of Mary. Each census tract was handled as a unit and each square block as a subunit. A time-consuming mistake was made in trying to utilize already existing maps of streets which cut through several blocks. Of course such maps could be used, but the chance for confusion and error existed. With the maps completed, copies of an "address and religious-affiliation record" were mimeographed on paper $8\frac{1}{2}$" x 11" in size and inscribed with the address (and apartment number, if necessary) of every household in the parish. Each sheet is identified by its census-tract number and its block number. After the address is space for the household's family name, for designating the family's religious affiliation, and for indicating the Catholic family's acceptance or rejection of the census schedule and its ultimate submission or retention.[13] There is a space for any comment of possible significance for the pastor, such as reasons for rejecting the schedule, manifestation of a friendly or hostile attitude, and so on. The plan was that each census worker would find on two or three of these sheets the 70 or so households for which he alone would be responsible, and be able to organize his own work most effectively in accordance with his own convenience and with no chance of interference with or by any other census worker.

Meanwhile planning the census continued on two levels: the technical or material, involving factors of cost, personnel, time, and materials; and the psychological, directed toward preparing the parishioners to help in taking up the census, or at least to cooperate in filling out their own family schedule in due time. All these details are mentioned here for the benefit of those readers who might wish to consider them in preparing or executing their own parish census.

---

[13] As stated in Chapter 6, any family in which any member was Catholic was designated as Catholic.

Cost can be feared as a prohibitive factor in census work. If such excellent census workers as Parish Visitors, Trinitarians, Missionary Helpers, or other religious groups are engaged, there is at least the obvious and necessary cost of their support during their time of work. Materials for our purpose were not too expensive. It was found that $250 was more than sufficient for having printed some 6,000 family census schedules (including 2,000 more than the expected need, so that every census worker would be certain to have enough at his disposal), covering letters for each household which included some specific and helpful instructions from the pastor, gummed envelopes within which each household would seal its own filled-out schedule, 300 identification cards to be carried by the census workers, 150 large envelopes and folders for their use in covering their territory, and about 7,000 sample filled-in census forms.[14] These sample forms, containing on the blank side a message from the priests of the parish, were for distribution at all the Christmas Masses, when, it was expected, many people would be in church who did not ordinarily attend.

An additional item, not included in the $250 and not quite absolutely necessary, was the use of the parish bulletin for two months almost exclusively for census purposes. This is explained below, but is mentioned here as an additional optional item of expense.[15] If the parish has a regular bulletin, there is

---

[14] If the cost of materials seems low, it must be remembered that printers often make special prices to parishes.

[15] All further cost was due to research analysis: planning a research card, purchases in sufficient quantity to provide one for every individual in the parish, transcription of the data from family schedules to individual cards, and punching and analyzing the cards. Actually such analysis is the most effective method of utilizing census data. Many a parish has fairly complete census files, but their use is restricted to providing information about individual persons or families. Analysis of data is explained more fully later in this chapter. It is mentioned here as another cost factor if the parish wishes to take that further step.

no reason why the cost for the census issues could not be included in the normal bulletin budget. Another optional item could be, and in fact was for OLM, catered buffet refreshments for the assembled census workers on the night of the final preparatory meeting.

The particular census schedule chosen (see the sample copy between pages 80 and 81) was almost the very same as that used by Fathers Kelly and Coogan in their Florida study. Other parish studies in the Fordham University Sociological Research Laboratory were using the same schedule. It was decided that the use of the same schedule would be helpful in the development of parish sociology, since the data presented in the various studies would thus be more easily comparable. Experience has taught us that some revisions would be preferable, particularly in view of our own particular procedure.[16] On the other hand, its basic comparability with other studies and the data in census reports made it extremely valuable for social analysis.

---

[16] Despite all the repeated instructions, whether given orally in church or written in the bulletin, the pastor's letter, and the sample schedules, some people found the schedules either too long or too involved, and either required help or left portions unanswered. Failure to ask for the place of reception of various sacraments, as well as of participation in parochial activities, was later regretted. The question about validity of marriage should have been phrased more tactfully. This would not be necessary if a priest or nun were conducting the census by interview: the proper psychological approach to the particular person concerning that question would be assured by personalities and circumstances. But since the OLM census schedule was filled out in privacy by the individual family, more tact was called for. Again, if the census were to be taken up by priest or nun, the schedule need not have appeared too involved. As it was, many persons showed that, despite the explanations, the schedule was too much for them. Even if nine out of every ten answer suitably, a 10 per cent deficiency ratio is quite costly when a census covers almost 5,000 families. A humorous reaction to the schedule was expressed by one parishioner who suggested that, just as citizens could find an office for help in filling out income-tax forms, so the parish might set up an office for advising applicants on filling out their parish census. On the other hand, most persons did cooperate extremely well, and most schedules were filled out carefully and intelligently.

Not dissociated from cost in the planning of a parish census is the matter of personnel to be used in taking up the census. There are various possibilities. All or some of the priests might be assigned to the work, either on a long-term, continuing basis, or on a short-term, concentrated one. This is probably the ideal method (except for some persons whom a priest simply cannot reach), but frequently it is quite impracticable, particularly in a large city parish, where priests oftentimes can hardly keep up with their ordinary duties. Of great help to parish priests in the census, if their services can be obtained, are religious groups who have specialized in that work. They have developed perfected techniques and often enough can and do reach and open hearts which would remain locked to anyone else. But these groups are usually in great demand, sometimes being booked up for years in advance. Besides, they do represent a cost factor, and in their thoroughness must take several months for their task. Frequently seminarians are assigned to this work. It is excellent practice for them, and the people are usually not unwilling to cooperate with them. On the other hand, summertime is not the best time for taking a census, since many people are away, and besides, a couple of summer months cannot suffice for a complete census undertaken by a team of two or three seminarians. Sometimes the Legion of Mary or some other parish organization such as the Sodality is charged with the census responsibility. They often do excellent work; but by the very nature of their situation—limited time, limited personnel, and other obligations—the census of a sizable parish takes them years to complete.

The final choice of personnel consists of the parishioners themselves. It has its disadvantages as well as its advantages. Despite training and good will, unevenness in ability and application spells unevenness in effectiveness and results. Since, rightfully enough, people cannot be expected to relate their personal spiritual affairs to fellow laymen (nor are laymen competent to do much about them), the effectiveness and accuracy of the census depend in large measure on the ability and willingness of the mass of respondents to cooperate in their private filling out of the schedules. Undoubtedly there are many self-answered census schedules which are not nearly so accurate, sometimes not even so truthful, as they would be if a priest, sister, or even experienced Legionary recorded the answers to judicious questioning. On the other hand, having volunteer trained parishioners do the job has several important compensating advantages. If the project is carefully planned, the work of each individual team exactly defined, and the parish sufficiently prepared to cooperate, lay census takers can do the job quite efficiently and speedily. Many parishes have used with some success the so-called "forty-eight-hour method," in which the entire forewarned parish is visited on two prearranged nights, first to receive the census schedule, then to return it.

At OLM we adopted that system partially; but since our aims were broader than simply collecting census schedules, we did not limit ourselves to forty-eight hours. We viewed our parishioner helpers not merely as runners or messengers, but as parish representatives. It was physically impossible for the priests of the parish to visit the whole parish, and a real value was seen in having parishioners call on their neighbors as personal representatives of the pastor and parish. Our plan called for a visit not only at all presumed Catholic homes, but at *every* home in the entire parish. In view of certain anticlerical prejudices which still exist here and there, among disaffected Catholics as well as among some non-Catholics, it was expected that laymen might receive a more ready welcome at some doors than a priest or sister would. This turned out to be true.

But speed, the unity engendered by a community project, and an entrance into difficult homes were not the only advantages of our parishioner-helper policy. The lay helpers themselves were expected to derive much real profit from their enterprise, and they did. First, they played an integral role in a parish project which was honestly described as important. Thus they were participating in a vital phase of Catholic action and the lay apostolate. They received responsibility in a field which many American laymen unfortunately still think must be tilled exclusively by the clergy. Every time they knocked on a non-Catholic door, or even at the door of Catholics who had had no personal contact with the parish staff, they were bringing a greeting from their pastor in the name of Christ, and they were serving as a medium for the neighbor to deal personally with the parish if need be. Many members of OLM's census team grew enthusiastic about their role in exercising this function.[17] A second benefit which they experienced, connected with the first, was the opportunity of getting at least a first superficial view of how their neighbors lived: an old blind woman who was delighted to have someone call on her, foreign born who were still suspicious and could speak no English, families of their own respective social situation who were glad to converse with a new

---

[17] As a matter of fact, persuading them to volunteer did not prove easy. Despite invitations to all from the altar and to members of parish societies by mail, very few presented themselves at the first preparatory meetings. Our original intention had been to invite only men to do the actual census work and to ask the women to join in the subsequent paper work. We overestimated the men and underestimated the ladies. As time for the actual census taking drew near we had to enlist their aid, and we were still far short of our desired 150 two-man teams. With that number we planned that no team would have to call on more than, on the average, 60 of the 8,537 households reported in the 1950 United States Census. Finally the curates in the parish decided that personal invitations by themselves after all the Sunday Masses were our last chance of gaining our assistants. The plan was completely successful, bringing us well over the 300 mark, and it reminded us of a single lesson in human relations which we had overlooked. People like to be asked personally, and an invitation to taking up a census was no exception. With all our assistants registered, the parish priests joined in pairing teams and assigning districts in accordance with the census-tract and block-map scheme. The work load for every team was so designed that no one even had to cross the street in covering his area from the first household to the last. Each of the curates assumed responsibility for a proportionate share of the parish according to census-tract divisions.

parish acquaintance. This experience, too, generated a real gratitude and interest in our assistants, a growth in their social consciousness and parish-mindedness.

The final element in the technical planning of the census was time: when should we start, and how long should we take? Owing to several parish activities, which would make attempts to execute the project before Christmas of 1954 unfeasible, we decided to start immediately after that date. It was a fortunate decision. The friendly spirit of the season and the fact that many people were home for the holidays (or, if away, would return soon thereafter) helped immeasurably. We did not put any time limit—forty-eight hours or a week—on our census assistants. We simply told them that the responsibility of covering their area was completely their own, and we depended on their effectiveness in getting the job done. The parish was advised that they would be calling. In only a few instances was it necessary for the priest captain to spur the lagging or send in reinforcements. The great majority of the returns were made within three weeks after New Year's Day, so that filing and transcribing could begin immediately.

So much for planning the census in terms of cost and materials, personnel and time. Psychological preparation of the parish was also of fundamental importance. On the first Sunday of December, one month before the beginning of the census, the pastor had the author preach on the subject at all ten parish Masses.[18] On the same day the December issue of the *Parish*

---

[18] It seems pertinent at this point to say something of the author's association with OLM Parish. One of the criticisms directed against Father Fichter's *Southern Parish* was that he, though a priest, had no parish experience and therefore had no right to publish a book about a parish. Though the objection can have some value, it is more specious than sound. True, as a neighboring parish priest told the author, one would have to serve two years in a parish before he could hope to know it; and it would be possible to serve many times two years and still not know a parish. The question is simply this, whether one is by training and at least some pertinent experience receptive to parish

Monthly, completely given over to an explanation and discussion of the census from many viewpoints, was distributed at all Masses. Despite the printing of an extra 1,000 copies beyond the normal Sunday complement, we ran short and had to supply an extra 1,000 the following week. A copy of this issue of the *Parish Monthly* is found in Appendix II, and contains in more fully developed form most of the ideas expressed in the special census sermon, as well as a cover drawing of the parish map. After this Sunday the priests of the parish spoke regularly and earnestly on the importance of the census and of the need of cooperation by all parishioners. Meanwhile a few meetings were held at which the early volunteers received lectures (replete with colored slides which illustrated parish geography, land use, neighborhood population characteristics, and other items discussed in Chapters 5 and 6) on the value and methods of parish research and the importance of their role in it. We went through the entire census schedule with them, and outlined the proper

---

knowledge through observation (even better, participant observation) and effective interrogation. The author is not a parish priest, nor has his parochial experience been very broad. However, it has been varied, in some ways beyond the experience of the normal parish priest. For two years he was on regular week-end call at a large urban parish other than OLM. One year was spent as chaplain of a military "parish" in British-occupied Germany, a role which involved a good number of the usual parish priest's obligations and relationships. Another year was spent in serving week ends at over twenty-five different parishes, which enabled him to accumulate a great deal of varied if superficial experience and insights. Another period of several months was spent in observing French and German parishes. The author has preached almost eight hundred parish sermons, heard many thousands of confessions, prepared converts for reception into the Church, baptized, prepared a parish for confirmation and first Communion, prepared couples for marriage, and so on. At OLM itself he had the opportunity of preaching a parish novena, of saying a parish Mass often enough, of participating in several parish activities and organizations, and of enjoying a most instructive and fraternal relationship with the priests of the parish. Since completing the study of OLM, he has served as an unofficial but very intimately engaged assistant to the pastor of another parish, this one in the suburbs. While "the more experience, the better!" is generally true, it is doubtful if either sociologist or religionist could find fault with the lack of it in this study.

approach to different types of parishioners. Although the census schedule was to be filled out privately, still the census takers had to be prepared in the event that some parishioners needed help. The confidential nature of the census was emphasized.

As mentioned previously, a sample copy of a filled-out census schedule with an explanatory note and Christmas greeting on the reverse side was distributed at the crowded Christmas Masses. The final meeting of the census workers occurred a couple of days later, and within a few days after the census had begun the January issue of the *Parish Monthly* (see Appendix II) was distributed at all the Sunday Masses. A personal letter from the pastor occupied the front cover, instead of the usual religious picture. The sample copy of the schedule was photographed and published in the middle fold, together with specific instructions for filling out each column. Several questions concerning the census were posed and answered; for example, why so many personal questions in the census, why are laymen taking it, why the questions about marriage, business, and education. Several comments of Pope Pius XII on the importance of the parish census were included, as was a copy of the parish map with each census tract and block clearly designated. After such measures we were hopeful that the parish was psychologically prepared to join wholeheartedly in the census project.[19]

Our first aim, that of compiling a complete address and religious-affiliation file, was 91 per cent effective. The census

---

[19] Those hopes were far less than 100 per cent fulfilled; rather only about 75 per cent. But the machinery was in operation to finish the work if, as, and when the parish staff had the opportunity. The actual work of the census takers included three steps: (1) calling on every address listed on one's address file sheet, ascertaining and marking the family's religious affiliation, and leaving a census schedule, covering letter, and gummed envelope at every home in which a Catholic family or individual resided; (2) arranging a date with every Catholic party for collecting the census schedule, collecting the schedule, and marking the result on the address file sheet; (3) bringing all returns back to the priest captain of one's district.

takers located 8,520 households,[20] but despite repeated calls, by phone or in person, just over 750 of the 8,520 families, or 9 per cent, made no answer, nor could adequate information about them be guaranteed by neighbors. Actually it is believed that the majority of the missing 9 per cent were not Catholics who would be among registrants of OLM Parish, for about two thirds of the nonanswering addresses were located in two neighborhoods: those in which Catholic parishioners of the local national parish predominated and those where the Jewish population was very heavy. Complete data concerning the number of households in each census tract, the number of Catholic households, and the number not contacted are shown in Table I.

TABLE I

Households in OLM Parish by Census Tracts

Tract Number	Number of Households Visited	Number of Catholic Households	Number of Households Not Contacted
383	819	576	69
385	243	205	9
387	1,112	869	115
397	391	281	31
399	3,334	1,876	278
401	1,447	474	109
237	1,174	393	142
Total	8,520	4,674	753

Of the 8,520 families living in OLM Parish, 4,674 were Catholic, of which 3,674 attended OLM and 1,000 belonged to

---

[20] The control provided by the 1950 census served very well. It showed 8,537 households to be within OLM limits at that time, and the OLM 1955 census revealed 8,520. Since OLM is in a very stable, already developed, neighborhood, we were satisfied that the few residential changes accounted for the slight shift in total households. Thus one novel phase of our parish census proved its worth, and it might be suggested that it would be generally useful as a control in any urban parish census. This could be said only with reservations of rapidly developing suburban neighborhoods.

the national church or other neighboring parishes. Each Catholic family was requested to fill out and return the census form. Of the 3,674 OLM Catholic households, 2,704 (73.6 per cent) returned completed forms; 414 families accepted the forms but either failed to return them or returned blank forms; 441 families refused to fill out the forms; and 115 families were never at home. Of the 1,000 Catholic families that professed membership in the national church located within the parish boundaries or attended other neighboring parishes, 619 (61.9 per cent) returned the census form. In addition, 69 families that lived outside the parish but attended OLM Church voluntarily requested and returned a census form.

There were 8,371 persons, including 216 non-Catholics, in the 2,704 OLM families that returned the census forms. The remaining 970 families (26.4 per cent) represent unfinished business. From the pastoral viewpoint the census records plus the information on the address and religious-affiliation sheets clearly and exactly define the work still to be done.[21] This is usually part of the follow-up work after a parishwide census and would be undertaken either by the parish priest or by an organization similar to the Legion of Mary.

The next step in our parish study was the analysis of census returns. Often enough the rich resources of information in parish census records remain untapped. How many youngsters four years old can expect to enroll in the parochial school in another year or so? How many unemployed are there in the parish, how many invalid marriages, how many college graduates, Catholic

---

21 This is a far better situation, pastorally speaking, than merely finishing a census project with half or less of the expected forms, and not knowing where the others are! Not a few parishes find themselves in such a situation. From the sociological viewpoint, having the records of over 73 per cent of the parish membership, over 2,700 families, provides a more than adequate sample of the parish population, not only in numbers but, as it turned out, also in geographical, socioeconomic, religious, and educational distribution.

or secular, how many students in non-Catholic schools? The identity of members of these and many other groups is often sought by the pastor for all sorts of apostolic reasons. The information is contained, he knows, in his thousands of census cards, but seeking out any one item would take dozens, even hundreds of hours. Even if an original analysis has been made and results have been tabulated, once the cards have been returned to alphabetical (or other) order, searching out all the members of one or other category becomes a time-consuming enterprise. To make our data available for analysis, we transcribed all the information in the census schedules on the key-sort research cards described on pages 329-30.[22] There was a card for each family member, punched for sex, place of birth (native or foreign born), education, marital status, and so forth. Actually this transcription to cards, the most time-consuming and costly part of the study, could have been avoided if we had used the cards for the original recording of census data.[23]

It was because of this use of cards that we were able to satisfy quickly the parish's first request for information. The priest moderator of the Legion of Mary asked for all the names and

---

[22] There was question of using IBM cards for the purpose, but in view of the relatively small number of cards (about 8,500) and doubt as to frequency of use, the cost factor seemed prohibitive and the periodic hiring of the necessary machine impractical. Instead, with the help of the McBee (now Royal McBee) Company, the Sociological Research Laboratory of Fordham University devised a parish census card capable of recording all the information contained on the detailed census schedule, so that any item of information could be sorted from several hundred cards simultaneously by the simple operation of a hand keysorter (a steel needle set in a plastic handle). See pp. 329-30 for a further description and explanation.

[23] There might be a problem in this connection. We used family census schedules, then transcribed the data onto individual research cards. What we should have done was either to construct a research card suitable for coding both family and individual data, which faced some technical problems in view of the extensiveness of our data; or have the parishioners fill out two sets of cards, one for the family and one for each individual. This might appear cumbersome; but at the cost of a little more instruction of the parish, the pastor would then have a perfect research file of his parish for a relatively small monetary cost.

addresses of parishioners attending non-Catholic high schools, so that they might be interviewed for registration in the religious released-time program. In about fifteen minutes, using the keysorter, he was able to find the names he sought.

There were in all 8,569 cards—one for each of the 8,371 individuals in the 2,704 OLM families that returned the census forms and for the 198 individuals in the 69 families who attended OLM but lived outside the parish. The three divisions of the parish, east, central, and west,[24] were analyzed for their respective records in religious observance, marital status, status as Catholics (born Catholic or convert), age and sex differentials, education, economic status, and occupation. Records of the parish were compared with those for the entire OLM neighborhood as given in the 1950 census, except, of course, with respect to religious observance and converts. Then religious observance was compared with each of the other factors, and the other factors with one another.

Each Catholic family received in its census packet an invitation to answer a questionnaire on Catholic religious and parish life.[25] The twelve-page questionnaire sought information on practice and attitudes, religious and social thinking and policy, social relations, moral views, evaluation of parish services, religious knowledge, motivation, and so on. Respondents were assured that their answers would remain anonymous. Since one might assume that only the more interested and religiously active parishioners would answer, this voluntary sample ran the danger of being biased. On the other hand, one could not very well hope to get the others anyway, particularly those who refused even to fill out the census forms. In view of the opportunity in OLM Parish the author wished to take as much advantage of the situation as possible.

---

[24] See Figure 2.
[25] See Appendix II for copies of the questionnaires and the letters.

Of the more than 1,000 persons who agreed to respond, almost 300 actually did so. The length of the questionnaire no doubt discouraged many pledged respondents from answering it. Few of the questions, however, could have been omitted without loss. Despite pretesting, which exposed some technical deficiencies, several questions had weaknesses which were revealed too late to have them changed.

Actually, the almost 300 who generously and carefully responded represented almost 30 per cent of the pledges and over 10 per cent of all the families in OLM which had cooperated with the census. When classified according to parish area where they lived, age, sex, length of residence in the parish, education, economic status, occupation, and religious observance, they formed a good cross section of the parish. The variety of their backgrounds and situations and the fact that only one questionnaire was accepted from a family guarantee as close to an unbiased sample as could be expected in this kind of interrogation. Much of our knowledge of OLM is derived from the responses to this questionnaire. Results are discussed in Chapter 6.

In addition, a short questionnaire was administered at meetings of each of several parish societies: the Holy Name, Altar-Rosary, and St. Vincent de Paul societies, the junior and senior Sodalities, and the junior and senior units of the Legion of Mary. Other questionnaires were prepared for the junior and senior Altar Servers societies and for the Nocturnal Adoration Society. Our purpose was to collect as much data as possible which would be interpreted according to the elements of a parochial social system as delineated in the previous chapter. Thus we could assess OLM's qualifications as a social system and the extent of its members' participation therein.

The brief but very important questionnaire directed to the Nocturnal Adoration Society sought the conscious motivation of mature men for their constant, unobserved, and devoted practice of nocturnal adoration of Christ in the Blessed Sacrament. It was thought that here most certainly there would be least danger of mixed, obscured, or misstated motives. If value acts as a bond of social living, religion too must have its values. The question of motives for religious participation is discussed in later chapters on parish services and parish societies.[26]

In this chapter we have considered the various methods used elsewhere in surveys of religious practice and have recognized the importance of an extensive and administratively maneuverable census in such a study. Reasons for choosing OLM as the subject of the study have been presented. The census, which was 91 per cent effective, and the census forms returned by 73.6 per cent of all OLM Catholic families supplied information and insight into OLM Catholic life. An introduction was given to the auxiliary questionnaires which were returned by 300 parishioners. We are now ready to analyze this parish as a social system. The next two chapters will consider the OLM neighborhood and the people; that is, its ecological and demographic structures, respectively.

---

[26] As a methodological note it might be mentioned that the Nocturnal Adoration Society respondents did not answer in church and give their replies to the marshal, as the author had intended, but answered later at home and mailed in their forms. Some 140 men, about 15 per cent, took the trouble to answer (anonymously) despite lack of any previous persuasion. Since the various other society questionnaires were administered in the respective societies' meetings, response was not so voluntary as in the case of the two previously described questionnaires. On the other hand, there was no coercion, and some did choose not to answer.

CHAPTER V

Location and Physical Setting
of the Parish

Location and physical setting comprise one of the basic elements of a social system, together with its interactive and purposeful functioning, its aims and values, and the structure of its relationships. Both location and social structure are essentially static; hence they are considered first. In this chapter we discuss OLM's ecological situation, in the next its demographic composition, and in Chapters 7 and 8 its social structure. Subsequent chapters view OLM in its dynamic and interactive functioning.

The very name parish and its origin as an administrative unit in Catholic Church history derive from an ecological situation. Ecology refers, sociologically speaking, to the response of society to its physical environment. With the spread of the faith and the expansion of Christian communities beyond the concentrated urban communities groups that were easily shepherded by their respective bishops came the need of establishing suburban, even rural, pastorates under the bishops' care. These came to be known as parishes.[1]

---

[1] Christians requiring pastoral care were living in the country beyond the limits of the city bishop's ready accessibility. The response was the creation of parishes, something new in the Church's administrative and pastoral structure. Incidentally, the words parish and ecology are derived from the same Greek word referring to place of abode.

We recall from earlier chapters the importance of physical setting not only for social life in general, but likewise for something presumably so personal as religious practice. Particularly such studies in religious sociology as Boulard's analysis of rural French Catholicism and the gradual decline of urban Christianity in many sectors,[2] Kerkhofs' study of the gradual erosion through industrial dechristianization of Catholic Limburg,[3] and Ligier's inquiry into religious practice in Jura's city and country,[4] all make it clear that ecological factors share the responsibility for religious health and illness. We cannot overemphasize this influence; but poor housing conditions, long distance from churches and chapels, and other unfavorable conditions have a high correlation with below-average religious practice.

---

[2] Not to be forgotten is Father Boulard's graphic picture of a walk through the breadth of France, in which one would experience almost universal practice from Brest to Angers, almost universal negligence between Angers and Nancy, and general practice again from Nancy to Strasbourg. He pointed out also not only the effects of city conditions on religious life, but likewise the similar effects of living along the routes of communication and trade, wherever a new changing civilization challenges the values, customs, and interests of an established one. Despite exceptions which he himself indicated, the phenomenon is general enough. As a matter of fact it was thus that Christianity first spread its faith and new ideas so rapidly, along the routes of travel, in seaports, in centers of thought and learning.

In discussing the weakness of religious practice in many parts of rural France Boulard explains further why, from an ecological viewpoint, so many parishes are without priests. The staggering number of over 15,000 is cited. Yet almost invariably these parishes number less than 300 inhabitants, the parishes themselves are relics from policy established in the time of Charlemagne, and thousands of priests are assigned to care for more than 2 parishes. It is this ecological situation—a rural environment, plus thousands of small communities with their respective churches and claims to continued social unity—which Boulard attacks with his proposal to establish priest teams for the rural pastorate.

[3] Kerkhofs showed in his study of Catholic Limburg how the inroads of dechristianization stem from an ecological condition: its proximity to areas exploited for industrialization and the already existing dechristianization of these areas.

[4] Ligier found in his study of a small city in the Jura that, although religious practice was bad in the bourgeois neighborhoods, it was worse in working-class sections near the edge of town, and worst in the center of town.

Local circumstances of a more minor character can influence the effectiveness of the functioning parochial system. The absence of certain types of stores and other conveniences can prompt parishioners to go across parish lines to another parish church for their religious observance. Virton tells of a practicing Catholic in a French suburb whom his pastor never saw at church. When the latter asked why that was, he answered that he went to the church near a tobacco shop where he could buy a cigar for his Sunday-morning smoke.[5] A simple anecdote, but indicative of the type of ecological influence.

Parish boundaries sometimes ignore ecological realities and split natural neighborhood social groupings. Group cohesiveness acts strongly against the incorporation by parishes of separated parts of the group. Either the entire group ignores parish lines and adheres to one parish or the other, or group unity is dissipated through adherence to the respective churches in accordance with parish boundaries, or the group maintains the cohesiveness while its members attend their respective parish only insofar as obligation requires them to do. In the first instance the bypassed parish is weakened; in the other two the parishes fail to exploit a potential source of parish strength in ignoring an already existing social unity. Sometimes the parish boundaries, though frequently made to coincide with main thoroughfares and other natural dividing lines, ignore such suitable guideposts. The effect may not always be the rupture of social groupings, but it does make for frequent and confusing disregard of parish territorial limits. Ineffective setting of parish lines is often explained by uncontrollable and unforeseeable factors.[6] A new highway, housing project, or shopping center can

---

[5] Virton, *Enquêtes de sociologie paroissiale*, "L'emplacement des paroisses."
[6] In rural areas the situation is somewhat different. Parish boundaries should not usually be along highways which join rather than separate neighbors, but through woods and open fields, thus to keep communities and neighborhoods parochially intact.

make formerly good boundaries practically inoperable. The point is that ecological factors affect the functioning of a social system—of a parish no less than of other systems.

Let us keep in mind the deep extensive changes wrought through the process of massive urbanization during the last century. The small all-inclusive group has yielded in function and importance in the individual's life to several restricted-purpose secondary associations. Each of the latter stands for certain values, often in conflict with those of other associations, and competes for the individual's adherence. This accounts for much confusion in people's lives: they are committed or at least strongly drawn to contradictory values and interests. Father Fichter developed this idea in discussion of the marginal parishioner.[7] Here again the point is that life *in the city*, an ecological as well as a social fact, prompts this conflict, this insecurity, the lack of attachment and anomy which sociological writers have constantly ascribed to urban life.[8]

The original church of OLM Parish was actually the college chapel on the Fordham University grounds, then, over one hun-

---

[7] Fichter, *Urban Parish*, Chapter 5.

[8] On the other hand it must be kept in mind that the great portion of today's urban population were born and raised in the city. They are not migrants from the country. They have not known and could not be affected by the change from rural to urban life. The ways of the city are normal to them. The city might have a disruptive impact on them, but it provides no less an opportunity for integration of many values into one's total frame of life. One significant fact of parish life in the city which is traceable directly to urban characteristics is the nonidentification of the parish with the neighborhood. This is true at least in our own country, though in some other places neighborhoods and parishes are even named the same. This need not prevent the formation of social groups across parish lines, but at least residents of a neighborhood cannot well forget the identity of their parish. Many American city dwellers do not even know the name of the parish in which they are, and the number is relatively rare of those who know their parish boundaries. The height of surrounding buildings prevents sight of their supposedly unifying parish steeple. The implication is that the sense of community, the feeling of belonging to the same group as all other members of the juridically bounded parish, is not often aided by the parish's geographical location in the heart of a large city.

dred years ago, called St. John's College. The church was intended to serve those at the college, but for some forty years it served also residents of the surrounding neighborhood. As the population increased it became necessary, a few years before the turn of the century, to build outside the college gates. The original parish covered a far greater area than OLM does now, for as the inhabitants increased in the upper Bronx it became necessary to split the old parish territory to form new parishes. The relationship between parish and university has been consistently cooperative.[9]

OLM Parish is right in the heart of the upper Bronx, one of the five boroughs (or counties) which comprise New York City and supply residence for its 8,000,000 inhabitants. The Bronx itself has about 1,500,000 inhabitants, slightly more than half of them residing in its upper section, which is often called "the bedroom of New York." Despite the usually stable aspect of a residential area, the upper Bronx continues to undergo change. (See Figure 4.) This is particularly (and almost entirely) true of the eastern half; that is, east of the Bronx River, where some undeveloped tracts remained available for building. Seven housing projects supply homes for over 30,000 persons in the lower and middle income brackets, while the privately financed Parkchester apartments, the largest single apartment community in the world, house 40,000 more. Private homes continue to be built in the northeastern sector. Altogether there has been an increase of over 200,000 in the upper Bronx's population since 1930. Extremely little of this increase can be found in the OLM neighborhood, however, for it is already quite fully developed.

---

[9] The annual Corpus Christi procession and triple benediction, sponsored by the Bronx Nocturnal Adoration Society (see Chapters 6 and 14) and conducted by the parish, occurs annually on the beautiful Fordham University grounds. Many of the university students board in the parish and attend Sunday Mass in OLM Church, which is only two minutes from the college gates, and in the center of the parish.

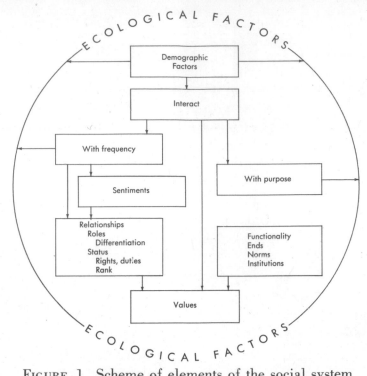

FIGURE 1 Scheme of elements of the social system

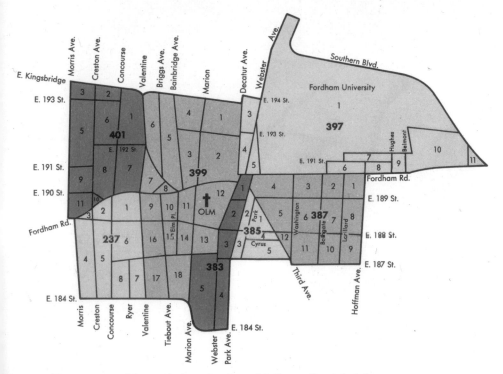

FIGURE 2 Map of Our Lady of Mercy Parish by census tracts

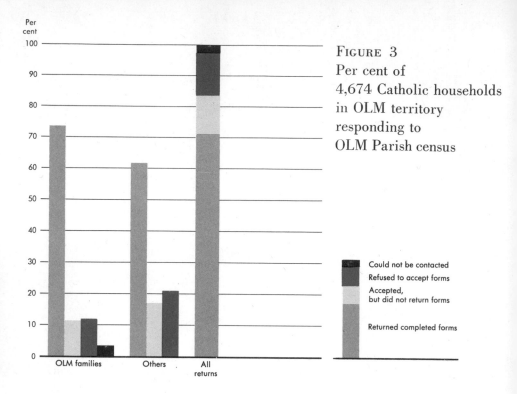

Per cent

FIGURE 3
Per cent of
4,674 Catholic households
in OLM territory
responding to
OLM Parish census

Could not be contacted
Refused to accept forms
Accepted,
but did not return forms

Returned completed forms

OLM families   Others   All returns

1914

1954

FIGURE 4
Looking north
from Fordham Road along the Concourse,
1914 and 1954

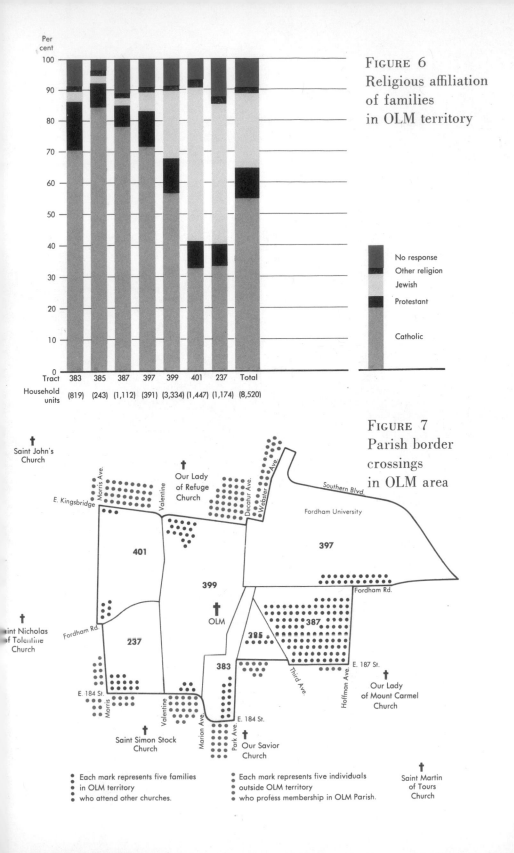

FIGURE 6
Religious affiliation
of families
in OLM territory

Per cent

No response
Other religion
Jewish
Protestant
Catholic

Tract	383	385	387	397	399	401	237	Total
Household units	(819)	(243)	(1,112)	(391)	(3,334)	(1,447)	(1,174)	(8,520)

FIGURE 7
Parish border
crossings
in OLM area

Saint John's Church

Our Lady of Refuge Church

E. Kingsbridge

Morris Ave.
Valentine
Decatur Ave.
Webster Ave.

Southern Blvd.

Fordham University

401

399

397

Saint Nicholas of Tolentine Church

Fordham Rd.

OLM

Fordham Rd.

385

387

237

383

Third Ave.

Hoffman Ave.

E. 187 St.

Our Lady of Mount Carmel Church

E. 184 St.

Morris
Valentine
Marion Ave.
Park Ave.

E. 184 St.

Saint Simon Stock Church

Our Savior Church

Each mark represents five families
in OLM territory
who attend other churches.

Each mark represents five individuals
outside OLM territory
who profess membership in OLM Parish.

Saint Martin of Tours Church

FIGURE 5
Land-use map of Our Lady of Mercy Parish

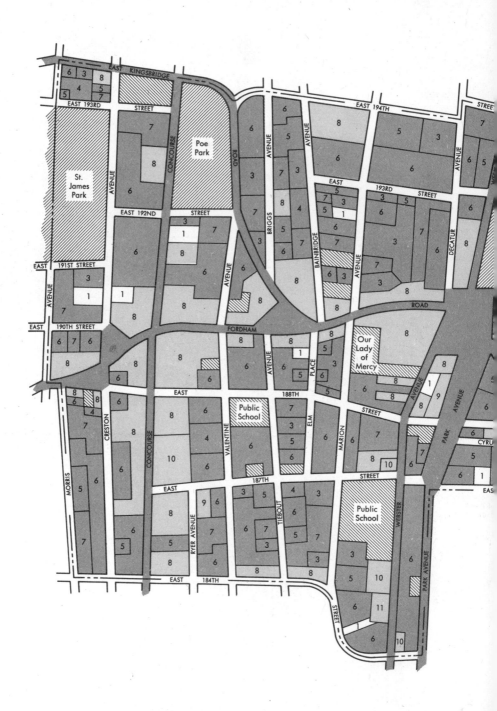

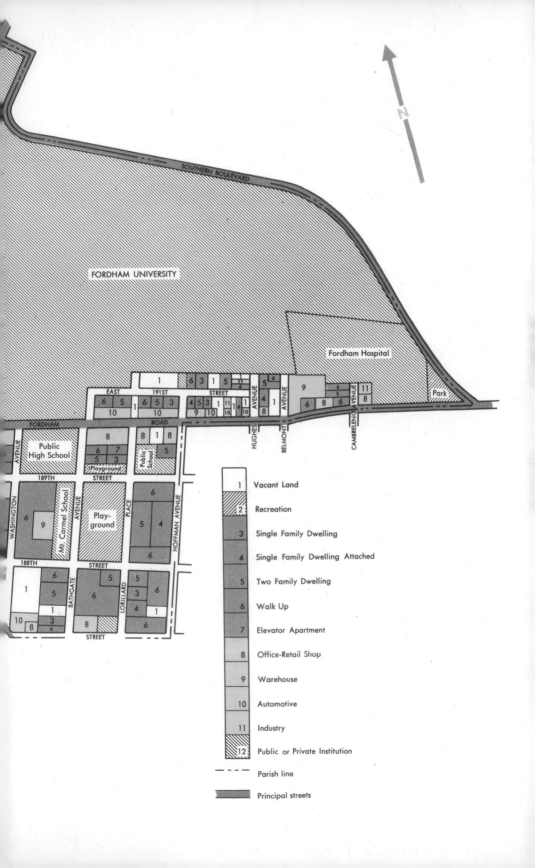

FORDHAM UNIVERSITY

SOUTHERN BOULEVARD

Fordham Hospital

Park

EAST 191ST STREET

FORDHAM ROAD

Public High School

Playground

Public School

189TH STREET

Mt. Carmel School

Play-ground

188TH STREET

WASHINGTON AVENUE

BATHGATE AVENUE

LORILLARD PLACE

HOFFMAN AVENUE

HUGHES AVENUE

BELMONT AVENUE

CAMBRELENG AVENUE

1	Vacant Land
2	Recreation
3	Single Family Dwelling
4	Single Family Dwelling Attached
5	Two Family Dwelling
6	Walk Up
7	Elevator Apartment
8	Office-Retail Shop
9	Warehouse
10	Automotive
11	Industry
12	Public or Private Institution

– – – Parish line

▬▬▬ Principal streets

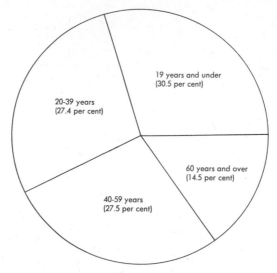

FIGURE 8

Population of OLM Parish by age groups

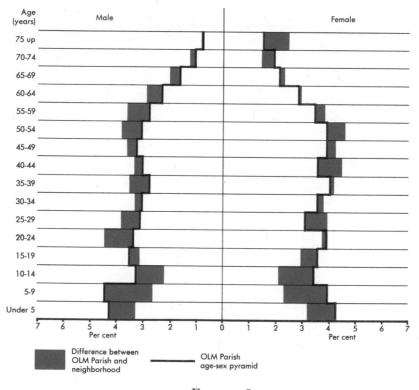

FIGURE 9

OLM Parish and OLM neighborhood population by age and sex

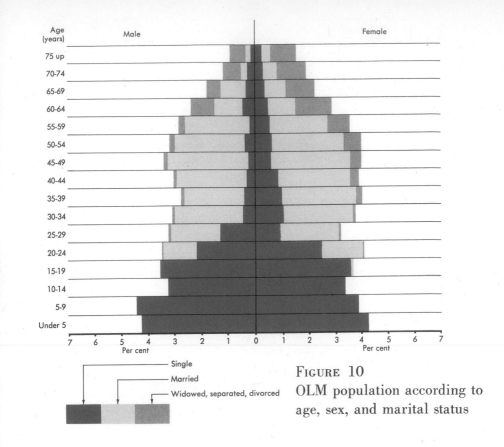

Single
Married
Widowed, separated, divorced

FIGURE 10
OLM population according to
age, sex, and marital status

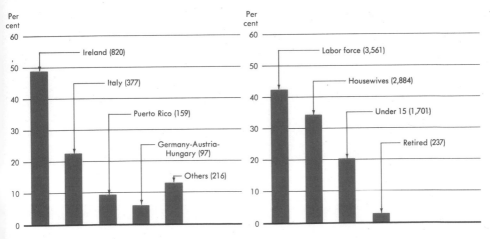

FIGURE 11
Country of birth
of 1,669 foreign-born
and Puerto Rican parishioners

FIGURE 12
Occupational status
of 8,383 OLM parishioners

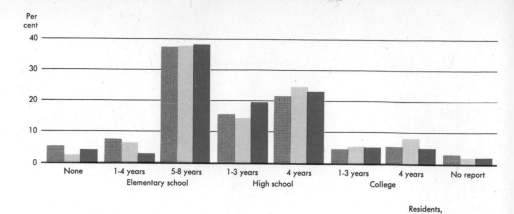

FIGURE 13
Years of schooling completed
by population over 25
in Bronx County,
OLM neighborhood, and OLM Parish

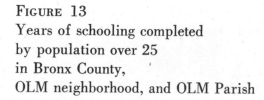

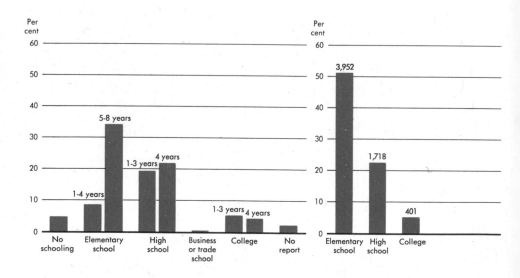

FIGURE 14
General educational attainment
of OLM parishioners
over 5 years

FIGURE 15
Type of Catholic schooling
received by
7,689 parishioners

Indeed, the OLM census for 1955 showed a total of 8,520 household units as compared with 8,537 units listed in the United States Census for 1950.

OLM's territory (consult the map shown in Figure 2) includes all of one census tract (399), most of three others (401, 387, and 397), and parts of three additional tracts (237, 383, and 385). It consists of 51 inhabited square blocks containing just over 8,500 households and 27,000 persons. It happens that the central section, Tract 399, contains by itself some 40 per cent of the whole parish (over 3,300 households out of 8,500), 40 per cent of all Catholic households (almost 1,900 out of 4,700), and over 50 per cent of the Catholic households registered in the OLM census. By joining Tract 401 with the OLM part of Tract 237, retaining Tract 399 separately in its entirety, and grouping Tracts 383, 385, 387, and 397, we contrive three fairly homogeneous and ecologically similar divisions corresponding to the western, central, and eastern sections, respectively. We will refer hereafter to these three divisions.

Several Bronx expressways and parkways almost touch the parish, and Fordham Road itself is part of U. S. Route 1 from Maine to Florida. It has developed rapidly into one of New York City's most important shopping centers. (See Figure 4.) One subway line and one elevated line cut through the parish on their way to and from downtown New York City, and another passes just outside the parish boundary, while the Fordham Station of the New York Central Railroad is just twenty-five minutes from the heart of Manhattan. The routes of some ten local bus lines pass through the parish.

Of the universities and colleges which have earned for the Bronx the title of "Borough of Universities," three of the most important are close to the parish: Fordham University is actually within the parish territory, and Hunter College and New York University are within moderate stone's throws of the parish boundaries. A new medical school and hospital center have just risen on Fordham Road's eastern extension, Pelham Parkway. Almost one fifth of the Bronx's land area is given to its famous parks, though for most youngsters who live on streets without empty spaces these parks do not satisfy the need for play facilities. Several parks and the famous Bronx Zoo and Botanical Gardens are within easy reach of—even border—the parish, providing fresh air, the glories of nature, and enjoyment.

OLM has no housing projects in its neighborhood; but if one walks off the one-mile stretch of Fordham Road, which divides the parish's northern and southern halves, or from Webster and Park avenues across the Grand Concourse, the three most important thoroughfares which cut through the parish's half mile from north to south, he will find a due proportion of the upper Bronx's six hundred elevator apartment houses, its more than fifty thousand one-family and two-family homes, and its innumerable walk-ups. The map (see Figure 5) shows the use of land in OLM, the important arteries of traffic, and the public institutions in the area.

We might observe that such a land-use map, with the different types of use indicated either by colors or by hatchings, could profitably be made part of the equipment of every parish. It could adorn a wall in a parish meeting room, as is the case in many parishes, and it would serve to familiarize parish members, and particularly parish workers, with the composition of the parish.

A check of the data collected in our study shows that the central sector (Tract 399) provides a very adequate cross section of the parish, allowance being made for a couple of distinct peculiarities proper to the eastern and western sections. Just a block away from the eastern section of OLM is the church of Our Lady of Mount Carmel (hereafter called OLMC), the national parish (that is, without assigned territory) for Italian-speaking Catholics. It is the center of an area heavily settled with people of Italian ancestry, including many of course from

OLM territory. Nearby, actually within OLM territory, are the magnificent newly enlarged OLMC school, capable of holding over 2,200 students, and the modern auditorium.[10]

The western sector of OLM lies on both sides of the Grand Concourse. (See map, Figure 5.) Here the parish has its greatest proportion of Jewish residents. This conforms with the prevalent opinion that Jewish people tend to choose for their homes well-serviced apartments close to economical transportation. The Grand Concourse, a good road modeled on Paris' Champs Elysées with convenient bus connections and a subway line and replete with fine apartments, satisfies those requirements.[11]

One other group in the parish, the new arrivals, have been attracted by the physical fact of lower-class and therefore cheaper housing. One sixteenth of New York City's inhabitants (500,000 out of 8,000,000) are now Puerto Ricans, mostly more or less recent arrivals from their native islands. Following the ever-renewed New York pattern, these newer migrants have started on the bottom rung of the ladder and have already begun the climb upwards. One step in this upward direction is leaving the worst parts of Harlem for low-type, but in their eyes better, housing. Some of this housing is available in the southern end of the eastern sector of the parish. Others have been crowded into a middle-class apartment house in the central section—the

---

[10] It seems fairly clear that these physical expressions of the thriving parish activity of OLMC are a strong attraction to most Italians to retain membership in OLMC even though, as living within OLM territory, they have the right to membership in the territorial parish. This is significant because, although many Italians do belong to OLM, the great majority in the eastern section belong to OLMC, despite a trend in American Catholic history for foreign-language groups to attach themselves sooner or later to the territorial parish. This is generally true, even though about 9 per cent of all 16,500 parishes in the United States are still national.

[11] This does not mean that only Jewish people have these characteristics; otherwise no one else would be living on the Concourse. Actually, Jews predominate there, but there are others; though most of the Catholics living in OLM tracts along the Concourse live off the Concourse itself.

house having been hastily reconstructed to accommodate more families. Over 250 persons are squeezed into space intended for less than one third that number.

A bar graph (see Figure 6) shows the distribution of OLM's population according to religious affiliation. The purpose of noting it here is to see the impact of ecological factors on OLM's population. The eastern tracts are almost solidly Catholic owing to the heavy Italian population associated with their national parish; the western tracts show a heavy Jewish concentration, thanks to the Grand Concourse.[12]

OLM's territory is rather hilly, with one slope rising rather uncomfortably (on a hot day) toward the Grand Concourse from the narrow plain between Webster and Park avenues; another rises more gently from the same plain to the eastern extremity of the parish; and a third drops mildly away from the Concourse area toward the western end. Inclines in the north-south direction are relatively slight.

Two hospitals, one of them being Fordham General Hospital, are located in the parish and receive pastoral care from the priests of OLM.[13] A very large public high school and a couple of elementary schools provide some of the recreational facilities which the parish would like to supply its parishioners, especially the young, but which it at present lacks. Many Catholic children attend these schools, and both a priest of the parish and its Legion of Mary unit are kept busy trying to make up for these youngsters' deficiency in religious education.

Thanks to organizing our study of OLM according to census tracts, it would be simple enough not only to compare Catholic

---

[12] The map (Figure 2) and Figure 11, which shows OLM's foreign born, should be viewed in the light of the foregoing ecological indications.

[13] This particular ecological factor is of direct pertinence to the structure and functioning of OLM, as will be discussed more fully later; for the hospital responsibility takes much time and effort, yet has little to do with the stable parish community as usually understood.

with general data for each section of the parish, some of which is done in the following chapter, but to present a rather thorough comparative analysis of the parishioners in the three divisions of OLM Parish.[14]

Some of these ecological implications might well be indicated, if only to emphasize further the impact of place on the total system. It is first of all clear that OLM Parish is, territorially speaking, an administrative and pastoral urban division in the Catholic Archdiocese of New York. Its boundaries, dictated apparently by the need of some equitable division of numerical population among parishes, are not especially in accord with natural divisions, except for the wide and busy Kingsbridge Road in the northwestern part and a short section of Fordham Road in the east. This facilitates crossing of parish lines by members of neighborhood parishes. Actually 1,000 families within OLM claim membership in other parishes, or close to 20 per cent of the parish. This figure is of course misleading, for well over 700 of these families (actually 73 per cent) belong to the national parish of Our Lady of Mount Carmel. However, those attending OLMC are at least to be considered as Catholics within OLM territory *but not members of OLM*, and therefore not directly concerned with the functioning and structure of OLM Parish.

The other 27 per cent (about 270 families) are juridically members of OLM, but practically are not. They participate in the life and activity of the parishes which they actually attend. No study was made of the reasons why these families attended other parishes, although enough volunteered their reasons to give us a fairly accurate picture. Fundamentally the most im-

---

14 For example, such analysis could show not only the differences in national origin, but also related comparisons of religious practice, age, fertility, education, type of employment, and types of responses to over one hundred questions on the parish questionnaire. (See pp. 316-28.) These comparisons would indicate quickly areas and types of parish strengths and weaknesses.

portant reason is an ecological one, but there are instances of others too, usually of an understandable personal nature. Several families living in the southernmost part of the parish (see Blocks 4 and 5 of Tract 383 on the parish map) find it more convenient to walk a couple of short level blocks to Our Savior's Parish rather than a couple of longer blocks and up a short hill to OLM. This might seem strange, since the distance to OLM is little more than a quarter of a mile. But people are accustomed to "give their trade" to the competitor who makes service more readily available. The attitude likewise affects the search for religious service, though it may be to a far less extent. Once the choice is made, personal and social attachments can and do cement a relationship begun on an ecological basis.

Similar reasons explain why several other families farther to the west on the southern border attend St. Simon Stock Church, and others in Tract 237, Block 4 attend St. Nicholas of Tolentine. In the north of the parish quite a few families from Tract 399, Blocks 4, 5, and 6 prefer the relatively level equidistant walk, without heavy traffic crossings, to Our Lady of Refuge Church (hereafter called OLR) to the hill and crossings on the way to OLM. Some apartment houses in this area are more or less evenly divided between families who attend OLM and those who go to OLR. Clearly this situation cannot contribute to a sense of parish solidarity. Perhaps this is not an unmixed disadvantage, since parish solidarity can sometimes degenerate into parochialism; but from the viewpoint of parish unity it is anything but helpful.[15]

---

[15] An obvious problem arises in matters which require parish membership. If the parish school is overcrowded, members' children have first choice. In building-fund campaigns and in the diocesan Catholic Charities collections, such families are at least approached twice, sometimes give to both, sometimes avoid giving to either, and sometimes feel unnecessarily put upon when asked by a second group. Only understanding and constructive cooperation by the respective pastors can solve that kind of problem.

Crossing parish borders is not a one-way affair. Though no census takers called at their homes, members of some 70 families living outside OLM voluntarily came to the rectory to request census schedules. There are many others not registered in the census. Some 14 per cent of OLM's 1,000-plus school children come from outside the parish—thanks in large part to the generous policy of the pastor. This incrossing of OLM's borders likewise has an ecological explanation. Above the northern border, for example, just a little east of the section where OLM parishioners prefer to go to OLR, many persons not only from OLR but also from the next northern parish, St. Philip Neri, prefer a longer walk or bus ride to OLM to climbing a hill in order to attend their own respective parish churches. Since OLM's church is just off Fordham Road, which is on the route of several bus lines, it draws nonparishioners from several directions. Figure 7 gives an indication of some of these parish border crossings.

The questionnaire, Part 2, Questions 15 and 16 (see Appendix II, page 322), asked about physical difficulties and advantages in the parish. Few difficulties were listed aside from the hills and crossings already mentioned. Only one was listed with any frequency: the fact that confessions in the lower church necessitated climbing up and down steps, which was a hardship for the older parishioners. Half the respondents, about 150, said there were no physical difficulties and another 125 gave no answer. Four times as many as the 25 who did list difficulties cited physical advantages of OLM. The great majority cited central location and proximity of the church, abundance of transportation in inclement weather, and conveniently situated upper and lower churches. This fits in with the comment of many that the large number and varied time of Masses offered a desirable service. Others mentioned the provision of bus service for the blind and of baby-sitting facilities; the back entrance to the church, which reduces the climb from Webster Avenue to

Marion Avenue; paved streets; and proximity to the Fordham Road shopping center.

One respondent mentioned the OLM church bells. This parish service was also included in the questionnaire, Part 2, Question 13, which asked whether the Angelus bell (the traditional ringing thrice daily as a reminder of the angelic annunciation to Mary and the incarnation of the Son of God) was heard, and whether it reminded the hearer to recite the Angelus prayer. Of the nearly 300 respondents 165 answered that they did hear it, and 82 that they were thus reminded to say the prayer. Here is a minor but typical instance of parish purposes being abetted by use of an areawide physical facility—the ringing of a bell suggestive of a prayerful thought.[16]

Life in a city parish implies spending much of one's time, energy, talent, and interest outside the parish orbit, thus making more unlikely close acquaintanceships and relationships with many fellow parishioners. It is one of the primary ecological considerations in the structure and functioning of the urban residential parish. Concerning OLM parishioners' time spent outside the parish, answers to the questionnaire's Part 4, Question 1 showed the following facts. Of the 300 respondents some 120 (40 per cent) spent all their working hours outside the parish, including most of the breadwinners who answered; almost 60 (20 per cent) did all their studying outside the parish; and 45 (15 per cent) went outside the parish for all their play and recreation. The remainder of the respondents were divided between

---

[16] Two thirds of the respondents from the central section, two fifths of those in the east, and three sevenths of those in the west heard the bell. Of those who heard the bell, 50 per cent in the center, less than 40 per cent in the east, and more than 60 per cent of those in the west were thus reminded to pray. Of course a large number of those who did not hear the bell were usually not at home, being occupied outside the parish. Hence the above figures are not significant in their comparative aspect (except perhaps in the percentages of those reminded by the bell to pray), but absolutely in their indication that a large part of OLM's people receive and utilize this parish service.

those who spent some time and most of their time in the parish for these activities.

In view of the time spent outside the parish in urban life, the respondents were asked whether and to what extent they made use of downtown churches for their religious practice and devotions. The churches in the downtown business sections of the city have hardly a handful of resident parishioners, and provide service mostly for business people who find it more convenient (and/or desirable) to attend there than in their home parish churches. Only rarely do such churches have baptisms (except usually for adult converts), or confirmations, marriages, or funerals. Clearly the marked differences between the two types of churches and parishes derive from their respective ecological situations. The residential parish is affected in that, while its parishioners are thus provided for religiously, still the claim of relationship between parish and parishioner is further weakened through displacement of another link. The home parish is that much less important in the parishioner's religious need fulfillments. This is no argument against downtown churches: they perform a valuable function and provide an appreciated service. But the fact is, in terms of parish analysis, that the tie between home parish and parishioner is thereby weakened.

Of OLM's nearly 300 questionnaire respondents 115 (38 per cent) make use of downtown churches. Their use ranges from daily Mass and other devotions, in a few instances, to monthly confession or occasional visits of devotion.[17] The pro-

---

[17] Before First Fridays and holydays, and on those days themselves, the crowds are often so immense that city police kindly assist in guiding traffic. And on ordinary weekdays too there is a steady stream of persons going to confession, attending early and midday Masses, making visits of devotion to the Blessed Sacrament, or seeking the advice and help of the parish priests. Yet on the week ends there is no work comparable to the rush in the ordinary residential parish. The author has himself experienced the activity in these downtown churches, having assisted in confessional work for First Fridays in one of them for over a year.

portion from each section of the parish was about the same, in each instance being between 35 per cent and 40 per cent.

A final ecological consideration pertains to the physical equipment of the parish—church, school, parish house, auditorium, and so on. The church of course is the very center of parish life—the house of God and God's people, the place of divine worship and public prayer. Cardinal Gasquet writes in the concluding paragraph of his chapter on "The Parish Church":

> What is most remarkable about the documents that have come down to us . . . is the consistent story they tell of the universal and intelligent interest taken by the people of every parish as a whole in beautifying and supporting their churches. In a real and true sense, which may be perhaps strange to us in these later times, the parish church was *their* church. Their life, as will be seen in subsequent chapters, really centered around it, and they one and all were intimately connected with its management. The building was their care and their pride; the articles of furniture and plate, the vestments and banners and hangings, all had their own well-remembered story, and were regarded as in truth they were, as the property of every man, woman, and child of the particular village or district.[18]

The physical fact of the parish church is something with which the parishioner grows up: its reaching-to-heaven steeple, its distinctive bell, its altar and sanctuary light signifying the Eucharistic real presence of Christ his Lord, its stations of the cross, its confessionals and baptistry, its Communion rail, its sacristies where priests and altar servers vest for divine service, its choir, its statues of heroic and exemplary saints, its pictures of religiously significant facts and events, its artistic decorations, its light, its prayerful and restful quiet. These are part of his experience and are usually capable of inspiring his loyal attachment to the religious truths, ideals, practices, and way of life for which they stand.

---

[18] Gasquet, *Parish Life in Mediaeval England,* p. 70.

OLM's church is certainly capable of such attraction and inspiration. All of the above features it possesses in significant, pleasing, and beautiful fashion. It is large enough to hold some 800 adults seated, and its beautifully appointed lower church can hold a like number. Counting standees, some 10,000 persons can thus be accommodated in its ten Sunday Masses, while more room, if necessary, could be provided by adding to the number of Masses and/or utilizing the school auditorium. Fans are in action during the summer to alleviate the effects of the heat. A loud-speaker system enables the voice of any preacher to be heard readily throughout the church. The installment in relatively recent years of this mechanical help for making the preacher's voice audible to all has had a pronouncedly beneficent effect, as those can testify who remember the days of straining for and missing snatches of the Sunday sermon. The church's newest acquisition is a series of six stained-glass nave windows picturing, as the *Parish Monthly* expressed it, "the reason for which and by what means God's eternal wisdom chose the Virgin Mary as a tool for His infinite mercy."[19]

The parish school, next to the church, wearing the motto "For God and Country," contains some twenty classrooms, including two which now serve as kindergartens; an auditorium with stage; and several multiple-purpose rooms which serve as lunchrooms, parish meeting rooms, and so on. Over 1,000 youngsters attend school through the eight grades, together with

---

[19] Each of the windows, featuring a manifold variety of related pictures, contains a wealth of religiography: from the Old Testament history of Adam's fall and the promise of the Redeemer, through the scenes of the incarnation and nativity, Christ's life at home, His public life and teaching, His redemptory passion and death, His triumphant resurrection, concluding with a representation of Pentecost. The teachers in school were provided with explanations of this iconography so that the children might associate the pictures with their religious studies—a method of religious teaching which recalls the masterpieces of the great artists of medieval times, for they too were installed for purposes of public teaching.

another 100 or so in the kindergartens. In necessity, room could be made for another 150 pupils. A modest paved schoolyard is available for recess and lunchtime recreation.

The parish house or rectory, the home of the six priests of the parish, is on the other side of the church from the school. Its three small office-parlors are for the priests' consultations with parishioners or other callers at the rectory; and in such a parish as OLM they are well used. Half of the rectory's ground floor is given over to large rooms which also serve parish functions such as the weekly meetings of societies and the daily office transactions of the parish's highly successful credit union, employment bureau, and social-welfare bureau. Behind the rectory is a small garden, a memorial in honor of a former beloved pastor, and a set of steps and walk between the church and Webster Avenue— a convenience for those coming to church from the east.

All these physical facilities are exploited by the parish in the course of performing its functions. Did they not exist, or were they less serviceable, these functions could not be handled so well. The ecological features not only of the parish territory, but also of the parish's own facilities, are of obvious importance to the effectiveness of OLM's and of any parish's operations. The one apparent weakness in OLM's system of facilities is its current lack of a recreational hall. Of itself this is not a parish necessity, and many parishes exist quite well without one. For reasons to be explained later, however, OLM could use one; and when the opportunity presents itself will probably take advantage of it to make even more functional its physical plant.

The parish social system depends for its functioning upon its physical structure. We have seen the main lines of OLM's ecological situation. It must be kept in mind in assessing other elements in parish life and activity.

CHAPTER VI

The Demographic Structure
of the Parish

Catholic parishes contain these four elements: assigned territory, church, people, and pastor.[1] Chapter 5 discussed the assigned territory and church of OLM, which corresponded to the characteristic of social systems called *locus*. In the present chapter we consider OLM's people, with the emphasis of course on those people in the OLM territory who actually identify themselves with OLM. This distinction is necessary in the American urban parish, for many persons in the religiously mixed neighborhood, even though generally included in the pastor's potential responsibility at least, have practically nothing to do with the parish and are often unaware of its existence. Likewise the parish, though always ready to welcome the non-Catholic neighbor and to make its services available to him, has usually little to do directly with those who do not identify themselves with it.

Thus we examine the demographic data of OLM parishioners compiled from both census and questionnaire and view

---

[1] These four elements are verified in all *territorial* parishes. For certain reasons parishes have been set up in which jurisdiction does not extend to territorial borders, but to certain persons or classes of persons independent of ordinary territorial jurisdiction. This is provided for in *Codex iuris canonici*, Canon 216, 4. Depending on their situation, such parishes are usually called national, racial, or personal parishes.

them against the background of comparable data compiled in the national census for all the people of the area.[2]

If the physical setting and equipment have much to do with fashioning a parish's physiognomy, this is even more true of its members. Are there many new families with a large number of young children and few older folks? Is the sex ratio balanced in the several age groups? What are the economic level, the educational background, and the national or racial origin of the parishioners? Are they for the most part white-collar workers, tradesmen or professional people, or largely blue-collar workers?[3] Boulard found that in the same predominantly practicing area of northwestern France certain industrial workers were consistently far behind their neighbors in religious observance despite identical education as children, long residence in the same community, and membership in the same parishes.

1. FAMILIES AND INDIVIDUALS

Within OLM's borders, according to both the United States Census of 1950 and the OLM census of 1955, live just over 8,500 families numbering some 27,000 persons. Of these totals,

---

[2] The clergy of OLM might well be included here; but since their importance to the parish derives more from their status and roles, we consider them in the next chapter on OLM's social structure. Here we but refer to their number and that of three groups of religious women who teach in the parish school.

[3] It might be said that studying only the 2,773 families, both within and outside OLM territory, who attend OLM and submitted census schedules might not represent the entire parish. Admittedly this does involve a difficulty. However, our purpose calls for a study of OLM insofar as it is actually a functioning social system. The participation of 2,773 families in OLM's life and activity would seem clearly to suffice for that purpose. Besides, a response of almost 75 per cent, including most diverse variations, would appear to be scientifically adequate. It might also be maintained that those who filled out their census schedules were very probably more closely attached to the parish. Yet this supposition cannot be accepted unreservedly. In the course of taking the census we found several loyal parishioners who "just didn't get around to it," and conversely, many who filled out the schedules showed, in their honesty, that their attachment to the parish was anything but ideally close.

which included over 750 families who made no response to OLM census, almost 4,700 families (55 per cent) and over 14,200 persons (53 per cent) are Catholic. The disparity between the percentages of families and persons derives from the fact that a family in which any member was Catholic was designated as Catholic. Undoubtedly a certain number of the irresponsive 750 families (9 per cent) are Catholic, but for purposes of our study they are not here considered, though the parish continues its efforts to have them included in the census. Over 2,000 families (24 per cent) are Jewish, over 800 families (10 per cent) are Protestant, while some 200 families (almost 2.5 per cent) profess either some other or no religion. These facts are summarized in Table II.

TABLE II

Response of Families in OLM Territory to Parish Census

	Number	Per Cent	Returned Forms	Refused	Failed to Return	Not at Home
OLM families	3,674	43.1	2,704(1)	441	414	115
Other Catholic families	1,000	11.7	619	221	170	—
Jewish families	2,051	24.1				
Protestant families	841	9.9				
Other religions	160	1.9	Not requested to fill out forms			
No religion	41	0.5				
Not contacted	753	8.8				
Totals	8,520	100.0	3,323	662	584	115

(1) Another 69 forms came from people outside OLM territory, making a total of 2,773 recorded families.

Not all of the nearly 4,700 Catholic families in OLM territory, however, belong to our study of OLM Parish as a social system. Over 1,000 of these families profess membership in either the local national parish for the Italian-speaking or in other border parishes. Over 600 of these filled out census schedules, thanks largely to the cooperation of the pastor of Our Lady of Mount Carmel Parish. The claim of the majority is definitely honest, while the parish adherence of the others would have to be evaluated by pastors. For our purposes they are considered as not belonging to OLM Parish.

Thus almost 3,700 Catholic families within OLM territory should be considered members of the parish in some form. But no census schedules were received from 970 of these families: 115 were never at home, over 400 refused for various reasons (25 because the questions were too personal) and more than 400 probably intended to complete the schedule but failed to return the form to the census taker or the rectory. The remaining 2,700 families loyally and cooperatively filled out the census forms. These, together with another 69 families who live outside OLM territory but receive the parish's services and consider themselves members of the parish, comprise the OLM families analyzed in this study.

Included in these 2,773 families are 8,570 persons, 8,352 Catholics and 218 non-Catholics. Since the non-Catholics are inseparably part of their families in everything but Catholic religious observance, they must be included in all demographic statistics except those for religious life.

As stated previously, OLM is an old parish. It does not have a predominantly young-family composition, as have some newer parishes in the east Bronx, though young families are by no means lacking. The numerous apartment houses provide ideal quarters for many elderly people, whether married or single, a situation which manifests itself in the older age-group concentrations on the accompanying age-sex pyramids. OLM's neighborhood is part of that large residential area where second- and third-generation children of immigrants (German, Irish, then Italians and central Europeans) settled as soon as they could get away from the teeming slums and tenement districts of lower Manhattan. In more recent times the upward migration has brought both Negro and Puerto Rican to the upper Bronx, though very few Negroes are to be found in OLM territory. Many families have the desire to move away from the Bronx altogether for the roomier neighborhoods of Westchester and Long Island. But there are very many too who are quite contented with this residentially established, urbanly convenient, and economically booming part of the Bronx.

2. AGE AND SEX STRUCTURE

The life of a community depends very much on the composition of its people. A community with many old people has different interests, activities, and problems than one in which young people predominate. Likewise, if the sex ratio—that is, the number of males per hundred females—is badly out of balance (as it was in postwar Germany and other war-torn countries), there are difficulties quite different from those in a community where the number of men and women is pretty much in balance. The pie chart (Figure 8) and the age-sex pyramid (Figure 9), both of which were printed with explanatory comments in the *Parish Monthly* toward the end of our study, give a good idea of OLM's age-sex composition.

Figure 8, based on 8,371 members of the parish (some respondents failed to list ages) reveals that 30.5 per cent were less than 20 years of age as compared with 14.5 per cent who were 60 or over. Almost three fifths of the parish members (58 per cent) were less than 40 years of age. This age distribution is roughly similar to that of all the persons in the entire Bronx, although the Catholic percentages are a little higher for both youngest and oldest groups.

In Figure 9 the age-sex distribution of the Catholics who filled out census forms is contrasted with that of the entire territory. For the United States as a whole the age-sex statistics form a very neat pyramid, going from a broad base to a narrow top, the only exceptions being indentations for the groups born during the depression years. The heavy line in Figure 9 shows the age-sex distribution for OLM Catholics; the shaded areas indicate differences between the parish and the neighborhood percentages. Ideally, 50 per cent of the population would be male and 50 per cent female. Of the 8,371 recorded members of OLM, 46.3 per cent are male and 53.7 per cent female, for the entire neighborhood the percentages are 48 per cent and 52 per cent respectively. A study of the pyramid reveals that in OLM Parish almost 4.3 per cent of the population are boys less than 5 years of age, and approximately 4.2 per cent are girls less than 5 years old. For the entire neighborhood the percentages are 3.3 per cent boys and 3.2 per cent girls. In the 5-9 year age group the percentages for OLM are: boys, 4.5 per cent; girls, 3.9 per cent. For the neighborhood: boys, 2.7 per cent; girls, 2.4 per cent.

It must be remembered that the OLM neighborhood—that is, all the persons in OLM territory—includes the OLM parish members; hence the statistics for the neighborhood include those for the parish. It should be recalled that the neighborhood includes 1,000 Catholic families attending other parishes and 969 families in OLM Parish that did not fill out census forms. Thus if Catholic age-sex patterns are consistent in the neighborhood, as a check of 619 census schedules submitted by Catholic non-parishioners who live in the territory would indicate, then the implied variations between Catholics and non-Catholics are far greater than those shown by the shaded areas on the pyramid. At any rate, variations between OLM Parish and the total neighborhood are clear, even when allowance is made, as it should be made, for the difference of five years between the 1950 national census and the 1955 OLM census. The parish is far stronger in its younger age groups than the neighborhood.

Analysis of age-sex composition is not meant to be a sort of hobby or diversion for the statistically minded. Such data contain valuable leads for understanding parish needs and fashioning parish policy. A glance at the young age groups on the superimposed age-sex pyramids of OLM neighborhood and parish, for example, makes it clear that the overwhelming majority of young persons within OLM territory are Catholics. The priests of the parish therefore, even though they cannot be expected to know everyone personally, could well adopt the attitude that a spontaneous greeting would be welcomed and appreciated by any children they happened to meet, since the chances are so high that the youth are members of the parish. This could help to counteract the impersonal anonymity which unfortunately characterizes relationships in many large urban parishes.

The age-sex pyramid also indicates that some 9.5 per cent of the parishioners are over 65 years of age and that about three fifths of these older persons are women. The OLM neighborhood has about the same percentage for this age group, while the Bronx and New York City both have somewhat lower percentages.[4] The OLM age-structure pattern mirrors the findings of the Population Reference Bureau concerning the proportional increase of the aged (those over 65) in the general population. The bureau found that persons over 65 rose from 4 per cent of the population in 1900 to 8 per cent in 1955, with women especially predominant. The article further commented: "In terms of voting power, ownership of land and corporate equities, the United

---

[4] A comparison of the OLM Parish age-sex pyramid, already contrasted above with the neighborhood pyramid, with such pyramids as those for the total Bronx, for New York City, and for the United States, shows a basic wholesomeness in the parish's age structure. There is a general likeness to the Bronx structure. New York City, though equally strong in the group of children under 5 years, is weak in all other youth groups, and is thus roughly comparable to the OLM neighborhood structure. The United States as a whole presents a fairly well-balanced pyramid, with its only sharp irregularities manifested in the small age groups born in the depression years of the 1930's. The sex structure shows a larger female imbalance in OLM Parish than in neighborhood, county, city, or country. The female percentages are: for the country, 50.5 per cent; for the city, 51.6 per cent; for the Bronx, 51.5 per cent; for the neighborhood, 51.6 per cent; and for the parish, 53.7 per cent.

States could be on the road toward a gerontomatriarchy—control by ageing females."[5] Recognition of the large group of elderly people in the parish (9.5 per cent) has led the pastor of OLM to establish a well-received Senior Club as an answer to some of the needs of the aged in our society.

3. MARITAL STATUS

Complete data concerning marital status were not received for 42 of the 8,570 recorded parishioners of OLM. Of the remaining 8,528 persons, 3,932 are single, 3,838 are married, 665 are widowed, and 93 are separated or divorced. Of the 3,932 single persons, 1,402 were 20 years of age or over, while 7 of the married women were under 20. Complete data are presented in Table III.

TABLE III

Marital Status of OLM Parish Members

Status	Male	Female	Total
Single (below age of 20)	1,271	1,259	2,530
Single (20 years and over)	609	793	1,402
Married (including 7 girls under 20)	1,912	1,926	3,838
Widowed	114	551	665
Separated or divorced	18	75	93

It will be noted that there are more female married persons than male, owing to the fact that some spouses living separately from the married partner failed to give any information concerning absent partners—in military service or in hospitals, for example. One observation that might be made at this time is that 1,926 of the 2,773 OLM households from which census forms were received (almost 70 per cent) are presided over by hus-

---

[5] *New York Times*, May 9, 1955.

bands and wives in the normal family pattern. The remaining households are headed either by widowed or separated parents, and there are also individuals living alone or together on a non-family basis.

A check of the figures in Table III reveals that much of the female overbalance in OLM Parish derives from the five-to-one ratio of widows over widowers (551 to 114) and the four-to-one ratio of divorced and separated women over divorced and separated men (75 to 18). Although there are a few more boys than girls under 20 years of age, there are almost 200 more unmarried women than men over 20 (793 to 609). The age-sex pyramid (see Figure 10) is a graphic representation of the marital status of OLM parishioners at each of the various age levels. The one conceivably weak spot is the plurality of 100 single women between the ages of 30 and 40.

As Father John Thomas has indicated, the types of marriages in a parish can be an index of parish vitality.[6] Since invalid marriages deprive the partners of participation in the sacramental life of the Church and often dispose them toward carelessness concerning their children's participation, the presence of a large number of such marriages suggests that the parish is not operative for many of its nominal members. This is particularly true of invalid mixed marriages, as both Father Kelly and Father Thomas have indicated. Conversely, functioning valid marriages provide the parish with the greatest portion of its closely identified members. The types of marriages in OLM Parish are summarized in Table IV, page 128. Data are available for 1,926 marriages, of which 100 (5.2 per cent) are invalid.[7]

---

[6] Thomas, "Family and Parish," pp. 291-96.

[7] Since Father Thomas has found a much higher rate of invalidity—sometimes as high as 30 per cent among all marriages in the parish and as high as 40 per cent among mixed marriages—and since Father Kelly found almost as high a rate among mixed marriages and 10 per cent among Catholic marriages in

The practical value of possessing the breakdown in Table IV lies in the possibility of adopting a uniform approach, or series of uniform approaches, to those who are invalidly married. Over 92 per cent of all marriages in OLM Parish (1,779 out of 1,926) were valid according to church law, whether both parties

TABLE IV

Types of Marriages in OLM Parish

	Catholic Marriages	Convert Marriages	Mixed Marriages	Total
Originally valid	1,609	68	102	1,779
Invalid, but later validated	26	5	16	47
Invalid in 1954	64	2	34	100
All marriages	1,699	75	152	1,926

were Catholic or not, and almost one third of the remaining 8 per cent (47 of 147) were later validated.[8] In the case of Catholic marriages only 5 per cent were contracted invalidly, a good portion of those being among a recent, still disorganized immigrant group. In the case of mixed marriages almost a third (50 of 152) were originally invalid, and of the 50 only 16 were subsequently rectified. For those who favor a more approachable paternal policy toward invalidly married parishioners

---

Florida, we might suspect either of two things about OLM: either the invalidity rate is very low, and thus not in conformity with the unfortunate pattern which Fathers Thomas and Kelly found; or the invalid marriages are to be found among the 27 per cent who did not respond to the census. Only completion of the census could determine where the truth lies.

[8] The term "Catholic marriage," as used in this study, refers to one in which both parties were Catholics at the time of the marriage, even though one or both partners may have been a convert to the Catholic faith. A "convert marriage" is one in which one of the parties, or both, was converted after the marriage ceremony. One of the parties in a mixed marriage is a Catholic and the other a non-Catholic.

(which this author strongly believes should be favored), possession of readily available data concerning this particular group
must be a valuable pastoral asset.

4. CONVERTS

At the time of our study OLM had 203 converts, 166 of
them converts for more than five years and the remaining 37
converted within the five years preceding our study. Of the total,
96 are males and 107 are females; 104 persons are over 59
years of age. The greater number of them are married, 144, and
another 35 are widowed or separated. The remaining 24 are
single. The fertility of the mothers among them averages less
than half that of their own mothers. As in most matters, their
religious observance is on a level with that of the rest of the
parish, though a relatively high 5 per cent have not made their
first Communion and 13 per cent have not been confirmed. More
details concerning their religious practices can be found in
Chapter 11.

5. THE FOREIGN BORN

As noted earlier in this chapter, immigrants and the children
and grandchildren of immigrants moved to that part of the
Bronx which is OLM territory as soon as they were able to leave
the tenement sections of Manhattan. Therefore immigrants and
the foreign-born children of immigrating parents comprise a
large block of Bronx residents. In fact, almost 26 per cent of the
1,500,000 inhabitants of the Bronx and 28 per cent of the residents in OLM territory were foreign born according to the 1950
United States Census. In 1955 it was found that 1,669 parishioners, about 19.5 per cent, were born outside the United States.[9]

---

[9] The differences between the OLM Parish foreign-born percentages and those of
the neighborhood and Bronx are easily explained. The Jewish immigrants
from central Europe are, with rare exceptions, not members of OLM Parish,

Table V shows the country of origin of the foreign-born residents in the entire Bronx, in OLM territory, and of OLM parishioners born outside the United States. Puerto Ricans are naturally not listed as foreign born in the United States Census, but are included in the 1,669 OLM parishioners born outside

TABLE V

Residents of Bronx County, OLM Territory, and OLM Parish
Born Outside the United States

Country of Origin	Bronx County [1950—26%]	OLM Territory [1950—28%]	OLM Parish [1955—19.5%]
Russia	23.3	11.9	——
Italy	16.7	16.5	22.6
Poland	12.1	5.2	——
Ireland	10.0	9.2	49.1
Austria	8.4	4.9	——
Germany	7.6	5.2	5.8(1)
Hungary	4.1	2.7	——
Puerto Rico	——	——	9.5
Other countries	17.8	44.4	12.9

(1) The 5.8 per cent includes all parishioners from Germany, Austria, and Hungary.

the continental or mainland United States. Blanks indicate that percentages were not large enough to be listed separately.

The high percentage of immigrants from Central European nations in the United States Census, both for the Bronx and for OLM territory, is accounted for by the Jewish population recorded in the parish address list census. Among members of

---

and relatively few of the Bronx immigrants from that area are Catholic. On the other hand, Catholic Ireland, Italy, and Puerto Rico have provided over 80 per cent of the parish's Catholics who were born overseas. Were all the Catholics in OLM territory considered, including those who attend other churches, then the Italian born would constitute the largest element of foreign born. But most of them attend their national church, Our Lady of Mount Carmel. A check of the names of OLM's school children shows a nationality background distribution pattern similar to that of the foreign born.

OLM Parish almost half the foreign born (820 out of 1,669) come from Ireland. Although many Italians attend the neighboring OLMC Church, 377 are members of OLM Parish. The following appeared in the *Parish Monthly* for May 1955.

OLM PARISHIONERS FROM OTHER LANDS

As is well known, the strength of America has come from the millions of immigrants who have come to our shores. After hard beginnings they have built a great nation. The same is true of the Church in America; some of the finest pages of American Catholic history have been written by Americans born in other lands.

Naturally New York City, including the Bronx, has typified that mixture of immigrant peoples into a new union, and our own parish, Our Lady of Mercy, mirrors that general development.

Of the 27,000 persons living within the borders of our parish over 28 per cent were not born in the United States. They were born abroad in many different countries: over 16 per cent came from Italy; almost 12 per cent from Russia; 10 per cent from Ireland; another 10 per cent from Germany and Austria; 8 per cent from Poland and Hungary. The remaining 44 came from other countries —the British Isles, Scandinavia, the Balkans, Canada, and Puerto Rico. The percentage of foreign born in all of Bronx County (26 per cent) is quite close to the 28 per cent of foreign-born persons living within the borders of the parish. The Bronx, however, has a higher percentage of immigrants from Russia, Germany, Poland, and Austria.

Among OLM parishioners the picture is a little different. Less than 20 per cent of our members were born outside the United States and almost half of these came from Ireland. Italy gave us 22.6 per cent, even though many other Italians attend the neighboring national parish. Almost 10 per cent of our parishioners were born in Puerto Rico.

The smaller percentage of Catholic than non-Catholic foreign born in OLM territory indicates that the third- and fourth-generation children of the old Irish and Italian immigrants are more numerous than the immigrants themselves and, in a sense, as American as they are Catholic. A new immigrant group has now come on the scene, in New York City, the Bronx, and OLM

Parish. Less than twenty-five years ago there were practically no Puerto Ricans in the upper Bronx; today there are nearly 20,000. Despite the usual and continuing struggle, disorganization, and heartache of the unacculturated new arrival, and thanks to more enlightened social policy, the Puerto Ricans have been moving more rapidly than any former immigrant group toward wholesome integration into New York life.

Most of the Puerto Ricans have moved up from the downtown and Harlem districts, and from the lower Bronx to the east Bronx. Some, however, have come more directly north. The total Puerto Rican population of OLM Parish, including American-born children, now numbers about 500. It is impossible to give a certain figure, for about three fifths of them are transients. Almost 200 live in the poorer houses toward the southern end of the parish, some of them already owning their own homes. The other 300—to a large extent broken and combined families—are, with some noble and notable exceptions, mostly city welfare cases.[10]

The Puerto Ricans manifest the renewal of the pattern of assimilating new ethnic groups into Catholic American social institutions, particularly church and school. The parish has tried to do what it could for these new residents. Both the Legion of Mary and the St. Vincent de Paul Society provide services. The few Puerto Rican children enrolled in the parish school have responded admirably. As far as OLM Parish is concerned, we notice the challenge to and response of the social system in the

---

[10] Puerto Ricans occupy one of a series of fairly good-looking middle-class apartment houses right in the heart of the parish, a house normally suited for some 100 occupants. They live four in a room, and about twelve families have at their disposal one tiny kitchen and two toilets. It would seem to be a typical instance of an attempt to obtain the greatest possible revenue from living quarters through overcrowding. Furthermore the neighbors, both those not well disposed toward ethnic groups and those who are, object to this defacement of their neighborhood through the usual effects of overcrowding.

face of demographic changes, new relationships, and new demands on its ability to function effectively.

6. OCCUPATIONAL AND ECONOMIC STRUCTURE

Mention has previously been made of the observations of European sociologists that certain occupational groups tend to be less associated with religious life than others. Hence the occupations of OLM parishioners are of interest to the study. Of 8,383 individuals in the parish from whom reports were received, 3,561 (42.5 per cent) are in the labor force; that is, they are either actively at work or are looking for work. (At the time the study was made 167 were unemployed.) Another 237 persons (2.8 per cent) have retired after a full life's work. Of the remaining 4,585 parishioners who are not or have never been in the labor force, 1,701 (20.3 per cent) are young people below the age of 15 and 2,884 (34.4 per cent) are housewives and mothers. Of course these housewives and mothers work, most of them harder than other people; but since they are not paid in dollars and cents, they are not technically considered as belonging to the labor force.

The type of work done by those gainfully employed is compared with the occupations of residents of Bronx County and the OLM neighborhood (as reported in the 1950 census) in Table VI, page 134. The percentage of women in the labor force is also included in Table VI. The figure indicates that the parish percentage of women in the labor force, where 37 per cent of those in the labor force are women, is higher than that for the county or the neighborhood. The census did not reveal the place of work, but the questionnaire indicated that 71 per cent of all the respondents in the labor force performed all their work outside the parish.

Examination of this table reveals that more than a fourth of the neighborhood workers are engaged in professional and managerial occupations. For Bronx County the percentage is 20.8, while only 14.6 per cent of the working population in the parish have professions or serve as managers. Engaged as craftsmen or operatives are 35.4 per cent of the Bronx workers, 28 per cent of the neighborhood labor force, and 26.2 per cent of the parish active labor force. A large percentage (39.6) of parish workers

TABLE VI

Types of Occupations by County, Neighborhood, and Parish

Occupation	Bronx County	OLM Neighborhood	OLM Parish
Professional and managerial	20.8	25.9	14.6
Craftsmen and operatives	35.4	28.0	26.2
Clerical work and sales	29.0	34.6	39.6
Manual labor and domestic service	14.8	6.8	19.5
Women in labor force	30.0	34.0	37.0

are engaged in clerical work or sales, as compared with 34.6 per cent for the neighborhood and 29 per cent for Bronx County. This higher percentage from the parish can at least be partially explained by two demographic facts already mentioned: the higher percentage of women in the parish population (53.7 per cent) than in either neighborhood (51.6 per cent) or county (51.5 per cent); and the higher percentage of women workers in the labor force (37 per cent as compared with 34 per cent and 30 per cent). The same observation can be made concerning the percentage of workers engaged in manual labor and domestic service. The neighborhood has a low of 6.8 per cent, the county has 14.8 per cent, and the parish has 19.5 per cent.

Of the 1,250 women in the parish labor force, only 325 are married. About 50 are engaged in some professional or managerial activity, 185 are employed in clerical or sales work, and the remainder work at various trades or services. Of the 325 married women, 123 have no children, 152 average just over two children each, and the other 45 who responded average almost five children each. In this small sample there is no significant pattern of fertility and no pattern of differences according to occupations.

It can readily be seen from the figures presented in Table VI that a large proportion of OLM's parishioners are somewhat behind their neighbors in certain socioeconomic achievements. This is not particularly important in itself, but it signifies a problem for the parish priests and societies in terms of communication and participation. As many Catholics move up the intellectual and socioeconomic ladder, the quality of sermons and society programs must likewise be elevated; yet a great number are still capable of absorbing much simpler fare. How to be "all things to all men" in Catholic parishes is a problem which taxes pastoral ingenuity.

Table VII presents data on the economic status of parishioners. While rents provide some indication of economic status, not too much insight is afforded by this amount, since rent controls have continued in effect and often enough the older and better homes in OLM Parish rent for less than newer and smaller ones. Just 2,650 of the 2,773 OLM families recorded the rental value of their homes. In addition, the questionnaire asked the

TABLE VII

Economic Status of OLM Parishioners by
Rental Value and Income

Rent or Income	Census		Questionnaire	
	Number	Per Cent	Number	Per Cent
Over $100 per month	60	2.3		
$10,000 or more annually			13	4.4
$80-$99 per month	90	3.4		
$5,000-$9,999 annually			114	38.9
$60-$79 per month	660	24.9		
$3,000-$4,999 annually			131	44.7
Less than $60 per month	1,840	69.4		
Less than $3,000 annually			35	12.0

respondents to indicate whether the total family income was more than $10,000 annually, from $5,000 to $9,999, from $3,000 to $4,999, or below $3,000.[11] Respondents were also asked to indicate whether the family owned a television set and an automobile. On the basis of these replies, the families were divided into four economic categories. Family income was the most decisive factor, but in borderline cases the possession of an automobile or a TV set also had some bearing.

While only 293 respondents furnished the data on family income, compared to 2,650 who listed the rental value of their homes, a consideration of both criteria gives the author the impression that family income is more indicative of the parishioner's economic status than rental value. Obviously, not much questioning on the subject was in order.

7. EDUCATIONAL BACKGROUND

The United States Census assumes that one's education is complete by age twenty-five. Looking at all OLM parishioners who are twenty-five years old and more, we see that there are few significant differences between the educational backgrounds of the residents of the Bronx, the OLM neighborhood, and OLM parishioners. Nearly 45 per cent of each group attained only elementary schooling; approximately 3 per cent of the OLM group had four years or less and 39 per cent had from five to eight years. Another 43 per cent had some high-school education; for the OLM group about 19 per cent had less than four years and 23 per cent graduated from high school. The OLM neighborhood has a slightly higher percentage of graduates than the parish. The neighborhood also leads in the percentages attending and graduating from college. Less than 10 per cent of the parishioners over twenty-five went to college, and half of these graduated. Of course a great many of the older people in

---

[11] See Part 1, Question 8.

the parish and community went to school during the days when elementary-school training was all that most persons received. Figure 13 presents data for Bronx County, the OLM neighborhood, and OLM Parish.

When all parishioners over five years of age are considered, almost 7,850 persons, there is an increase in the percentages of those who have attended or are attending school. This is to be expected, since the ranks of those with high-school and college training continue to swell in accordance with today's social policy and needs. The percentages in Figure 14 (for all parishioners over five years old) differ slightly from those in Figure 13 (for parishioners over twenty-five) because they are based on a larger population.

Of particular interest in this study is the amount of Catholic schooling which parishioners receive. About 51.5 per cent of the parishioners over five years old have had or are receiving Catholic elementary schooling; 22 per cent have some Catholic high-school training or have graduated from high school; just over 5 per cent have attended or are attending Catholic colleges. Almost half (193 of 401 college students) have graduated.

Education influences people's interests, desires, and efforts. The policies adopted by a community are therefore determined to some extent by the education of the people in the community. The general level and the variation of educational achievement are of obvious importance in the vital relationship of communication between priests and people—and among the people themselves—in cooperating toward the realization of parish aims. In a later chapter the educational factor is further considered in its relationship to religious practice.

8. RELIGIOUS PRACTICE

Analysis of a group's demographic structure should include an examination of every factor pertinent to identifying and understanding that group's characteristics—its physiognomy, as certain French writers like to call it. Particularly in the study of a religious society, though likewise in other social studies too, the religious activities of its members and their participation in the religious activity of the organization can by no means be disregarded.

On the other hand, the very religious activities and attitudes in which OLM's members participate are precisely those manifestations of social interaction and value orientation which bind the members of the parish, both clergy and laity, into a functioning religious society. Consequently all the demographic aspects of religious practice, the numbers and percentages of Mass attendance, reception of the sacraments and performance of one's Easter duty, and all the relationships between religious life and certain demographic categories—membership in a particular age or sex group, residence in a certain geographical milieu, employment in a certain occupation, educational and economic status, marital and family situation, and so forth—are discussed in later chapters on the use of the parish's religious services rather than here.

9. RESPONDENTS TO THE QUESTIONNAIRE

Information about age, sex, marital status, place of birth, occupation, rental value of homes, and education attained was secured from the census forms filled out by families in the parish. As mentioned in connection with economic status, some of the knowledge about OLM's members is derived from the responses to the lengthy questionnaire. A brief demographic view of these respondents will serve to indicate their typicalness as a representative sample of the parish.

Of the 293 respondents, 144 are men and 149 women, showing a somewhat higher proportion of male respondents than the percentages of 46 per cent male and 54 per cent female distribution of parishioners would warrant. They are a bit above the parish average educationally, since 83 have attended college

(41 graduated), 128 have attended high school, and 82 have a grammar-school education. Of the 83 with college training, 42 attended Catholic colleges (26 graduated); 61 of 128 attended a Catholic high school; and 73 of 82 among those who have only an elementary-school education went to a Catholic elementary school. In general religious observance they are above the average; 33 qualify as exceptional, 171 are above the required norms, 77 are average in that they satisfy the norms, and 12 are at best lax in their religious practice.[12] More than half of the respondents (169) come from the central district (Tract 399), 74 live in the western sector, and 50 live in the eastern sector. The variations would seem to indicate that the sampling of OLM parishioners was fairly valid.

---

[12] See Chapter 8, p. 171, for an explanation of these categories.

CHAPTER VII

The Parish Priests

We have noted Cardinal Cushing's reference to the parish as the "Church in miniature." Making allowance for various religious services, projects, and activities conducted on a diocesewide or a nationwide basis, we can nevertheless represent the parish's goals as being those of the Church within its own territory. These are, briefly, the spread and increase of knowledge of the truths of the Christian creed; the acceptance, both personal and communal, of a way of life in accordance with the Christian code which derives from that creed; the practice of the Christian cult, centered in the reception of the seven Christ-instituted sacraments and participation in His constantly renewed sacrifice of the Mass; finally a communion of the faithful based on the common possession of the values inherent in this creed, code, and cult. In short, the parish aims to assist people to achieve holiness—that is, union with God—and, because of it, fraternal community among men. This is another way of saying that Church and parish seek to implement what Christianity's founder designated as the two greatest commandments: love of God and love of neighbor.

The people joined, whether in the Church as a whole or in the parish, in striving for these goals are linked in a series of relationships structured accordingly. Religious truth, including the doctrines inherent in creed, code, and cult, passes constantly from teachers to disciples; norms of conduct are established by those in authority and accepted by subjects; liturgical officials conduct divine worship and the body of the membership assists therein. Each of these fundamental relationships and countless others based on them involve certain patterns of status and role. Teacher and disciple, ruler and ruled, liturgical leader and assistant, all have certain ways of acting which are expected of them, rights and duties, parts to be played. Thanks to the parish's values, definite norms govern the way these parts are played.

Having seen in previous chapters OLM's physical setting and the demographic structure of the parish, our attention now goes to the arrangement or organization of the relationships between these people; not of all their relationships, of course, but of those which are part of the parish life and functioning. In other words, we are here interested in the social structure of the parish. A society is a union of persons who cooperate for a certain purpose. A baseball team is a union of persons working together to score runs and to prevent an opposing team from scoring. Their working together, their interaction, implies a number of relationships structured in accordance with that purpose. The pitcher-catcher relationship derives from a common effort to prevent an opposing batsman from hitting successfully. Second baseman and shortstop are called a "pivot combination" because of their peculiar defensive role. Any social organization—educational, business, political—possesses a general structure of relationships deriving from its purposeful interaction as well as a web of particular relationships, depending on its extent and complexity, between members or groups of members in accordance with their respective roles.

The parish is in no way different from other societies in these respects. It has its purposes, its interaction to achieve them, and a structure of relationships implicit in and developed by that interaction. Relationships have a structure of their own, consisting of the respective statuses of their members and the roles which they play in regard to each other.[1] In this and the following chapter we consider OLM's social structure, and therefore its system of statuses and roles. Since the most important aspect of the parish social structure is the relationship between priests and people in their pursuit of parish purposes, we treat the priests' status and roles in this chapter, those of the parishioners in the next.

The overriding question in any social organization must be whether the structure of its relationships is adequate to achieving its purposes. Deficient structure means unfulfilled purposes, and the latter mean that the social organization itself is losing or has lost its very *raison d'être*. Circumstances of time and space, changes in attitudes or demographic conditions, a different historical tradition, can explain accidental variations in structure, or might necessitate them. Swoboda pointed out that a precondition for effective pastoral activity was some sort of numerical balance. He recalls that the Council of Trent used as its norm in this respect "that he [the pastor] can know them [members of the parish]."[2] Pope Pius VI (1791) was unwilling that any pastor should be responsible for more than 6,000 souls. Pope Leo XII (1824) considered that a parish of 3,000 was neither too large nor too small, and could be suitably shepherded by a pastor and an assistant with the further help of a sacristan and two priests to help with confessions. The Provincial Council of Vienna (1858) judged 10,000 souls to be the very most which should be included within one parish. In our own day Dutch and Canadian proposals would limit a parish to 7,000 or 8,000 members.[3] The point is that an unbalanced numerical ratio between pastor and flock calls for a change in the structure and role pattern. Thus most religious education of

---

[1] See Figure 1.

[2] Swoboda, *Grossstadtseelsorge*, p. 6.

[3] See Léon de Coninck, *Problèmes de l'adaptation en apostolat*, p. 97. Paris: Casterman, 1949.

school children is not cared for today so much by the priest as by religious women teaching in the parish school and by generous laymen in the Confraternity of Christian Doctrine and other groups.

In similar vein space can be a determinant of structure. Boulard pointed out that many French priests have to care for two or more parishes and lose much of their time in simply traveling between churches and repeating services.[4] Missionaries often have large tracts of land to cover and hence make use of catechists to relieve them of some elementary teaching. From a different aspect the so-called liturgical movement in some places has led to increased active participation of the congregation in divine worship; for example, in the dialogue Mass and the community-sung Mass. This implies changes, even though relatively minor, in the liturgical roles of priest and people.

The most obvious, important, and multiple relationship in a Catholic parish is that between priest and people, between pastor and flock. This can hardly be questioned, for each of the three fundamental relationships mentioned above—teaching Christian truth, interpreting Christian morality, and leading Christian worship—necessarily involves priest and people. All others of his parish roles, as priest, derive from these three. Hence in considering the social structure of a parish our attention must go first to the parish priest.

It must be recognized that the role of the priest, the part he plays in relationship with other Catholics and particularly with his parishioners, is rooted in Catholic theology. So is the status to which his priestly rank elevates him. In his deservedly famous pastoral "Priests among Men" Cardinal Suhard said:

> The priesthood is not a derivatory function. It cannot be artificially constructed at our pleasure from the confusion and partial

---

[4] For a summary of Boulard's work, *Problèmes missionaires de la France rurale,* see Appendix I, pp. 285-86.

order of society. It is not a supererogation or a ritual garb. It changes the priest in his very essence. It is given from on high. It is unique, permanent, eternal. It must be accepted for what it is, not as something rising from experience but as both the original source and the fulfillment of all the imperfect foreshadowings of it found in the history of religions. This priesthood is the priesthood of Jesus Christ, Son of God. Being a priest in the social order is not a matter of inventing functions but of continuing by Christ's grace His unique priesthood in His Mystical Body which is the Church.

To be a priest means to perpetuate Christ just as He is, throughout time and space. It means to preserve Him unchanged, throughout the course of history, identical under the most diverse forms of social life, without subtracting anything from His priesthood, without adding anything to it, but not without making Christ perceptible and communicable. . . . To be a priest in the social order means to perpetuate the immutable and essential elements of Christ's priesthood, that is to say His mysterious mediation, under the constantly recurring aspects of time.[5]

The Catholic priest, then, is not a priest in his own right, as a lawyer might be a lawyer in his own right through having studied the law and being admitted to the bar. But the priest, though he might be a theologian, canon lawyer, or church historian in his own right, can be and is a priest only insofar as he exercises the priesthood of Christ, only insofar as he causes Christ to be continued among men. It may be that many a sociologist and of course many non-Catholics generally do not believe or accept this; but to understand the role of the priest in the Catholic community or the parish they must recognize that Catholics do believe it and consequently conduct themselves in relationships with a priest, as a priest, accordingly.

For Christ in Catholic theology, which underlies the values of the Catholic community, is prince (or ruler), prophet (or teacher), and priest (or mediator between God and man). In Him is achieved and perfected the one, true, and effective priest-

---

[5] Suhard, *The Church Today*, p. 223.

hood, for His incarnate divinity and human-divine sacrifice alone were and are the effective mediation between God and man and the redemption of man for eternal life. No other priest or priesthood could take His place, for His priesthood is eternal. But men could and would, according to the will of the founder of Christianity, be ordained to His priesthood and thus continue Christ and that priesthood, visibly manifested among all men in all places.

Thus the foundation of the priest's role is that he is an *alter Christus:* in the name of Christ he offers the divine sacrifice and dispenses Christ's sacraments. In addition, since Christ's priesthood was and is aimed at men's sanctification (union with God), then His human minister participates also in those other prerogatives and functions, as Suhard says, which are attributed to the Word Incarnate and His own mission of sanctification; namely, those of ruler and teacher. Actually all of these prerogatives, if we may follow Suhard again, "merge in their turn into one function which comprehends them all, that of mediator. It is for that that a priest is ordained, for that that he accepts the priestly requirements of Church discipline, and on that that his status in the Catholic community basically rests."[6]

Thus the Catholic is trained from earliest parish consciousness (that is, those Catholics who are aware of the teachings of their faith) to see in the priest not merely a man playing an ecclesiastical role but the perpetuator of Christ's mission in His teaching, His exposition of a holy way of life, and His performance of the cult of divine worship.

To prepare for the priestly role the parish priest-to-be engages in a fairly lengthy period of training in the seminary. Generally it lasts some twelve years from the time he has finished elementary school, and proportionately less if he begins his training after high school or college. He is almost invariably

[6] *Ibid.*

satisfied that God has called him to priestly service and consequently, out of devotion to God, willingly foregoes certain legitimate human aspirations denied by church discipline (for important reasons) to the priest. The last six years of his training, usually in the seminary, are given primarily to a study of philosophy, Scripture, doctrinal theology, moral theology, church law, and pastoral practice. This practice is principally concerned with administering the sacraments, leading public worship, preaching, handling parish problems, and providing counsel and guidance. The priest-to-be looks forward to the day when he will be assigned to a parish church where he will be able to serve parishioners who come to it in their search for God and in their desire to receive the God-given benefits provided by the parish church. Unfortunately there is little evidence that his training includes the study of the social composition of the parish. We say "unfortunately" because so much of religious life and pastoral policy can be better understood in terms of the social milieu.

Once appointed by his bishop, the pastor, who has primary responsibility for the parish, and his assistant priests are occupied in the performance of a multiplicity of roles. Father Fichter, in a chapter entitled "Social Roles of the Parish Priest," lists and analyzes well many of these roles, which reflect not only the traditional needs of spiritual fatherhood and mediatorship but likewise "a whole complex of functional demands which appear to require a corresponding complexity and expansion of the basic transcendental roles of mediator and father."[7] Father Fichter suggests that these roles are projected into the parish priest's life because of the "predominantly associational and secondary types of group relations" which characterize modern urban living and because of the development of two conflicting value systems which impinge on priestly life, namely, "the ways

---

[7] Fichter, *Urban Parish*, p. 127.

of the world as accepted and practiced by the parishioners and the ways of God as taught and striven for in the Church."[8] Some of the roles which Father Fichter lists, and which provided the material for one of the questions in the OLM questionnaire, are those of father, mediator, member of community, administrator (running the parish and all its subsocieties and functions), businessman (financing the parish and keeping proper records), citizen and civic leader, reformer, educator, leader of spiritual societies, and liturgical leader.[9]

Many of those roles, however, are derivative; they are important, but subordinate to—and possibly exist only because of—prior roles more intimately associated with the priestly character. If the priest's greatest role is that of perpetuating Christ, and if Christ's mission was to join man to God, then obviously the most directly priestly activities which a priest performs in the parish must pertain to enabling or facilitating the parishioner's approach to God. In so doing he exercises the twin roles of father and mediator. Let us study them a little, remembering that they are roles formally established and imposed by the universal Church and hence to be met in the social structure of OLM as in that of every Catholic parish.

In Catholic theology the several sacraments are described—really, not in any mere symbolism—as means of God's grace coming to the faithful. A person is baptized and thus admitted into the Christian community and the supernatural fraternity of Christ; he is confirmed and thus receives strength to manifest publicly his devotion to Christ; in confession he receives absolution from his violations of God's law, thereby returning to or growing in divine friendship; by receiving the Eucharist under the sacramental appearances of bread and wine he enters into physical and intimate union with God; in serious illness and at

---

[8] *Ibid.*
[9] See Appendix II, Part 2, Question 29.

the point of death he receives with the last anointing extreme unction, the necessary spiritual and even, when necessary, physical help in man's final earthly test. In each of these sacraments, these conferrings of God's grace, it is the priest who administers to the parishioner—except for confirmation, which is usually administered by the bishop. Since grace implies participation in the divine life, as Catholic theology teaches, then the priest actually plays the role of father, a spiritual father, in administering the sacraments of God which confer that grace.

Each of the five sacraments just mentioned are primarily personal, in that the recipient's personal union with God is their primary aim—though his relationship with the community is also thereby influenced. The other two sacraments, though they too confer grace personally on the recipient, are given primarily to help him perform his social role in the Christian community adequately. One is ordination to the priesthood or holy orders, with which the parish priest has little formally to do, since it is the bishop who ordains. But in so many instances it is the parish priest who has first awakened, then encouraged, then sponsored a young man's interest in joining the ranks of Christ's priesthood, of spiritual fatherhood for the Catholic community, that here too his role can be accurately called that of father. And while it is happily true that the priest does not confer the sacrament of matrimony on betrothed man and woman, but rather that they confer it on themselves while he is but the Church's official witness, nevertheless it is the priest to whom they go for premarital instruction and often also for guidance, and it is from the priest that they receive God's and the Church's blessing on their new life.

But the role of father is not performed only in these official functions themselves. In and around each of them is often woven a complex of circumstances in which the fatherly role is further looked for, expected, and exercised. The Church requires of the priest in the confessional that he be not only the judge who forgives or retains sin, but, as occasion and penitent require, the teacher who instructs, the spiritual doctor who heals the distraught soul, and the father who understands, encourages, and sometimes must firmly insist. In addition to administering extreme unction he is expected to be father to the sick, the dying, and later the bereaved. No less than doctor, fireman, or policeman, he is expected to be ready at any hour of day or night when his spiritual children, his flock, his parishioners, need his fatherly care. The point to be noticed is that the role is both exercised by the priest and expected by the laity. It manifests the relationship which is cardinal to the Catholic parish system of social relationships; that is, the social structure.

Less closely connected with his priestly functions, but still derived from his fatherly role, are the priest's roles as counselor and helper-in-need. The tramp of the road and the ne'er-do-well do not call on the priest as on a father, but usually as an expected "soft touch." But this expectation came from the community's understanding that the priest is ready to help the temporally as well as the spiritually unfortunate parishioner. And the honestly needy do take advantage of that readiness, though modern public welfare services have reduced the priest's role in this respect considerably. Trouble at home with spouse or children, the fellow at home who can never keep a job, the girl "in trouble," the youngsters caught in some delinquency by the police—all these and more come with the routine calls at the rectory door. Nor is it only trouble that comes. Not seldom bride and groom like to have "Father" join in the joy of their wedding celebration. Fond parents invite him for their offspring's graduation, and parish celebrations are not felt to be complete without his presence.

The foregoing instances show the priest as father, particularly in his dispensing of goods—primarily spiritual, secondarily and subordinately temporal. He plays another role, his other most important role rooted intimately in the priesthood itself, in which he does not dispense gifts to them, but offers their gifts to God. Thus he mediates, as it were, in the other direction, bringing men to God, whereas in dispensing the sacraments he brings God to men. For such is the priesthood of Christ. Catholic theology teaches that Christ offered to God the one great acceptable sacrifice, a holy offering of praise and of thanks, of redemptive atonement and efficacious petition. It teaches further that Christ commissioned those who would continue His priesthood to renew constantly for men in an unbloody way His sacrifice of Himself on Calvary, as He first had done in the consecration of bread and wine at the Last Supper. So it is that the greatest act of the Catholic priesthood is the constant renewal, in parishes and on altars round the world, of the sacrifice of the Mass. It is the very center of Catholic worship, the ever-true reenactment of the most sublime religious act in the history of mankind. That is why the Catholic parish church is so crowded, Mass after Mass, on every Sunday of the year, and why so many Catholics assist at Mass not only every Sunday but even on every day of the week.

In this as in the far less important acts of Catholic public worship, such as Benediction of the Blessed Sacrament, the recitation of the rosary, Vespers, Compline, and other "devotions," the Catholic parishioner sees the priest in the role of mediator, the one who, in Christ's name and in theirs, joins their prayers and offerings with Christ on the altar and offers them unerringly to the throne of God. Any study of OLM, of any Catholic parish, must recognize these priestly roles and the relationships which they imply.

During Mass itself a constant series of interactions between priest and people occurs, though it must be admitted that many Catholics are still unaware of much of it. Every expressed prayer concludes with the congregation's approving "amen," every action of the congregation (standing, kneeling, sitting, listening, responding) corresponds to an action by the priest.

Every tinkling of the Mass bell brings (or should bring) priest and people to a united consciousness of a common sacred action. There is a performance of respective and expected roles culminating, at least liturgically speaking, in the distribution by the priest and the reception by the congregation of the sacrament of Communion, and the final blessing and brief exhortation to bring to the world outside the fruit of this divine worship and union with God.

It is such performance by the priest, especially in his roles of father and mediator and when colored by the realization that the priest has paid a high price (in human values) to be privileged to render such service, which forms the parishioner's concept of the priest. From childhood he has been brought up on it, and unless the relationship dies or withers, it is part of his mental equipment for life.

Two observations should be made here in view of two objections which could deservedly be made. In the first place, why so much theological explanation of a social role? Suppose a student of the priest's role either does not accept or does not even understand the theology? The answer is, in great part, very simple. Acceptance of or belief in the theology is not required, but some understanding of it certainly is essential before one can hope to understand the role of the priest, or indeed the corresponding role of the layman. The identification of the priest with the priesthood of Christ, who in Catholic theology is God Himself, and consequently the realization that the priest serves as a link between the parishioner and God in his own very life must be comprehended before one can possibly grasp the role of the priest in the parish social structure.

The second observation can be more serious. Do all Catholic parishioners share this concept of the priest, understand the theology behind it, and participate in the priest-parishioner relationship? The answer must depend on what we understand by a parishioner. As far as those whom Father Fichter would designate as dormant and Brother Schnepp as lapsed are concerned, the answer would be no. But for all others the answer would be in the affirmative, though not to the same extent. What was described above as the priest's place in the parish social structure and the theology underlying it do represent both what is to be found in the Catholic parish and the values and attitudes which explain its existence. It does not follow that every priest lives completely up to his role, especially in the more derivative functions, or that every parishioner is aware of it and responsive to it. That would be something to be determined empirically in any given parish.

The prevalence of secondary associations in modern urban life can easily lead the sociologist to a denial of community in the urban parish. But we question whether the denial is completely valid. Unquestionably those on the fringe of parish life, the lax or marginal parishioners, share rather little in parish community life. Unquestionably too it happens not seldom that parishioners living on the same street, perhaps in the same apartment house, do not know each other, even though they might be well known to the parish priest and active in one or more phases of parish life. But it seems just as unquestionable that any structure of social relationships so constant, so multiple, so centered around the roles of priestly father and mediator, and so involved in such functions as those delineated in the following chapters must imply at least a communal possession of values and a communal disposition to cooperative enterprise. It is far from unusual to find that there is more than this possession and disposition: all parishioners may not be fully aware of all other parishioners, but all are consciously related to some, and this web of partial unities makes the common purpose and functioning of the parish effective.

Certainly the degree of community consciousness and the closeness and extent of community ties in the parish can be determined only by empirical inquiry. But the evident existence of manifold ties and relationships of more than passing importance makes the denial of community subject to rebuttal. That, incidentally, is a value of the social-system conceptual scheme as applied to the parish. It involves far less subjective evaluation in the application of such concepts as community and group.

Other roles of the parish priest, as Fichter has pointed out, have expanded with the parish. The head of any society, unless merely titular, has an administrative role to play which calls for more ability and dexterity the more extended and complicated it is. Figure 16, which shows the organizational structure of OLM Parish, indicates many of the activities conducted under the direction of the parish, all of them with their own stories of group goals and personal interests. The growth of the parish can imply, as it has for thousands of American pastors, the need to build a new church, school, convent, or rectory. This involves him in the role of businessman. As Fichter has suggested, this involvement can occasion conflict with his other roles, at least in terms of time, energy, and attention.

Precisely because of his pre-eminent status in the minds of his parishioners, and likewise because of the total permeation of human life to which Christianity aspires, the priest often finds himself called upon to exercise his influence as a civic or social leader in matters less connected with his essentially priestly role. Depending on the wisdom and prudence of the priest, such relationships can help or hinder his priestly functions.

The priests of OLM can already be known, at least in their official parish roles, by much of what has preceded. They are six in number: the pastor, whose many years of effective priestly service has led him to be honored with the monsignorate; four full-time assistants; and one priest who teaches in the diocesan minor seminary and helps in the parish as much as that position allows.

The pastor, who once studied under Franklin Giddings, an early American professor of sociology at Columbia University, and who cooperated most enthusiastically in the present survey of his parish, had come to OLM some fifteen years before the study. Given a well-functioning, highly reputed parish, he built on what his predecessor had left and added to the parish services several welfare functions which have tied in intimately with the basic spiritual purposes of the parish. The credit union which he instituted has been called the finest parish credit union in the country. The parish's employment bureau and social-welfare service give further testimony of his pastoral interest and vision, for he could see that his people not only would be materially and sometimes thereby spiritually benefited by such services, but would take the opportunity to identify themselves more fully with their parish. If it is true that urban life introduces more competitors for the urbanite's interest and support, then, where possible, the parish might well sponsor such legitimate interests itself. Thus the parishioner can both satisfy expanded interests and integrate them into his parish life.

In addition to these not too ordinary commitments, the pastor runs the Holy Name Society, the usual spiritual organization for men in most American parishes; the St. Vincent de Paul Society, dedicated to helping the poor; the Ushers Society; and the recently formed Seniors Club. Beyond these parochial roles, in each of which he acts as spiritual guide and fatherly counselor, he serves also as chaplain of the local organizations of the Knights of Columbus, the Ancient Order of Hibernians, and the Catholic War Veterans. He is also chaplain of the Bronx County Chapter of the St. Vincent de Paul Society.

These activities, together with his priestly functions of offering Mass, preaching, hearing confessions, officiating at funerals and wedding services, being available to parishioners who call on him, and visiting the sick and attending wakes, show the pastor of OLM active in performing the roles described earlier in this chapter. His is the responsibility for the school, the education of over a thousand youngsters, and the management of their thirty teachers. His supervision of the parish as a whole and of the activities of his assistants casts him in the role of administrator; and he has contributed to the physical development of OLM, the latest addition being the windows described in Chapter 5. His concern includes the parish staff, such as the sexton, the sacristan, the secretary, and the housekeeping help. As pastor of a flock in a secular environment he has several times used his position to influence secular affairs; for example, in the closing of an unsavory theater and the blocking of the use of land for a parking space in favor of its retention as a playground for the parish's cramped children.

All in all, it is quite easy to see the appropriateness of designating the Catholic pastor's role as that of father and mediator to which the laity's roles correspond. All the subsidiary roles can add to his effectiveness in the two major ones, as is obviously true in OLM, though they could well interfere. To cite two not infrequently found examples of the latter, one pastor in his zeal for what he considered Catholic social policy espoused strongly, both in and out of the pulpit, one side of a political issue about which Catholics were properly divided in their opinions; another, in his businessman's zeal for financing a needed building program, let his sermons and parochial policy be almost exclusively dictated by this activity. In each instance subsidiary roles—one tolerable if restrained, the other important but still secondary—received disproportionate emphasis and lessened the effectiveness of the performance of the respective pastors' primary priestly roles.

Each of the four full-time assistants shares the role of the priest no less than the pastor, though without the extent of his responsibility or the right to make ultimate decisions in parish policy. As a matter of fact, with less administrative and executive responsibility they often perform proportionately more of the regular priestly work. They rotate days on duty (25 hours straight), which means that they are responsible for all parish calls during their respective days. In some places this can be and sometimes is a sinecure; in others the priest has hardly a spare moment from one end of the day to the next. In OLM, with two hospitals in its territory and a shopping center near the church, the priest on duty is kept busy. One of the hospitals is Fordham General Hospital, which, as is usual with such a hospital, has its fill of emergency and accident cases at night as well as during the day. The priest on duty at OLM can count on being awakened on the average of almost twice a night to attend a sick or dying person at Fordham General Hospital. OLM's assistants assure me that one never gets quite used to such a nocturnal schedule, and that the following day is usually anything but their most effective.

Each priest has a rather lengthy list of sick persons in the parish to whom he brings Holy Communion once or twice a month. Each has usually, at any one time, some three or four adults under instruction preparing for conversion. During the year about 125 weddings occur and almost 150 funerals. The former require almost an hour apiece for paper work and additional time for rehearsal and instructions, plus the time for the actual wedding Mass and ceremony. The priests try to attend every wake—a time-consuming service in view of the number of deaths each year. Offering the funeral Mass and accompanying the funeral party to the cemetery usually take the equivalent of an entire morning. Celebrating Mass in church or the sisters' convent and praying the Divine Office each day usually take close to two hours. Baptisms on Sunday afternoons, helping to distribute Communion at the Sunday Masses, hearing confessions each Saturday, before holydays and First Fridays, and on one other weekday (for the children), conducting evening devotions, visiting the sick and classes in school, and counting the Sunday collections are all regular tasks week after week.

With the exception of the last-named task, which in some parishes is satisfactorily handled by the ushers or other lay assistants, each of these functions involves the priests of OLM in a structured set of relationships with their parishioners. Though the transient patients in Fordham General Hospital are hardly parishioners, still they receive the ministrations of OLM priests in their priestly role as spiritual father. Many receive such ministration for the first time after a long lapse, and thus re-enter into the priest-parishioner relationship.

Mention of all these priestly functions calls our attention to three considerations. First, each of the involved relationships is a fully social one, in which both the priest and the parishioner plays his respective role for the achievement of a common purpose. This is further explained in later chapters which discuss interaction in services provided at OLM. Second, these relationships are the elements of the total parish social structure, which in turn is one of the major constitutive parts of a social system. The third consideration is a practical one: many of the relationships that have been described involve only one person or a small group of persons.

In an observant parish of some 10,000, more or less, it does not take long for the accumulated legitimate demands of individual parishioners to exhaust fairly well the priest's available time and energy. For example, the single item of funerals costs each OLM priest some 30 (or more) mornings each year. Add almost 90 mornings of days on duty, including visits to the hospitals, the 58 Sunday and holyday mornings, when the priest's time is fruitfully taken up in the church, some 15 to 25 mornings devoted to Communion calls, and already 200 mornings out of the yearly 365 are accounted for. A glance at the other tasks already mentioned suggests that there is a demand for the other mornings too. And there is more to come, as will be seen in the added responsibilities of each individual priest. The point is that we must assess quite carefully the parish priest's time load when we think about the necessity and desirability of the parish's assigned apostolate among its non-Catholic and lapsed residents, and its no less necessary interest in having pastors and flock know one another.

The first assistant, now twenty-five years ordained, achieved a master's degree in history in his earlier days and later the rank of major as chaplain in the Army during the last war. Aside from the roles common to all the priests, he is responsible for keeping the parish records, servicing and financing the pamphlet and magazine rack, and editing the regular edition of the *Parish Monthly*. More important is the time and energy he pours into the senior and junior units of both the Sodality and the Legion of Mary. Four hours on each of two nights a week are given to these societies, not to mention the hours during the day when the priest follows up the apostolic contacts made by the Legionaries. In addition he is chaplain of the Bronx division of the Legion of Mary, which takes more time, particularly in the preparation of meetings, talks, and trouble shooting. He teaches catechism each week in the released-time program to pupils in the public high school and sponsors the periodic drive to have parishioners donate blood to the Red Cross blood bank—a rather thankless task, but one which provides the parish with another service, since blood is thus made more readily available to its members in case of need.

The second assistant, a seminary classmate of the first, has served in OLM for all of his twenty-five years in the priesthood. His experience gives him a good grasp of OLM's territory and people, and many students in OLM's school ten or fifteen years ago knew him as their priest then and do so now that they head families of their own. Several activities keep him occupied, in time spared from regular duties, from one end of the year to the other. Twice each year the parish conducts a drive for financial help, once for its own needs in the annual bazaar and once as part of the diocesewide Catholic Charities appeal. For years he has led these drives, assisted by loyal and generous teams of some 150 parishioners. These drives are examples of the parish cooperatively in action, and their valuable by-product is the close relationship between priest and devoted lay helpers. The second assistant priest of OLM has been for years the moderator of the Bronx Nocturnal Adoration Society, which is discussed more fully in a later chapter. It is one of the most remarkable groups of men to be found in Catholic parishes. Other parish groups for which this priest is also responsible include three spiritual societies of children and teen-agers, several "dens" of Cub Scouts and the older Scouts, and the Propagation of the Faith Society. The hospital provides him with another group which he serves as chaplain—the Pasteur Guild, consisting of the Catholic medical personnel.

Assistant Number Three, ordained almost twenty years and a member of OLM's staff for five, had former experience in a large business-district parish and served with the archdiocesan matrimonial court. For many summers he directed successfully a large camp for Catholic boys. He works occasionally on an involved matrimonial case assigned him by the chancery and he has three parish groups which claim his attention: the parish women's Altar-Rosary Society, the senior and junior groups of altar servers (also called Mass servers and altar boys), and the various divisions of the parish's CYO (Catholic Youth Organization) teams. Each of these groups is discussed in more detail below.

The youngest full-time assistant, assigned to the parish a few years ago, has been gradually adding to his roles in OLM's parish life. From his predecessor he inherited the Cana Conference, the Christian Family Movement groups (for married couples), and the League of the Sacred Heart (promoters of the Apostleship of Prayer). He supervises teaching catechism in the released-time program of the public elementary schools, and more recently has been assigned broader responsibilities for the parish school children and for the parish phase of the new archdiocesan convert-instruction program.

The sixth priest in the parish, called in Figure 16 an auxiliary curate, can help with parish work on a limited basis only, for he travels downtown each day to teach in the preparatory seminary. Still he carries a full schedule of parish assignments on the week end—confessions and Masses—takes his turn at novena services, and spends a couple of hours each week preparing his sermons. His one free day and several evenings are taken up with parish appointments. He knows the youth of the parish fairly well despite his restricted availability, and was able to point out to the author several "hangouts" for youth, the attraction of which is often stronger in the youngsters' eyes than attending Mass or doing school assignments.

A typical week of the first assistant midway during our parish survey gives a more detailed view of the priest's role in the parish. Sunday found him offering two parish Masses, preaching at each, and distributing Holy Communion at two others; hearing some confessions; helping in the collection count; performing several baptisms; attending or presiding at two meetings, giving an hour's instruction to a prospective convert, and reciting the official daily hour-long prayer of the Church that is required of priests. On Monday morning he started a twenty-five-hour stretch of duty with Mass at the convent some blocks away, made the rounds at Fordham General and Union hospitals, serviced the pamphlet rack, received three or four rectory calls and as many hospital calls, held a meeting for his society officers, conducted novena services after supper, attended a wake, prayed the Divine Office, and answered the phone twice during the night to make trips to the hospital. Tuesday began with several Communion calls, followed with a funeral Mass and a trip to the cemetery (nearly an hour away). There were a few calls from Monday's day on duty to be followed up, an interview with prospective society candidates, the Divine Office to be read, preparation for two society meetings, and, after supper, the two Legion meetings themselves. Wednesday also began with

Communion calls and Mass, continued with editing the *Parish Monthly*, giving an instruction in school, praying the Divine Office, making reports of parish records, preparing for two more society meetings, and, after supper, holding meetings of the junior and senior Sodality groups. Thursday, after Mass and Communion calls, brought the semiannual diocesan conference for the clergy, visits to parishioners in several hospitals, Divine Office, public-high-school released-time catechism instruction, confessions in Union Hospital and confessions in church in the morning, afternoon, and evening in preparation for First Friday, an evening Holy Hour, instruction of a convert, and a wedding rehearsal. Friday was duty day again, practically the same as Monday except for the added First Friday devotions in the evening. Saturday brought another funeral and trip to the cemetery after Communion calls and Mass, recitation of the rosary occasionally with those in church in honor of Our Lady of Fatima, Divine Office, preparation of the morrow's sermon, and confessions from 3:30 to 9:30 P.M. (with time out for supper). It is only at odd times here and there and in preparation for talks and sermons that this priest finds an opportunity to catch up with any solid reading.

Such a schedule reveals both extensive occupation and cooperation with parishioners in several roles. The week was not unusual, but typical. During the time of the parish census that much more work was added. During the author's year and a half of familiar coming and going in the rectory he saw nothing, aside from the normal slackening in some matters during the summer, which at all indicated any slower pace than that just described. In not all parishes is it so; in many others and in OLM it is.

Two other aspects of the priest's status and roles in parish society can only be touched on here: the distinction between his official and unofficial position and his own concept of his priestly position.

With regard to the first, we might point out that such distinction exists in all kinds of social groupings. For example, the father of the family is officially recognized as its head, though often in practice it is mother who rules. A foreman might be formally charged with the leadership of his working gang, but in terms of actual leadership it might be a man from the ranks who, whether through personal competence or the informal personal influence of higher superiors, dominates the group. So a parish priest might simply perform his official duties and thus exercise his formal role as religious functionary, or he might have won respect as an intellectual leader, a favorite of youth, or a socially influential personage, and thus have achieved a status more prominent than that warranted by his official position. Of course the formal and the informal are distinct, though not separated. A more intense parish study than our own would have to assess this distinction in terms of social effectiveness. Sometimes it is of crucial importance in understanding parish vitality or weakness.

Also of potentially vital importance is the priest's understanding of what is required of him in his position. This can also involve the matter of formal and informal roles. More basically it is a matter of understanding the apostolic role of the parish priesthood itself. It must be available for the development of the spiritual lives of the practicing faithful while at the same time there exists a great need for priestly labor among fallen-away Catholics and non-Catholics. An article by Bertha Mugrauer reflects this dilemma.[10] One mentality adopted by many priests is that they have a role of helping to save individual souls rather than the social order as a whole, that the customary way of doing things is the best and only way, and that the closed parochial milieu should be safeguarded and maintained. A second concept of the priestly role is that of the builder of a

---

[10] Mugrauer, "Variations in the Pastoral Role in France," pp. 15-24.

Christian society, of one who helps to shape an ever-developing dynamic society according to Christlike and human culture. The third concept delineated by Mugrauer is that of the "witness" among the proletariat, among those who no longer know Christ; the priest who seeks to identify himself with the people through his presence and to develop a popular liturgy and other creative means for bringing them to Christ.

Obviously a parish priest's approach to his official duties must be affected by his understanding of them. If he commits himself to waiting for people to come to him, he can contribute relatively little to the progressive Christianization of the social milieu. If he does involve himself in that apostolic mission, almost certainly he must seek the assistance of the laity. This results in a new and broadened set of priest-parishioner relationships involving mutually ordered statuses and roles.

We could treat this subject far more extensively, and it should be so treated in a more thorough parish analysis. It is beyond the scope of the present study. We now proceed to a consideration of parishioners' roles in OLM. Since these are so intimately connected with those of the priests, we shall consider also their understanding of and response to the status and roles of their priests. This too is part of OLM's social structure.

CHAPTER VIII

The Parishioners

Parishioners are as essentially part of the parish as is the
pastor. Without either of them there is no parish. Study of the
priest's place in the parish social structure has already implied
coordinate roles of others in the parish. These roles might be
divided into two classes: that of receiving the services which the
Church commissions the priest to give, and that of actively participating in the apostolic work of the parish. The latter involves
all those who in any way contribute to the communication of
Christian ideals, values, and example to the world about them,
but especially those who share in the organization, administration, and execution of the work of the various parish societies
and other agencies. These include the parish schools and the several lay groups banded together for common spiritual and/or
social purposes in a setting of parish unity.

In this chapter we glance briefly at several of these lay roles
auxiliary to the clergy, the proliferation of parish societies, and
some evidence of the laity's awareness of priestly roles and implicitly, their own roles in response.

Among the most important parish agencies are its schools
and instructional services. OLM's school, as parish schools everywhere, plays a double role: education for secular life and
religious education, which is intended to permeate a person's
entire approach to life. In its latter role particularly it is an

extension of the priest's role of teacher. Groups of religious women (nuns or sisters), less often of religious men (brothers) and lay teachers, in dedicating themselves to the teaching profession and apostolate, relieve the priests of much of what would be a most difficult and overburdening task: communication with and the religious instruction of thousands of parish youngsters. One of the parish functions has thus been institutionalized as part of the elementary school, the students being recipients of the instruction and the teachers being auxiliaries of the priest. The role of teachers in the parish is obviously important, since on them depends in large measure the formation and socialization of not only the citizen but, more pertinent to our present inquiry, the growing parishioner. The teaching sisters are responsible for much of the young parishioner's religious knowledge, attitudes, habits, and practice. Strong and lasting loyalties derive from this early relationship. In OLM a faculty of some 30 persons (mostly sisters from three groups of religious women, the Dominican, Ursuline, and Maryknoll orders) is entrusted with this office. The boys are taught by the Dominicans and 2 Maryknollers, and the Ursulines teach the girls. The Dominican sisters have a convent in the parish—not, as is often the case, next to the school, but a few blocks away—and the OLM priest on duty offers Mass there each morning. The Ursulines live outside the parish in a large convent housing members of the order. Through an eight-year cycle over a thousand young parishioners graduate from OLM school with the impress of the sisters' devoted training.

Emphatic evidence of the important role which the parish school and its teaching personnel have come to play in Catholic life is found in the personalities of millions of parochial-school graduates who have been formed and socialized in their classrooms as American Catholics, not only in OLM Parish but especially in many currently burgeoning suburban parishes lacking their own schools. For generations Catholic practice and parish policy have so emphasized parochial schools that Catholic communities in many suburbs feel lost without them. On the other hand, a standard measure of Catholic growth in many other suburbs has been the far-flung school-building program so costly in terms of added financial sacrifice, fund-raising efforts, and so on. The point is that the parochial school has been so intimately incorporated into the American parish value system that those responsible for its conduct are themselves recognized as playing vital roles in the life of the parish. OLM's school and teachers qualify for this recognition, though only a more profound study could assess adequately their merits and debits in terms of proximate and ultimate parish values.

In former times, as Gasquet shows, the parish was served by several other officials and craftsmen.[1] The schoolmaster has been supplanted by a complete faculty of teachers. The system of churchwardens, still of considerable importance in the French-Canadian parish, is nonexistent in most American parishes today. The wardens had charge of many of the parish's temporal concerns, but the unfortunate excesses of trusteeism in American parish history eventually led to the liquidation of the office, except in a merely juridical sense, and the absorption of the role by the parish clergy. Several other functionaries mentioned by Gasquet—the bell ringer, bookbinder, painter, carver, silversmith, gilder, tinker—either have no place in the modern parish, or their functions have been absorbed by the sexton. The sexton is still, as he was in the days described by Gasquet, an important functionary in the parish. Responsible for all custodial services in the parish plant, he can be a strong right arm for the pastor and represent the difference between a well-kept, attractive church and school and the contrary. OLM's sexton died during our parish survey, after many years of faithful and efficient service. It was revealing to witness the affection and ap-

---

[1] See, for example, Gasquet, *Parish Life in Mediaeval England*, pp. 102-23.

preciation shown by both clergy and laity during his wake and at his funeral Mass.

The sacristan of the parish is to the altar, sanctuary, and sacristy of the church what the sexton is to the entire physical plant. Sometimes this office is held by one or more of the teaching sisters, sometimes by a layman or laywoman. In OLM the post is held by an efficient and devoted laywoman. The importance of her role and its coordination with the roles of the parish priests are evident to even a casual observer of OLM's religious functioning. The preparation of the altar, altar linens and accessories, sacred vessels and vestments, and all of the other items needed for the performance of divine worship, which the priest presupposes are in readiness when he comes to the church, is the concern of the sacristan. About the best way to appreciate the value of a competent sacristan is to experience some oversight: the candles not lit, the cruets unfilled, the ciborium not prepared, the linens not replenished. Such occasional experience elsewhere points to the satisfactory condition of this phase of OLM's social structure. The sacristan receives some assistance from the ladies of the Altar-Rosary Society, to be found in many parishes, in laundering, in sewing, and even in providing altar linens and vestments.

Active only while religious services are in progress, the parish ushers have a coordinated role in the functioning of the parish. They facilitate the keeping of proper order among the congregation, particularly during the parishioners' entrance into and exit from the church; they take up the collection; and they are usually available for answering minor questions or referring matters to the priests. They could be useful in spotting new parishioners and having them meet the priests. Such services as providing proper ventilation, regulating the heat, and setting the loud-speaker system usually come from the ushers.

Also part of the parish staff in OLM are those who work in the rectory: secretary, housekeeper, cook. Their roles are aimed at leaving the priest free for work more peculiar to his office. Spic-and-span rectory parlors have their influence on parishioners who call, and satisfactory meals at home save the priests many hours of time. Such things are often taken for granted, but experience in less fortunate parishes underlines their contribution to the parish's functioning and their place in its social system. Phone calls are channeled by the staff to the requested priest or recorded for him if absent. Secretarial service saves an enormous amount of time, and the management of the credit union and employment bureau by one of the staff provides OLM with some of its most valuable features.[2]

All of these persons—sexton, sacristan, secretaries, ushers, and housekeepers—have their own places in the OLM social structure, with roles tuned to the basically purposeful roles of the parish priests. The persons toward whom and for whose benefit all these parochial relationships and roles are structured are the parishioners themselves, the laity of the parish. They are the flock whom the pastor tends, the spiritual children of the priestly father, the people whose mediator with God the priest is. The priest teaches and preaches, the people heed and learn; the priest interprets God's law and governs his assigned portion of God's kingdom, the people try to obey and fashion their lives accordingly; in the Mass he offers the gifts which they bring to God, and in the sacraments he dispenses God's gifts to them.

The people who are thus related to their priests are those described demographically in Chapter 6. Their roles, however, are not merely passive. They not only receive but also contribute positively to the functioning of the parish, to the growth of Christian life in their neighborhood. Every head of a household, every parent, has the responsibility of making his home and his family living supports of the parish. His children are to be so reared as to be good parishioners, capable and desirous of re-

---

[2] See Chapter 13, pp. 259-60.

ceiving the spiritual benefits which the parish can give them. Someone said once that, as the parish is the Church in miniature, so is the family the parish in miniature. The comparison is not quite accurate, but it does suggest the analogous roles played by the members of the family.

To even more active roles are the laity invited. Both to enable them to share positively in Christ's, the Church's, and the parish's mission of spreading the faith and Christian life, and also because their help is needed, the parish provides several societies and activities in which they can participate more fully in its life and work. Each of these societies has its place in the parish social structure, contributing to its achievements and making more varied and more closely bound its relationships.

The respective roles of the various societies have been suggested in the discussion of the parish priests who direct them, and the organizational chart, Figure 16, indicates how the societies fit into the general structure of the parish. The two societies found in practically every parish are the men's Holy Name Society and the women's Altar-Rosary Society, and these are usually given the opportunity of being the most important societies in the parish. But most commonly, in OLM as elsewhere, the active membership is but a fraction of those listed as members, usually because the program is not vital enough to command general attention and support.

Several OLM organizations are almost exclusively spiritual, providing opportunity for and encouragement of spiritual development and further use of the spiritual facilities of the parish. These include the Nocturnal Adoration Society, the Catholic Youth Adorers, the Society for the Propagation of the Faith, the League of the Sacred Heart, the First Saturday Club, and the school children's Crusaders and Angels.

Other societies aim at providing opportunity for both personal spiritual development and apostolic work. The St. Vincent de Paul Society is everywhere known for its help to the poor, and the spiritual wealth to be found in its meetings is no less significant to its members. The two divisions of the Legion of Mary are most active in apostolic work, its members obliging themselves to spend at least three hours weekly in the Legion's work.[3] They actually extend the arm of the priest moderator, multiplying his time and availability, for they do much of the contacting and winning back of fallen-away Catholics and problem cases. The Sodality too is built on the double principle of personal sanctification and apostolic enterprise. The two Christian Family Movement groups, consisting of some half-dozen married couples each, have a similar purpose. Several societies exist primarily to serve. The Ushers Society, the choir, and the Altar Servers Society are entrusted with intimate roles in public worship. Others contribute to material activities of the parish, such as the OLM Federal Credit Union, the employment bureau, and the teams of workers for the annual bazaar.

A final group of societies exists primarily to provide a recreational or other religiously indifferent service within a Catholic atmosphere and with people whose Catholic philosophy and morals of life can contribute to the respective members' integration of various aspects of their lives with Catholicism. Such are the OLM Cub Scouts, Boy Scouts, the CYO, and until recently the OLM Catholic Club.

So much for the arrangement of parish societies within the parish structure. Each has a certain status and a role to play in the parish life, and their members add accordingly to their parochial status and roles. We discuss most of these organizations in later chapters when we consider them as services rendered by the parish and used by the parishioners.

Earlier in this chapter reference was made to the laity's implicit recognition of their own roles in responding to the roles

---

[3] Since our parish survey was completed a third Legion unit had to be established, thus testifying to the group's vigor and successful apostolate.

of the priests. Several questions in the OLM questionnaire sought the parishioners' understanding of the priest's roles. It was found that 156 out of 293 respondents (53 per cent) at least knew the names of all six priests, and the great majority of the remainder were able to list at least some of the priests' names.[4] A special analysis was made of the 156 who knew the names of all six priests with respect to religious observance, economic status, general education, and Catholic education. Could any notable variations be found? It should be explained, as indicated in preceding chapters, that the respondents, on the basis of their replies to the questionnaire, were divided into four groups in each category studied. The classifications in the categories considered here are:

> *Religious observance:* Group A—outstanding in religious observance; Group B—above the required norm; Group C—observe the required norms only; Group D—very lax.
> *Economic status:* Group A—yearly income of $10,000 or more; Group B—income of $5,000-$9,999; Group C—income of $3,000-$4,999; Group D—income less than $3,000.
> *General (and Catholic) education:* Group A—(Catholic) college graduation; Group B—some (Catholic) college education; Group C—(Catholic) high-school education; Group D—(Catholic) elementary schooling only.

Table VIII on page 172 presents the results of this study of respondents. The number in each group who correctly named the six priests is followed by a number in brackets, which indicates the total number of respondents in that group. Thus 22 [33] means that, of the 33 respondents who were outstanding in religious observance, 22 correctly named six priests.

Table VIII shows significant differences between the groups only in the case of religious observance. Over 60 per cent of those in Groups A and B (superior in religious observance)

---

[4] In Part 2, Question 18, respondents were asked to name the priests of the parish and at least five parish organizations or activities. See Appendix II, p. 322.

were able to name the priests, while only 30 per cent in Group C and 17 per cent in Group D (lax in fulfilling their religious duties) could name six priests. Those in Groups A and B of the economic and educational scales were not more familiar with the names of the priests than those in Groups C and D.

TABLE VIII

Knowledge of Names of Parish Priests by Social Categories and Ranks

	Group A	Group B	Group C	Group D	Total
Religious observance	22 [33]	109 [171]	23 [77]	2 [12]	156 [293]
Economic status	7 [13]	66 [114]	63 [131]	20 [35]	156 [293]
General education	20 [41]	22 [42]	64 [128]	50 [82]	156 [293]
Catholic education	13 [26]	10 [16]	31 [61]	43 [73]	97 [176]

A tentative assumption that can be drawn from this table would seem to be that variations in economic and educational status do not affect the simplest phase of the priest-people relationship—the latter's knowledge of the priests' names. Those educated in Catholic schools (55 per cent correct answers) have only a slight advantage over the entire group (53 per cent).

A surprising variation was found in the breakdown according to geographical areas. More than 50 per cent of those in the east and west sections named the priests, while less than 50 per cent of those living in the central section, where the church is located, named all six priests. The figures are listed in Table IX, which also includes responses to a question about parish societies and organizations. When respondents were asked to list the names of at least five parish organizations, residents of the center tract had a higher percentage of correct responses (62 per cent) than they did in listing the names of six priests (47 per cent), but they still trailed residents in the east and west zones. There were practically no variations when the responses were analyzed for religious observance, economic status, and educational attainment.

It might be mentioned that the parishioners are expected to be more familiar with the names of parish organizations and societies, since the activities of these organizations are constantly being brought to the attention of the congregation in parish an-

TABLE IX

Knowledge of Names of Parish Priests and
Organizations by Geographical Areas

Section	Priests	Organizations
East (Tracts 383, 385, 387, 397)	29 [50]	30 [50]
Center (Tract 399)	79 [169]	105 [169]
West (Tracts 237, 401)	48 [74]	51 [74]

nouncements. Names of parish priests are not so publicly or constantly mentioned.

The questionnaire also sought to ascertain the parishioners' understanding of the time available to parish priests.[5] More than five sixths (250) of the respondents expressed an opinion. In view of the time schedule of OLM's first assistant priest described in Chapter 7, it is significant to note that almost 90 per cent (221 of 250 respondents) checked the response indicating their belief that a priest in a large parish has so many activities that he might be otherwise occupied when someone calls; 25 persons (10 per cent) signified that they believe that there is always something for the priest to do, but he is never really hard-pressed for time; only 4 persons checked the response indicating that a priest has little to do beyond his day of duty. The 25 persons who thought that the priest always had something to do, but was never really hard-pressed for time, were concentrated in the

---

[5] See Part 2, Question 27, p. 323.

west and central districts, were mostly in the B and C grades in religious and economic categories, and in the lower two educational grades (C and D). This concentration, however, does not imply high percentages in any instance since the population in these respective categories is quite large.[6] The 4 who believed that the priest had little to do beyond his day of duty lived in the central section, were evenly divided in the four groups of religious observance, were in the lower three economic grades, and in the lower two educational grades.

The conclusion is that OLM's parishioners seem convinced that their priests are busily engaged in their role of spiritual shepherds. This need not be, and as a matter of fact is not, always the case in all parishes. But although some priests could certainly be more active in their parish roles, many persons who assume that a priest has little to do might well ponder the roles already described.

In another section of the questionnaire the parishioners were asked why they greeted a priest if they did.[7] Of 293 respondents 287 replied that they do greet a priest on the street, although 80 said they do so only if they know the priest. Of these 287, the great majority (189) claimed that they greet a priest "because he represents Christ to me and through him I greet Christ." Other reasons given were that they greet the priest out of habit (56), because of the priest's social position in the community (27), and for various other reasons (15). The reply of the majority indicates that the parishioners have some understanding of the priest's role in the parish.

In the following question eleven roles of the priest were listed, including most of those cited by Father Fichter: father, administrator, civic leader, recreation leader, educator, reformer, preacher and teacher of God's word, mediator, litur-

---

[6] Refer to Table VIII for the number of persons (in brackets) in each category.
[7] Part 2, Question 28, p. 323.

gical leader, counselor, and social leader. Respondents were asked to place the numbers 1, 2, and 3 beside those roles which they considered the priest's most important duties and to use the letters x, y, and z to indicate the roles which they considered least important.[8] The results are summarized in Table X.

TABLE X

Parishioners' Estimates of Relative Importance
of Priest's Roles

| | Most Important | | | | Least Important | | | |
	1	2	3	Total	x	y	z	Total
Preacher and teacher of God's word	209	59	8	276	—	—	—	—
Counselor	2	80	78	160	4	4	8	16
Father	60	37	23	120	8	3	3	14
Liturgical leader	6	41	36	83	6	11	13	30
Educational leader	5	24	48	77	3	6	8	17
Mediator	7	11	29	47	11	9	12	32
Administrator	4	12	15	31	17	20	16	53
Reformer	11	10	21	42	33	36	34	103
Recreational leader	1	5	7	13	53	55	42	150
Social leader	1	—	8	9	46	39	67	152
Civic leader	1	1	4	6	72	65	37	174

Named as the priest's most important role by 209 respondents was "preacher and teacher of God's word," with 59 others placing it in second place and another 8 in third place. No one considered this one of the least important roles. The role that received the second largest number of votes was that of counselor; of 160 votes designating its importance, 2 considered it most important, 80 placed it second in importance, and 78 listed it as the third most important role. On the other hand, 16 parishioners listed counselor as one of the priest's least important roles. The role of father received 120 votes of importance, 60

---

[8] Part 2, Question 29, p. 323.

naming it as the most important role, 37 in second place, and 23 in third place. This role also received 14 votes in the least important group. The role of liturgical leader received 83 important votes (6 in first place, 41 in second, 36 in third) and 30 votes for being least important (13 in last place, 11 in second last, and 6 third from last). The only other role to receive a fairly strong vote on its importance, a total of 77, was that of educational leader; but 17 votes also put it in the least important class. The roles of mediator and administrator were not strongly slanted either as roles of great importance or as roles of least importance.

The response to this question, which was described in Chapter 4 and Appendix II as being partially ineffective as a result of some of its terminology, indicates that the terms "mediator" and "liturgical leader" were not understood by the respondents, despite the finding of an expected response in a pilot study. The author is persuaded that, if "liturgical leader" had been expressed as "leader of divine worship" and "mediator" as "offerer of men's prayer to God and dispenser of God's grace to men," the respondents would have designated them as important roles more often than they did.

Responses indicated that the least important roles were those of civic leader (174), social leader (152), recreational leader (150), and reformer (103). The conclusion seems valid that OLM's parishioners consider their priests' spiritual roles as most important and their derivative social roles as least important in the life of the parish. Conversely, this implies recognition by the parishioners of their own roles as recipients of spiritual goods and the right of those in their status to receive them.

A final test of the parishioners' evaluation of the role of the priest can be seen in their response to the question that followed. Calling attention to the shortage of priests, particularly in missionary and dechristianized lands, and to the many duties which priests must perform in places where Catholic practice is good, the questionnaire poses the question asked by Cardinal Suhard in his letter on the priesthood: "Should today's priest spend his time mostly in being priest to the faithful or in being prophet and teacher to those without the faith?"[9]

OLM's respondents showed much difference of opinion. Some 30 parishioners, over 10 per cent, answered that there could be no "either . . . or" in the priest's role in this respect; he had to aim at both objectives. Many chose not to answer, saying they could not decide. About 130, nearly half of those who expressed an opinion, thought that the parish priest should be mostly concerned with being a priest to the faithful. In educational attainment just over 60 per cent of the two higher grades (graduation from or attendance at college) and less than 50 per cent of the two lower grades (education limited to elementary or high school) were among these 130 parishioners. In economic grades, 10 out of 13 with high incomes were in this group of 130; less than half of each of the other grades were represented. The same tendency was noted among the various classifications of religious practice. Among the 130 who claimed that the priest should minister primarily to the faithful were 20 of the 33 persons who were outstanding in religious observance. Among those whose religious observance was superior, normal, and very lax, less than 50 per cent were represented.

It would seem that a great number of OLM's parishioners have a definite concept of the priest's role as being important to their own spiritual welfare. Others realize the dilemma of the priest-parishioner relationship clearly; hence the double answers and the refusal to decide.

---

[9] Part 2, Question 30, pp. 323-24. For Cardinal Suhard's question see *The Church Today*, p. 273.

CHAPTER IX

Providing Service
in the Parish

P arish analysis involves studying the parish in its structure (what it is) and in its functioning (what it does). Professor
Timasheff designates these two aspects of the same social reality
as the static (structural) and kinetic (functional) isotopes of a
social system.[1] Chapters 3 and 4 discussed in some detail the
nature of the parish as a social system, with the major emphasis,
however, on the structure of the parish rather than on its active
functioning. The subject of the present chapter is the active functioning of the parish, or the service that it seeks to render for
the benefit of its members.[2]

The purposes, ends, and values for which a system functions are of a system's very constitution. They comprise the
raison d'être, the final cause, of the system's existence and the
bond of unity which ties the members together. What are they?
In general, as Loomis and Beegle put it, they are "the changes
(or perhaps the maintenance of the *status quo*) which members
of the system expect to accomplish through operation of the system."[3] A value may be that which attracts (positive) or that

---

[1] Timasheff, "The Basic Concepts of Sociology," p. 178.
[2] See in this connection Schuyler, "The Parish Studied as a Social System," p. 4,
parts of which are here quoted or paraphrased.
[3] Loomis and Beegle, *Rural Social Systems,* p. 5.

which repels (negative). Those things have value for men which satisfy needs. These needs may be biological, economic, educational, psychosocial, recreational, religious, and so forth; and insofar as a social system satisfies them, it contributes to the functioning of the total social order and serves as a bearer of society's culture.

Relationship in the system implies that the related members have a certain position, status, or rank. A person invested with the status of leadership receives a certain ranking of preeminence and is expected to conform to the groups' expectations (norms) of leadership. Accordingly he has a certain authority, certain rights and duties necessary for the effective performance of his role. Role has been called the dynamic aspect of status: status refers more to position, role more to action. Status and role do not belong only to the leader: followers too have a quite necessary position in the social system, roles to play which are essential to the system's functioning.

A social system may well question whether merely passive roles in its followers contribute to effective functioning. Peter Drucker has said: "If the individual is not given social status and function, there can be no society but only a mass of social atoms flying through space without aim or purpose."[4] In very similar words Pius XII, speaking of the universal brotherhood of mankind, says: "In the light of this unity of all mankind, which exists in law and in fact, individuals do not feel themselves isolated units, like grains of sand, but united by the very force of their nature and by their eternal destiny, into an organic, harmonious mutual relationship."[5]

As for the Church, she has spiritual gifts even for infants and for others who are unaware that they are receiving them, but

---

[4] Peter F. Drucker, *The Future of Industrial Man*, p. 25 (New York: John Day Company, 1942). Cited by Homans, *The Human Group*, p. 47.

[5] Pius XII, *The Unity of Human Society (Summi pontificatus)* [1939], p. 11. New York: America Press, n. d.

her great work is done with those who are capable of interaction. She wishes to make all men, old and young alike, recipients of divine favors and to see them develop into forces for the betterment of mankind. Pius XII has said:

> Not only through her ministers, but also through every one of the faithful thus imbued with the spirit of Jesus Christ, the Church strives to make this spirit pervade the whole of human life—individual, domestic, social, and even economic and political—in order that all that are called sons of God may more easily attain their appointed end.[6]

Without a dissenting voice philosophers and theologians accept the fact that the Church is a society or social system. We may therefore study it as such, but we must not overlook the differences between the Church and merely natural societies. The end of the Church is supernatural, and the means that she uses for achieving her end are primarily supernatural. Interaction is necessary for her successful operation, and few evils have been more vigorously condemned by the popes than a merely passive participation in her rites. But if interaction is for most men and under normal conditions necessary for fruitful life in the Church, it is necessary more as a condition than as an efficient cause. Effects which in natural societies may be due to interaction are, when we are speaking of the Church, due to grace and to the life that flows from Christ into the members of what is called His mystical body. If these distinctions are kept clearly in mind, we may safely study the functioning of the parish as a sociologist would study the functioning of a natural social system. As a matter of fact, the application of sound sociological principles to religious life has had much to do with some of the finest developments in parish practices within the last fifty years. How, then, does the parish function?

---

[6] *Christian Worship: Encyclical Letter (Mediator Dei) of His Holiness Pius XII* [1947], translated by G. D. Smith, p. 21. London: Catholic Truth Society, n. d.

In a letter to the French Canadian Social Week in 1953 the then papal prosecretary of state, later Archbishop Montini, wrote of the parish:

> . . . and so the parish is bound to an area, intimately linked with local traditions and definite points of view. In the heart of this area, surmounted by its belfry, stands the parish church—with its baptistry, its confessional, its altar, and its tabernacle; the church, symbol of unity, center of the community.
>
> It is important to keep in mind that the parish is above all the hearth of religious life and missionary expansion; its true members can be counted at the foot of the altar when the priest distributes the Bread of Life. The pastor is not the head of his people in the secular sense of the term (Matthew 20:25-28), but he is rather the servant of the people of God, having received spiritual authority over his flock only to be for it the "dispenser of the mysteries of God," so that "it may have life and have it more abundantly" (John 10:10). Jesus known, loved, served by all: such is according to the very words of the Holy Father, the purpose of all parish life. And His Holiness does not hesitate to insist: "Everything else should be valued insofar as it contributes and in the extent which it serves the realization of the purpose which the Church wishes to achieve." . . . Now it is precisely such a parish, a really living and active cell of the Body of Christ, which is called by its very fidelity to its proper religious mission, to play a role of first rank in the regeneration of modern society.[7]

This purpose of the parish—to have Jesus known, loved, and served by all—how is it achieved? We have seen the milieu in which OLM exists, its people, the social structure which comprises it. Now our interest is in OLM in operation, functioning to achieve its aims. Its action is interaction, for among its members there is cooperative effort in the communication of knowledge, direction, and benefits.

A Catholic parish is convinced that it already possesses the religious life which it is its purpose to give. It is convinced that

---

[7] Quoted in the December 1954 issue of the OLM *Parish Monthly*.

the true creed, code, and cult are the source of that life, of union with God, and of the consequent communion among its members. It is convinced, finally, that its creed, code, and cult are the true ones because it has received them from the Church, whose two thousand years of unity, holiness, universality, and apostolic tradition support that conviction. It is immensely important to appreciate that mentality, for it alone can explain the consistency of the interactional patterns which constitute the functioning of a Catholic parish.

A Catholic parish, whether new or old, has certain advantages in its manner of operating which accrue from the very fact that it is a Catholic parish. Adaptation to local requirements and satisfaction of particular needs must always demand a certain amount of enterprise, prudence, and ingenuity. Sometimes they are lacking. But the main lines of parish operational policy have been developed through many years of experience: teach the creed, preach the commandments, celebrate Mass, and administer the sacraments. An established parish like OLM profits besides from its own experience, its own accumulation of physical equipment. We have already seen OLM's favored position in having adequate church, school, rectory, and other facilities.

We have noted previously, in discussing the social structure and the roles of the parish priests, a great number of parish operations. Now we wish to catalogue them in a more orderly way to get a total concept of the parish at work. Since every social operation is functional or purposive and hence renders a service, we consider the services which OLM makes available to its members, noting meanwhile the interaction involved in some of them. Most are not unique to OLM, but typical of all Catholic parishes. These services can be classified into two types, those primarily religious or spiritual in nature and those auxiliary to religious aims; both classes can be either institutional or personal. Other services which the parish performs are directed beyond the parish itself; for example, contributing to Catholic

Charities, to the welfare of the home and foreign missions, and so on. In the present chapter we are concerned only with the proffering of services by the parish; in the following one we consider the use made of these services by the parish membership and some of the latter's attitudes concerning parish service and religious life as manifested in the several questionnaires.

In Chapter 8 we saw that OLM's questionnaire respondents overwhelmingly chose as the priest's major role his teaching and preaching of God's word. Allowing for whatever change a clearer designation of his liturgical and mediatory roles might have effected, nevertheless the teaching-preaching role is important. How does OLM perform this function?

We have already briefly discussed the parish school.[8] Here, together with the full curriculum of elementary studies followed by pupils in public and other schools, the young parishioner in OLM receives a course in Christian doctrine and the Bible, adapted to his age right through his eight years. He has regular assignments in religious study for homework, is subject to regular daily recitation, and must pass his midterm and semester examinations. In his very first years he is prepared for his first absolution in the sacrament of confession and his first Holy Communion. There is a definite pattern of interaction to be followed in the confessional, discussed below, and it is the mutual function of both teaching sister and learning pupil to prepare to follow that pattern intelligently and usefully. The interaction involved in the other sacraments which the young Catholic receives—Communion, which he will receive often in his life, and confirmation, which he receives but once—is much simpler, but training for it is necessary.

This same educational interaction is at work in the formation of normal Catholic attitudes in the youngster, which the sociologist would call his socialization or social integration.

---

[8] For a study of a parochial school see Fichter, *Parochial School.*

Thus he comes to have a great reverence for sacred persons, places, and things, a special respect for priests and nuns both in the parish and in general, and a devoted loyalty to the various institutions in Catholic society—the papacy, the hierarchy, the missionary, Catholic symbols, and so on. Deeper than this socializing process, and really its purpose, is the formation of a consciousness of God as present in one's life, a conviction of God's personal interest in each individual, and a personal devotion to and love for Jesus Christ.

Here again it is necessary to remark that Catholic practice— for example, the positive willingness of a 10-year-old or a 50-year-old to go to Mass every morning—cannot be explained except in terms of such values, learned sooner or later in life and made the motives of his actions.

No Catholic youngster capable of elementary-school work is refused admission to OLM's school. Almost 14 per cent of its enrollment comes from outside the parish. It charges no tuition, although there is a small charge for books and stationery. Yet OLM's enrollment of over 1,000 pupils does not include some 250 young parishioners who attend public school elsewhere. For them the parish provides religious instruction during released time and also a Sunday-school class. In some parishes, where the school cannot care for all children despite double sessions and crowding, these released-time programs assume major proportions and impose a heavy burden on the teaching staff.

In addition to their teaching in the school, the parish clergy are constantly occupied with instructions. The instructees might be parishioners seeking intellectual enlightenment in religious matters, members of the society's organizations which have set up a program for their development in religious knowledge, or prospective converts. The last provide an interesting subject for interactional study, for there are so many varieties of would-be converts. They vary in backgrounds, preconceived notions, intellectual capacity, and motivation. For each the instructing priest must adapt his approach and his teaching technique. Each comes voluntarily, and only a voluntary ultimate decision is valid: a convert must declare himself convinced of Catholic truth and desirous of becoming a Catholic.

In Chapter 6 we saw that only 10 per cent of the residents of OLM Parish are Protestant and almost 25 per cent Jewish. Despite an unending trickle of Jews into the Church and an apparent increase in recent years, they are generally not very amenable to conversion. This fact and the small number of Christian non-Catholics found in the parish greatly reduced the need for an organized convert apostolate in OLM. There are American parishes which have received phenomenal numbers of converts in recent years, some well over 500 annually, and organized convert courses have become both popular and fruitful. OLM twice sponsored within recent years a public course for converts, and it is now one of many regional parish centers for courses sponsored by the archdiocese. These group courses have gained a couple of dozen converts each time. But OLM's priests claim that they total as many converts with private instruction in any given year as they gained through group instruction. The advantage of private instruction is its greater suitability for the individual candidates' needs and for frank questions; public courses save a great amount of time and also create the favorable and valid impression of popular interest—always an encouraging circumstance. Public courses also usually make provision for private consultation when a prospective convert makes such a request.

The instruction of a convert and his admission into the Church are a particularly fine example of specific interaction between father and spiritual child, between guide and follower in a spiritual enterprise, between baptizer and baptized, confessor and penitent, priest and layman.

A major phase of the priest's teaching role is his preaching of sermons at Mass. In OLM, as in most parishes, the priest celebrating Mass reads the assigned scriptural selections for the day's Epistle and Gospel, continues with the week's parochial announcements, and proceeds to his sermon. Occasionally a guest preacher speaks at all the Masses for a definite purpose, but this is not common. Many American dioceses now have schedules of sermon topics to be followed in each parish, thus assuring the laity of a periodic instruction on the doctrines of the Creed, the commandments, the Mass and sacraments, and different Christian virtues. Together with many others, the New York archdiocese does not have an assigned program, leaving it to the individual preacher to select his topic according to need and circumstance.

Preaching has connected with it several fairly constant problems which often curtail its effectiveness. We must remember that preaching is but the priest's action in an interactional function. The congregation meanwhile is listening with, presumably, the same purpose as the preacher: that the listeners may receive knowledge or perhaps be persuaded to a course of action. A fine sermon to the ladies' Altar-Rosary Society could be meaningless to the young men's Sodality. At most parish Masses, except for those provided especially for the children, the congregation can be quite heterogeneous educationally, socially, in age and sex, and from the viewpoint of religious interest, vitality, and knowledge. The preacher has either to find a note of common pertinence, or make at least some remarks meaningful for different types of hearers. Wider participation in higher education and in the lay apostolate has been making many Catholics desirous of more mature sermons, while at the same time a large number of pious folk can be reached only with a simple exposition or exhortation. The seriousness of the problem is increased by the fact that the total time of all weekly sermons during a year amounts to about five hundred minutes (at ten minutes per sermon)—the equivalent of about eight hour-long television programs. In addition, parking problems around our city churches and the need of maintaining a close schedule of many Masses make it often difficult to preach more than ten minutes.

But preaching is fortunately not limited to sermons during Mass. OLM offers preaching at its evening devotions and often invites a visiting preacher to conduct a special triduum or novena in preparation for a major feast. Every second year it invites a "home-mission" team to conduct the parish mission for four weeks.

The parish's teaching function is not limited to school, rectory, and pulpit. Its pamphlet and magazine rack is replenished regularly. Attention is sometimes called to new books in a nearby Catholic bookstore. Occasionally the parish promotes a sale of Bibles at popular prices, and its members are reminded of available spiritual retreats for different groups in the parish. One of its most effective techniques in communication is its observance of the liturgical year, the annual sequence of seasons or cycles, analogous to the equinoctial seasons, of ecclesiastical significance, beginning with Advent, Christmas and Epiphany, and proceeding through Lent, Eastertide, and the season of Pentecost. All of these seasons recall important episodes in the life of Christianity's founder or the early Church with a special meaning for Christian life. Church decorations, the color of the altar vestments, the reminders in sermons, the *Parish Monthly*, perhaps a school pageant, are all institutional reminders both of the season and its portent. In OLM, as in every parish, the religious year is structured around these recurring seasons and other great feasts. The cooperative response of OLM's parishioners is reflected in the greater religious activity during certain seasons that inspire greater devotion.

Religious activity implies attendance at Mass and reception of the sacraments. The performance of the liturgy, together with the preaching of the gospel, is a major function of the Catholic parish. As expressed previously in the discussion on the fatherly and mediatory roles of the priest, the sacraments are God's established ways of coming to the Catholic, and the Mass is His way of having men come to Him. Other expressions of public divine worship are of minor importance compared to them. In all of them, as the parish offers Mass or dispenses the sacraments, it is involved in functional interaction. This purposeful interaction, the parish is convinced, contributes to the conferring of spiritual life and strength on its members in the manners that we have already explained.

Each of the sacraments instituted by Christ consists of a sensible sign accompanied by a pertinent verbal expression. Conferred by the proper minister on the properly disposed recipient, it gives the latter, according to Catholic theology, a share in God's friendship and a type of divine grace or help clearly symbolized by the same sign. For example, baptism consists of pouring water on the head of the candidate while the ministering priest simultaneously says the words, "I baptize you in the name of the Father and of the Son and of the Holy Spirit." Both action and words indicate cleansing, which is precisely the nature of the grace which is given; namely, the cleansing of the candidate from original sin and his consequent initiation into the pure kingdom of God. The baptismal rite consists of many subsidiary ceremonies expanding on that theme. Priest, candidate, and the latter's godparents cooperate in performing the rite which is spiritually so valuable to the candidate. The usual time for baptisms is Sunday afternoon, though it is performed at any time in case of necessity. The priests are available to perform baptisms also in the two hospitals.

Each of the other sacraments has its sensible sign: the anointing in confirmation, signifying the strengthening of the Christian warrior; the absolution in confession, signifying pardon from sin and reconciliation with God; the consecration of bread and wine in the Eucharist, signifying the food of spiritual life; the mutual giving and receiving of each other by husband and wife in matrimony, symbolizing the union and love between Christ and His Church to be reflected in marital love; the imposition of hands in ordination, a symbol of the conferring of authority and power; again the anointing in extreme unction, a sign of strengthening in sickness or in life's final battle. And in the conferring of each of them (all regularly take place in the parish church except ordination and extreme unction, which is conferred where the sick person happens to be) there is purposeful interaction of minister and recipient.

The parishioner who desires to go to confession, for example, as he must at least each year if guilty of serious sin and as many freely do each month or even each week for their greater spiritual growth, enters the church, reflects for a few prayerful moments on whatever he has to confess, expresses in his prayer sorrow for having violated God's law, then walks to the confessional. Through parish usage both priest and people expect the other to be there at scheduled times. If others are already waiting, he joins the line; if not, he walks immediately into the confessional. He knows, or should know, that the only reason the priest is there is to dispense divine mercy in a way specified by Christ Himself. The priest is aware, or should be, that the penitent's definite purpose is to regain or increase his favorable relationship or friendship with God. On that mutual basis the confessional dialogue commences, though some of it, particularly the Latin prayers of the priest, may be lost on the penitent. The priest first confers his blessing and offers a brief prayer that the penitent might confess properly, with God in his heart and on his lips. The penitent, having asked for a blessing and mentioned the length of time since his last confession, accuses himself of his sins according to type, number, and seriousness, then expresses his sorrow and requests forgiveness. The priest offers a word of advice or encouragement or enlightenment, assigns a penance, recites the form of absolution, and usually concludes with a final blessing. The penitent, usually expressing his thanks, departs to do his penance and enjoy his new-found peace. Should it have been necessary or desirable for either priest or penitent to ask a question or make a comment, each would have appreciated its suitability.

This interaction between parish priest and anonymous parishioners occurs thousands of times each year, and year after year. In an average year a priest at OLM hears almost fifteen thousand confessions. Parishioners have the regular opportunity to go to confession almost five hours every Saturday afternoon and evening, on the days before First Fridays and important feasts, and daily during tridua, novenas, and missions. In addition a parishioner may call at the rectory any time for that purpose. School children are provided time for confession weekly, and one of the priests of the parish covers the two hospitals each week.

The greatest event each day in the parish church is the consecration of the Mass. The Mass, or Eucharistic sacrifice, is the central act of Catholic worship. In Catholic theology and conviction it is the constant renewal of Christ's sacrifice on Calvary. Being offered at every second somewhere in the world, it is the fulfillment in Catholic eyes of the biblically prophesied sacrifice to be offered "from the rising of the sun even to the going down" (Malachias 1:11). As mentioned previously, Catholics understand it as the God-given, divinely accepted way for men to go to God with their praise, their thanks, their contrition, and their requests. Even if Catholics do not know what each part of the Mass means—unfortunately many do not—they at least do know its essential importance in itself and for them.

This is not the place to discuss the theology and liturgy of the Mass in detail, but a brief delineation is essential for an understanding of its cardinal position in the values and functioning of OLM Parish and in the lives of OLM parishioners. Youngsters learn reverence for the Mass even before they know what it means. Culpable omission of Mass on Sundays and feast days of obligation is considered a very serious offense. Many devoted persons, men and women, young and old, try to attend Mass, not only each week but every day, thus sacrificing an hour's sleep or other ordinary occupation.

For the Catholic, Christ ordained priests at the Last Supper and gave them the power to do what He had just done, to pronounce efficaciously the words of consecration and change bread and wine into His own body and blood. At the Last Supper Christ offered His body and blood which was the next day to be sacrificed for the redemption of men; His priests were thereafter to offer His body and blood which had been immolated on Calvary. Christ died once and can die no more; but as the divine victim who once was slain He is offered anew each day. And since all Christians are united through baptism to Christ in His mystical body, and since it is Christ who, through the agency of the priest, actually offers the Mass, then the laity too are actually co-offerers of the Mass. With Christ they offer the Mass through the mediation of the priest; with Christ they are offered in the Mass to their heavenly Father. Thus the significance of the Mass to a Catholic, to any OLM parishioner; that is, it is the significance which the Mass should have for all Catholics and does have for a very great many.

The great moment of the Mass is the act of consecration when Christ is brought to the altar and offered to God. But the Mass lasts more or less one half-hour and on Sundays a quarter of an hour more. Actually it consists of five parts: two of preparation, three of completion. Mass begins with a prayer service, when man's word of humility and praise goes to God. It follows with an instruction service; when God's word comes to man in the scriptural selections from the Epistles (or Old Testament) and Gospel, in the sermon (if there is one), and in the recitation of the Creed. Thereafter, in the Offertory, the priest takes the bread and wine of men and offers it for use in the divine sacrifice; at the Consecration God, through the words of the priest, changes the bread and wine into the Lamb of God; some moments later, in the Communion banquet, this Lamb of God is made available to men as the Bread of God, thus satisfying the yearning of man, evident in every age, for union with his God.

In each part of the Mass there is, at least theoretically, dialogue between priest and people. He often uses the first person plural in his words, thus showing the union between priest and people in their common action. Actually, except where the so-called dialogue Mass has been restored, the Mass servers take the place of and speak for the people in this dialogue.

The interaction and relationship between priest and Mass servers comprise a sort of subsocial system by themselves. Sometimes priest and server can almost prescind from each other in making their memorized responses. But when the verse-response pattern is done at all reflectively, priest and server depend on each other for stability and smoothness in the flow of the vocal prayers. They are mutually dependent more obviously in their actions, for their roles are interactive. A well-served Mass seems to be the simplest thing in the world until it is compared with a Mass in which the Mass server is not well trained and makes several wrong moves. In the author's experience the average American Mass server would seem to be midway between the solemn, exactly spoken, deliberately moving German boy and the quickly moving and quickly speaking French boy. There are minor differences in Mass servers, as in the ways in which priests celebrate Mass. For liturgical functioning which best conforms with the norms and with the congregation's expectations, priest and Mass server must coordinate their actions.

Some few years ago OLM introduced a congregational high Mass, at which not only the choir but the whole congregation joined in singing the responses. It represented an awareness of many persons' desire to participate more fully in public worship, and an attempt to satisfy that awareness. This congregational high Mass, which is regularly celebrated in a great number of German and French churches and some others, went along splendidly for several months, and then failed. Perhaps some day, when the people are better prepared for it, it will be tried again. At any rate, the service was offered as a parish function, and at least for a while was utilized.

One valuable service which OLM, together with many other parishes, has rendered its people is the provision of hand Missals (Mass books) and the explanation of how to use them. This is mentioned to indicate how the congregation can coordinate its own thoughts and intentions with those of the priest. The children often join the priest in the dialogue Mass on Sundays. Thirty years ago Missals were rather uncommon; today they are rather expected, especially, but not only, among the younger parishioners and those with a Catholic education.

There are at least three early Masses offered every morning at OLM, not counting the Mass in the convent, and sometimes more. Masses at seven o'clock and seven-thirty o'clock are mostly for those who later go to school or work. Another Mass at nine o'clock is attended by a great number of mothers of school children, shoppers, and retired persons. During Lent a Mass at noon is added, a service greatly appreciated by shoppers and business people. Ten Masses are celebrated each Sunday, and almost as many on holydays. During the course of a year in OLM the Mass, the great act of Catholic religious devotion, is offered some thirteen hundred times.

It is not necessary to discuss other types of public worship in OLM as we have done for the Mass. Evening devotions, whether for the Holy Hour or the miraculous-medal novena, the exposition of the Blessed Sacrament for public veneration on First Fridays, and the occasional special devotions are all part of parish life in which priest and interested people play their expected roles with the common view of developing the intimacy between God and His people. The parish church is open all day on every day so that people might enter to pray in quiet and visit with their Eucharistic King. Private services, such as the blessing of women after childbirth, the blessing of religious objects, and the signing of Mass-intention cards, are provided on request. As we have seen in Chapter 5, OLM's Angelus bell rings out regularly each day to direct the thought of its people toward history's greatest event, the Incarnation of the Son of God.

Meanwhile OLM is making available to its people other opportunities for living a richer religious life. In noting the roles played by the priests of OLM in the last chapter, mention was made of the parish organizations in their charge. The exclusive or chief purpose of many of them is the spiritual betterment of their members. The men's Holy Name Society and the women's Altar-Rosary Society receive Holy Communion one Sunday each month in a body, as do several other groups on their respective Sundays. The Nocturnal Adoration Society has a standing invitation to the men, accepted by many, to join in an hour's quiet adoration of their Eucharistic King during one night each month; it also sponsors the annual public procession and triple benediction of the Blessed Sacrament in commemoration of the Feast of Corpus Christi. The Catholic Youth Adorers provide an opportunity for teen-agers to join in a similar hour one Sunday afternoon each month. The senior and junior sodalities and the grammar school "Angels" have their members join in spiritual exercise, as do the Legion of Mary units, the St. Vincent de Paul Society, and the League of the Sacred Heart, which also makes a holy hour of adoration each month. The elementary-school Crusaders share the bond of going one day extra to Holy Communion. The Cana Conference and Christian Family Movement groups join in corporate Communions. Ushers, choir, and Mass servers have the opportunity of contributing their services and of joining more intimately in divine worship.

And beyond mutual participation in religious activities, several of the parish societies offer their members the opportunity of sharing directly in the work of the apostolate. This is particularly true of the Legion of Mary units, the St. Vincent de

Paul Society, the Society for the Propagation of the Faith, which collects funds for the missions, and the Sodality units. For some strange reason the Sodality, whose constitution is as apostolate-minded as any organization for lay people, is less active than the other groups in this respect. It has only girls' units, and its program of action, at least in OLM, is far less vigorous than its sister organizations. At any rate, each of these groups represents another OLM institution for enabling parishioners to identify themselves more actively in the work of Christ, Church, and parish.

Turning to activities which are less directly spiritual in themselves but which abet spiritual purposes, we find first of all the school, which provides an education within a Catholic context and sponsors much spiritual activity among the children. The Scouts, Cub Scouts, and CYO provide useful and/or recreational opportunities under parish auspices with fellow parishioners. As explained in Chapter 4, parishioners were invited to play a major role in taking up the parish census. The annual parish bazaar and Catholic Charities drive are other parish institutions in which parishioners, young and old, can assume the roles of active participants. The Junior Legion provides a baby-sitting service during Sunday Masses, and a bus is made available for transporting the blind to Mass each Sunday.

The OLM Federal Credit Union, rightfully the pastor's pride and joy, has been saving and lending money for parishioners for thirteen years and has gone over the $1,200,000 mark in total loans granted. Its interest rate is a strikingly low one half of one per cent of the unpaid balance. It lends $400 without security and up to $10,000 with security. On innumerable occasions it has rescued individuals and families not only materially, but thereby also spiritually. The employment bureau and the social-welfare service have similarly good records.

Why is the parish concerned with these at first less obvious spiritual activities? Because they fit into the pattern of the total parish life and its purposes. Spiritual harm has often come upon people on the occasion of material misfortune. If ordinary temporal channels are such that these people are not helped, then it makes sense that the spiritual organization should take up whatever slack it can in view of its higher goals. Besides, even prescinding from need, the parish recognizes that its people are often drawn away through conflicting values under secular auspices. Insofar as these religiously and morally indifferent values can be integrated into parish services, the parish believes it can contribute to its people's spiritual as well as material prosperity by providing them.

This chapter has hardly done justice to the extent of OLM's social functioning, but the services mentioned and partially explained should be proof that OLM is indeed a social system with a coordinated structure and functioning, and that both these latter are aimed clearly in the direction of its fundamental purpose, the Christian formation of its members.

On the other hand it has not been our intention to imply either that everything is being done that could be done to achieve OLM's objectives or even that every service which is offered is already so perfect that it could not be improved. As a matter of fact OLM would receive a rating much higher than average on both the number and the quality of its services. But our only aim in this chapter has been to consider an important element in any social system: interactive functioning for the achievement of its goals. The services rendered by OLM are one expression of that functioning. The following chapters study another expression: the extent to which OLM's functioning is effective, as seen in the use of its services by its members.

CHAPTER X

The Mass
and the Sacraments

Running a motor while the car stands motionless can imply waste of investment, energy, and power. A parish social system which provides the services described in forerunning chapters proves its existence, but its effectiveness is tested by the extent to which it realizes its purposes and secures the participation of its members. In this and the following four chapters we see the use which OLM's parishioners make of the parish services and consequently the level of effectiveness which the parish social system has achieved in its functioning. This chapter records the parishioners' response to the availability of Mass and the sacraments; Chapter 11 analyzes the relationship between religious practice and various elements of its demographic composition; Chapter 12 centers on the Blessed Sacrament; Chapter 13 inquires into the parish societies; and Chapter 14 probes the attitudes and the realization of values of parishioners. These chapters not merely report on OLM but exemplify in a small way the use of the social-system concept as a tool for parish analysis, whether the parish be OLM or any other.

It will be remembered that the intention of the author was not to pronounce judgment on the degree of OLM's effectiveness or its approximation to the parochial ideal suggested in Chapter 3. His purpose was rather to present facts on the existence and activity of OLM as a social system, and to show that it can be analyzed accordingly and that the tool of analysis is applicable to parishes in general. The recording of statistics of religious practice in OLM suggests a certain level of effectiveness, but we must recall that effectiveness in spiritual matters cannot be assessed adequately through external considerations. But while external practice need not conform with inner sanctity in all cases, it does serve as a useful norm, even if not as a completely accurate one.

The tabulation here of data on OLM practice and attitude is intended primarily as a contribution to parish sociology in general. Reference has been made previously to the need for positive data in assessing parish life. Some of the remarkable and valuable hypotheses in the initial studies of Fichter, Kelly, Schnepp, and Thomas cannot be tested without available data. These OLM data can be joined with their own in a growing fund of empirical parish studies.

The subject of Mass attendance brings us, strictly speaking, beyond the bounds of the definition of OLM parishioners used in preceding chapters. Heretofore only those parishioners have been considered who were members of families that filled out the census forms. These comprised 73 per cent of all Catholic families listed in the address and religious-affiliation file who did not claim membership in other parishes—approximately 2,700 out of more than 3,670 families. There were also 70 families living beyond the parish limits, but attending OLM Church, who filled out census forms. The total number of persons represented by these 2,773 families is 8,570.

A meaningful estimate of parish practice must also include: (1) those families listed in the address file as Catholic families who failed to fill out the census form and (2) at least a portion of the 750 families for whom no data concerning religious affiliation were obtained. Not all of the 970 Catholic families who failed to return census forms would be members of OLM Parish.

By a projection based on both parish and national census data it was calculated that the OLM Catholic families contained some 2,620 persons. It can be estimated, therefore, that there were 11,190 persons in all OLM families listed in the address and religious-affiliation file. But it was also pointed out in Chapter 4 that while the religious affiliations of some 750 families were unknown, ecological considerations indicated that a large percentage must be either Jewish or members of other parishes, particularly of the Italian-speaking national parish. At the very most possibly 300 of these households would belong to OLM. Since the average number of members per household in both OLM territory and OLM Parish is 3.1, the address-file total would thus be increased by 930 persons if these 300 families were included. The estimated number of persons in all OLM families thus totals 12,120.

In evaluating attendance at Sunday Mass deductions must be made for non-Catholics (almost 220 of the 8,570 registered parishioners), children under seven years of age (approximately 1,000 of the registered parishioners), and those who are legitimately excused—the old, the infirm, and those necessarily at work—estimated at 10 per cent. The estimate of 10 per cent legitimately excused is not completely arbitrary. Almost 6 per cent of OLM's registered population are over 70, and several of the priests have as many as 40 regular Communion calls for the sick. A Sunday trip about New York City, where almost half the population is Catholic, shows the observer so many active persons in the transportation, recreation, and concession industries that he cannot be surprised if many of them are Catholics whose necessary work prevents them from attending Mass. Finally, European figures have ranged from 10 per cent to 20 per cent, including children. If anything, 10 per cent is probably an underestimate.

In Column 21 of the census form the parishioner is requested to state how many times he has missed Mass in the last four weeks through his own fault. Deducting non-Catholics, children under seven, and 10 per cent legitimately excused, 6,620 of the 8,570 registered OLM population are expected to be present at Sunday Mass. Census returns indicated that 5,270 (79.6 per cent) were regularly present, another 650 (9.8 per cent) at-

TABLE XI

Sunday Observance in OLM Parish

	Census Returns	Address File	All OLM Families
Number of persons	8,570	11,190	12,120
Non-Catholics	220	290	310
Under 7	1,000	1,300	1,410
Excused (10 per cent)	730	960	1,040
Expected average attendance	6,620	8,640	9,360
Average attendance reported	5,920(1)	6,020	6,020
Percentage	89	70	64
Not attending	700	2,620	3,260
Percentage	11	30	35

(1) The 5,920 includes 5,270 who were regularly present and 650 who attended irregularly.

tended irregularly, and 700 (10.6 per cent) did not attend Mass at all. Thus 89 per cent of the registered parishioners attend Mass either regularly or irregularly. Average attendance at Sunday Mass as reported by ushers and recorded each week in the parish book is 6,020. On the average, therefore, an additional 100 persons beyond the total called for by the parish census attend Sunday Mass. The general picture of Sunday Mass attendance in OLM Parish is presented in Table XI. All figures in the column headed *Census Returns* were derived from the parish census and apply exclusively to OLM registered members. The figures under the head *Address File* refer to the members of Catholic families listed in the religious-affiliation file, which included 970 families who did not return census forms. The third column, *All OLM Families*, adds to the second column the estimated 930 persons in the families missing from the address file.

The second and third columns are based on estimates. All figures have been rounded to the nearest 10. If they err, it is probably on the side of slightly underestimating practice.

Several observations may be made concerning the foregoing data. It cannot be maintained that OLM's census returns included only practicing Catholics, for almost 11 per cent of these respondents admitted to not attending Mass on any Sunday during an entire month and 10 per cent were present irregularly. Nor can one claim that all practicing Catholics were included in the census returns, for another 100 persons attend Mass on an average beyond the total accounted for by the census respondents. At the same time it must be admitted that these 100 represent hardly 5 per cent of the nonrespondents. At the very most 35 per cent of the parish members—and more probably 30 per cent and possibly less—omit Sunday observance. Of these the merest handful stated that they no longer had anything to do with the Church. The 441 families who refused to fill out the census forms, even though they had designated themselves as Catholics, gave no intimation of such an attitude.

The parish has an observance rating of nearly 70 per cent in terms of the members for whom and with whom it functions successfully. The remaining 30 per cent belong evidently to the same ecological, educational, recreational, occupational, and cultural milieu as the 70 per cent, yet the functioning of the parish does not extend to this group. Therefore the 30 per cent must be the object of a special apostolic endeavor of the parish, presumably proceeding from the completion of the census. Perhaps the parish has not succeeded in communicating to the 30 per cent the pre-eminence of its values; or perhaps that statistical group exemplifies the effect of what Father Fichter calls institutional inconsistency, or again we may think of the biblical parable of the seed falling on different types of ground.

A second observation has to do with those who practice irregularly. Proper and required religious observance calls for, among other practices, regular weekly assistance at Sunday Mass. Can those who are partially delinquent be said not to practice their religion? The answer must be, quite obviously, that they do practice, but not as much as norms require. Their roles in the functioning social system are being played only partially. But the social system *is* meaningful to them and supplies a value to them, at least to the extent that sometimes they respond to it. It is the parish's main function to help its members get to God. Those practicing irregularly, in accordance with their own acceptance of values, are included among those members and are helped by the parish at least as much as they will permit it to help. Presumably it would be wise to view European studies of Mass attendance in that light; namely, that the total present at Mass on any one Sunday, no matter how "typical" the Sunday, probably does not include a fairly large number of other persons who are likewise members of the parish system.

Strict comparison between the results of the OLM study and other parish and national studies is not possible in all respects, despite attempts to keep categories comparable. The findings of the more important American urban-parish studies are summarized in Table XII. Although nonparochial, the *Catholic Digest* study of Catholic adults and the Kelly study of white Catholics in Florida are included because they contribute to the overall picture of religious observance based on attendance at Sunday Mass.[1] Two sets of OLM data are recorded: Mass attendance as reported in census forms, which includes both regular and irregular attendance; and Sunday observance based on all persons listed as Catholics in the address file. Three sets of data are

---

[1] Beginning with the November 1952 issue the *Catholic Digest* published a series of thirty articles entitled "Religion in America," based on replies from 23,700,000 Catholics. Father Kelly's study, *Catholics and Practice of the Faith*, embraced some 40,000 white, English-speaking Catholics in the Diocese of St. Augustine, Florida. For a summary of studies made in the United States see Appendix I, pp. 292-97.

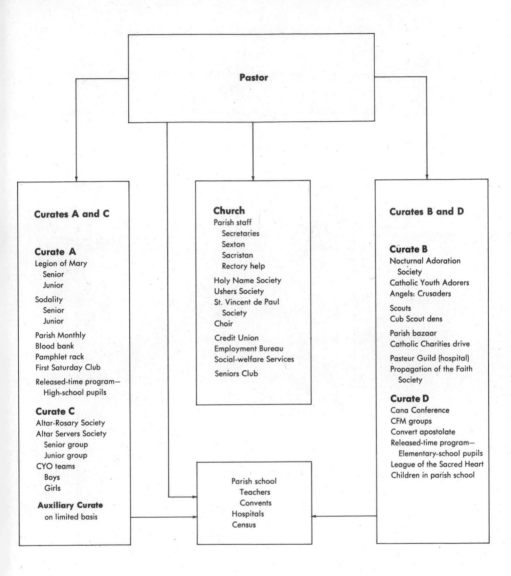

Pastor

Curates A and C

Curate A
Legion of Mary
  Senior
  Junior
Sodality
  Senior
  Junior
Parish Monthly
Blood bank
Pamphlet rack
First Saturday Club
Released-time program—
  High-school pupils

Curate C
Altar-Rosary Society
Altar Servers Society
  Senior group
  Junior group
CYO teams
  Boys
  Girls

Auxiliary Curate
  on limited basis

Church
Parish staff
  Secretaries
  Sexton
  Sacristan
  Rectory help
Holy Name Society
Ushers Society
St. Vincent de Paul
  Society
Choir
Credit Union
Employment Bureau
Social-welfare Services
Seniors Club

Parish school
  Teachers
  Convents
  Hospitals
  Census

Curates B and D

Curate B
Nocturnal Adoration
  Society
Catholic Youth Adorers
Angels: Crusaders
Scouts
Cub Scout dens
Parish bazaar
Catholic Charities drive
Pasteur Guild (hospital)
Propagation of the Faith
  Society

Curate D
Cana Conference
CFM groups
Convert apostolate
Released-time program—
  Elementary-school pupils
League of the Sacred Heart
Children in parish school

FIGURE 16
Our Lady of Mercy Parish
organizational chart

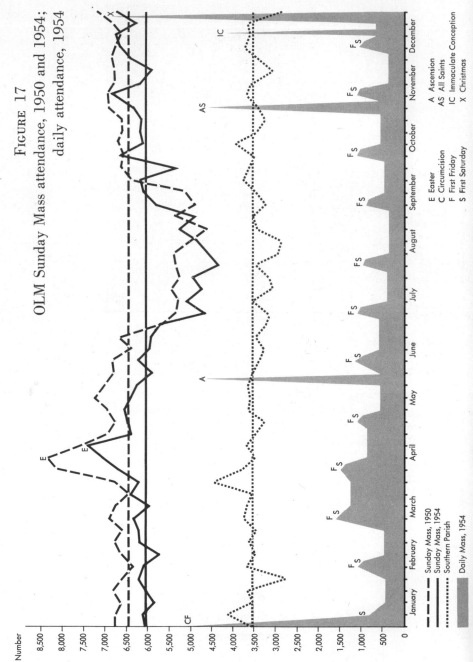

FIGURE 17

OLM Sunday Mass attendance, 1950 and 1954;
daily attendance, 1954

Number

8,500
8,000
7,500
7,000
6,500
6,000
5,500
5,000
4,500
4,000
3,500
3,000
2,500
2,000
1,500
1,000
500
0

January February March April May June July August September October November December

- - - - Sunday Mass, 1950
——— Sunday Mass, 1954
········· Southern Parish
▓▓▓▓ Daily Mass, 1954

E Easter
C Circumcision
F First Friday
S First Saturday

A   Ascension
AS All Saints
IC Immaculate Conception
X   Christmas

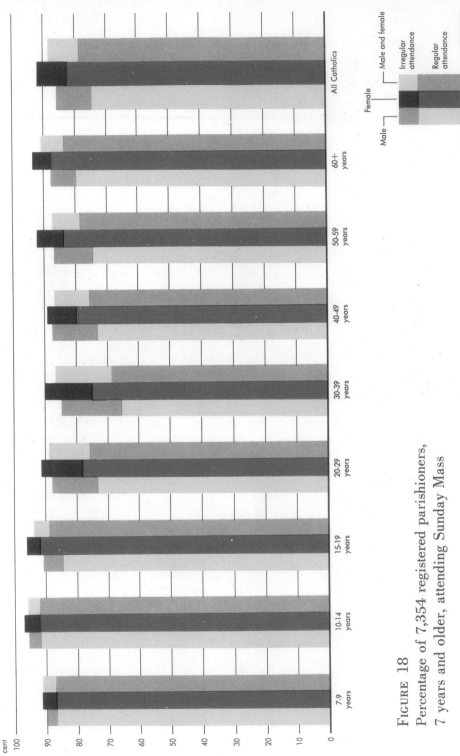

FIGURE 18
Percentage of 7,354 registered parishioners,
7 years and older, attending Sunday Mass

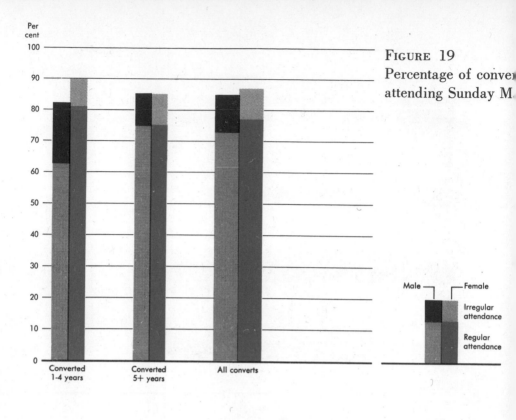

FIGURE 19
Percentage of conver[ts]
attending Sunday M[ass]

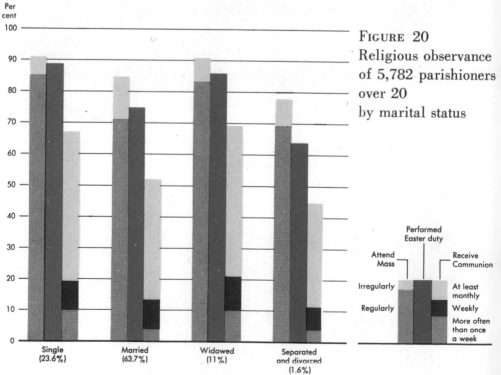

FIGURE 20
Religious observance
of 5,782 parishioners
over 20
by marital status

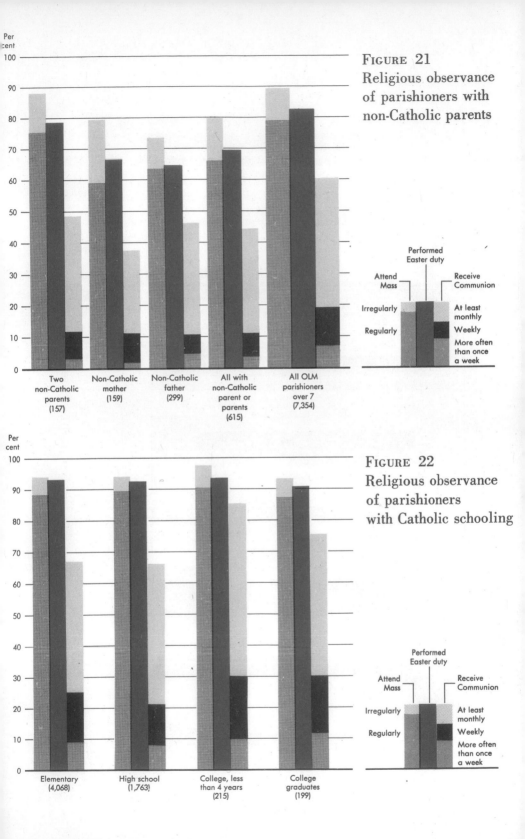

FIGURE 21
Religious observance
of parishioners with
non-Catholic parents

FIGURE 22
Religious observance
of parishioners
with Catholic schooling

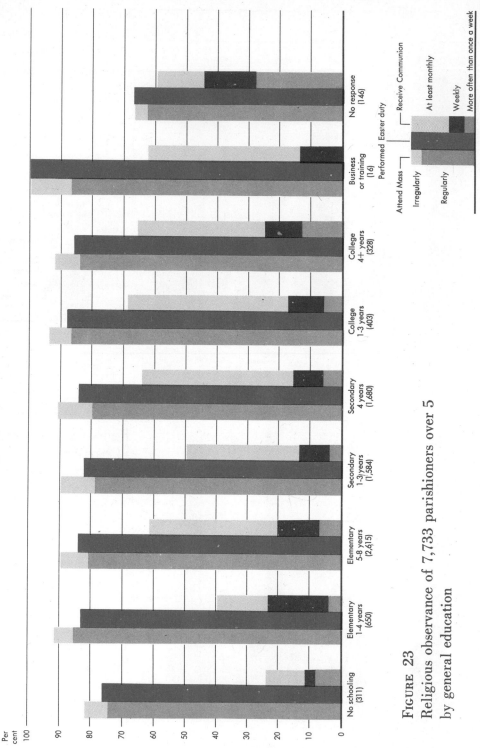

FIGURE 23

Religious observance of 7,733 parishioners over 5
by general education

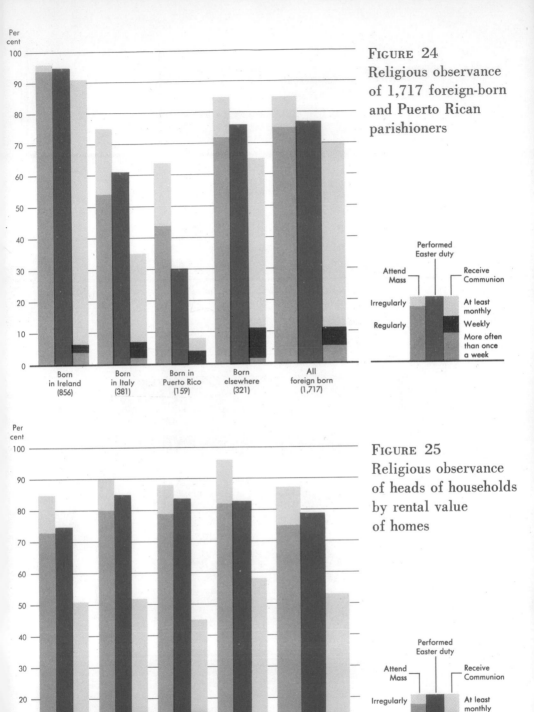

FIGURE 24
Religious observance
of 1,717 foreign-born
and Puerto Rican
parishioners

FIGURE 25
Religious observance
of heads of households
by rental value
of homes

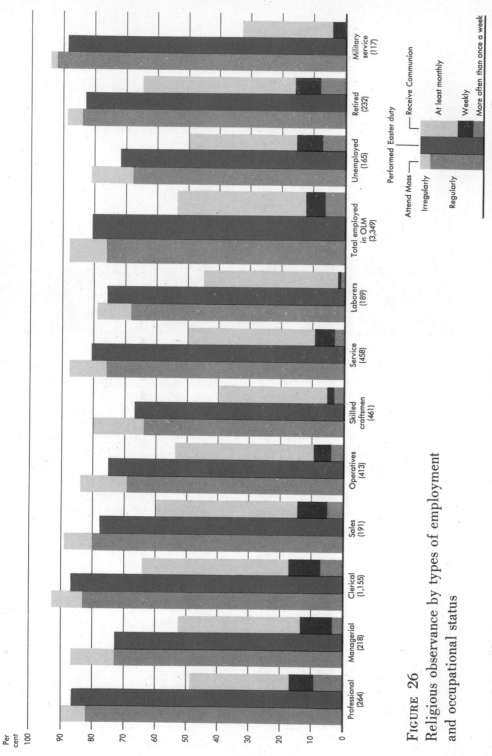

Per
cent

FIGURE 26
Religious observance by types of employment
and occupational status

recorded for the Fichter studies of a southern parish: the claims
of 6,500 parishioners on census forms; the Fichter findings concerning these same 6,500 parishioners; and the percentages calculated for all Catholics in the parish.[2]

TABLE XII

Sunday Observance, Compiled from Several American Studies

Study	Location	Number of Catholics	Per Cent Attending Mass		
			Regularly	Irregularly	Not at All
Catholic Digest	United States	23,700,000	62	20	18
Fichter (census reports)	South	6,500	81	7	12
Fichter (actual practice)		6,500	57	31	12
Fichter (all Catholics)		11,000	34	18	48
Kelly	Florida	40,000	75	12	13
McCaffrey	Midwest	2,800	71	—	—
OLM (census reports)	Bronx	8,350	80	9	11
OLM (address file)		11,190	70	—	30
Schnepp	East Coast	3,720	80	16	4

Allowing for the wide range of results in European urban
parishes (Mass attendance between 15 per cent and 30 per cent),
it can be said that the survey of American studies made thus far
shows a distinct superiority to the level of Mass attendance in
European cities. The claims on the respective census schedules
of the parishioners of Fichter's southern parish and those of
OLM, a northern parish, are almost identical. These percentages
of 81 and 80 per cent regular attendance closely approach the
findings of Schnepp, though the percentage of nonattendance is
higher in both cases than the 4 per cent found by Schnepp.[3] At
the same time the census-form claims surpass the findings of
McCaffrey, Kelly, and the *Catholic Digest*.[4] However, the disparity between the claims of the parishioners and Fichter's find-

[2] Fichter, *Southern Parish*, pp. 136-53.
[3] Schnepp, *Leakage from a Catholic Parish*.
[4] McCaffrey, *Youth in a Catholic Parish*.

ings in the southern parish were not experienced in OLM, where the records of parishioners correspond quite well with their census claims. Likewise, Fichter's findings of almost 48 per cent nonpractice and 40 per cent dormancy have no counterpart in the OLM study.

Records of attendance at Mass in OLM Parish for each Sunday of the years 1950 and 1954, and average daily attendance for the year 1954, are shown in Figure 17. By way of comparison Mass attendance on Sundays in Father Fichter's southern parish is included.[5] The first thing to be noticed on the graph for Sunday Mass is that attendance follows a consistent pattern in the two years studied and that it drops sharply during the summer months. This can be partially explained by the negligence of some children, who are not required to attend the assigned school children's Mass, and also by the negligence of adults who yield to early calls from the golf club or beach. The major consideration, however, is the fact that many people who can possibly afford it leave the parish for the summer, in whole or in part, and others spend week ends away from the city or attend Sunday Mass along the way to the summer resort.

An examination of Figure 17 reveals that if the summer months were excluded, the average attendance at Sunday Mass, calculated for the purpose of assessing religious observance, would be close to 6,300 per week rather than the 6,020 cited in Table XI and depicted in Figure 17. A similar adjustment, apparently, could also be made for average attendance in Father Fichter's southern parish. Another fact made clear by the OLM graphs is that attendance is extraordinarily high on two successive Sundays, Palm Sunday and Easter Sunday. This rise in attendance suggests that the seasonal observants may well be attracted by other than religious values, for there are secular values attached to these two spring occasions. It is possible that

---

[5] Fichter, *Southern Parish*, p. 151.

the religious values are fundamentally little different from those involved on any other Sunday. Interestingly enough, the graph for the southern parish dips at Palm Sunday, which is apparently to be explained by the local traditions and the ethnic backgrounds of the parishioners.

A comparison of figures for the years 1950 and 1954 reveals that weekly attendance has decreased by almost 500 over the five-year period. Mobility could account for some of the decrease and also the replacement of some Catholic families by the Puerto Ricans, who are as yet not too well established. The fact is that another condition affecting the parish is thus called to the priests' attention through the census. They will wish to investigate and to seek a remedy for the situation if the facts indicate that one is needed.

The graph for daily attendance rises sharply on holydays, suggesting that religious values are attached to these occasions, at least for very many of the 5,000 OLM parishioners who attend Mass. No attendance figures are given for the Feast of the Assumption since it coincided with the Sunday in 1954. Except for the feasts of Christmas and the Circumcision (New Year's Day), these are days of ordinary secular business. Thus most working people surrender an hour of their own convenience, in addition to the demands of travel and business, to satisfy religious demands, or, to put it in another way, to achieve religious value. The parish operates to provide this value by scheduling early and noonday Masses. Recently OLM inaugurated two additional early Masses on holydays and found that the total attendance rose almost 500 above the usual holyday rate—a clear instance of the functioning social system's provision of service in accordance with the parishioners' need and the use of the service by parishioners.

Attendance at daily Mass increases during Lent and on the First Fridays and Saturdays of the year, but it is rarely over 1,500 persons.

Thus far in this chapter we have been discussing the total record of Sunday observance in OLM. The purpose was to allow OLM to be viewed within the same framework as other parishes studied for religious practice. Let us return to our previously defined parish, consisting of the 2,773 families and 8,570 individuals registered in the parish census. Although Mass attendance is of prime importance in parish life, let us now see how these individuals make use of other religious services provided by the parish. Fulfillment of Easter duty and the reception of Holy Communion, however, will be deferred to Chapter 12.

Baptism has been explained previously as the initiation of the would-be Christian into the Church. Of OLM's 8,350 census-registered Catholics,[6] practically all have been baptized, less than 1 per cent being listed as not having yet received the sacrament. Over three quarters of the latter (64 out of 81) are in the 9-and-below age category. A few were but very recently born at the time of the census, and others were children in disorganized and broken Puerto Rican families. The parish Legion of Mary has been working diligently and with some success to combat this problem. As to the other nonbaptized, almost invariably the census schedules of the few indicated nonbaptized adults suggested faulty responses. The first service utilized by the parishioner is that of being baptized. With the recent approval given to the United States for the use of English in a large portion of the baptismal rite, more and more parishioners of OLM and elsewhere have been appreciating not only the major benefit of the sacrament but also the sense of its liturgy more completely.

The priests of OLM baptize almost 400 persons each year. The average for the five-year period 1950-1954 was 381; the total for 1954 alone was 422. These include nearly 30 adult converts, about 90 persons privately baptized in the parish's two hospitals, and newly born infants brought to the parish church

---

[6] It will be recalled that almost 220 of OLM's 8,570 parishioners are non-Catholics.

by their parents or godparents. The attempt is sometimes made to estimate fidelity to and lapse from Catholic practice in childhood through comparison of baptisms with first Communions some seven years later. This can indeed be a helpful index, and Father Fichter made use of it in *Southern Parish*. However, some variants which often are not easily controlled, especially in a highly mobile society, must be considered. As an established and highly regarded parish, OLM naturally attracts former parishioners. Some who have moved away return for the baptism of their children. As a residentially saturated parish, OLM sees many of its young families move away before their children have reached first-Communion age. Since OLM has its share of the 30,000,000 Americans who, according to the United States Census Bureau, change their dwelling in any one year, only an accurate parish file of long standing could provide adequate information for an index based on a comparison of baptisms and first Communions.

The Catholic population of OLM Parish is large enough to require having the sacrament of confirmation administered each year. (Some parishes have it only every second or even every third year.) One of the bishops of the archdiocese is the confirming prelate, and the occasion is a religiously very festive and joyous one for the parish. Choir and altar servers are both specially prepared. The responsible sisters in the school work hard with the student candidates both to make them intellectually appreciative of the event designating them public witnesses of the Christian faith and to make the religious celebration dignified, colorful, and even beautiful. The author was privileged to participate in an OLM confirmation ceremony during the time of this study, when some 200 school children aged 9 years and some 20 recent adult converts received the sacrament. The parish norms for their acceptance, and the success of the candidates in measuring up to those norms with the help of their teachers, exemplify the effective functioning of the parish system.

Almost 7,000 OLM parishioners above the age of 10 have been confirmed, but over 175, about 2.5 per cent, have not. Some 20 of the unconfirmed are converts (about 10 per cent of all OLM converts), while 86 are immigrants from a foreign country or from Puerto Rico. Just half (43 of the 86) come from Puerto Rico and the others are mostly from Ireland and Italy. The disproportionate ratio of unconfirmed among Puerto Ricans, those born in foreign countries, and converts is indicative of the interdependence of parish functions. Had these persons passed through OLM School, they would have received the sacrament. Of course a preponderant number of converts and foreign born have been confirmed despite nonattendance at the parish school, but there is a positive relationship between attendance at a Catholic school and reception of the sacrament of confirmation. About 50 of the 175 who are not confirmed are in their teens, both boys and girls, and the others are distributed more or less evenly among the other age groups.

While 97.5 per cent of OLM parishioners over 10 have received the sacrament of confirmation, 99 per cent of those over 7 have made their first Holy Communion (7,225 out of 7,350), another positive response to a service offered by the parish. This sacrament, as its name signifies, implies union between the recipient and Christ, the Catholic firmly believing that this union is a physical one, since Christ's presence in the sacramental species of bread and wine is likewise physical. Reception of the Eucharist is intended to be the recurring high point of a Christian's life, precisely because of this intimate union between man and his Maker, creature and Creator, the redeemed and his Savior, the Christian soldier and his Lord, the human with his divine friend. Hence the first reception of this sacrament is marked with no less preparation and joyous festivity than the reception of confirmation. In certain ethnic areas where religious practice has fallen to a type of social formality, this first reception of Communion is often the last, except perhaps at

Easter each year and on one's deathbed. In OLM, as in most other healthily functioning parishes throughout the world, it is actually the first of many Communions. Some youngsters take up the practice of receiving every day, which many adults too have either continued from youth or more recently undertaken. Here is where the communication of values to the young parishioner, his socialization within the parish community, and the influence of God's grace on him and his response thereto are inextricably woven. On the other hand, the difference between a parish with many and frequent Communions and one with but few can be explained in terms of parish policy, emphasis, and its training of its youth for their first Communion.

Just as the Eucharist is a sacrament that is received often in one's life, so confession is intended to be repeated often. Church law—and to the Catholic mind common sense—makes it obligatory at least once a year if a person has sinned seriously since his baptism or previous confession. But very many Catholics go to confession frequently, monthly or even weekly. Their preparation for this sacrament was received at the same time as the preparation for first Holy Communion, and again their use of this sacrament depends largely on the values they have been helped to recognize. Many find confession not easy, which is understandable, since few enjoy confessing their faults into a fellow man's ear. Nor is it easy from another aspect, that of emendation; a penitent must not only be sorry for his wrongdoing but must sincerely intend to refrain from it hereafter.

It was mentioned in the previous chapter that a priest at OLM hears almost 15,000 confessions annually. An accurate estimate for the entire number of confessions heard in OLM during the year would probably be well over 70,000. Many of these were made by nonparishioners, since shoppers along Fordham Road find OLM convenient for confession on a Saturday or preholyday afternoon, but it would be almost impossible to ascertain how many.

The OLM questionnaire asked respondents why they went to confession, if they did, more often than church law required.[7] Motives suggested as possible reasons included: to receive absolution, to receive an increase of grace through the sacrament, to ask priestly advice, to keep a check on oneself, to keep up with

TABLE XIII

Reasons for Going to Confession More Often than Necessary

Motive	Per Cent
Grace	34
Absolution	22
As a check	20
Advice	16
Habit	4
Other	4

a habit, or some other. Some five sixths of the respondents (248 out of 300) answered this question, the percentage checking the various reasons are listed in Table XIII.

The important first conclusion from these responses is that the ritual act performed by the OLM parishioner in going often to confession is motivated by positive values in his life. This is taken for granted by the Catholic, but can hardly be appreciated by the non-Catholic social scientist. Only 4 per cent who profess to go out of habit give a nonsupernatural explanation, though the motive of some of those who go for advice or as a check on themselves might be subject to a natural interpretation. The 4 per cent who checked "other" for their motive either did not explain or mentioned some such reason as divine command, peace of soul, the direction of a confessor, and so on. The valuable consideration, from the viewpoint of the parish as a social system, is the cooperative use made of this parish service.

------

[7] See Part 2, Question 10, p. 321.

Every year some 125 marriages take place in OLM. Roughly five sixths of the marriages are between Catholics and one sixth are mixed marriages (that is, one of the spouses is Catholic and one is not). About one third of the Catholic marriages are performed at nuptial Masses, in which the Church adds to the usual Eucharistic liturgy the prayers, blessings, and rite of matrimony. The religious tone, the joyous solemnity, and the emphatic linking of the couple's marriage with the sacrifice of Christ and the central act of Catholic worship are the reasons why ardent Catholics are most desirous of having a nuptial Mass, and why it stands long in their memory as a recollection of values attained and still to be achieved. Anyone who has witnessed or participated in a nuptial Mass must be convinced of an exposition of values and a manifestation of religiously social approval and encouragement which no mere wedding ceremony of itself could have, despite its intrinsic significance and value. Certainly all couples who receive the Church's blessing on their marriage, especially those who join in a nuptial Mass, cooperate in functional interaction to achieve values of importance.

One further phase of parish cooperation for the attainment and protection of Christian marital welfare is the required announcement of the banns of marriage. Thus on three occasions before the marriage ceremony the parish is notified (usually at the parish high Mass on Sunday, or its equivalent) of the intended marriage. Should anyone know of an impediment to the marriage, he is morally bound to inform the pastor that it might be investigated and harm be averted.

As in the joyous religious experiences of life, so in times of sorrow, in sickness and in death, the priests are at the service of their parish, and the parishioners utilize and cooperate in that service. During the five years beginning with 1950 the priests of OLM brought spiritual ministration to the sick an average of 1,050 times each year (1,596 times in 1954). This has included Communion visits to the sick, when the priest brings the sacrament of the Eucharist to a sick person in his own home. The better a priest comes to know his people, and vice versa, the more occasion there is for priestly service of this sort to be requested. Perhaps this accounts for the gradual rise in sick calls from 788 to 1,596 through the five years.

Not included in these figures are the 14,350 average yearly sick calls made in the parish's two hospitals. This number has remained rather constant through the five years, varying from 14,100 to 14,950. A moment's reflection shows that this has meant an average of almost 40 ministrations (often including confession, Viaticum or Communion for the dying, extreme unction) every day and night of the year. Many of these are attended to on the daily round to the hospital, but others are not. This service must be assessed in terms of both the parishioners' use and the parish's provision of it.

Another item of parishioner cooperation must be considered here. Although the daily round of the hospital follows an institutionalized pattern as do many of the Communion calls, all other sick calls do not. They are instituted by the sick person himself or someone associated with him. This lay initiative prompts the priestly response. In addition, the parishioner prepares for the priest's coming. In the hospital this is habitually cared for by the staff; in individual homes it must be provided by the parishioner. The *Parish Monthly* prints this statement regularly: "Sick calls.—At any time. The priest should be called whenever the person is considered dangerously ill."

A parish bulletin other than OLM's prints the following detailed instructions regularly on its directory page:

> Sick calls should be sent to the Rectory before 9 A.M. but in case of sudden illness call the priest immediately at any time, by phone or messenger. A good rule to follow is: If the patient is sick enough to have the doctor he is sick enough to have the priest. In preparation for the administration of the Sacraments at home, the following should be in readiness before the priest enters: a table

covered with a white cloth on which should be arranged a Crucifix; two Blessed Candles lighted; Holy Water; a glass of drinking water; a teaspoon and a napkin. If possible an attendant should meet the priest at the entrance with a lighted candle when he brings the Blessed Sacrament.[8]

Thus the parishioner plays his own important role in enabling the parish to be of service. The OLM questionnaire asked whether the respondent had in his home equipment for a priest's visit to the sick.[9] The question is not a key test of a parishioner's Catholic practice or union with his parish; yet it is one of those fairly trustworthy, though minor, telltale signs of Catholic responsibility, conformity, and maturity in religious practice. Almost two thirds (192 out of 293) answered affirmatively. The religious, economic, and educational background of respondents making affirmative answers is summarized in Table XIV.

TABLE XIV

OLM Parishioners Having Equipment for Priest's Visit to Sick, by Social Categories and Ranks

	Group A	Group B	Group C	Group D	Total
Religious rank(1)	31 [33]	124 [171]	37 [77]	0 [12]	192 [293]
Economic rank	8 [13]	75 [114]	83 [131]	26 [35]	192 [293]
General education	19 [41]	25 [42]	85 [128]	63 [82]	192 [293]
Catholic education	17 [26]	9 [16]	41 [61]	57 [73]	124 [176]

(1) The system of classification is explained in Chapter 8, p. 171. As in previous tables, the numbers in brackets represent the total number of individuals in each group.

Several interesting observations follow. The possession of equipment follows expectations based on religious rank almost perfectly. Of the parishioners who rank highest in religious observance, Groups A and B, 71 per cent have the necessary sup-

---

[8] Bulletin of Saint Thomas the Apostle Church, Woodhaven, New York City.
[9] Part 2, Question 14, p. 321.

plies as compared with less than 50 per cent in Group C and none in Group D. In economic rank the variation runs from 62 per cent in Group A to 74 per cent in Group D, indicating no relationship between income and preparations for sick calls. Those who had grade-school or high-school education, whether general or Catholic, have a higher percentage of affirmative response than those with a college education.

After sick calls there is often the burying of the dead. For the five years preceding this study the priests at OLM attended the wakes, offered the funeral Mass, blessed the remains of the deceased, and accompanied the funeral party to the cemetery some 175 times each year. Usually the deceased is a parishioner, though occasionally it is the wish of a former parishioner that he be buried from OLM—not an unusual occurrence in established parishes which have served their people well. This practice, though not too widespread, would obstruct attempts to measure any difference between Catholic death rate in OLM and OLM funerals, not to mention the crossing of parish boundaries and the presence of a nearby national parish. The priests of OLM, who would be expected to hear of deaths in the parish perhaps more surely than anything else, are satisfied that no parishioner dies without Catholic burial, except in unique and known circumstances. Here again parishioner and priest join in bringing succor to the bereaved and in performing a corporal work of mercy to the dead.

Having discussed briefly several of the more important religious functions of OLM and the useful participation therein of the parishioners, we can have some understanding of the unending activity, interaction, derived relationships, and pursuit of spiritual values which characterize the functioning of a lively Catholic parish such as OLM. Obviously our study has been only introductory, but likewise indicative of areas of further inquiry. We proceed next, in Chapter 11, to an analysis of the people who cooperate in this parochial functioning.

CHAPTER XI

Characteristics of Active Parish Members

Catholicism is catholic for many reasons, one of the more important being the universality of its mission. Its aim is to win the minds and hearts of all men everywhere, all kinds of men in all kinds of circumstances. We have seen that, except for the summer months, about 6,300 persons participate at the holy sacrifice of the Mass each Sunday in OLM's parish church. Nearly half that number again should be participating, but neglect to do so. Is it that people in certain socioeconomic groups go to church and others do not? If so, a particular apostolic approach would have to be developed and used toward the latter. Thus it is that in some places the poor go to church and the wealthy do not bother; in other places the opposite is true. The same can be said of educated and ignorant, natives and foreigners, men and women, young and old. What is the breakdown of parishioner participation in OLM?

Let us return to the use of the Mass in OLM, together with those other two fundamentals of Catholic religious life and observance: making the annual Easter duty and receiving Holy Communion frequently. We noted previously that of the nearly 6,300 persons who are in attendance at OLM's Sunday Masses the great majority are the 89 per cent of OLM's registered parishioners who attend either regularly (80 per cent) or ir-

215

regularly (9 per cent). We have already seen, although briefly, the interaction of priest and people at Mass—the responses, the communicative movements, the role of the altar servers, the community of interest in the liturgical sacrifice. Now we intend a correlational analysis for the purpose of understanding the parish population of OLM as an element of the social system. What kind of people are OLM's churchgoers?

A great majority of European and most of the few American studies of religious practice have emphasized age and sex factors in analyzing characteristics of the religiously observant. We recall the warning cry of Père Daniel that the churches of Paris were filled with women and children,[1] a situation not uncommon, especially in many Latin areas. Figure 18 shows the percentage of 7,354 OLM parishioners over 7 who reported attending Mass regularly and irregularly. The age and sex composition of OLM's attendants is almost exactly comparable with the table compiled by Father Fichter, though the latter makes no distinction between the later and earlier teen-agers.[2] The data too are very similar.

Fichter found the sex difference, always in favor of female regular Mass attendance in all age groups, to vary from 5 per cent in the teens and twenties to 13 per cent in the thirties, 15 per cent in the forties, about 10 per cent in the fifties, and 13 per cent in the sixties-plus. OLM Parish, where over-all practice shows a female predominance of 83 per cent regular Mass attendance to 76 per cent for the males, exhibits a fairly similar pattern. When irregular is joined with regular attendance, the female dominance is 93 per cent over 87 per cent. Up to the end of the early teens (age 14) there is little choice between boys and girls, less even than Father Fichter's 2 per cent. In the late teens, however, while the girls retain a percentage over 90, the

---

[1] Daniel, *Aspects de la pratique religieuse à Paris*, pp. 111-12.
[2] Fichter, *Urban Parish*, pp. 85 ff.

boys fall off to 85 per cent. The gap is closed a bit in the twenties, but OLM's young ladies retain a 4 per cent edge in those twenties also. The difference expands again to 9 per cent in the thirties and varies from 6 per cent to 9 per cent from then on. OLM does not show the range of variation in religious practice according to sex which Fichter found in the South (9 per cent as opposed to 15 per cent). However, there is further confirmation for the common assumption that women practice more faithfully than men. On the other hand, a necessary and scientific conclusion warranted by these figures is that a 7 per cent difference, which might appear important in itself, loses a great deal of its significance when one considers that it refers to regular practice on the part of 83 per cent of the women and 76 per cent of the men. In other words, it would be clearly a poor conclusion to assert that male practice is poor because it is 7 per cent lower than female practice when, as a matter of fact, over 75 per cent of the men attend Mass regularly. When those who attend irregularly are added to the regular attendants the percentage is over 85. This does not mean that 24 per cent laxity or lapse among men in a parish is not serious, just as 17 per cent deficiency among women is not insignificant, but it should prevent undue emphasis on a relatively minor consideration.

In fact, we might look at it quite the other way. The priest facing his Sunday congregation at OLM cannot afford to proceed as if men were a mere minor faction among his listeners. Actually they are close to half, allowance being made for the absolute female imbalance which shows 100 female parishioners for nearly 85 males. In rounded generalities, one could say of the OLM parishioners who filled out the census forms (nearly 75 per cent of all persons included in the religious-affiliation chart) that slightly better than 8 out of 10 women practice regularly (and another one irregularly), and slightly less than 8 out of 10 men practice regularly (and another one irregularly). American parishes thus far studied give little indication of being beset by Père Daniel's worry about lack of men, though undoubtedly it remains an interesting sociological and psychological problem to explain what difference does exist between male and female religious practice.

The age factor might be similarly analyzed. Fichter finds a gradual dip from 91 per cent Mass attendance among male teenagers to 62 per cent among men in their thirties, then a gradual rise to 83 per cent among men over 60; among the females practice dips from 95 per cent to 75 per cent, then rises to 96 per cent for, respectively, the same age groups.[3] In OLM we find a similar pattern. Regular attendance at Mass dips from 92 per cent in the early teens to 66 per cent among men in their thirties (75 per cent for women), then rises to almost 80 per cent for men over 60 (almost 90 per cent for women). OLM shows not quite the range of variation which Fichter found, but the similarity of pattern lends confirmation likewise to the observation that practice is at its ebb in the thirties.

Father Kelly came to practically the same conclusions about the relation of age and sex to religious practice in Florida.

> For all married people, there is a certain falling off in religious observance between the ages of thirty and thirty-nine. Except for this decline, increasing age generally brings with it a more faithful observance of religious duties. A certain laxity appears for single people, both men and women, between the ages of twenty and twenty-nine.[4]

Again, however, we might strive for balance. Even when the dip in practice is at its sharpest, in the thirties, well over 60 per cent of the men and 70 per cent of the women in OLM Parish remain faithful. Unless a trend showing that these levels represent a stage along a consistent decline is demonstrated, which would of course be sociologically and religiously significant, the

---

[3] *Ibid.*, p. 91.
[4] Kelly, *Catholics and Practice of the Faith*, p. 160.

important sociological fact would seem to be the evidence of positive practice. On the other hand, it must be a pastoral concern to adapt the functioning of the parish system to strengthen its weak spots.

It might be pointed out that in Figure 18, showing OLM Mass attendance by age and sex, the percentage of male irregular attendance, which is usually larger than the per cent of female irregular attendance, tends to close the gap a little between male and female practice when the latter includes both regularity and irregularity.

There is little need to show that observance of the Easter duty by age and sex follows quite the same pattern as does that of Mass attendance. Fichter's table shows it, and it is verified in OLM data. Generally the percentage making their Easter duty is somewhat higher than that for regular Mass attendance and somewhat less than the percentage for combined regular and irregular attendance.[5] Usually, too, those making their Easter duty are those who attend Mass regularly, with the exception of a few of the latter who are separated from Communion because of some difficulty. Some of the irregulars also perform their Easter duty.

The OLM parishioners who answered the questionnaire were requested to state whether they believed that religious practice was least good among people in their thirties, as some studies had shown, and to express an opinion on why they believed it was true.[6] More than 75 (nearly 25 per cent of the respondents) agreed that the thirties comprise the weakest religious group; 40 suggested that the late teens were worse; a few more named the twenties as the lowest in religious practice; about 5 nominated older groups; and a dozen denied that age had any effect. Those who agreed that the religious practice of persons in their

---

[5] See, for example, Figure 20.
[6] Part 4, Question 5, p. 327.

thirties was lowest admitted being puzzled, but offered the following reasons most consistently:

The prevalence of worldly interests, pleasures, and obligations
The age of greatest self-sufficiency, both financial and intellectual,
    resulting in forgetfulness of God's blessings
Birth control, often deriving from economic problems
Age of greatest problems and temptations in sex and business
Belief in a long life ahead of them; desire to have the pleasures of
    youth while they still can

Respondents were also requested to indicate why, in their opinion, studies had shown that women had a better record of religious practice than men.[7] Nearly half of the respondents expressed themselves on the subject, often with penetrating insight. Less than 10 disagreed with the studies, claiming that women's religious practice was not better than men's. In view of the fact that the sex differential in OLM is only 7 per cent, perhaps so simple a black-and-white proposal as the sex factor should not have been included. One respondent, himself a male college graduate, answered:

I don't know, but suggest that a man's ego impels him to try to
    solve his own problems on his own account, whereas woman, as
    helpmate, housewife, and mother, is more keenly aware that
    she needs more powers than she normally possesses.

Quite a few answers conformed with that one. Others offered some expression (often quite sharp) of the following reasons.

More emotionalism in women.
Women are less inhibited.
Women have more to pray for: their family, its future and its pro-
    tection.
Women need religion as the protector of their social position.
Women are closer to their parish.
Need for motherly example.

---

[7] Part 4, Question 6, p. 327.

Women's family obligations, intimacy with young life, responsibility for spiritual formation.

A relief from daily routine at home; religion provides a social outlet.

Women are more humble.

Woman tends to be dependent, man to be self-sufficient.

The double standard for men and women is still in vogue.

Man's work is material, woman's is spiritual.

Women are smarter, hence more religious.

In temptation to sin, men stay away, women go to God.

Men feel more inhibited, believe church is for women and children, fear reputation as sissy if they manifest their religious interest.

Men feel responsible in matters pertaining to sexual sin and birth control.

Men are distracted by more external activities and responsibilities.

Women have more time (mentioned quite frequently).

Converts, checked for fidelity to Mass attendance by sex and length of conversion, show about the same level of practice as all parishioners with minor variations, as indicated in Figure 19. Of OLM's 203 converts (96 men and 107 women) 166 had been Catholics for five years or more, while 37 had been converted within the past four years. About 75 per cent of all converts attend Sunday Mass regularly, which is 4 per cent below the percentage for the entire parish. The record for the men converts is 73 per cent and for the women 77 per cent, 3 and 6 per cent less respectively. Recent male converts have the poorest record; only 64 per cent attend regularly. Approximately 80 per cent of the recent women converts attend Sunday Mass regularly. Both the men and women whose conversion had taken place five years or more before the study was made maintain records of 75 per cent attendance.

Not only are Catholics required to attend Mass on Sundays and holydays of obligation, but they must also receive Communion at least during the Easter time. The faithful Catholic, however, receives Communion more frequently than once a year. As may be seen by referring to Table III in Chapter 6, page 126, most of the adults in OLM Parish (64 per cent) are married, including seven girls who are less than 20 years old. Single persons over 20 account for 23.4 per cent of the parishioners, 11 per cent are widowed, and 1.6 per cent are separated or divorced. The practice of each of these four groups with respect to attendance at Mass, performance of Easter duty, and the reception of Communion is shown in Figure 20.

In general, the single members of the parish have the best record of religious observance, topping even the widowed in all practices except the reception of Holy Communion weekly or more frequently. Thus 85 per cent of the single persons and 83 per cent of the widows and widowers attend Sunday Mass regularly; 89 per cent of the single persons and 87 per cent of the widowed receive Communion during the Easter time; about the same per cent in each group receive Communion monthly; but almost 10 per cent of the widowed and 9 per cent of the single receive Communion weekly, while those who receive more frequently include slightly less than 9 per cent of each group. Altogether, 69 per cent of the widowed and 67 per cent of the single receive Communion at least once a month.

The separated and divorced have the lowest records of religious observance. Some 68 per cent attend Sunday Mass regularly and another 10 per cent irregularly; 64 per cent performed their Easter duty; 45 per cent receive Communion at least once a month, including 11 per cent who receive weekly or more often. Here again a positive view is worth considering: some 65 per cent of OLM's parishioners who are separated and divorced have maintained religious vitality. This group, by the way, is the only one in which a larger percentage attend Sunday Mass regularly than comply with the Easter duty. In all other cases a higher percentage fulfill their Easter duty than attend Sunday Mass regularly.

Of the married parishioners, 71 per cent attend Mass regularly and another 15 per cent attend irregularly; 75 per cent received Communion at Easter; 45 per cent receive Communion at least once a month.[8] Although separate statistics are not reported for men and women according to marital status, OLM practice is quite similar to that found by Father Kelly.

> The women show themselves to be more faithful to all religious obligations than men. The difference between the men and women is greatest in the reception of monthly Communion, which is a voluntary devotion. Large variations occur, also, between the men and women in mixed marriages. The women are not so influenced in a harmful way by the environment of mixed marriages as the men. The single women in all classifications are better than the men.[9]

The number of OLM parishioners in three types of marriages who attend Mass, comply with the Easter duty, and receive Communion frequently is given in Table XV, page 224.[10] The table reveals that the religious practices of those persons whose marriage was originally both Catholic and valid—actually 87 per cent of all married persons in the parish—is not noticeably higher than those of all married persons: 74 per cent in Catholic marriages attend Mass regularly and 14 per cent irregularly; 79 per cent performed their Easter duty; and 52 per cent receive Communion at least once a month.

Although allowance must be made for the relative smallness of the population, one tentative conclusion to be drawn from the

---

[8] Catholics know that persons living in a state of unforgiven serious sin may not receive the sacrament of Eucharistic Communion. Thus Catholics living otherwise apparently good lives, but continuing without repentance one seriously sinful practice, have no right to go to Communion. Two not infrequent examples are the sins of artificial birth control and living in an invalid marriage.

[9] Kelly, *Catholics and Practice of the Faith*, p. 160.

[10] The classification in Table XV is the same as that used in Table IV, Chapter 6. "Catholic marriages" are those in which both parties were Catholics at the time of the marriage, even though one or both may have been a convert to the Catholic faith. The term "convert marriage" refers only to those in which one (or both) of the parties was converted after the ceremony. Thus a convert marriage may originally have been a mixed marriage (one of the parties was a non-Catholic). If one of two non-Catholic partners is converted after marriage, the marriage is classified as a mixed rather than a convert marriage.

table is that the percentage of OLM Catholics in valid mixed marriages who receive Communion monthly (52 per cent) and make their Easter Communion (76 per cent) is about the same as that of persons in fully Catholic marriages, though there is a falling off in Sunday Mass attendance (63 per cent regular and

TABLE XV

Religious Observance of 3,686 Parishioners by
Types of Marriages

Type of Marriage	Number of Catholics	Sunday Mass Attendance Regular	Irregular	Easter Duty	Monthly Communion
Catholic					
Valid	3,204	2,365	436	2,542	1,653
Validated	52	30	9	32	18
Invalid	128	40	19	——	——
Convert					
Valid	136	100	17	103	61
Validated	10	6	2	105	63
Invalid	4	1	——	——	——
Mixed					
Valid	102	63	20	77	53
Validated	16	6	5	10	6
Invalid	34	11	6	——	——
Totals					
Valid	3,442	2,528	473	2,722	1,767
Validated	78	42	16	47	27
Invalid	166	52	25	——	——

20 per cent irregular). This corroborates the tentative conclusion of Fathers Kelly and Thomas from their data that the danger of leakage from the faith comes not so much from mixed marriages in themselves as from mixed and invalid marriages outside the Church. This would have to be further studied, however, for the vitality of Catholic life cannot be judged only by these few criteria, important though they are.

An interesting revelation in Table XV is that 77 out of 166 persons involved in invalid marriages nevertheless attend Mass either regularly or irregularly. This indicates the partial functioning of the parish system even for some of its members for whom it cannot function fully. It also suggests the continuation of these persons' religious values, which could lead to full reconciliation. The parish census brings the identity of such persons to the notice of the pastoral staff, and the latter are often able to seek for a suitable occasion to make the first move. OLM's census was productive of such pastoral assistance in several cases.

The table reveals something more obvious: the number of homes in the parish for which the parish system is functioning either adequately or partially, as well as those parishioners for whom its functioning is apparently without meaning. The former manifest the existence and effectiveness of the system; the latter represent the parish system's lack of completeness in terms of its own goal, the sanctification of each member of the flock. This consideration is a standing reminder to the parish not only of work still to be done but also of the need for fashioning apostolic policy accordingly. Which of the flock are missing? What kind of people are they? What are their circumstances? If there are so many and the priest cannot do it all, or at least in the first instance, how prepare parish lay apostles to act? That is the value of the foregoing and following tables, as well as so many others which could be constructed from both census and questionnaire data.

Just over 600 OLM parishioners are the children of either mixed marriages or non-Catholic marriages. Over 450 have a non-Catholic father or mother; that is, only one parent is a Catholic. About three fourths of the converts in the parish have two non-Catholic parents; the remaining one fourth of the converts have one lapsed Catholic parent. Figure 21 indicates the religious observance of all parishioners who have a non-Catholic parent or parents. These figures are further subdivided to show the practices of parishioners with two non-Catholic parents, with a non-Catholic mother, and with a non-Catholic father respectively. Both children between the ages of 7 and 20 years and adults are included in these categories. For purposes of comparison all parishioners over 7 are also included.

Of all parishioners over 7 almost 80 per cent attend Sunday Mass regularly and the percentage is increased to 89 when those who attend irregularly are included; 83 per cent made their Easter duty; and 61 per cent receive Communion at least monthly (14 per cent receive once a week and another 9 per cent even more frequently). The average practice of the 615 children of non-Catholic parents is lower. About 66 per cent attend Mass regularly and another 14 per cent attend irregularly; almost 70 per cent satisfied Easter-duty requirements; and a little over 47 per cent receive Communion at least once a month. Parishioners with two non-Catholic parents have almost the same average practice as all converts (Figure 19), of which they are the major portion. Those of mixed parentage have a much lower average, though not much difference separates persons with non-Catholic mothers from those with non-Catholic fathers. The children of Catholic mothers have a better record of regular Mass attendance and reception of Communion than the children of Catholic fathers, but they trail in performance of their Easter duty and in irregular Mass attendance. It would be interesting to ascertain what percentage were children of invalid marriages, for we recall that one fourth of OLM's mixed marriages are invalid (Table XV). Actually, over 65 per cent of the children of mixed marriages satisfy both Easter-duty and Mass-attendance requirements, while over 40 per cent receive Holy Communion at least monthly, as shown in Figure 21. Here again wisdom in analyzing data is called for. Since their average is less than the parish's, one might too quickly draw conclusions concerning the extent of the harmfulness of mixed marriages. Yet over 65 per cent of the children born of such marriages have been brought up to practice their religion, to function as parts of the parish system. In Chapter 14 the thinking of OLM parishioners concerning mixed marriages is discussed within the context of parishioner response to parish values.

An indication of the effect of Catholic education on religious practice is seen in Figure 22. Though 89 per cent of all parishioners attend Mass at least irregularly (79 per cent regularly), 83 per cent perform their Easter duty, and 61 per cent receive Holy Communion at least monthly, those with a Catholic education have higher rates. The figure shows the religious practices of parishioners with elementary, secondary, some college, and complete college training in Catholic schools. The religious-observance rates of those with Catholic college training might be compared with those of all college-trained parishioners (Figure 23). Of particular noteworthiness is the high percentage (approximately 80 per cent) of Catholic-college-trained parishioners who receive Communion at least monthly.

Figure 23, showing religious practice according to educational backgrounds, reveals few significant variations for Mass attendance or Easter duty. Those without any schooling and the college educated are below and above average, respectively, by several points. This slight trend toward better practice in accordance with educational attainment is more pronounced in the reception of Holy Communion. Over 65 per cent of the college educated receive at least monthly and almost 20 per cent weekly or better. In general, it might be observed that the unfortunate record shown by several European studies, that the less educated were among the masses separated from the Church, is not reflected here; nor was it reflected in other American studies, though the better educated do show a slight superiority in religious practice.

We saw in Chapter 6 that not quite 20 per cent of OLM's parishioners are foreign born or Puerto Rican. When returns of those persons living outside the parish but attending OLM are included, the total number of parishioners born outside the continental United States is 1,717, almost half of whom are of Irish origin. Figure 24 shows the religious practices of this group. The fidelity of the Irish born is clearly indicated; their averages for Mass attendance, the performance of the Easter duty, and the reception of Communion monthly or more frequently are not only much higher than the averages of all foreign born, but of the entire parish. Those of Italian and Puerto Rican origin have much lower percentages, and all the other foreign born are slightly lower than the Irish and total parish averages.

The figure's steplike representation of Irish, Italian, and Puerto Rican religious observance suggests a few observations. If descendants of the Irish born have not quite the record of their forebears, Italian descendants have been improving on the heritage left them. Both would seem to have been affected by the impact of American culture on Catholic life, the Irish being distracted from their parents' high record and the Italians being gradually drawn into full participation. And just as the Italians have been moving upward in the steps of the Irish, so now the Puerto Ricans are making their start. Many Irish and later the Italians were disorganized during the beginning of their stay in a new country. With acculturation came organization and renewed participation in Catholic life. The Puerto Ricans are undergoing the stress of disorganization now, but there are definite signs that their acculturation will be neither so long nor so painful as was that of the other migrants to New York. Two small recent studies (unpublished) showed that in some Puerto Rican groups in New York religious practice was better than in Puerto Rico, and the men actually were leading the women in their observance.[11] OLM's Puerto Ricans are not numerous, and half of them are such transients that the parish cannot do too much lasting good for them. But the parish's Legion units have

---

[11] These unpublished studies were made by students at Fordham University and Loyola Seminary.

effectively opened the door to genuine parish membership for several of the groups.

Rental value of the home can be one factor in determining socioeconomic status. The relationship between this measure and the religious practices of the heads of households is shown in Figure 25. It will be seen that the average practice of those who pay less than $60 per month in rent (over two thirds of the parish) is less than the parish average for Mass attendance and Easter duty, but practically the same in the frequency of reception of Communion. On the other hand, those in the three upper rental categories have higher percentages of practice, although only the top rental group has a significantly better Communion record. It will be observed also that the heads of households who pay from $80 to $99 per month rent have the lowest Communion index. Once again it must be recalled that the Puerto Ricans live almost exclusively in the lower-cost homes and that their religious practice is affected by their disorganized condition. If this group were disregarded, it is doubtful that economic differentiation would have much significance as far as participation in OLM's religious life in concerned.

Another difference between the results of many European studies and our own is evidenced in the religious observance of those who are gainfully employed. Figure 26 shows the relationship between religious practices and the socioeconomic factors of employment and type of occupation. Almost 3,350 of OLM's Catholics are employed; 165 are unemployed and looking for work; 232 are retired; and 117 are in military service. A slight decline in average practice from that of all parishioners derives from the elimination of young persons from the occupational chart. Actually, the decline is quite minimal; 76 per cent of the employed attend Mass regularly; slightly over 80 per cent performed their Easter duty; and 54 per cent receive Communion once a month or more frequently (for all parishioners: over 79 per cent regular attendance at Mass, 83 per cent fulfillment of Easter duty, and 53 per cent reception of Communion at least monthly). The important point is that, with the exception of skilled craftsmen, 70 per cent in all the occupational groups made their Easter duty and that all except three groups —operatives, craftsmen, and unskilled workers—maintain at least 70 per cent regular Mass attendance. In the frequent reception of Holy Communion the percentages vary from 40 for skilled craftsmen to 62 for clerical workers. The unemployed, retired, and those in military service follow similar patterns. The unemployed are slightly below the employed in all three measures of religious practice, and the retired have better records than the employed. The parishioners in military service are above the average of the employed in Mass attendance and the performance of their Easter duty, but below in frequent reception of Communion.

Here again we find that for the employed in many occupational groups the functioning of the parish is meaningful. If the index of participation is derived from Mass attendance and performance of one's Easter duty, an average of 80 per cent participate in that functioning; in no occupational groups do less than 70 per cent participate. While it can be worthwhile to look into those groups whose participation is least strong, there is no group which is not strongly represented in parish life, in whose ideals and values those of the parish are not in some way included and integrated. This fact is clearly at variance with the results of several European studies.

A similar conclusion could be drawn from most of the comparative analyses made in this chapter. In terms of parish policy their result is rather negative; namely, that no special program need be developed for any uniform group. On the other hand, the sociologist of religion is positively interested in this evidence that American parish vitality cuts across various class and group lines, unlike the situation that exists in other parts of the world. The pastor, too, can draw some practical value from these evidently unalarming analyses. For example, contrary to the often-heard expression that "converts make the best Catholics," OLM's converts are not quite up to the parish average in religious observance. Conceivably a pastoral program might be directed specifically at that one group of deficient converts, whose shared experiences might well make them susceptible to a common approach. Likewise the Catholic college graduates, whose obligatory and voluntary religious observance is higher than average, might well be approached as prospective auxiliaries in the more thought-requiring aspects of the lay apostolate. Parents in their thirties, who manifest a dip in religious practice, might well be the object of special pastoral regard. Thus the parish might promote days of recollection, Cana Conferences, or something similar specifically for the parents of children just entering school, or preparing to receive Communion or confirmation, or about to graduate.

The point is that knowledge of parish uniformities can be the basis for planning and implementing pastoral policy directed specifically toward meeting their needs.

CHAPTER XII

Motives
in Eucharistic Devotion

T hus far in our study of OLM Parish, in the heart of New York's populous Bronx County, we have seen something of its basic purposes, the organization of its elements into a functioning social system, and various aspects of its spiritual life. Socioreligious studies must, however, go farther than observable conduct, for the peculiarly human characteristics of conduct derive from the motives behind it. Why do persons performing the same religious rituals, for example, go on to achieve opposite types of conduct, one of which might involve the very rejection of his assumed religious principles?

In Chapters 7 and 9 an analysis was made of the functioning of OLM Parish in the services it afforded. But the mere provision of service does not give evidence of a functioning social system; the use of that service through purposeful cooperation on the part of those for whom it was intended is likewise necessary. Chapters 10 and 11 offered evidence that OLM parishioners do respond to the provision of religious services. The heart of OLM's spiritual life is, of course, the parish church, where the parishioners carry out their religious observance. Those who perform only the required religious exercise spend approximately four hours a month in OLM church—nearly one hour each Sunday.

In terms of human values, however, mere external provision and use of service need imply merely minimal achievement of the objectives of a social system. Once the human being has reached a degree of mature intelligence, his internal convictions and values should conform with his external behavior. The properly coordinated society of intelligent men is one in which the norms and values of the members are those of the society.

Many writers, including Father Fichter,[1] have emphasized the need to study values in order to explain socioreligious conduct. One critic claims that, in the midst of "pervasive secularism and mounting religiosity . . . the religion which actually prevails among Americans today has lost much of its authentic Christian (or Jewish) content" and that the "religiousness characteristic of America today is very often a religiousness without religion . . . a way of sociability or 'belonging' rather than a way of reorienting life toward God."[2] This chapter will therefore study values—those good things which motivate conduct. We will assess briefly the Eucharistic devotions of OLM's members and the motives which inspire those devotions.

In these matters it is necessary to ask people why they do what they do. Is it merely out of habit, because of social pressure, or for any other natural reason that people attend Mass, receive Communion, and visit the Blessed Sacrament? In some instances their motives may be natural; and it could be that this is the case more often than they themselves suspect. But while it is sometimes extremely difficult to identify and establish motives, even one's own, still the individual's testimony remains the best first evidence of the motive for his actions unless the contrary can be firmly established.

---

[1] Fichter, *Urban Parish,* pp. 2-3. See also Joseph B. Schuyler, "Religious Behavior in Northern Parish: A Study in Motivating Values," *American Catholic Sociological Review* 19:134-44, June 1958.

[2] Will Herberg, *Protestant-Catholic-Jew,* pp. 14-15, 276. New York: Doubleday and Company, 1955.

The questionnaire that was answered by 293 OLM parishioners requested the respondents to indicate their motive for
attending Sunday Mass regularly; for receiving Holy Communion more than once a year as required by church law; and, since
confession is so closely related to Communion, why they went

TABLE XVI

Motives of OLM Parishioners for Attending Sunday Mass

Motive	Number
Required under pain of mortal sin	98
Desire to join in the Lord's sacrifice	185
Out of habit	25
Because people I know go	4
Other reasons	7
I don't go regularly	11

to confession oftener than required.[3] Each question was both
structured (reminding the respondent of several probable
choices) and open end (leaving him free to express himself in
other ways).

As indicated in Table XVI, the overwhelming reason for attending Mass was the importance of the Mass—or as expressed
in the questionnaire, the desire to join in the Lord's sacrifice.
The significant second choice was the fact that Sunday observance is required under pain of mortal sin. Both are spiritual
motives and are, of course, included in the church and parish
roster of values. The former is more positive and the second
rather negative, but both evidence the vitality of these motives
in the functioning of OLM Parish. Since several respondents
listed more than one motive, the total in Table XVI is greater
than the number of respondents.

Believing that possible self-deception might be uncovered or
that honest self-analysis might be confirmed through an estimate

---

[3] Part 2, Questions 8, 10, 11, p. 321.

of the motives of others, the questionnaire also asked respondents to check the reasons why fellow Catholics whom they knew went to Mass.[4] Honestly enough, many said that they did not know; the reasons attributed to others most frequently are listed in Table XVII.[5] Though respondents mentioned natural motiva-

TABLE XVII

Motives Attributed to Others for Attending Sunday Mass

Motive	Number
Necessity	75
Importance of the Mass	110
Out of habit	45
Because people they know go	11

tion a little more frequently for others than they admitted in themselves, the importance of the Mass and the obligation of attending under pain of mortal sin remained the most frequently mentioned choices. It is interesting to note that, whereas only 25 listed habit as the reason for their own attendance at Mass, 45 listed it as the motive of others. Conceivably the second estimate is closer to the truth. No one, however, can gainsay the significance of the preponderant frequency with which the first two motives were mentioned. Nor should we overlook the fact that all religious training has as one aim to make habitual the performance of virtuous actions. Attending Mass "out of habit" does not necessarily exclude the higher motives.

The percentage of OLM parishioners receiving Communion monthly, weekly, and oftener has been shown in Chapter 11.[6] In

---

[4] Part 2, Question 8, p. 321. In the tables the motives are listed in the order in which they appear in the questionnaire.

[5] "Necessity" and "Importance of the Mass" in Table XVII are analogous to "Required under pain of mortal sin" and "Desire to join in the Lord's sacrifice" in Table XVI.

[6] See Figure 23.

addition, we have data on the approximate number of Communions distributed each month in the year 1954. The data were supplied by the Ursuline sister who filled the monthly order for hosts. In order to receive Holy Communion a person must be free from serious sin and that he must be fasting.[7] Hence these Communions imply a conscious effort to live within the framework of the Church's moral law, as well as personal devotion and sacrifice. The average number of Communions distributed each month was 17,917. The orders for the individual months were: January, 21,000; February, 17,000; March, 21,250; April, 19,500; May, 17,250; June, 17,000; July, 11,500; August, 14,500; September, 21,000; October, 21,000; November, 15,500; December, 18,500. It will be noted that the month-to-month pattern resembles quite closely the pattern of Mass attendance, which drops considerably during the summer months.[8] We have already seen that over 60 per cent of the parishioners receive Holy Communion at least once a month and that 20 per cent of the parish receive every week or oftener. OLM will not be satisfied until the percentage of monthly and weekly communicants approaches the 100 per cent mark.

The questionnaire asked respondents to check reasons for receiving Holy Communion frequently and also their motives for going to confession often.[9] Responses are shown in Table XVIII. Again the evidence points to the fact that the highest values in the church and parish system of values are those which motivate the OLM parishioners in their reception of these two sacraments: to be more intimately united with God and because the sacrament increases God's grace. In listing motives in the questionnaire the ideal response was not always in the same or in first position. Thus the ideal answer for motives in receiving

---

[7] The mitigated fast of three hours from solid food and one hour from liquids was not in effect when the study was made.

[8] See Figure 17.

[9] Part 2, Questions 10 and 11, p. 321.

Communion, although in fourth position, nevertheless received the most votes. Holy Communion (and confession) provides the means of achieving those values for which OLM and every Catholic parish exist.

Catholics believe firmly that Christ abides, in sacramental form, in the tabernacle on their altars. The Blessed Sacrament

TABLE XVIII

Motives for Frequent Communion and Confession

Motives	Number
For Communion:	
As a sign of Catholic living	28
To ask favors of God	38
Because it increases grace	84
To be more intimately united with God	115
Other motives	10
For Confession:	
To receive absolution	58
To receive an increase of grace through the sacrament	91
To ask priestly advice	41
To keep a check on oneself	48
Out of habit	9
Other motives	11

is Christ the Lord really present. Some persons in the religious state dedicate their entire lives to personal and collective adoration of the Blessed Sacrament. Practically every Catholic church is open all day so that members can use it for their own quiet prayer and worship. The author does not remember any time, whether morning, noon, afternoon, or evening, when he visited OLM church without finding worshipers present. Regularly during the year OLM conducts various pious services for those who wish to participate. The Novena of Holy Hours, made in both adoration of and reparation to our Lord for one's own sins and those of the world, is attended regularly by almost 200 parishioners. Approximately 400 persons join in the regular weekly

devotions in honor of our Lady's miraculous medal, while somewhat fewer are present for night prayers on Sunday evenings.
Close to 700 persons attend the daily services during the novenas in preparation for the feasts of the Sacred Heart in June
and of the Immaculate Conception in December.

Throughout the entire night between the First Saturday and
the following Sunday of each month from 800 to 1,000 adult
males can be observed entering the church in OLM Parish. After
spending an hour at religious exercises they emerge again into
the night and return home. These are members of the Bronx
Nocturnal Adoration Society, which consists of lay membership
and exists to promote devotion to the Blessed Sacrament, particularly at night when otherwise there would be little adoration,
and to develop a spirit of reparation.

In the United States there are some 50,000 members of the
Nocturnal Adoration Society in about 350 parish centers. The
members adore the Blessed Sacrament enthroned upon the altar
throughout one night each month. Each member agrees to
"watch" one full hour, so that one team is present for each hour
of the night. Membership involves inconvenience and sacrifice,
for obviously an hour spent in prayer from midnight to one
o'clock or from three to four o'clock in the wee hours of a winter
morning, not to mention the time spent and the discomfort un-
dergone in getting to church, is hardly the sort of pastime that
most men freely choose. Participation is completely voluntary;
it involves no sanctions and imposes no obligations. In the ob-
scurity of the night their worship attracts no attention and can
win no human plaudits.

The Bronx Nocturnal Adoration Society is not, strictly
speaking, a parish organization. OLM Parish organized the society some twenty-five years ago and it continues to function in
the parish, even though other parishes have begun to form their
own groups. About one tenth of the 1,100 actively participating
members are OLM parishioners. The worship of these men

manifests the fruitful functioning of OLM at, perhaps, its spiritual highest. Of all OLM's societies the Nocturnal Adoration Society might be designated the most exclusively spiritual. What the members do, though done together, is purely spiritual; the religious exercises take place at night, when no men observe or honor its members. In addition, the Bronx society organizes the annual procession of the Blessed Sacrament which takes place near the Feast of Corpus Christi.

Without warning, the nearly 800 men present on one of the First Saturdays were given copies of a special questionnaire.[10] Few interrupted their prayers to answer that night, but over 140, 18 per cent of those who received copies of the questionnaire and 13 per cent of the entire membership, went to the trouble of taking it home, answering it anonymously, finding a stamp and envelope, and returning it to the author by mail.

There were three factual questions: age, length of membership, and parish. In addition, the men were asked to say why they joined or remained members of the society. Data about the age and the number of years in the society are given in Table XIX, page 240. The 141 men who returned the questionnaire came from 38 different parishes, about 28 of them from OLM. Four parishes had 10 or more members and there were fifteen parishes that had only one representative. The average age of the members was 54 and the average number of years in the society was 12.

The motives for belonging to the society listed by the men are revealing, particularly because of the nonmaterial nature of the organization's values and purposes and the anonymity of the respondents. A total of 220 motives were listed, and there were 70 different but often allied motives in the 220. Upon analyzing the personally expressed motives it was found that they could be separated into the following categories: "giving to God" (ex-

---

[10] See Appendix II, p. 316, for the complete questionnaire.

amples: adoration, reparation, thanksgiving), 70 per cent of the replies; "giving to the Church" (examples: helping Catholic action through good example, joining in the common prayer of the Church, praying for vocations, the companionship of inspiring and devoted men, the attractiveness of this type of spiritual service and ritual), 15 per cent; and "getting something from the group" (examples: doing something of spiritual value together, contributing to the effectiveness of a satisfying spiritual

TABLE XIX

Age of Members of Nocturnal Adoration Society and
Length of Membership

Age	Number	Years in Society	Number
18-29 years	7	3 years or less	27
30-39 years	12	4-10 years	40
40-49 years	27	11-20 years	50
50-59 years	51	21 years and more	24
60-69 years	27		
70-79 years	15		
80-89 years	2		

organization), 5 per cent. In addition, there were a few unclassified motives, including the memory of a deceased relative or friend, the need to belong to some society, and so forth.

Some of the answers expressed more frequently were:

Love, adoration, honor, and thanksgiving to the Blessed Sacrament; realization of the real presence of the Eucharistic King
Reparation for the world's sins against God and reparation for one's own sins
Thanks for blessings received
An answer to Christ's words, "Could you not watch one hour with Me?" and "Come . . . and rest awhile."
Spiritual benefits and uplift; personal sanctification
To pay adoration owed to God
Opportunity for making some sacrifice of time and comfort
Prayer for others: the work, the departed, vocations

Peace of mind

Doing good for oneself and God

Common effort in purposeful prayer

The spiritual nature of the society, the way it is run, and the efficiency of the director

In memory of a deceased son or other relative

The example of one's father or friend

Liking for an hour spent with Christ

Two conclusions that might very probably be drawn from the statistics of the Nocturnal Adoration Society and the expressions of the members' motives are: first, as far as general condition of life is concerned, its members are rather average adult men; second, these men find in a service provided by the parish the opportunity to achieve certain spiritual purposes and values which are as real to them as they are unconsidered by persons outside the parish system. As expressed by a colleague to the author, such a group of men and the satisfaction of their spiritual interests by the parish comprise in themselves sufficient reason for recognizing in the parish an effectively functioning system. The emphasis on spiritual and exclusively religious motives indicates that members of this society do not contribute to the secularism in religion of which Herberg speaks.

Whereas Nocturnal Adoration societies are found in only a minority of parishes, every parish has a group similar to the Altar Servers Society in OLM Parish. In the early morning hours youngsters between the ages of ten and fifteen can be seen trudging along quiet, perhaps still darkened, streets to the parish church. After assisting the priest at Mass they return home for breakfast just as their age mates are rolling out of bed. What is the motive behind this unusual behavior? Their duties, voluntarily undertaken, often involve a quite generous commitment of time, for which play, sleep, and other interests in a youngster's life are usual competitors. Altar boys frequently go to bed earlier and almost always rise an hour earlier when they serve Mass, as our study and other experience show.

Often enough parish altar boys are drafted from among willing or volunteer lads in the higher grades of grammar school. The system has several advantages: the availability of the boys, their interest, the example of their older schoolmates, the encouragement of the teaching sisters, the opportunity to develop the youngsters' interest in matters religious and priestly, and so forth. Frequently other grammar-school pupils take the places of those who graduate from the parochial school. OLM Parish, however, also has a unit for older boys, for it is anxious to capitalize on the veteran altar servers' experience and interest, particularly in the middle and late teens when association with priest and altar can be more influential. The altar boys number about 50; 35, with an average age of 13, are in grammar school; 15, ranging in age from 14 to 20 years, belong to the Senior Altar Servers Society. Recruited to serve the priest in his liturgical functions, especially at Mass, the acolytes usually receive weekly assignments for serving daily Mass and irregular assignments for funerals, wedding services, and other devotions. The older boys receive from the priest moderator post cards which inform them of their new assignments. The society meets for a social occasion several times a year.

Since the Mass is the central liturgical function of the parish, it seems proper that the priest's assistants should be those who are most intelligently aware of what they are doing. In earlier centuries it was always so, for ordained acolytes served on the altars. A cultural development led to the use of smaller boys, and this has led to the widespread assumption that the altar server's role is most fit for schoolboys. While the youngest lads do well enough, the role seems to be especially suited to adults, even to fathers of families. Military chaplains know that men in service vie for the privilege of serving Mass, and a few parishes have adult men as altar servers. The dignity of the liturgy is frequently enhanced thereby, as the author's present parishioners and others have experienced.

The questionnaire constructed for the altar boys was answered by 25 members of the Junior Altar Servers Society and 14 of the senior group, almost 80 per cent of all the altar servers in the parish. Information was sought regarding the age, schooling, time of retiring and arising when serving early Mass, reception of Holy Communion at Masses served, attendance at Mass when not serving, motives (seven suggested with space for additional reasons), whether serving has helped in the understanding of the Mass, ability to use a Missal, knowledge of Latin in the responses, and benefits received (none suggested).

The juniors who answered the questionnaire were all pupils in the parish school and ranged in age from 12 to 14 years. Half of them stated that they go to bed an average of one half to three quarters of an hour earlier than usual when they have an assignment to serve Mass. All rise about three quarters of an hour earlier when they serve Mass. All usually receive Communion at the Mass they serve, and all but one make it a practice to assist at Mass oftener than they actually serve—some assist every day, others a couple of times a week, and a number an extra day or two in Lent and Advent. Of the 25 respondents, 21 checked as their major motive "serving brings one very close to Christ and the Mass" and 3 that they both "liked to serve and it was a good thing to do"; 2 checked the statement that they liked to serve; 2 checked the influence of parents or priests. Two boys suggested other motives: "It's an honor to serve Mass" was listed as a chief motive; a desire to join some activity as a secondary motive.

The boys in the senior group ranged from 14 to 20 years old, with an average age of 16, and all of the 14 respondents were graduates of the parish school. One now attends a Catholic college, 1 works (2 others work part time), 10 attend a Catholic high school, and 2 are in a non-Catholic high school. Half of these respondents go to bed about an hour earlier than usual when assigned to serve Mass, unless it happens to be a late Sunday Mass; all rise an average of one hour earlier than they otherwise would. All receive Communion when they serve; 10 attend Mass voluntarily oftener than they serve—daily, periodically, or occasionally. The chief motive checked by 8 respondents is closeness to Christ and the Mass; by 3 respondents because they like to do it; by 2 both because they like to do it and because it's a good thing; and 1 because of parental influence. Checked as auxiliary motives were: liking for Mass serving, 6; priestly influence, 2; closeness to Christ and the Mass, 3; might as well serve, 1.

Thus the motives of both younger and older boys are almost universally quite spiritual. Clearly these youngsters find that the parish provides them with the opportunity to discover and achieve values important in their lives. Their sacrifice of time and sleep indicates the importance of those values. Since the participation of the older lads is more evidently and completely voluntary, it is a further indication of the effective functioning of the parish system.

All of the seniors and all but one of the juniors claimed that serving Mass helps them to understand the Mass better than their nonserving comrades; 11 of the seniors and 21 of the juniors claimed that they know how to use the Missal quite well, and the others are able to use it a little; about 40 per cent of both groups checked the response that they understand the meaning of the Latin used by the priest and themselves at Mass, another 40 per cent do not understand, and the remaining have some understanding. Such responses imply a large amount of cooperative interaction between the priests and servers (and sometimes between parents or school sisters and servers) for the achievement of a parish purpose and a deepening of social relationships. All the respondents numbered friends among their fellow altar servers. However, only 5 seniors and 18 juniors believed that friendship was strengthened through mutual membership, 9 seniors and 2 juniors were uncertain, and 5 juniors denied that friendships were strengthened. It might be suggested that, although the boys were not aware of it, their activity as altar servers provides them with both role and status in the parish and among their friends, and it increases the occasions of interaction among the servers.

The respondents were also asked if they were acquainted with any former Mass servers and whether they knew why they served no longer. Over half the respondents knew former altar servers. Although many did not know why the former servers were no longer active, the following reasons were suggested as possible: unavailability of time while going to high school, laziness or dislike for early rising, the belief that Mass serving is "for grammar-school kids" or "sissyish," lack of interest.

The benefits which the altar servers derive from their service are further illustrative of parish values that are recognized and achieved. The first two benefits in the following list were mentioned most frequently.

> The happiness of being closer to Christ on the altar or in the Blessed Sacrament
> The joy of serving Christ
> Closer contact with the priests
> Occasional monetary tips when serving at nuptials and funerals
> Better appreciation of the Mass ("so that it is not boring even when I am not serving")
> Pleasure of exercising a privilege
> Closer association with Christ
> More intimate participation in the Mass
> More grace and merit

Half of the respondents had no suggestions about serving Mass or membership in the Altar Servers Society. Those which were made included:

> Care of own cassock and surplice by each boy
> More reverent movements; hands always folded
> Raising the age limit for membership to ten years (refers to beginners, long before they actually serve Mass)

A few specific ceremonial corrections (minor)
Little boys should not serve Mass (suggestion of a 13-year-old)
Two new boys should not serve together
More neatness and attention
More appointments for seniors
Stricter standards

Although more could be written about OLM's altar servers, enough has been said to show their role in the parish operation, the benefits they derive from participation in the parish's most sacred operation, and the use they make of parish services. A similar study could have been made of the parish choir, which is composed of both student and adult parishioners and directed by a devoted layman subject to the pastor. It was felt, however, that such a study would yield data rather similar to those found in the study of altar servers, and probably to a less degree.

The members of the Holy Name Society and the Altar-Rosary Society, both dedicated to spiritual purposes, responded to a questionnaire that was common to a number of societies. Discussion of the results of this questionnaire will be taken up in the following chapter.

CHAPTER XIII

The Parish Societies

Particitation of members in the full life of the parish almost always presupposes the existence of those organized sub-groupings which are called parish societies. In Chapter 3 an ideal parish is defined as one in which "there exists the practical and exploited opportunity for the spiritual and derivatively temporal richness of the faith to be brought to its every actual and potential member and to every institution of its coextensive civic community." This calls for both pastoral holiness and managerial astuteness of high order, particularly when the typical American Catholic parish rubs elbows daily with a secular environment. Moreover, the parish contains its own share of the millions of born Catholics who no longer profess the faith, as well as many whose practice of the faith is negligible at best. It must be clear, as popes have insisted, that the work of the parish requires a great measure of help from the laity.

How do parish societies fit into this picture? One might expect their role to be almost essential in terms of helping their members grow in knowledge and practice of the faith, in the strength of Catholic spiritual and social fellowship, and in the charitable apostolate of building the parish, spreading the faith, and Christianizing the community. Indeed they have contributed immeasurably to all the wonderful achievements of the Church in our country. In both parish sociology and pastoral policy it is emphasized that one of the most important elements must be a careful analysis of parish societies in terms of parish effectiveness. How many societies are there? How much do they cost in terms of time and man power? How much can and do they contribute to parish vitality and growth? The brief study of OLM societies made in this chapter can only serve as the beginning of such an assessment.

One objective of the analysis of the parish social system is to learn whether parish management has realized a proportionately high return on its investment of priest power and time spent on these societies. The parish organizational chart, Figure 16, indicates that both the pastor and his assistants, no doubt at the cost of considerable time, serve as moderators of the various societies and organizations in the parish. One of the first steps is to determine to what degree OLM parishioners join in the activities of these subbodies.

Approximate membership in the various societies, as shown by the official roster of each organization, is as follows: Holy Name Society, nearly 400; Altar-Rosary Society, nearly 250; Catholic Charities Club, about 150; Our Lady's Sodality (two units), about 100; Legion of Mary (two units), about 50; St. Vincent de Paul Society and Auxiliary, nearly 75; League of the Sacred Heart (promoters of the Apostleship of Prayer), nearly 75; Ushers Society, about 40; Christian Family Movement, 12 couples (24 individuals). Enrollments in the Nocturnal Adoration Society and the Altar Servers Society were given in the preceding chapter dealing with devotion to Christ in the Eucharist.

In actual participation in society activities, however, the members are fewer than those given here, at least in many instances. About one tenth of the members of the Holy Name and the Altar-Rosary societies attend monthly meetings, for example, although many more join the respective societies in their monthly corporate Communion and in their social affairs. It has been estimated that 600 parishioners actively participate in the various spiritual organizations and thus utilize the services offered by the parish in maintaining these societies. They represent somewhat less than 10 per cent of the parishioners who would qualify for membership, the very young being excluded. The members of most of the organizations average less than three or four hours a month spent in the society's activity, mostly in attending a meeting and/or religious service. Exceptions are about a dozen ladies in the Altar-Rosary Society who contribute as much as twenty or thirty hours a month working in the sacristy and sanctuary, all the members of the Legion of Mary units, several members of the St. Vincent de Paul Society, the ushers, and officers of all the societies.

Can any conclusions be drawn concerning parish organizations from the fact that only 10 per cent of the parishioners participate? A former curate at OLM strongly advised that attention be given to the disproportion between the relatively few members in parish societies and a curate's expenditure of time and effort in running these societies. If some 90 per cent of the parish has little or nothing to do with the parish societies and if those societies take up so much of the moderators' time, how, institutionally speaking, are the priests to get to the rest of the parish? OLM's situation is not peculiar, but rather typical of many if not of the great majority of parishes. It seems, in fact, to be in a better position than many parishes in the vigorous and successful functioning of a number of its groups: the Nocturnal Adoration Society, the Legion of Mary, the Christian Family Movement groups, and the Cub Scouts (a youth organization).

A special view of the Legion of Mary will illustrate the effectiveness of this parish organization. At the time this study was made there were two units of the Legion and a third has since been established. Its members average over twenty hours each month in society work, and it is really work too. Every week each team of two receives an assignment, which may be to check on census reports, to visit lapsed families or welcome new ones, to instruct prospective converts, or to teach catechism. The assignments require at least two hours, usually more. All of the senior members are working people or college students, yet all spend at least four hours each week, including the weekly meeting, in active parish work. There are additional spiritual activities and an occasional social gathering, both of which tend to implant the Legion and its work strongly in their daily living and system of values and to establish them in a spiritually and apostolically satisfying parish role. The author joined in their meetings and work often during the parish study and was consistently impressed by their participation in parish life, its meaning to them, and the help which their activity was to the priests' own apostolic work. The Acies, their annual ceremony of rededication and consecration to our Lady in conjunction with all Legion units of the Bronx, was an inspiring occasion and one which must have impressed the members with a renewed spirit of common apostolic purpose and personal service.

Brief explanation was given in previous chapters of the spiritual and temporal services offered by several of the parish societies: stimulus to increased and corporate religious practice, social fellowship bound with religious communion, and the opportunity to join in the work and apostolate of the parish. Why, then, are there not more members? The opportunity is available to all to join and participate, and the parish makes it known often that all are invited. In the general questionnaire that was answered by 293 parishioners the respondent was asked whether he was a member of the Holy Name Society if a man or the Altar-Rosary Society if a woman[1]—the two organizations to which it is desired that all adult men and women parishioners belong. Those who were not members were asked to explain why. Many young parents expressed themselves as being regret-

---

[1] Part 3, Question 8, p. 327.

fully unable to join the Holy Name and Altar-Rosary societies because of the press of business and the care of growing children. Other parishioners blamed themselves for "just never getting around to it." Others, especially among the women, claimed (as is heard in so many parishes) that the same "old-timers" ran things and did not welcome younger blood. Many charged that the programs of meetings and activities are not stimulating or interesting.

Responses to another section of the questionnaire[2] indicate that 44 per cent of the respondents had visited a priest in OLM rectory during the preceding year (a very high percentage) and that 57 per cent had engaged a parish priest in conversation outside of confession, though less than 9 per cent did so frequently. Much of this social contact between parishioner and priest involved members of parish societies, for 35 per cent were members of some OLM society, 28 per cent being members of the Holy Name Society or the Altar-Rosary Society. The point is that membership in parish societies facilitates this generally desirable contact, and for this very reason increased memberships must be a constant parish aim, especially in the modern urban parish where the demographic situation is such that many parishioners never get to know their priests, and vice versa. Incidentally, a further breakdown of the responses of those who had occasion to visit the rectory showed that all religious, economic, and educational categories (except religious Grades A and D for opposite reasons) were well represented, ranging from over 30 per cent to 50 per cent.

Several societies—Holy Name, Altar-Rosary, Sodality, Legion of Mary, Ushers, St. Vincent de Paul—took time in their meetings to answer a special society questionnaire.[3] A total of 84 persons responded, 31 males and 53 females. Of those who

---

[2] Part 2, Question 27, p. 323.
[3] The questionnaire will be found in Appendix II, pp. 313-14.

filled out the questionnaire, 6 were below the age of 16; 17 were between 16 and 20 years old; 9 were between 21 and 31; 17 were between 31 and 50; and 35 were over 50. No members in the Holy Name and Altar-Rosary societies were below 30 years of age and most of the members were over 50. The St. Vincent de Paul and Ushers societies followed the same patterns.

The motives for society membership and activity listed by respondents to the special questionnaire are given below, often in the words of the members. Often enough motivation for membership in a society—such as personal prestige and status, the desire to have something congenial to do, and the influence of friends' memberships—can be quite natural. Be that as it may, the presumption of objectivity must be considered tenable until there is evidence to the contrary.

> *Holy Name Society:* Stimulates clean living; "Makes me a better Catholic" (mentioned often); to honor the Holy Name and participate more fully in religious life (often); to fulfill my obligation to Church and parish (a few times); Catholic fraternization (mentioned by several); because the Holy Name Society and Knights of Columbus comprise the lay right arm of the Church in America; "I like it"; to help the parish priests and be in their company.
>
> *St. Vincent de Paul Society:* Several as above; to help the poor; spiritual growth through union with Christ in helping others.
>
> *Altar-Rosary Society:* The privilege of working about the altar (mentioned frequently); chance to work for God, help the priests (mentioned frequently); "I'm able to help, and I love to do so"; "I enjoy being around the church"; the custom of saying the daily rosary; "It gets me out of the house"; "My mother made me"; influence of friends; opportunity for more prayer and increased blessings, indulgences; a chance to work and stay out of mischief; opportunity for social relationships with Catholic women.
>
> *Junior and Senior Sodalities:* The desire to be more closely associated with our Lady and to know more about her; to honor Mary, and her Son through her; need for further religious development beyond school years; for pleasant Catholic com-

radeship and social satisfaction; "Was pressured to join in grammar school and remained"; "The Sodality gives me a way of life which satisfies my needs as a Catholic."

Legion of Mary (Junior and Senior Praesidia): The ideals of personal sanctification and helping others (mentioned often); to participate in Catholic action, help myself and others to God; the glory of God and the salvation of souls; desire to join Mary in the apostolate of her Son; "I had time on my hands, so joined; like the work, so remained"; "Priests couldn't do it all, so I joined to help"; to take a more active part in the life of the Church; to get more spiritual direction; to maintain social contacts; to join the apostolic life of the parish; to participate in the lay apostolate.

When asked whether their reasons (motives) for joining or remaining in the societies were being satisfied, fewer than 10 respondents listed only partial satisfaction and none recorded dissatisfaction. All mentioned some general or specific contributions they were making to the society, thus gratifying their own desire to be of help to the parish through the society. One or more benefits which the respondents were deriving from active membership, usually conforming to the motives for belonging, were listed on all the returns.

Quite a few respondents thought that active membership in the society should be increased, but not too many other suggestions were offered for improving the respective groups. Many members of all societies said that no improvements were needed. The suggestions included:

Holy Name, St. Vincent de Paul, Ushers Societies: Need for more spiritual emphasis; more definite assignments and clearer programs; more meetings for constructive criticism; resume hospital work in St. Vincent de Paul Society.

Altar-Rosary Society: More attention by ushers at the society's corporate Communion Sunday; no annual Communion breakfast.

Junior and Senior Sodalities: Do and pray more together; enthusiastic program to draw new members; more apostolic interest and participation by members; more mission work.

Legion of Mary: Better means of communication, such as a society bulletin board and suggestion box; more definite plan for the members' own spiritual lives; less formalism in meetings; more training in methods, both apostolic and ascetical.

In the light of Father Fichter's shrewd observation on organization,[4] the society members were asked whether they thought that the society had become more concerned with conserving formal organization than achieving its fundamental purpose.[5] Admittedly this is a puzzling question for nonprofessionals, and the problem it implies is extremely difficult to recognize, particularly in one's own society. Yet one of the gravest problems of parish organizations is precisely the overemphasis on retaining past methods and structures despite the need for change in current circumstances. An example is the fact that modern public welfare work has made minimal the care for the poor that is requested of the St. Vincent de Paul Society in most parishes. Nevertheless the Vincentians, who are deeply spiritual, apostolic, and parish-minded men, often continue to restrict their efforts to helping the poor, whereas spiritual problems based on temporal needs are to be found in every parish. The same can be said of the Sodality, which is often restricted to girls and young women. Although its solid spiritual constitution and apostolic flexibility are its finest assets, the Sodality lags far behind the Legion in parish work and the vitality of its membership. Only 12 of the 84 persons answering the society questionnaire indicated that it was partially true that concern over formal organization took precedence over concern about the successful accomplishment of the society's aims and purposes.

Such responses on motives, satisfactions, and activities indicate that members believe the societies are functioning purposefully. A most probable explanation for lack of members in

---

[4] Fichter, *Urban Parish,* p. 156.
[5] Appendix II, p. 314.

parish societies would seem to be that the various subgroupings in any neighborhood or population tend to exert a pull more attractive than that of a centralized parish society, which often cuts across categories of age, occupation, education, geographical proximity, and other interests. Many persons do not feel at home joining a new group and going through a period (longer in anticipation than in fact) of making new acquaintances, particularly when they are satisfied with their existing social relationships. Yet these are the people for whom, too, the parish would like to increase its meaning and service.

One answer to this difficulty is carrying the parish to these subgroupings. OLM already does this in two relatively small but important areas. It has two groups, totaling 12 couples, of the Christian Family Movement and it has eight 7-member "dens" of Cub Scouts.

The CFM couples have a natural affinity for association: they are young, married, have growing families, live near one another, and share a common interest in both sanctifying their married lives and profiting from one another's experience. Their groups are small and manageable (once they get large, they split up), they meet in the informal setting of one another's homes, the parish chaplain comes to them instead of their going to the parish hall. Their meetings combine spiritual, apostolic, and sociocivic interests. They get together with other CFM groups periodically, make use of their parish church for occasional corporate Communions and of the parish hall for dances. Their effective functioning seems to be a superb solution of the problem of how to bring parish values and service to parishioners in terms of their own needs and social situation.

Decentralization has other values too. Meetings are in the members' homes, where surroundings are particularly congenial and suitable for free discussion in an informal atmosphere. The priest is welcomed into these homes. He brings his blessing and leaves his imprint. Children get used to the priest on a more familiar, though certainly respectful, basis. The Chicago priests who have been managing CFM groups for over a decade have noticed a wider and warmer interest in the priestly vocation. The CFM members themselves develop a sense of parish interest and responsibility, and in the course of the give-and-take of prepared meetings they learn and exercise themselves in the ways of leadership.

Thus a parish becomes alive in groups of people geographically removed from the parish center. A parish with several healthy CFM groups provides its priests with additional sets of eyes, ears, and hands so that they can be more intimately present to all the parish life.

One CFM group in the author's neighborhood considered reports on the following activities in its most recent regular meeting: the three fall Cana Conferences, the book club and library acquisitions, the results of the CFM-sponsored Missal display and sale, preparations for the Thanksgiving Day family Mass, home discussions on religion with priests and neighbors, participation in town and school-board meetings, developments in the neighborhood recreational program, another day-at-home for youngsters in the local orphanage, plans for the parish Advent party, care of the parish's "mission" church, and organizational matters. Not all of these activities are 100 per cent successful as yet. Perhaps some will not be. But there is no doubt about the group's involvement with Christ in the institutional apostolate of the parish and no doubt about its community vitality. Such is the CFM's opportunity and apostolic mission.

The Cub Scouts operate on a somewhat similar basis. Each "den" consists of seven youngsters, each of whom must have at least one parent actively interested in the activities of that den. Youngsters and parents share common interests. The meetings are in the members' homes, a constructive enterprise is regularly in progress, and periodical demonstrations are held in the parish hall. Again, the chaplain goes to them, and they function in a milieu of natural interest. The success, not only of their social events but likewise of their religious celebrations, attests to the effectiveness of this subsystem within the total parish system.

Could OLM further exploit these natural subgroupings? Unquestionably it would take time, and we have seen that OLM priests have not much time to spare. Yet a careful study of the possibilities might well indicate an opportunity so fruitful that time would have to be made. In addition, any plan would necessarily involve greater use of lay cooperation. Planning would not be easy at first, but eventually it would utilize the time, energy, and talents of many parishioners interested in doing something but not knowing what to do. Parish exploitation of such natural subgroupings as occupational, educational, neighborhood, and other units would increase far beyond current levels the significance of the parish to many members.

The general questionnaire asked respondents whether they would like to belong to a decentralized group, giving as examples of such groups the Christian Family Movement and the Cub Scouts.[6] Owing to limitations of space the question could not be phrased in sufficient detail, and many respondents indicated that they did not understand it. Extremely few, however, checked the negative response and almost 40 per cent (more than 100 of the 293 respondents) affirmed that they would be interested in a decentralized group connected with the parish.

Investigation has shown that the societies in OLM Parish include but a small minority of the parish and that the priests' occupation with most of them limits their opportunities to get to the rest of the parish. The suggested solutions, ranging from liquidation of all or most of the present societies to drives to expand the memberships, are not promising for four reasons. First, the societies are already serving a good purpose, as the over-all 10 per cent membership testifies. Second, they are a

---

[6] Part 4, Question 4, p. 327.

ready-made organizational framework for periodical functions undertaken by the parish, such as publicity and fund drives, the parish census, newsstand-cleanup campaigns, and the like, all of which lean heavily on the cooperation of parish societies. Third, it is doubtful whether many of the other 90 per cent would avail themselves of even the most suitable opportunity to participate in a revised organizational structure. Many persons lack either the time for or interest in parish activities that go beyond ordinary religious practice. (The old adage about leading a horse to water and the parable of the seed falling on different types of ground are applicable here.) Fourth, even if it is feasible to develop parish societies on a more naturally decentralized basis, a large part of the present centralized structure (or some form of it) would have to remain for the sake of unity and stability.

There are other societies and activities in OLM Parish which do not have a directly spiritual aim. These include the CYO (Catholic Youth Organization), the Credit Union, the Employment Bureau, and Social Welfare Service. The facilities of the parish are also utilized by such groups as the Catholic War Veterans, a Bronx chapter of Alcoholics Anonymous, the Ancient Order of Hibernians, the Catholic Daughters of America, and others. Though parishioners are members of these nonparochial groups and the pastor is chaplain of some of them, this study will consider only parish activities.

The parish's CYO athletic teams were in the past quite successful and famous, though recently, owing probably to lack of home facilities, they seem to have dropped in importance. But successful playing is of course a secondary consideration. The chief concern is parish sponsorship of and identification with youth's normal interests, including the social and athletic. The reason for this concern is the desire for the integration of religious values with any other wholesome, normal values in the parishioner's life. Sometimes being sports director of his young people is a time-consuming task for a parish priest, who might prefer to be more directly involved in the apostolate. Yet the loyalty of these young people to the parish in later days frequently derives from their association and identification with priest and parish in earlier social interests.

Of probably even more significance has been the phenomenal success of the OLM Federal Credit Union. This parish bank service, which was the inspiration of OLM's pastor in 1941 and is now his pride and joy, provided an effective answer to parishioners who had been victimized, or could be victimized, by the ubiquitous loan sharks. To supply money at cheaper interest rates than elsewhere is not the only purpose of the service. In line with the most important spiritual interests of the parish, the loans made by the bank make it possible for persons whose disadvantageous material condition was harming, or could harm, their spiritual condition to "get on their feet again." Story after story could be told of homes that have been saved, families that were held together, and individual lives that regained some order and hope, thanks to the help of the Credit Union.

Of course the Credit Union does not do business only for hardship cases. Providing capital for new jobs, for meeting the expenses of a family vacation, for a child's education, or for repairs on the family home is normal procedure. The organization does not dispense charity; it could not exist if it did and the federal charter would not last. But often the St. Vincent de Paul Society or one of the priests puts up collateral in a hardship case, thus enabling the Credit Union to lend money cheaply. A report issued in 1957 reveals that loans totaling more than $1,200,000 have been granted since its organization.[7]

Yet despite the years of successful operation and the help and happiness that loans have brought to so many parishioners, only a little over 700 parishioners (less than 10 per cent) are members of the Credit Union. The voluntary purchase of shares

[7] See Appendix II, p. 331.

by the school children has taught them some of the principles of saving and credit. Some are able to save enough to pay for their high-school education. Despite the regular notice about the Credit Union in the *Parish Monthly* and mention of its weekly meeting in the Sunday announcements there are parishioners who have either not heard about it or have hesitated to seek a loan because of some fear or other. Laymen conduct the business and keep the records of the Credit Union, the treasurer being a woman of great devotion and remarkable competence. Their work is a superb exemplification of devoted lay cooperation. They need some younger blood, and have made that fact frequently known; but as yet younger parishioners, with two or three exceptions, have not stepped forward to share the load.

The parish Employment Bureau and its Social Welfare Service, both handled capably by the same person who is treasurer for the Credit Union, have also been utilized by a proportionately large number of the parishioners. Not seldom have unattended old persons who know nothing about social-security laws or pension technicalities received needed information, help, and directions. As with the Credit Union, so it has been with the Employment Bureau when there was question of coming to the aid of distressed and unemployed breadwinners.

Without exaggeration, a fruitful book could be written about each of OLM's societies and activities: their history and achievements, their successes and failures, their roles in parish life. Responses to the questionnaires indicate that these societies provide OLM with opportunities of offering service and give the members opportunity to cooperate with the parish in attaining both parish goals and their own. Some societies are very strong with vigorous programs; others are weak and in need of support. But each organization forms part of OLM's social structure and participates in its functioning.

CHAPTER XIV

Imparting Values
and Attitudes

V alues, consciously recognized and sought, distinguish the human being's conduct from the animal's stimulus-response pattern of behavior. The mission of Christianity is to preach the truth revealed by God so that men may freely, though with divine assistance, govern their lives and conduct accordingly. A value is something worth having; true values must be in accord with divine truth, divine law, and divine destiny. Thus the parish has the responsibility of imparting and parishioners of accepting true value motivation.

We have already discussed the motives of OLM's parishioners for their Eucharistic devotion.[1] We resume the discussion of motivating values now, extending it to a wider area of religious, moral, and social issues.

One parish service which is basic to its operation and purpose is the communication of the Church's and parish's system of values and doctrines. We have seen that this service is provided especially in school and pulpit. Now we are interested in seeing to what extent the parishioners have responded to the service by incorporating what they have heard in the areas of religious, moral, and social issues into their own body of knowl-

---

[1] See Chapter 12, pp. 232-46.

edge and norms of conduct. A series of questions on the OLM questionnaire were designed to give some picture of the Catholic mind formed by OLM Parish, or, in the case of newcomers, by other similarly functioning parishes. Many of the questions used by Father Fichter were modified and asked of the OLM group.[2]

To discover the respondents' knowledge of fundamental Catholic doctrines they were asked to match five doctrinal expressions (such as Incarnation, Nativity, consecration) with corresponding explanations or equivalent terms.[3] It is possible that some of the more simply educated persons in OLM might have had difficulty with the matching technique, and the question was not the simplest possible, for some of the terms are frequently confused by intelligent persons. Actually, a great many respondents matched all but two sets correctly, but only those who matched all five pairs perfectly were credited with correct responses. Of the 293 respondents, 206 (70 per cent) answered correctly. When these respondents were divided into four categories according to religious practice, economic status, and education,[4] it was found that 70 per cent of those whose religious practice was excellent answered correctly as compared with 25 per cent of those who were delinquent in practicing their religion. Only 50 per cent from the highest economic class and almost 70 per cent from the other economic classes scored correct answers. Classification according to education showed an irregular pattern; the college trained, whether in Catholic colleges or others, made no better marks than other parishioners. We conclude that, since 70 per cent answered correctly, the parish or some other agency (perhaps the parochial school) succeeded in communicating exact theological doctrine.

---

[2] Fichter, *Southern Parish*, pp. 261-66. In this study priests conducting interviews with a selected group of 68 parishioners who had demonstrated the "most Catholic" behavior asked sixteen questions without advancing any explanation.

[3] See the general questionnaire, Part 2, Question 32, p. 324.

[4] See Chapter 8, p. 171, for an explanation of the four categories.

Asked whether they thought the Church should make exceptions from its laws pertaining to divorce and birth control in difficult cases, 64 per cent of the respondents indicated that the Church should not make exceptions in the case of divorce and 15 per cent stated they did not know. Just over 60 per cent said that the Church should not make exceptions in the case of birth control.[5] The responses of those with a Catholic education were the same for both questions, 62 per cent. Father Fichter, using the expression "unhappily married" instead of "difficult cases" found that 87 per cent thought that the laws should not be relaxed.[6] Apparently the OLM respondents who thought that the Church should make exceptions (about 20 per cent) do not know that it is not within the power of the Church to change those laws which it teaches are divine. At any rate, the parish's teachings and values on divorce and birth control are known or accepted by more than 60 per cent of the 293 parishioners who answered the questionnaire.

The OLM questionnaire included two questions on mixed marriages; the first asked whether the respondent agreed with the Church's stand on mixed marriages, and the second asked how the number of mixed marriages might be reduced.[7] It might be explained here that the Church's opposition to mixed marriages and its reluctance in permitting them when necessary have several well-founded reasons. First, that complete union between husband and wife which the sacrament of matrimony symbolizes and is meant to achieve can hardly be attained when the spouses differ on something so fundamental and all-pervasive as religious belief and practice. One who doubts this simply does not understand the unifying nature of Catholic belief. Second, the Church knows from experience that the Catholic spouse

---

[5] Part 2, Question 33, p. 324.
[6] Fichter, *Southern Parish*, pp. 261-62.
[7] Part 2, Question 39, p. 325; Part 5, Question 6, p. 328.

runs a far greater risk than usual of losing his religious belief or practice, or both. Third, it often happens that children of mixed marriages are brought up in religious confusion or with no religion. On the other hand, it cannot be denied that many mixed marriages work out very well, at least with regard to the second and third points just mentioned.

Over 83 per cent of all respondents (244 out of 293) agreed definitely with the Church's stand on mixed marriages. Several of the remaining 17 per cent were not sure and had doubts, and a few favored a more liberal attitude. The breakdown of affirmative responses is shown in Table XX.

TABLE XX

Agreement of OLM Parishioners
with Catholic Attitude on Mixed Marriages

	Group A	Group B	Group C	Group D	Total
Religious rank (1)	32 [33]	146 [171]	65 [77]	1 [12]	244 [293]
Economic rank	13 [13]	99 [114]	105 [131]	27 [35]	244 [293]
Education completed	36 [41]	39 [42]	104 [128]	65 [82]	244 [293]
Catholic education	21 [26]	16 [16]	51 [61]	62 [73]	150 [176]

(1) The numbers in brackets represent the total number in each group.

The percentage in agreement with the attitude of the Church ranges from 79 for the lowest educational group to 100 (in highest economic rank and students with 1-3 years in Catholic colleges). Only the members of Group D in religious rank, those who are deficient in religious practice, tend to disagree with the attitude of the Church. Those who have attended Catholic schools are not in much closer agreement with the church attitude (85.2 per cent) than are all the respondents (83.3 per cent). In view of urban living in a religiously mixed society, this percentage of agreement with the Church is very high.

Thus the members of OLM Parish manifest a different degree of conformity with church values than did Father Fichter's respondents from a southern parish. Only 35 per cent of the 68 persons interviewed by priests were opposed to mixed marriages. It should be noted, however, that Father Fichter's question implied a decision concerning habitual policy.[8]

Almost 230 of the OLM respondents gave reasons for their answers. Those few who wanted a more favorable attitude toward mixed marriage invariably cited their own or some known experience in which a mixed marriage worked out successfully, frequently with the conversion of the non-Catholic party. It is of course true that a very great source of adult conversions to the Church is precisely mixed courtship and mixed marriage, for often the non-Catholic party sees the Church for the first time, is attracted, investigates, and seeks admission. But the great majority of those who agreed with the attitude of the Church pointed out that experience lies heavily on the side against mixed marriage. The Church's three reasons for opposing mixed marriages were cited frequently. Some simply mentioned that the Church, with all its experience and authority, had the right and wisdom to take such a stand and that they agreed. Others claimed that marriage and the rearing of children were difficult enough without starting under the handicap of religious disunity. Positively speaking, it was stated that marriage and family life, to be successful and happy, require the union of mother, father, and children worshiping God together. Such frequent causes of conflict as the Church's law on divorce, birth control, fast and abstinence, and the religious upbringing of children were cited often. A point which several wisely made is that in a home of mixed parental religions neither the religious tone of the home nor the children's development can be as fully Catholic as two Catholic parents could make them.

---

[8] The question asked by Father Fichter was: "When two young people are very much in love, do you think that they should marry even if they are not of the same religion?" (*Southern Parish*, p. 283).

In answer to the question asking how the number of mixed marriages might be reduced the three suggestions made most frequently were: more variety and regularity in mixed recreational events offered by the parish; more frequent, detailed, and mature instruction—citing the difficulties and frequent unfortunate results of mixed marriages—to all age groups; a stricter attitude toward such marriages. Respondents not in agreement with the Church's attitude suggested means of making mixed marriages more fruitful: understanding that mixed marriages are to be expected in a mixed society; showing a friendly sympathy toward the persons involved, so that Catholic attitudes might be recognized and perhaps accepted.

OLM's respondents seem to have accepted the values for which the parish system operates. Even those who favored mixed marriages or were undecided manifested an attitude in agreement with many values of Church and parish. To most respondents the parish exists not only as a dispenser of religious services, but also as the formulator of value patterns which have been integrated into their own lives and social norms.

When asked whether they believed that it was better to raise two children in extra comfort or five children in decent but more difficult circumstances,[9] 75 per cent of the OLM respondents favored the larger family. Several others said that they did not know. As Father Fichter points out, the question "offers a choice between popular secular values and Catholic values, between a higher material standard of living with fewer children, on the one side, and a lower standard of living with more children, on the other. Anyone who understands and accepts the supernatural criteria of Christianity would not place comfortable advantages above children."[10] OLM respondents showed a generally good grasp of the Christian sense of values.

---

[9] Part 2, Question 44, p. 325.
[10] Fichter, *Southern Parish*, p. 263.

When asked whether the Church has said definitely that workingmen have the right to form unions,[11] less than 60 per cent answered affirmatively and most of the remaining 40 per cent said they did not know. Apparently the Church's teachings on industrial and economic life are not too well known.

The questions relating to racial attitudes had several parts.[12] A record 95 per cent believed that colored people should have the same rights in the Catholic church and school as white people. This contrasts with Father Fichter's findings that only 12 per cent of the respondents in the southern parish wanted integrated rather than segregated Catholic parishes, and that only 26 per cent would send their children to a racially mixed Catholic kindergarten.[13] OLM respondents were also asked whether, if they lived near Jewish, Puerto Rican, or colored people "whose moral life and conduct were as good as your own family's," they would encourage their children to associate with children of other races. Replies indicated that 45 per cent would encourage association with Jewish children, 34 per cent with Puerto Rican children, and 35 per cent with Negro children. Just under 50 per cent stated that they would neither encourage nor discourage association with any of the three groups. On the other hand, only 7 per cent would discourage relations between their children and Jewish children, while 18 per cent and 19 per cent, respectively, gave the same answer regarding association with Puerto Rican and Negro children.

The reasons and comments added by the respondents in defending their positions on race relations filled seven typed pages. Some few gave as their reason for discouraging interracial association their conviction that the moral standards of other ethnic groups were dangerously lower than their own, in-

---

11 Part 2, Question 34, p. 324.
12 Part 2, Questions 35 and 36, pp. 324-25.
13 Fichter, *Southern Parish*, pp. 265-66.

dicating that they had entirely disregarded that part of the question which specified that it was limited to those families whose moral life and conduct were as good as the respondent's. Another small minority, without admitting their own prejudice, simply stated that other ethnic groups are socially and morally inferior, or at least different. All of these persons, somewhat less than 10 per cent of all respondents, either missed the point of the question or manifested ignorance or lack of acceptance of the Church's teaching on universal human unity and universal fraternity under God and in Christ.

The remainder of those who would discourage interethnic association among their children gave as their reason the possibility that such association might lead to religiously mixed marriages. No superiority attitude or prejudice determined their decision and, faced with a choice of apparently conflicting values (nondiscrimination and concern for their children's religiously unified marriages), their personal prudence dictated selection of the one in preference to the other. All the others, those who would either encourage or remain neutral, gave vigorous expression to their conviction that discrimination was opposed to God's law, that Christ made no distinctions, and that no moral or religious harm need result.

This manifestation of a Catholic attitude is further exemplified in the respondents' answers to the question of whether they thought that a person of a different race or nation should be prevented from taking a job or joining in other aspects of social life. Only 15 persons, just over 5 per cent, answered affirmatively. Again a great many reasons were advanced, most of them including the thought expressed by one respondent: "All human beings are equal in the sight of God as well as in the concept of the United States democracy." Others added such qualifications as: "It might be cruel to accept them and have them ignored by the majority"; "No, but each individual has a right to balance his own economic and social convenience against the right of the minority member"; and "He must stand on his own feet and not expect others to carry him."

In general, over 90 per cent of the respondents in OLM Parish show a wholesome Catholic attitude on the race question. This probably reflects the difference in social milieu between this northern parish and Father Fichter's southern parish. It is an encouraging indication of the communication and acceptance of parish sociomoral values.

Answers to the question about the recent relaxation of the law concerning the Eucharistic fast[14] revealed that 60 per cent had taken advantage of it and over 92 per cent of the OLM respondents knew of it. A majority of the others said they would take advantage of it if there were reason for doing so.

In an effort to discover whether the respondents' political views derived from religious convictions, they were asked whether the government should provide more low-cost housing for poor people if private builders cannot or will not provide it.[15] The answers showed 87 per cent in favor of government housing and almost 13 per cent opposed. But whereas only 12 per cent of those who opposed public housing advanced reasons in whole or in part religious, 37 per cent of those in favor alleged at least partly religious reasons. Of those who had Catholic schooling, 50 per cent who favored and 4 per cent who opposed government housing cited religious reasons.

Asked whether they believed that the devil was someone real,[16] 75 per cent of the OLM respondents indicated that they did and several said they did not know. A comparable 75 per cent of the respondents with Catholic schooling replied affirma-

---

[14] Part 2, Question 40, p. 325. The changes referred to are those contained in the apostolic constitution *Christus Dominus* of January 6, 1953. These have been more recently extended in *Sacram Communionem*, which went into effect on March 25, 1957.

[15] Part 2, Question 41, p. 325.

[16] Part 2, Question 42, p. 325.

tively. Even though Catholic theology, teaching, and prayer formulas are very definite in affirming that the devil is real, many people apparently think of a real person as possessing a human body. Father Fichter experienced the same lack of understanding, for only 54 per cent of his respondents believed that the devil was a real person.[17] Even the substitution of "someone real" in the OLM questionnaire for Father Fichter's "real person" left some respondents with the notion of a human body.

It was found that 88 per cent of the OLM respondents (87 per cent of those with Catholic schooling) were opposed to mercy killing.[18] This compares rather closely to results in Father Fichter's southern parish, where 91 per cent gave a negative response to almost the same question.[19] One further question that sought to establish the degree of acceptance of Christian values referred to calling a priest when a person was seriously ill.[20] The Catholic norm, to call a priest as soon as one knows that the illness is serious, was the choice of 88 per cent of the OLM respondents. Only 34 (11 per cent) preferred to save the sick person from worry by postponing the call for a priest until death was almost certain. In view of the widespread secular attitude favoring the second choice, the percentage in agreement with the Catholic norm is quite high.

While the replies to the OLM questionnaire indicate that the parish cannot be completely satisfied with the parishioners' knowledge and acceptance of Christian teaching and values, it is difficult to conceive of any parish that would ever be in a position to be completely satisfied. Acceptance of religious values is achieved despite competition from secular values and the falling

---

[17] Fichter, *Southern Parish*, p. 262.

[18] Part 2, Question 43, p. 325.

[19] "In the case of prolonged and painful cancer do you think that it would be all right for a doctor to give the patient an overdose of sleeping pills?" (Fichter, *Southern Parish*, p. 261).

[20] Part 2, Question 14, p. 321.

of religious seed on different types of ground. On the other hand, there were never less than 62 per cent of the respondents who were in agreement with church and parish teaching; in most instances well over 70 per cent of the parishioners, sometimes as high as 90 per cent, were in agreement. Most of these questions involved issues in which secular values differ radically from Catholic ones. The extent to which OLM parishioners accept these Catholic values and reject the secular is one index of the effective functioning of the parish system.

One tentative conclusion to be drawn from the analysis of the data must disturb the Catholic educationist: the 176 parishioners who had the benefit of Catholic schooling did not show greater acceptance of Catholic attitudes toward religious, moral, and social issues than did all the 293 respondents to the questionnaire. It suggests that there is much work still to be done in the schools and parishes.

These responses of OLM parishioners draw attention to one of the foremost functions of the priesthood, preaching at Sunday Mass. In another part of the questionnaire the respondents were asked whether they actually listened to the sermons or discussed them outside of church; their opinions were also sought on whether the sermons should remain the same, contain more explanation of the Church's moral and doctrinal teaching, or have less explanation and more inspiration.[21] As a matter of fact, the priests themselves had requested comments and criticisms of their sermons a few years previously and had received some helpful suggestions at that time, another example of OLM's cooperative functioning.

Just about everyone, 289 out of 293 respondents (99 per cent), claimed that he listened to the sermons. Undoubtedly many priests in many other parishes will marvel at this favorable response! Apparently this figure included most of the re-

---

[21] Part 2, Question 21, p. 322.

spondents rated Grade D in religious practice; presumably they meant that they listen the few times they bother to attend. And almost everyone (94 per cent) discussed the sermons outside of church, at least occasionally, most saying that they did so rarely. Preferences on types of sermons were indicated by 263 respondents: 46 per cent were pleased with OLM's sermons as they were and wanted them to stay that way; 44 per cent wanted more explanation of the Church's moral and doctrinal teaching; on the contrary 5 per cent wanted less explanation and more inspiration and devotion; another 5 per cent had some other criticism. Since this was the opportunity to express themselves both frankly and anonymously concerning the sermons which they listen to each week, we may presume that OLM parishioners are generally well satisfied with what they hear—rather a fine tribute to the pastor and other parish priests. The request of the 44 per cent who wanted more information and explanation in the sermons could conceivably be satisfied by the adoption of a system of scheduled topics, which is used in many dioceses.

A few of the additional comments on the sermons included these points:

A sermon at every Mass all year round, including the summer
Connect Church's moral teachings with current social issues
More instruction on the history and liturgy of the Mass and sacraments
A less elementary approach
Some question-and-answer sessions

The difficulty in satisfying everyone, especially those of different educational backgrounds, must be obvious. Frequency of repetition is another problem. New parishioners, for example, would not be expected to know that the parish recently conducted a lengthy series of instructions on the Mass during Sunday Mass. But such an incident is a reason for communication between priests and people, that each may know the other's expectations and needs.

A further view of OLM's functioning and the parishioners' cooperation was gained by paging through a year's issues of the *Parish Monthly*.[22] On the editorial staff of this news organ were 13 parishioners who were closely identified with the parish. The following types of material found in the monthly indicate that it played an important role as a very effective medium of unity in the parish community:

Frequent use of parishioners' names and pictures of parish interest

Recording of birthdays, weddings, and other anniversaries

Explaining technical announcements in attractive ways

Publicity given to each of the parish societies: personalities, events, dates, coming programs

Such services as printing the Consumers' Union advice, the Legion of Decency ratings, an exchange for baby furnishings

Parish-area advertisements

The banns of matrimony

Cartoons, sports, letters to the editor, including some frank criticism

Popular explanation, in installments, of the annual American bishops' statements

Calling attention to parish outings to Jones' Beach and to class-reunion celebrations

Special articles on items of current interest

An examination of the Sunday announcements for an entire year produced evidence of the vitality and social functioning to be found in a Catholic parish. Activities called to the attention of OLM parishioners indicate the types of activities engaged in and reflect the interests and responses of the people. Items in the parish announcements included:

Talks for non-Catholics

Teen-age dance sponsored by the Sodality (a monthly affair)

---

[22] After this study was completed the *Parish Monthly* yielded to the current commercially edited monthly, but in a recent move the parish has resumed a policy of the inclusion of extensive parish news under parish editorship, while retaining the commercial format.

Dances sponsored by the Catholic War Veterans or other groups
(frequent)
The people's high Mass (sung by the entire congregation)
Red Cross blood bank
Monthly times of adoration for members of the Nocturnal Adora-
tion Society and Catholic Youth Adorers
Irish night
OLM School reunion
The cardinal's appeals for funds for such worthy causes as Cath-
olic Charities, war victims, Peter's pence, bishops' relief drive
for the destitute, the archdiocesan high schools, the seminary,
the cathedral, the national shrine of the Immaculate Concep-
tion in Washington
The Passion Play
Released-time program
Mailing list for relatives in service
Cana Conferences
St. Vincent de Paul Society's penny sale for the Home for the Blind
School registration
May crowning of our Lady
Occasional collections; visiting missionary priests, charitable causes
Altar servers outing
Anniversary of Bronx parent group of Alcoholics Anonymous
Cooperation with civil authorities in such matters as air-raid warn-
ings, request of police for help against certain types of juve-
nile delinquents
Resumption of evening dances on Sunday nights
Invitation to see improvements in school and kindergarten
Celebration for the pastor's investiture as right reverend monsignor
Day of prayer for the Church persecuted behind the Iron Curtain
Reports on the Credit Union
CYO activities
Sale of lenten Missals
Advertisement of pertinent activities on the campus of Fordham
University
An appeal not to shop or do business during the three hours on
Good Friday
Altar-Rosary Society activities for altars, sanctuary, and vestments
Investiture of Boy Scouts
World Sodality Day

How do the members of such an active parish as OLM, and such a generally religiously observant parish, estimate the values they have received from the parish? A list of some of the responses throws light on this question.[23] The services mentioned include the following:

Provision of Mass, sacraments, prompt service on sick calls
Everything which a person could or should want in his religious life
School for my children; Catholic education
The awareness of what it means to be a Catholic, to have a Catholic
    philosophy of life
A lovely place to worship God, a fine school, and wonderful priests
The missions given every second year
The great example, teaching, and inspiration of the nuns in school
Daily Mass
The Credit Union
Such activities as the Cub Scouts—for parents and children
The availability and understanding of the pastor
The weekly high Mass and Holy Hour
Return to the Church
Conversion of my husband (wife)
General willingness to help: the sick, the financially distressed
The friendliness pervading the rectory and parish activities
Edification by our priests
Beauty and cleanliness of our altars
Frequency of Masses
Excellence of the parish school
Good spiritual direction
The Sunday nursery
Parish social activities for young and old
Opportunity for participation in lay apostolate
Help in finding a job
Good sermons
Visits to the sick and Communion calls

The above list lacks the emphasis felt when reading page after page of the OLM parishioners' own responses. Their con-

---

[23] Part 2, Question 23, p. 322.

stant reference to Mass and the sacraments, to spiritual guidance and uplift, and to the Catholic education of their children makes it evident that OLM stands for something very big and important in their lives.

The respondents were asked too whether there were any benefits which they thought OLM could provide but did not.[24] About 75 took the opportunity to offer suggestions. They include:

A parents' club, to bring about closer association with the teachers in school

More activities for the teen-agers and young people (mentioned frequently)

A study group on both elementary and advanced levels

Priests to visit each home, if only once

Not only an Irish night, but also an Italian night, Polish night, and so forth

A club for young unmarried people

Additional daily Masses at six and eight o'clock

A parish high school

An annual parish report, with financial, religious, and vital statistics

Better athletic facilities

Confessions in the upstairs church

The parish priests have long considered, and have good reasons for not accepting, several of these suggestions. Others, already known to them, they accept but are not yet ready to take action. This is particularly true of the need to revive and expand the youth program for which OLM was until recently famous. War and especially postwar social changes caused this youth program to founder. To be conscious of the needs of the social system and of its members, with the aim of adapting policy to satisfy them, is characteristic of a social system. OLM, which is already functioning so extensively in many areas of providing service and realizing values, is also aware of its need to provide even more service and to find the way to do so.

---

[24] Part 2, Question 24, p. 322.

The Parish
in the Balance

P revious chapters have called attention to some of the details of life in OLM Parish. It is most difficult to add a concluding chapter when the study has really just begun. Most of the data concerning parish life that we have gathered and briefly analyzed are of the more readily obtainable kind. The underlying influences which either affect such parish phenomena or derive from them can be discovered only by further research and by analysis. There are, besides, vast areas of parish activity which have not even been touched.

Since over half the neighborhood is Catholic and consists principally of OLM's parishioners and since OLM's members have religious values and moral habits which impinge upon social life, then, obviously enough, the parish must exert some influence on types of recreation, education, and other public conduct. What has been the mutual impact of neighborhood and parish on each other in recreational, moral, and cultural values? That too manifests the social system at work: its influence outside itself and its ability to withstand or absorb the influence of the outside upon itself. The fact that hundreds of places of business in the parish area close for the three hours on Good Friday during which Christ's death on the cross is recalled, derives from direct parish influence. A neighborhood theater closed its doors when OLM ruled it out of bounds for OLM parishioners because of its unacceptable programs. The city abandoned its plan of using some free space for a parking area because OLM fought to have it reserved as a playground. In each instance social roles were played, statuses exploited and matched, ecological situations considered, and policy implemented through interaction and social functioning for the achievement or protection of OLM's values and those of its members.

Over 75 per cent of OLM's respondents think that the parish has an influence on the neighborhood educationally and morally,[1] and over 80 per cent think it has influenced recreation in the area. Over half of those who think so believe that the influence is more than trifling. It would be valuable to study both the validity of this claim and the extent to which Catholic values impinge upon the urban secular culture. There is strong evidence to show that secular values influence the parishioner; it would be valuable to study how much and why.

Questions that might be asked concerning OLM influence on the neighborhood educationally are: How have the parish school and the neighboring public schools influenced one another? Is the OLM student more or less conscious of civic values than his public-school friend? Is the Catholic boy or girl in a public school less aware of religious values, or not? How much money does OLM save its neighborhood by having its own school?

His Eminence, Francis Cardinal Spellman, archbishop of New York, pointed out that in 1953 the archdiocesan school system represented an outlay of over 233 million dollars and an annual expense of almost 64 million dollars for teaching staffs and maintenance.[2] The elementary and secondary schools in the Archdiocese of New York care for over 200,000 students, stu-

---

[1] Part 2, Question 38, p. 325.
[2] Letter of August 1953. These outlays have continued to swell over the past five years, as have the numbers of teachers, students, and schools.

dents for whose schooling the city authorities do not have to provide a penny. A recent survey conducted at Manhattan College shows that in the country as a whole Catholics will be called on to build more than 4,000 new elementary and secondary schools during the next decade at a cost of over a billion dollars.[3] Public-school systems are already deeply embarrassed financially. How much more serious would their condition be if the respective Catholic dioceses and parishes did not save them the cost of providing for all the children being educated in the parochial-school systems? It would be valuable to know how many standards are now observed in parochial schools because public schools introduced them, or in public schools because parochial schools took the initiative.

How can the laity be more and more integrated into the parish's apostolate—not a mere handful of them, but enough to bring the parish and its message consistently to every corner of the parish? It would be of great importance, both in theory and practice, to study the feasibility of increasing interaction and social relationships through the identification of the parish with various decentralized subgroupings, such as the Christian Family Movement groups and the Cub Scout dens.[4] Could the parish afford having its priests drawn away from the rectory to such groups at just the time, usually in the evening, when parishioners find their opportunity to come to the rectory? Since so many people do come to church and rectory, and since the priests' time is so very often taken up with those functions performed in church and rectory, it is not surprising that so many persons view the parish in terms of the church.

In this connection, with no particular reference now to OLM, an apparently sound hypothesis of both Père Georges Michonneau and Father Paul Furfey would be worth investigating. The

---

[3] See the release of the Religious News Service, August 9, 1955.
[4] See Chapter 13, pp. 247-60.

two writers suggest that it might be asked of parish priests in general whether they envision their pastoral role, both in seminary days and in the actual apostolate, as responsibility for a church to which parishioners come or responsibility for a parish within which a church is.[5] Here is no subtlety, but a difference in outlook and role appreciation which can, and probably does, seriously affect their apostolic attitude and policy. The need for the acceptance of the second alternative is one of the practical assumptions on which this study was undertaken. For a parish is not merely clergy and church servicing people who happen to come to them (except for peculiarly situated business-district parishes), but a system comprised of geographical area, priests, and parishioners functioning together in accordance with their respective statuses and roles for the achievement, protection, and development of definite values, and utilizing certain definite institutions toward that end.

The church, the parish's house for God and God's people, together with the entire liturgical system of sacrifice and sacraments, is the most important of those institutions. But it is not the only one; another important one is mutual knowledge of shepherd and sheep, not merely as individuals but as partial products of particular social milieu. A third is the legal assignment of all residents of the parish to the shepherd's staff, whether they follow it or not. And still another is both the invited and the needed participation of the laity in the parish work, on a scale large enough for the parish to accomplish its task: the evangelizing of every resident and the sanctification of every member. The use of such institutions requires the type of knowledge that was incipiently discussed and analyzed in the previous chapters.

It is not difficult to understand why many priests tend to view their apostolate as church centered rather than as parish

---

[5] See *Sociology of the Parish*, edited by Nuesse and Harte, p. 306.

or area centered. There can very easily be a disposition to visualize the parish in terms of the church. Yet that almost necessarily involves practical unconcern with those persons and families, sometimes distressingly numerous, who do not come to church or whose Catholic practice seems to be limited to performance of minimal religious obligations. Not that this church-centered disposition is universal, but it is certainly widespread enough to be seriously considered. In discussions with many active, dedicated parish priests, held in different situations and in various geographical areas both here and abroad, the author found that parish priests were often quite surprised at the dichotomy, had never previously considered it, and agreed with the wisdom of adopting the parish-area conceptualization of their apostolate.

Despite its unfinished character, our study of OLM as a functioning social organization has made some contributions. The methodology employed will be used by others, probably with improvements, for it is basically sound. The use of national census data provides both initial information and a constant control. The McBee Keysort research cards are both manageable on a parish basis and very helpful for discovering parish uniformities and relationships and in directing policy toward them.[6] The possibilities of using such an efficient procedure are almost without number. The structured compilation of parish data, mostly following Kelly, Schnepp, and Fichter

---

[6] It has been noted on pp. 98-99 that one of the curates of OLM was able to sort through the entire parish file in a few moments to obtain the names of prospective students in released-time classes. Should the pastor desire to communicate a message of specific pertinence to any group—the converts, the foreign born, certain educational or occupational classes, those weak in the practice of their religion, or any group—he can obtain all the names and addresses in a few minutes and is able to send his message with a minimum of search, expense, and time. Should he be desirous of discussing a matter of parish or public interest with a group of doctors, union officials, teachers, and so on, the same procedure could effectively be utilized.

but with additional features, both contributes to previous parish studies and broadens the path for future ones.

The Church's battle with the undying materialism, secularism, and indifference to God of succeeding generations will not be won by some master stroke of Vatican policy. The master strokes have, indeed, already been struck: the revelation of divine truth, the establishment and constitution of the Church, and the commission to carry Christ's redemptive word, the Mass, and the sacraments to all nations. It but remains to implement that commission. The divine appointment of the apostles as bishops implies a diocesan division of the Church's ordinary work in meeting that commission; the Church's appointment of pastors to rule and guide parishes is a further refinement of that division.

Though there are auxiliary apostolates, all presuppose and eventually depend upon the existence of the parish. In this day of advanced scientific techniques and social consciousness it is incumbent upon our parish leaders, clerical and lay, to accept the challenge of ever-increasing and realized responsibilities with all the possible equipment and advanced techniques at their command. This study of OLM Parish as a vitally functioning social system has been aimed at contributing to the development of that equipment and of those techniques.

Studies
in Religious Observance

The following paragraphs are intended to supplement the cursory view of studies in religious observance in Chapter 2. Almost all the information found here is taken from the various studies cited in Chapter 2 for the countries there mentioned. In addition summary material and a few more recent tabulations can be found in two excellent articles in *Actualité religieuse dans le monde*, no. 32 (July 15, 1954) and no. 52 (May 15, 1955), this last being the final issue of the periodical under that name. Thereafter, with practically the same format and purpose, it has been known as *Informations catholiques internationales*. Its issue for September 1, 1956 (no. 31) has a particularly valuable review of "Trois ans de sociologie religieuse en France." We look first at continental Europe and Latin America, then after summarizing those findings at the United States and England.

1. FRANCE

The survey made in Paris in 1954 showed that of its five million diocesan inhabitants, excluding non-Catholics, some 15 per cent attended Sunday Mass. Youths below the age of 14 accounted for anywhere from one fourth to three fourths of the attendance in the parishes of Paris. Adult attendance varied from 4 per cent to 20 per cent. Individual parish surveys confirmed this and also indicated the rate of women's observance. Of St.-Germain's 15,000 people, 23 per cent practiced Mass attendance, women outnumbering the men by two to one (67 per cent to 33 per cent). St.-Laurent showed almost the same sex ratio in observance. Of St.-Séverin's 11,000 people, 19 per cent attended Mass, again women leading men by two to one, and children comprising 20 per cent of the total. At St.-Sulpice, 20 per cent of whose residents attended Mass, the ratio was five to three in favor of women. St.-Hippolyte, situated in a working people's quarter, sees only 6 per cent of its 23,000 inhabitants at Mass, a great portion of them being children; 3.6 per cent of its factory workers and 4.5 per cent of the white-collar employees attend, women excelling the men by a ratio of four to one within both groups. In a middle-class section St.-Pierre at Neuilly, just outside Paris, welcomes 7,000 of its 32,000 people (22 per cent). One concerted survey, covering six parishes in the more or less typical fifteenth ward *(arrondissement)*, found that, of 230,000 people living within the six parishes' boundaries, 13 per cent attended Mass, the percentage of women in those attending ranging from 61 per cent to 68 per cent.

In general it was found that in good parishes observance was about 20 per cent, in more populous areas it was a bit under 10 per cent, and in the crowded sections inhabited by working classes it fell under 6 per cent. The 30-to-40-year age group was low in observance, and working people themselves (that is, manual laborers as opposed to white-collar employees) were represented at Mass by anywhere from 1 per cent to 3 per cent of their number. Invariably the conviction found expression: "Too great crowds, too few priests." Apparently a rather universal phenomenon of religious behavior, the late Masses were far more fully attended than the earlier ones.

Marseilles and Lyons, France's second and third largest cities with about 700,000 apiece, including suburbs, have rates of 13 per cent and 19 per cent respectively. In Marseilles women lead men by two to one; in Lyons by three to two. Marseilles' parishes range from 7 per cent to 29 per cent in Sunday observance. Practice diminishes with the years till old age, and women comprise over 65 per cent of the observants. Only 3 per cent of the workers attend Mass, though 23 per cent of the higher-placed attend. Of every 100 Marseillais at Mass, 75 are economically unoccupied—women, children, students—although such groups constitute only 50 per cent of the population.

In the Jura region studies were made of both rural and urban areas. The 45 parishes in the 4 rural cantons have an observance ratio of 38 per cent for their 77,000 adults (above 14 years), women outscoring men by almost nine to five. The range is quite great however, for it goes from 105 men per 100 women in one parish to 11 men per 100 women at the other extreme. Children comprise one third of the total observants, and farmers lead nonfarmers by four to three. In the small Jura city of Dole, with a population of 18,000, practice is 20 per cent, with females, both girls and women, outranking men and boys in practice by better than two to one. As against the over-all 20 per cent average, 26 per cent of the nonoccupied practice as compared with 21 per cent of the independent professionals and only 10 per cent of the workers. The author of this study thus summarizes religious observance by groups: the adults more than the young, men rather than women, the occupied rather than the economically inactive, workers as opposed to employers and professional people, and slum dwellers rather than the better housed. The superiority of slum dwellers to the better housed is a rather unusual characteristic.

The Grenoble ratio is better than 16 per cent of its 130,000 population. In its 15 parishes women outrank men better than two to one, comprising 68 per cent of the observants. Children are 17 per cent of all those attending Mass, and those between 14 and 20 years of age comprise another 15 per cent. At Nancy the ratio is just over 30 per cent. Only 6 per cent of the manual laborers attend Mass as contrasted with 43 per cent of the professionals and others in higher places and 35 per cent of all employees. Women comprised 68 per cent of the observants.

Across the Mediterranean a Tunis survey in 1952 showed 18 per cent practice for its 100,000 Catholic inhabitants, and Casablanca 13.5 per cent for its 150,000. In the latter women predominated three to two. In other French cities the story is more or less the same. In Rheims 16 per cent of its 90,000 attended Mass, 64 per cent of the observants being women. This 64 per cent, actually 9,000 women, was just 20 per cent of all the women; the 5,000 male observants represented 11 per cent of the men. Though its workers comprised 28 per cent (25,000) of its population, they made up only 3 per cent of those attending Mass. Almost 60 per cent of those attending Mass were not active in any economic occupation, being either retired, students, or housewives. In three of Rouen's downtown parishes, situated in working-class sections, 9.5 per cent for the 20,000 residents attended Mass, and of the workers just 3 per cent, chiefly women workers. Most of those in attendance were students, children, and housewives. Of the marriages 55 per cent were blessed in church. The parishes of Lille vary from 3.5 per cent to 64 per cent in observance, with an observance rate for adults (over 14 years) of about 20 per cent. Toulouse has a 15 per cent observance rate for its 265,000, with adults (15 years and over) achieving 12 per cent; and Saint-Etienne, with 180,000, has a rate of 28 per cent. This is relatively high for cities. But again we notice that only 5 per cent of the miners and 10 per cent of other manual workers attend Mass as contrasted with over 50 per cent of those in higher professions and 25 per cent of tradesmen and white-collar employees. Strasbourg shows a 45 per cent rate in Sunday practice, and the Diocese of Sees 40 per cent, but Calais only 13 per cent. In each of these last three cases women retain their three to two or two to one lead over men.

In rural France, thanks to Boulard's extensive work, we know that, of almost 20,000,000 residents, about 38 per cent attend Mass regularly, 57 per cent at least make their Easter duty, almost 2 per cent are Protestants, and the remaining 3 per cent range from little practice to nothing. Total France, cities and rural areas included, has a rate of some 34 per cent for those over 14 years making their Easter duty, which implies about 30 per cent for the adults. It would seem that the rate for Sunday Mass attendance is just about 20 per cent or a little more.

2.   THE LOW COUNTRIES

Catholic Belgium's religious-observance map for the whole country, based on Sunday Mass attendance, shows that its total population of almost 9,000,000 has an observance rate of 49.6 per cent, practically 50 per cent if adjustment is made for the legitimately excused. The Flemings 4,500,000 have a rate of 60 per cent as compared with the 3,000,000 Walloons' 41 per cent and 35 per cent for the inhabitants of Brussels and its environs. The limited study of La Louvière, in the least practicing province of Hainsult, shows 13 per cent practice among 1,169 persons, with adults achieving 11 per cent, women outranking men by five to three, children making up 16 per cent of the observants, and only 4.5 per cent of the workingmen in attendance. In the Kerkhofs study of devout Limburg we see that almost 80 per cent of its nearly half-million inhabitants practice regularly; the cities are less strong than the country, and the southern part of the province is weakened through disaffection in less devout Liége. Its numerous vocations come from the areas where practice is highest. Liége (the city) and Brussels both have rates higher than 25 per cent—26 per cent for Brussels, 27 per cent for Liége. The disparity between this figure for Brussels and the 35 per cent given above is probably due to the lower figure's lack of adjustment for the legitimately excused and the higher figure's inclusion of parishes in the environs of Brussels. Liegois women outscore the men by three to two (61 per cent to 39 per cent). Children up to 20 account for 40 per cent of the observants; practicing women are 23 per cent of all Liége women and practicing men are 17 per cent of all Liége men. Of Liége's occupational groups 6 per cent of its workers go to Mass, 18 per cent of its white-collar employees, 12 per cent of its self-employed, and 34 per cent of its secondary-school graduates (presumably in the professional classes). The limited study of engaged couples in a single Brussels parish shows women leading men in religious practice almost four to three (56 per cent to 44 per cent). Antwerp, with a population of over half a million, has a relatively high practice rate of almost 32 per cent.

The available religious-observance map of Holland shows areas of different rates of practice but does not make calculation possible. The cities constantly show the lowest rates. The single study of Amsterdam, 23 per cent of whose 759,000 are Catholics, shows a Mass-attendance rate of over 48 per cent and an Easter-duty rate of 62 per cent.

3.   GERMANY AND AUSTRIA

German religious statistics could give more information than those of any other country, but they have not been analyzed very extensively. The recent breakdown according to dioceses shows that West Germany's 23,000,-000 Catholics have a Mass-attendance rate of not quite 48 per cent and an Easter-duty rate of almost 55 per cent. Russian-controlled Germany's 2,100,-000 Catholics have rates of 29 per cent and 37 per cent for Easter duty. Köln (Cologne), the largest German diocese, with 2,700,000 Catholics, has Sunday-attendance and Easter-duty rates of 41 per cent and 43 per cent; and Breslau, in the Russian zone and the smallest diocese, with 94,000 Catholics, has rates of 31 per cent and 41 per cent. The dioceses with the highest rate of practice are Passau (almost 500,000 Catholics) with 56 per cent and 78 per cent, and Regensburg (over 1,125,000 Catholics) with 60 per cent and 76 per cent. The lowest rate belongs to the Russian-zone Meissen, whose 550,000 Catholics have a 25 per cent Mass-attendance rate and a 29 per cent Easter-duty record.

A recent Austrian survey shows a 43 per cent Easter-duty rate and 30 per cent Sunday-observance rate.

4. ITALY

Not enough is available in published documents for us to have a broad-scale picture of Italian religious life. Father Droulers and Father Rimoldi refer to some studies showing variation in Mass attendance and Easter duty ranging from 10 per cent to 95 per cent and 16 per cent to 98 per cent, respectively. More specifically, to quote Droulers and Rimoldi, "In the parishes of Venezia (even in the towns), the Marches, and to the south of Piacenza, the percentage of practicing Catholics is from 80 to 100%, while in the towns of Emilia (even in the country), Tuscany and Liguria it falls to 30%, even to 10-15% with women in the majority, but with a general predominance of the paschal observance over Sunday Mass. . . . In the south of Calabria, in the large towns, the percentage of men fulfilling their Easter duties is estimated at about 35% and attendance at Sunday Mass at 30%, while in the smaller centers it is 50% and 40% respectively, the proportion of women being much higher. . . . In Sicily, ten years ago, fulfillment of the paschal precept and attendance at Sunday Mass by men and youths in some parts did not go beyond 10%, some times much less . . . a revival has taken place since."[1]

Figures for Rome are not available, and the same authors merely refer to "experienced people" who judge that about 10 per cent of men and youths make their Easter duty, women having a much higher record, and the rate continues to decrease. Mention is made of parishes which are too large and other parishes which are far too small. Swoboda's study in 1908 showed no Roman parish to have as many as 20,000 souls, but Droulers

---

[1] *Lumen vitae*, Vol. 6, nos. 1-2, January-June 1951, p. 82.

and Rimoldi say that some have 50,000 to 60,000. A visitor to Rome can see quite easily this wide variation between populous parishes in residential districts and parishes with few parishioners in the center of the city.

In Milan, to quote Droulers and Rimoldi again: "The figures for the men making their Easter duties seem to vary between 25% and 17%. At Varesotto, to the north, the large towns are better in their centers than in their immediate neighborhood (55% against 35%), the country parishes better than the hamlets (85% against 60%). In the agricultural zone to the south the proportion is 50%. Generally speaking, except in the parishes of the town itself, there is a predominance of the performance of the paschal precept over Sunday Mass."[2]

The Diocese of Mantua has an Easter-duty rate of 60 per cent. Generally speaking, the working class has a 25 per cent rate contrasted with a 47 per cent rate for farmers and landowners. Women and children raise the general average. Mass attendance varies from 47 per cent in the north of the diocese to 26 per cent in the south, women making up from 60 per cent to 75 per cent of the total.

5.   SPAIN

Available are recent studies of Bilbao, Madrid and its environs, and a few Barcelona parishes. Madrid's 1,750,000 population has an 18 per cent rate of practice (Mass attendance) among its adults (18 years and over), according to a survey in 1942. Ten years later a survey showed Bilbao's 250,000 to have a rate of Sunday Mass attendance of 54 per cent, with parish rates ranging from 25 per cent to over 70 per cent. Four Barcelona parishes were surveyed: one with a mixed population of 5,000, mostly workers and small farmers; another of 20,000 with predominantly bourgeois middle-class residents; a suburban lower-middle-class parish of 9,000; and a suburban working-class community also with 9,000 people. The worker-farmer parish showed 30 per cent of the men and 60 per cent of the women regular in observance. The middle-class parish has an observance rate of 20 per cent; the lower-middle-class parish rose in recent years from 1 per cent to 12 per cent; and the suburban worker parish had less than 1,000 regular observants, somewhat less than half being children, and only one man in forty being a regular observant. Most of the foregoing figures indicate higher rates than those found less recently in some individual parishes in various cities: in many rural parishes in southern Spain only 10 per cent are regular in their practice; in some rural parishes in the dioceses of Madrid, Cuenca, and Toledo practice is as low as 5 per cent; in some industrial parishes in Madrid, Seville, and Bilbao, declares Father Delaa, one

---

2 *Ibid.*, pp. 83-84.

comes across great sections of the population which are completely pagan. In the outskirts of the capital a parish like St. Ramon de Vallecas has a Sunday Mass attendance of 4 per cent, including 3,000 school children; 6 per cent receive their Easter Communion; 10 per cent receive the last sacraments; 25 per cent of the children are not baptized; 20 per cent of the marriages are civil marriages, and of the couples who are married in church 40 per cent do not know the Our Father. These conditions exist despite numerous "contact" schemes inspired by Catholic zeal. Father Delaa cites discouraging figures from Father Sarabia, who wrote in 1939, but it must be remembered that in 1939 Spain was still recovering from the effects of its cataclysmic civil war.

Many of the reports and estimates present a rather dark picture. The sociologist can learn from them, but he cannot be satisfied with them. The emphasis is rather constantly on the negative, whereas the sociologist should be concerned as much about what is good as about what is not good, about communities where religious practice is high as about those where it is quite minimal. It would be sociologically interesting, as well as pastorally helpful, to study the difference in outlook on life between inhabitants of the Basque country, where practice is high, and southern Spain, where apparently practice is low. Are there any contributing sociological explanations for the rise in practice in Madrid since 1939? At that time Mass attendance was as low as 6 per cent, whereas in 1946 it had risen to 19 per cent in several parishes under study. For one thing, some of the mammoth parishes have been divided into as many as six smaller parishes.

6.   BRAZIL

One knowledgeable evaluation of Brazilian Catholicism reports that there are over 40,000,000 Catholics being served by just over 3,000 parishes, which represents a rapid increase of 800 parishes between 1929 and 1947. This still means, however, an average of some 13,000 persons per parish, often in very difficult terrain, as contrasted with the American average of a parish for about 2,500 persons. Vocations are insufficient and much superstitious cult apparently has a part in many Brazilians' religious customs. A study of the marital situation of 1,400 Brazilians in the industrial city of Bahia showed that 38 per cent of them were involved in free unions, and that of the 32 per cent who were married, 41 per cent were married civilly, 18 per cent were married only in a religious ceremony, and 41 per cent were married in both civil and religious ceremony.

7.   SUMMARY

Before proceeding to American studies it seems well to summarize some of the more evident uniformities apparent in the foregoing reports, as indicated in the analyses of various commentators. Of first importance are uniformities and variations in the rate of religious practice itself. With the exception of some cities (Bilbao, Antwerp, Strasbourg, a couple in northern Italy, apparently a few in both Holland and Germany) with a relatively high adult practice rate of more than 30 per cent, most cities range between 30 per cent and 15 per cent, or even lower. One cannot speak of a law or generalization in simple terms of city and country practice, for some cities far surpass some rural areas even within their own environs. Indeed, there are sizable variations within the same city. But the findings that have been reported are an invitation, first, to determine the extent to which all cities share in the characteristic of 15 per cent to 30 per cent practice and second, to search for the reason for the fact that observance is so poor or is erroneously thought to be so poor.

It should be mentioned here that many of the statistics cited thus far are to be accepted with caution. Are percentages taken of the total population, the total Catholic population, or the Catholic population obliged to practice? In many instances, obviously, these varying methods of calculating percentages will lead to widely varying conclusions. Then, too, many of the surveys were based on answers to inquiries handed out to all present at the parish Masses on one or other "typical" Sunday. All sorts of extrinsic circumstances might have made that particular Sunday unexpectedly atypical. On the other hand the very fact that one survey after another showed conformity with the same general pattern suggests that the method was at least a serviceable guide. Then, too, the assumption that all those present on the particular Sunday should be considered regular practitioners may not be valid. What of those who attend one, two, or three weeks out of four? It would seem that any true picture of practice in a parish, diocese, city, or country should take account of those who are part-time practitioners.

One uniformity that is almost universal in the surveys already cited is the predominance of women over men in religious practice. And this predominance is almost always in terms of two to one. Why is this? Is it due to something in woman's nature? If so, how explain the fact that practicing women are themselves only a fraction of those women whom their ecclesiastical society obliges to practice? Or, since there is also a close relationship between observance and freedom from economic activity, perhaps the answer is to be found rather in women's sociofunctional role. At any rate, the fact implies a problem for the parish in terms of preaching, guidance, and policy in auxiliary activity, for two thirds of the Sunday congregation can be expected to be women.

A similar question arises from the disproportionate number of preadults and elderly adults who practice. In those surveys in which apposite information was given, both young and old practiced in a higher ratio than their proportion of the total Catholic population would warrant. This was why Abbé Daniel warned that churches were allowing themselves to cater to women and children. Age analysis indicated that lapsing from practice came largely after either reception of solemn Communion, or at the end of elementary school, or at the commencement of marriage. Since it can be doubted that these events cause an immediate change of values or norms in young people's minds, one might ask whether their practice is motivated merely by social example rather than conviction, and if so, whether the religious society can do anything to win adherence of its members on a more personally voluntary basis. Of course there always remains the fact, which must be explained no less than that of lapsing, that many people, whether minority or majority, do remain faithful to religious practice.

One uniformity in the lapsing of youth from religious practice seems to be that children of bourgeois families lapse less frequently (33 per cent to 47 per cent) than children from worker families (50 per cent to 79 per cent). This might indicate that age is not the important determining factor, but rather social role and status. For whereas the worker's son in European society moves into the worker's milieu after elementary school, the bourgeois son continues at school and in various other middle-class groups where the Church's role is well established.

Another uniformity, regrettably widespread, has been implied in the previous paragraph: religiously observant workers have a ratio far below their proportion of the total Catholic population. With the exception of those few cities which have an extremely high rate of practice and in which workers practice almost as well as any other group, their lack of practice shows how much truth there was in Pius XI's plaint that the Church has lost the working class. Of course, as suggested previously, this must be understood correctly. At no time did the Church reject or turn its back on the working class; rather, the working class sprang up in the industrial age without the Church's being effectively aware of its growth. Again we might ask whether being workers has anything to do with nonpractice, or whether nonpractice is more causally connected with overcrowded living in slum housing, with minimal wages, and with lack of education, all of which also have a high degree of relationship with nonpractice.

Indeed, almost any European parish map of religious practice shows the least observant people living precisely in the overcrowded areas. Overcrowding plus nonattendance at Mass means, perhaps paradoxically, that too few parishes and too few priests are assigned for the ministry needed by these people. The result is the well-known vicious circle: no more priests are assigned because the parish is dead, and the parish remains dead because there are not enough priests to enliven it. Incidentally, as a result of the Grenoble study, Bishop Caillot and his clergy have instituted a new practical study aimed at realigning priests and parishes in accordance with population needs. Evening Masses and several of France's experiments to get in contact with the working classes derived from the exposition of similar parochial facts.

All the foregoing factors, and undoubtedly more, help to form the social structure of the city as seen from the viewpoint of religious practice in several countries. Certain patterns have become more or less evident, and it will be revealing now to see whether and to what extent the few American studies show conformity with those patterns.

8.   THE UNITED STATES AND ENGLAND

Aside from some earlier and somewhat speculative studies on leakage from the faith, and Bishop Shaughnessy's often quoted *Has the Immigrant Kept the Faith?*[3] the first parish study pertinent to our purpose is Brother McCaffrey's *Youth in a Catholic Parish.*[4] His parish, which suffered from a high rate of mobility and a fairly large national group not yet too well assimilated, included some 930 Catholic families with 2,800 members. Total parish observance rate was 71 per cent (2,000 out of 2,800). Fifty-one per cent of the adult men practice and 60 per cent of the adult women. Neglect in adult practice totals 44 per cent. Of the 280 young people (unmarried, aged 16 to 24), some 71 per cent practiced their faith regularly; 31 per cent of the boys and 27 per cent of the girls were negligent.

The Schnepp parish study[5] examined the practice record of 3,720 parishioners (1,115 families, over 90 per cent of the parish) according to the factors of nationality, marriage type, education, conversion (if any), social life, and economic life. Of all individuals, 80 per cent practiced regularly, 4 per cent were lax (practiced irregularly), and 16 per cent were lapsed (did not practice). The observants (those who practiced regularly) were 80 per cent of the parish and comprised 53 per cent women and 47 per cent men; the lax were 63 per cent male and 37 per cent female; and the lapsed were 56 per cent male and 44 per cent female. Single persons 15 years and over had an even better record than the whole parish, with an 86 per cent practice rate (81 per cent male, 92 per cent female). Economic condition did not appear to play too great a role. But whereas 70 per cent of the parish's families were recorded as practicing (everyone in the family was so recorded), only 60 per cent of workers' families were in that category, most leakage apparently centering in workers with least security and most mobility. Lapsed families had the greater proportion of children in non-

---

[3] Gerald Shaughnessy, *Has the Immigrant Kept the Faith?* New York: The Macmillan Company, 1929.

[4] Augustine McCaffrey, *Youth in a Catholic Parish.* Washington: The Catholic University of America Press, 1941.

[5] Gerald J. Schnepp, *Leakage from a Catholic Parish.* Washington: The Catholic University of America Press, 1942.

Catholic schools. There were more lapsed among mixed-marriage families (24 per cent, or 78 out of 330) than among Catholic-marriage families (6 per cent, or 26 out of 457). The widowed showed the highest rate of practice, followed by the single (including those above 15 years of age), the married, the separated and divorced. The confusion in parish membership registration occasioned by the presence of a national (nonterritorial) parish seemed to contribute to leakage, particularly among those who could be presumed to belong to the national parish.

Brother Schnepp reaches several other conclusions pertaining to mixed marriage, converts, public education, the effect of youth and adult programs on leakage and practice, social and recreational activities, and economic status, to which reference is made in our own study of OLM Parish. His parish study was the first of its type, more detailed and analytic than any of the European studies have yet been; and it is a veritable gold mine of statistical data for parish research. It seems regrettable that so little attention has been paid it in subsequent parish studies.

Father Kelly's extensive and intensive study of Catholics in Florida[6] provides much helpful information and many provocative indications. It embraces some 40,000 of the identifiable white, English-speaking Catholics in the Diocese of St. Augustine. Of all married Catholics (almost 18,500), including those in Catholic marriages, convert marriages, and mixed marriages, 75 per cent made their Easter duty and 75 per cent regularly attend Sunday Mass. Another 12 per cent attended Mass irregularly. In both Easter and Sunday observance those in convert marriages had the highest rate and those in mixed marriages the lowest. An interesting item, rather at variance with most European figures, is that, whereas persons in Catholic and convert marriages have a slightly higher rate for Easter than for Sunday observance, those in mixed marriages have a higher Sunday-observance record. There is little variation with age, though there is a slight dip in practice beginning with the thirties and a rise in later life. In neither variation is the range comparable to European age differentials. In each type of marriage women lead men in practice; this lead is about 6 per cent or 7 per cent in Catholic and convert marriages and about 15 per cent in mixed marriages. Except for the poor record of men in mixed marriages (about 50 per cent) each group is close to or well over a 70 per cent observance rate. Evidently the religious-observance leadership of American Catholic women, insofar as manifested in this diocesan survey, is minimal when compared with frequent European leadership ratios of two to one. If only valid marriages are considered, each marital group averages well

---

[6] George A. Kelly, *Catholics and Practice of the Faith.* Washington: The Catholic University of America Press, 1946.

over 80 per cent in both Easter and Sunday observance, even the males in mixed marriages achieving a 75 per cent rate.

Monthly (voluntary) Communion rates, which would be higher if only valid marriages were included, come close to 45 per cent for all types of marriage combined, women leading men by about 10 per cent. More specific data concerning converts, the widowed, the divorced, and the separated are considered, as was done in our study of OLM. As to mixed marriages, more Catholic women (about one in three) enter them than men (about one in five), but Catholic women's rate of invalidity in marriage is lower than men's, and their religious-observance rate is higher than Catholic men's in mixed marriages. Women in valid mixed marriages are very close to women in Catholic and convert marriages in rate of religious practice.

The fact that one parent is not a Catholic (unless the marriage is invalid, which adversely influences children's practice) has little effect on children's participation in obligatory religious exercises. Children of mixed marriages practice almost as well as others. But in voluntary acts, such as monthly Communion, the children of mixed marriages have not so good a record as the children of two Catholic parents. Sons born of mixed marriages tend to enter mixed marriages at the same rate as other men; daughters tend to marry non-Catholics at a higher rate (one in two) than other Catholic girls (one in three).

Education has little influence on the male rate of entering mixed marriages, but women with college education more readily marry non-Catholic partners, particularly if their education has been partly Catholic, partly public. On the other hand exclusively Catholic education tends to reduce women's participation in mixed marriages. Generally speaking, education tends to help religious practice. A high positive relationship between men's religious practice and a high-school education seems to imply some necessity for the latter. It would not appear to be so requisite for women. Catholic education is important, particularly above the seventh grade, in terms of men's voluntary religious practice. Reception of monthly Communion is some 30 per cent more frequent among those educated in Catholic schools.

Father Kelly found that native-born Americans tend to enter mixed marriages more readily than the foreign born. This is especially true of women, of people in the South, and of rural nonfarmers. Native-born Catholics have a slightly higher rate of religious observance, though a few foreign groups (Irish, English, Canadian) rate very high. A quite significant finding was that urban Catholics do slightly better in religious practice than their rural cousins, which is quite different from Europe's experience. Metropolitan areas in Florida and the diocese as a whole have almost identical religious-observance rates.

In economic matters little difference was found religiously between employee and employer or self-employed, though employed women tend to be involved in mixed marriages more than those who are not employed outside the home. Career women have as good a rate of practice as housewives, though women in the service trades tend to be more lax. Those workers engaged in manufacturing, and especially the unskilled, have the highest rate of marriage invalidity and the lowest rate of religious practice. Home ownership as contrasted with renting has no religious significance, but mixed marriages are more prevalent among those paying lower rent. Renter and owner have about the same rate of practice except in the lowest bracket, where the renter is more observant than the owner.

The Kelly study will prove to be an invaluable source of comparison for future studies of religious observance. Rather diocesan than parochial, it provides a wider backdrop than would most parish studies. It is difficult to understand why European authors merely refer to it without comparing its data with their own and why Father Houtart and others make no reference to it in discussing American religious observance.

Father Kelly examined religious observance. Father Fichter's studies, while they included observance, were aimed more at a sociological understanding of the structure and function of the Catholic city parish. The first, *Southern Parish. Volume I: Dynamics of a City Church*,[7] examines religious practice in a large, well-reputed New Orleans parish, but the study of practice is not limited to Sunday Mass attendance and Easter duty. After describing both place and people according to aspects varying from race and nationality to the politics of the parish, *Southern Parish* discusses both the nature and use of each of the parish's religious functions and services: each of the sacraments, the Mass, particular devotions, and even the extent to which parish ideals were reflected in the parishioners' attitudes. Father Fichter's findings were less encouraging than those of Schnepp and Kelly. Of 11,000 born Catholics, some 6,500 considered themselves as practicing Catholics. The study concerns itself only with this approximately 60 per cent of the total number. As to the others, many never become consciously members of the parish, any connections they had with it having stopped right after their baptism in infancy. Hence a great deal of leakage occurred even in infancy.

Over 600 of Southern Parish's members went to confession at least monthly, another 3,500 at least annually (many more often than that), daily communicants ranged from 50 to 150 throughout the year, the latter figure coming during Lent; weekly communicants ranged from over 400 to over 800 (the latter being likewise a lenten figure); monthly Sunday Communions ranged from over 1,650 to over 3,500 (Lent and Easter). Other

---

[7] Joseph H. Fichter, *Southern Parish. Volume I: Dynamics of a City Church*. Chicago: The University of Chicago Press, 1951.

aspects of practice show similar variation from frequent use of the parish's religious services to nonuse. The findings of this study of religious practice would seem to indicate that there is a good deal of effective functioning, as well as a large area in which the parish's purpose is not achieved. Just over 3,000 of Southern Parish parishioners attend Sunday Mass regularly, almost 800 but monthly, over 850 once or twice a year, and over 600 never attend. This represents a regular Mass-attendance rate of somewhat less than 60 per cent without an adjustment for the legitimately excused.

The second Fichter study, *Social Relations in the Urban Parish*,[8] represents real progress in parochial sociology. The author constructs a series of parishioner types (nuclear or ideal, modal or average, marginal or lax, and dormant or lapsed), thereby enabling a study of religious effectiveness according to uniform types and the social influences most closely identified with those types. For example, a study of marginal parishioners (some 20 per cent of the author's study as compared with 10 per cent nuclear and 70 per cent modal, the dormant not being included) provided enough evidence to suggest the hypothesis that the marginal parishioner has committed himself to his social life to the conflicting values of other institutions, such as Sunday-morning golf, unchristian ethics in business, perhaps the anti-Catholic attitudes of his professional associates. He remains associated with his Church, rather on the fringe; but that association is made and kept weak by his acceptance of other relationships incompatible with his religious adherence. He therefore partially accepts and partially rejects, at least implicitly, his religious values. The pastoral approach to the marginal man as distinct from other types of his parishioners would be intelligent analysis of the reasons for attaching value to these institutions hostile to religious dedication and a counterattack against them.

Father Fichter found a sharper dip in practice in the 30-39 age group than did Kelly. Likewise, although the sex factor provides almost the same differential in required religious practices as Kelly found, Fichter notes that females have a far greater lead in voluntary practices. Residential mobility apparently plays little part in the practice ratio of American urban Catholics. The role analysis which Father Fichter structured for the parish priest enables religionist and sociologist to know the parish society more clearly through an understanding of its most important personality.

The *Catholic Digest* survey, conducted by a professional marketing and opinion-research firm and published in a series of thirty articles on "Religion in America" beginning with the November 1952 issue, showed that of 23,700,000 adult American Catholics 87 per cent considered them-

---

[8] Joseph H. Fichter, *Social Relations in the Urban Parish*. Chicago: The University of Chicago Press, 1954.

selves active in their religion and 82 per cent had attended church during the twelve weeks previous to the survey. This is hardly an adequate criterion for judging the amount or regular weekly attendance at Mass, but it makes one cautious in the face of general estimates to the contrary.

As a matter of fact, this survey also showed that 62 per cent of the Roman Catholics say that they have attended Mass every Sunday during the last twelve weeks. Thanks to the usual sampling devices the research firm is satisfied that the chances are 99 in 100 that the sampling error does not exceed plus or minus 5 per cent. In other words, had all American Catholics been asked this question, between 57 per cent and 67 per cent would have answered in this way. (See "Technical Information Research Method Used in the Catholic Digest Study of Religious Beliefs, Attitudes, and Practice of U.S. Adults" [mimeographed], the Catholic Digest Publishing Company.)

A most recent English study, *Youth and Religion,* published by the Young Christian Workers, presents the results of its "scientific inquiry into the religious attitudes, beliefs, and practices of urban youth." It reports a level of 76 per cent practice, which is comparable to the 68 per cent level of practice among adult (over 16 years of age) Roman Catholics as reported by the British Broadcasting Company. Girls lead boys by 77 per cent to 76 per cent. Mass attendance was lowest in London (less than 65 per cent); highest in Liverpool and Birmingham. Evidently England and the United States are more like each other than they are like the continent in their relatively high practice and in the relatively low lead of women observants over men.[9]

These few American and English studies suggest that, although Europe is far in the lead in the number and relative uniformity of socioreligious surveys, Europeans have not yet begun to explore so deeply as have, for example, Fathers Kelly and Fichter and Brother Schnepp. On the other hand the latter's contributions provide only a beginning. Many other simple quantitative studies are necessary to identify trends, characteristics, uniformities, and dissimilarities in religious practice which can profitably be made the subject of thorough analysis.

---

[9] A. E. C. W. Spencer, E. Mellon, and W. N. T. Roberts, *Youth and Religion.* London: Young Catholic Workers, 1958.

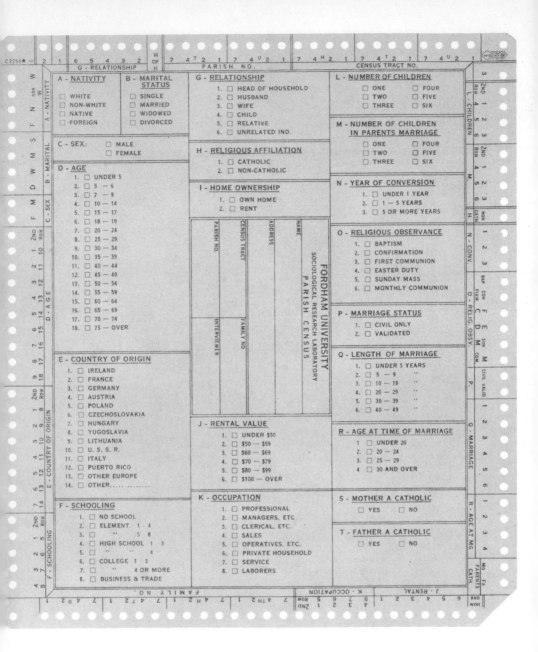

The Royal McBee keysort card,
described on pages 98-99 and 329-30,
reduces the time required for tabulations.

Parishioners received one copy
of this census form filled out as a sample
and a blank copy for their own use.
The form shown here has been enlarged
by adding space between the lines.

Census Materials

To avoid breaking the continuity of the text of Chapter 4 any more than necessary, few of the materials used in our OLM study were exhibited there. To satisfy the interest of many parish priests and lay leaders who may wish to examine models for possible studies of their own, and for the benefit of those readers desirous of following the references in the text more closely, materials not shown in Chapter 4 are reproduced here.

The first is a reproduction of the special issue of *The Parish Monthly* of OLM for December 1954. Its aim was to communicate to all parishioners both an awareness of the meaning and importance of their parish census and a sense of personal responsibility for participation. It is reproduced here since several parish priests throughout the country have found it suitable for their own purposes. While we knew that many parishioners would not take time to read it, we were confident that many of the more interested and responsible would read it with personal and parochial profit. The cover, title page, table of contents, and aspirations that were injected here and there have been omitted.

Do I Know My Parish?

Every tenth year the United States government spends many tens of millions of dollars taking the national census. All other governments take regular inventory. Large and small businesses do the same, and so do most social organizations of importance. To plan their operations, to know what services are needed, what their clients expect, what their own organization can provide, they willingly make these periodic investigations—even at great cost.

How many schools does a city need? How many roads will a state have to build? How many newlyweds will soon be looking for homes? The answers to these questions are important to social, political, and economic life—and the answers can be had only by knowing the facts. That's the value of taking inventory, or a census.

We all know that the Church is a social organization—a society divinely instituted by Christ and confided by Him to the care of His pope, bishops, and pastors. We know too, as Archbishop Cushing of Boston once expressed it, that the parish "with its pastor and priests, its altar and confessionals, its pulpits and schools, its good works, its sinners, its saints—the Catholic parish so constituted is . . . the whole Church in miniature, and through the parish Christ does for a limited group what He founded the Universal Church to do for the whole world."

There are of course some small parishes, mostly in the country, where the pastor will know his flock so well that he doesn't need to take inventory. But in the large city churches that is impossible. In a parish of more than 5,000 souls (and there are many such) a priest can't possibly know his parish thoroughly—what it has, what it needs, what its parishioners need—merely from personal contact. So, as the leader of any other large enterprise, the pastor too must take inventory—to know his parish as a whole, to have a record of all his flock. With that knowledge he can help, with the aid of his people, to make his "church in miniature" ever more effective in the work of bringing Christ to men and men to Him.

That is why the parish census is so necessary, so important. It is of course as valuable for the parishioners as it is for the pastor—even more so—for the parishioners benefit most from their church's effectiveness, and the facts from the census enable the pastor to assure that effectiveness.

So Our Lady of Mercy Parish is about to take up its next census. We hope to do it quickly and well, under the patronage of Our Lady's Immaculate Conception, on whose feast we'll begin. The cooperation of the whole parish is essential—both those who help take up the census, and everyone else. And we look for the parishioners of OLM to be as helpful in this work as they are in so many parish activities.

Church Law Requires the Census

Taking the parish census is not merely a matter of good sense and intelligent management on the part of the individual parish. Because the census is so important, the Church's official *Code of Canon Law* (Canon 470 No. 1) requires:

"The pastor should keep the parish books, that is, the book of the baptized, of the confirmed, of the married, of the deceased; in addition he should aim, as well as he can, to record accurately the book of the census; and, according to the usage of the Church, or the regulation of his own ordinary (bishop), he should keep all these books carefully up to date and in proper order."

Because of the many demands of a large and well-organized parish on the priests' time and attention, the above law is not always easy to keep. However, it is nonetheless important, and the parish's Legion of Mary has done most valuable work in compiling the census for several years. We intend now, however, with the parishoners' help, to bring the whole parish census up to date.

And Not Only Catholics!

Our holy father, speaking to the clergy of Rome this past February, recognized the great difficulty of maintaining contact between priest and so many parishioners in the large modern parishes. Citing our Lord's words, "the harvest indeed is great, but the laborers are few" (Matthew 9:37), the pope adds:

"We are a few priests who do not stop working, and do not rest; but what can we do? How is it possible to be mediators between God and the thousands of souls entrusted to our care. And how can we go into certain 'zones' spiritually more backward, if our presence there would arouse, we do not say hostility, but wonder in those very souls we are seeking?"

But then the Holy Father immediately answers: "And yet, even in those circumstances, you do not cease being pastors of *all the souls who live in your parish*."

An important part of the answer to this tremendous problem is, according to the pope, the help of the laity in the apostolate:

"From this there naturally follows, dear sons, the necessity of obtaining help, of finding collaborators capable of multiplying your strength and capacity, ready to supply for you where you do not succeed in penetrating. Hence the great importance of the apostolate of the laity which, as you yourselves know from your own experience, can become a powerful source of good."

As with so many large parishes, this applies also to our own parish. The 1950 United States Census shows that there are well over 30,000 souls living within the boundaries of OLM—in over 8,800 household units. Simply to take a complete census of all those homes is far too much for already very busy parish priests alone.

That's why it's utterly necessary for the parish to help with this census work, as the Church and our holy father intend.

In This, the Church in America Lags Behind!

For one reason and another (we wish it weren't so!) the United States Census doesn't ask us what religion we profess. Until 1936 it had conducted an additional but incomplete religious census every ten years, but even that has been, at least during the recent war, discontinued. Other democratic countries with people of different religious faiths include that question in their census, and the people naturally have no objection to it. But in this country we don't have it—and what a loss that means! Instead of having one simple additional question asked on the regular government census every ten years, every religious organization now has to take its own census. In terms of time, effort, and expense that means a tremendous cost. That's why so many dioceses and parishes in this country lag behind.

We don't even know how many Catholics are in the country, for the statistics compiled annually for the Catholic Directory are admittedly inaccurate. In fact, a recent scholarly estimate showed that there are probably 10 million more Catholics (about 41,000,000) than the figure currently given (a little over 31,000,000). We can be certain of neither figure, and it shows how inaccurate our knowledge is. And such knowledge is important, of course.

One parish in a large city thought it had almost 1,000 families; actually it had almost 3,000 Catholic families! We don't have anything like that uncertainty in OLM, for thanks to the census work of the Legion of Mary and the Rosary Crusade we have a fairly good idea of our parish population. But we want to be sure—and as exact as we can be.

In some other countries every diocese and parish has the necessary information to direct policy for building schools, hospitals, youth organizations, etc. They may have other difficulties, but at least they have the facts. Some of the statistical records in Germany, Belgium, Holland, and France are extremely helpful to the Church's apostolic workers—both priests and laity.

Naturally the dioceses depend on parishes for facts. In the Bronx alone we have 55 regular territorial parishes (not counting the national parishes). We want OLM Parish to be one on which the archdiocese can depend for accurate facts. We want to make our own contribution, in addition to benefiting the parish itself, to the collection of dependable religious statistics for the Catholic Church in the United States.

Those who help with this work will themselves make a valuable contribution to parish, archdiocese, and the Church as a whole.

OLM Has Experience!

We won't be starting our census project as if we were doing something entirely brand-new without experience. Several priests in the parish have had sizable census experience. In addition there's been consultation with others of experience, and there has also been consideration of different ways of taking the census used by other parishes elsewhere.

But of particularly valuable help, too, is the experience of many members of the parish who have participated in certain parish activities. For example, the energetic and zealous Legion of Mary members have been constantly working on a census for years, for it helps their effectiveness in their apostolic work. The present census aims to bring our records completely up to date. The Legionaries have too much other work to spare them for that purpose, and too few members. But their experience will be of great help. Another successful enterprise of a couple of years ago will stand us in good stead: the Rosary Crusade. Over 2,700 of 3,200 families pledged themselves in the all-out drive which covered every home in the parish. The concentrated experience of the teams who worked in that crusade will make our census that much more effective.

The annual Catholic Charities Drive, also depending on the hard work and cooperation of many teammates, has added to the parish experience and should make that much easier our efforts for a complete census. And the bazaar canvass, which resulted in the distribution of books to some 5,000 parishioners, gives us a substantial parish list with which to start.

Undoubtedly the joint efforts of those parishioners who have already been so helpful, plus the added assistance of new volunteers, can help OLM achieve an effective, quick, and complete census of the whole parish.

Your experience and help are essential to OLM success!

The Parish Is a Society

Something we don't want to forget is this fact: the parish, any parish, is set up as a society. Any society exists to help its members to acquire certain benefits. The parish is a religious society, and aims at helping its members acquire spiritual benefit. Because spiritual and religious life is so closely connected with the day-to-day living of our temporal lives, knowledge of material conditions is also important to the parish.

Naturally, then, the parish, as a good society, wants to know how well it is serving its members, how many of its members take full advantage of it, whether there are any material conditions interfering with healthy spiritual life, whether there might be any particular types of parishioners who could use special help or service, whether there's a situation that needs particular attention.

While our census can't tell us everything we want to know, it can help very much. That is why this census effort is so important to us all, and why the help of as many as possible is necessary.

The Census Is Strictly Confidential

The information you put down on the census form is for the eyes of the parish priests alone. The census forms will be kept in the parish file, reserved for their use alone. That's why you will receive an envelope with your census form. After filling out the form, you will put it in the envelope and seal it. Thereafter that information will be used by no one other than your parish priests.

The value of this information for the priest should be easy to understand. In the thousands of instances each year when the priest has dealings with families in the parish, all he has to do is refer quickly to the census form and he'll have at a glance necessary information which otherwise he wouldn't have or would spend precious time getting. And not only will the census file help in the great number of individual cases, but he can check the files quickly to find such necessary information as: how many children of such-and-such an age do we have? how many doctors? how many college graduates? how many vocations? how many unemployed? and so on. In fact, through a special coding device, thanks to Sociological Research Laboratory of Fordham University (which is in our parish), such information can be found within a very few minutes.

That's why the information requested on the census forms we are using is a little more than usual—though not much more. In many respects it's not nearly as much information as we're accustomed to give to our doctor, our insurance agent, often enough to our employer, the government census taker, and (during the war) to the rationing authorities. With the guarantee that the information is confidential, no one should have any reason to hesitate to make out his form as completely as possible.

Dedication to Our Lady!

Today is the Sunday within our novena of preparation for the feast of our Lady's Immaculate Conception. Since our parish is dedicated to our Lady, and since we'll begin our preparatory work for the census on the feast of her Immaculate Conception, the ending of the Marian Year, what more fitting patroness could we have for our census work than herself?

For she herself once answered a census call. Just at this time of year, looking forward to Christmas, we recall how Mary and Joseph were returning to their own town to register in the census of the Roman emperor Augustus. We can ask her help for a successful effort, and her guidance that all parishioners will "register in the census" as quickly and completely as possible.

Doing It Scientifically

The parish map on the front cover of this month's *Monthly* might be a little puzzling—with all those numbers and jagged lines. Actually they are an important help in our aim to know more about the parish. The jagged lines represent United States Census tracts, and each block within every tract has its own number.

But what do census tracts mean to us in a parish census? The fact is, the government has already done a great deal of work for us, and we might as well make use of it. The census material for the tracts within our parish enable us to know, even before starting our census, how many people are in the parish, including Catholics and non-Catholics; how many people are in every age group (under five years, and within every five-year group up to 80 years); the income and educational levels, the type of employment, the national origin of the 30,000 people in the parish. We don't know that individually, of course—nor is it our concern to know it individually. But businessmen, educators, and professional people, among others, find it extremely useful to have good information on the type of people in their neighborhood. That is no less true of religious leaders—especially since, as Pope Pius XII expressed it, the Catholic parish has a responsibility for everyone in it.

What we still need in addition, however, is the Catholic side of those statistics. For certainly the primary concern of the parish—in its religious and educational and cultural work—is the Catholic population. For example, we might know from the census that there are over 2,000 children under the age of 5 in the parish. But how many of them are Catholics? The parish should know in order to prepare its school facilities. We know that the people in the parish include more elderly people on the average than the whole of the Bronx. But is that true of Catholic parishioners? It too could be significant in parish policy.

Having the census figures of each block is a great help, too. For when we start to work on the census, in which we want first a name-and-address file of the whole parish, we'll know ahead of time exactly how to divide up the work for our census teams, we'll know exactly how many homes each team will have to visit. We can plan it in such a way that most teams will not even have to cross the street to cover their territory. Then, too, we can check our results.

The advantages of using census-tract material are almost incalculable. With the results of our study we can know our parish better through comparison with the total population of the city, the Bronx, the area, the total parish. Other parish studies could enable further comparison, so that we could build up a good amount of knowledge of our people. And, as we saw before, running a society effectively means, as a start, knowing it very well. Our OLM census will enable us to improve our knowledge of the parish even beyond our present knowledge. The next two pages will explain the procedure and timetable we hope to follow, and will give an explanation which will make filling out the census as easy as possible.

Procedure and Timetable

This Wednesday we celebrate the feast of our Lady's Immaculate Conception—and with it the beginning of our parish census project. The sermon at all the preceding Sunday parish Masses, preached by a Jesuit from Fordham's sociology department who is helping us with the work, is aimed at explaining the purpose and value of the census to our parishioners, asking their help in prayer and participation, and preparing them for filling out their own census schedules.

Our first important step is to enlist the aid of parishioners who will call at every household in the parish. There are many ways of taking up a census. In some parishes it is done by the parish priests themselves—a system with definite advantages, but practically impossible in a situation like our own. Many parishes use their sections of the Legion of Mary for the purpose, as does Our Lady of Mercy Parish. But we have already seen the limitations that other apostolic obligations put on their census work and how impossible it is, under that system, to have a census record that is both complete and up to date. Several religious congregations of sisters have done, and do, excellent census work, but their services are in great demand, and sometimes a parish's purposes are such as to make its own method preferable.

Our own intention is such that we wish parishioners to have the opportunity of sharing in this work. We want our own parishioners to be the parish's representatives in calling on every house in the whole parish. We are looking forward to having one hundred two-man teams (and more!) join in this parish project.

With that number of teams we can arrange each team's area so that it will call on only 85 homes. At several meetings between the Feast of the Immaculate Conception and the New Year we'll be planning both the distribution of these areas and the proper approach of the prospective census taker. Thus, when the census begins, . . . everything will be in readiness for doing an accurate, quick, and efficient job.

Each census team will have two tasks. First, to visit every household unit in his area, and tabulate its family-name, address, and religious profession (Catholic, Protestant, Jewish, other, nothing) on cards or sheets printed for that purpose. Second, in every home where there is a Catholic (whether a member of the family or not, whether practicing or fallen-away) to leave a family census form with instructions for filling it out, and later, at an agreed time—whether the same night, the following night, or other time—to collect the filled out form.

In other words, each team has as its total and sole responsibility the name-address-religion file of every household (about 85) in its area, and the filled out census form of all Catholics therein. How much time will it take? In advance we can't be too sure. Some parishes have actually had 80 per cent success with the so-called "48-hour method," in which almost the whole job is done in 48 hours. Our own purpose is a little broader than those methods usually achieve; we want as close to 100 per cent as possible; and since the census takers will be representatives of the parish in less a sheer business-like than Christlike way, they may wish to be a little less rapid when occasion requires. . . .

Some Explanations

It would be a good idea to save this issue of the *Monthly*, if only for this page of instructions. The census form is simple enough, though it includes more headings than most others. The reason is that we want to take advantage of the United States Census data which we already have available—as previously explained—and thus get as good an understanding of the parish as possible.

The form is a folded sheet which contains headings for almost all the requested information on the inside. This, plus the fact that you will receive an envelope in which you will enclose the answered form and then seal it, assures you that your form will be kept confidential. On the outside of the sheet is space for your name, address, phone number, and the name of the church you attend. Does this last item surprise you? Well, most parishioners of course attend OLM Church, but there are some who for various reasons attend elsewhere. For example, whereas OLM is a territorial parish with its own regular boundaries, there is a neighboring church which serves a so-called "national parish" whose members are drawn from several surrounding territorial parishes. It is helpful for parish administration to know that fact.

Most of the headings are self-explanatory. However, one or two might be a little confusing. If you have any doubt at all, don't hesitate to ask the census taker to explain. He will be willing to help you. For example, under the heading of education, there is space for schooling in general and for Catholic schooling. If your schooling has been all Catholic, mark both columns; if only non-Catholic, mark just the first column; and if mixed, mark accordingly.

Under "class of worker" (no. 13), you might use as abbreviations "S" for "self-employed," "H" if you are hired or employed by someone else—a company or other employer, "Un" for unemployed, "W" for housewife.

Under heading no. 14, religious affiliation, use these easy abbreviations: "C" for Catholic, "NC" for non-Catholic, "O" for no religion at all. Under home ownership (no. 16), for the "actual or estimated rental value" it would be well if you put down your answer to this question: "How much rent do you pay, or (if you own your home) how much would your home realistically rent for?"

Under religious observance there are three headings (nos. 21 to 23) referring to attendance at Mass and reception of the sacraments of confession and Communion within the past four weeks. They are simply to help us get a good cross section of parish religious observance. There is no implication that nonreception of the sacraments within four weeks in every case indicates any religious failure.

The headings under "marital description" need be answered only for the husband and wife. If married sons or daughters are still living at home with their own families, they should fill out a separate census form. If married sons and daughters are away from home, their names may be simply listed, mention made that they are married and absent. . . .

The above explanations will be repeated later. They are mentioned now simply to prepare the parish ahead of time and as an indication of our attempts to be as accurate as possible in this parish census.

A Further Step

With the completion of the census the major portion of the parish's objective will be completed. However, merely names and addresses, facts and figures, don't tell the whole story. We said before that the parish is a society. It is a neighborhood society that carries on its work among other societies in a changing world, and for people who are members of those other societies—business, educational, recreational, and so on.

Obviously the small country parish, particularly in a Catholic area—such as some portions of Louisiana, French Canada, France, Germany, Italy, Belgium, Holland, or Ireland—has a different meaning for its parishioners than a large city parish in New York, Paris, or Frankfurt. In those country parishes the people's social life is almost entirely tied up with the parish, and even in politics the priest is often as important as the mayor. That situation is rarely found in big cities.

Now the question arises, does the changed world in which the city parish functions mean that the work of the parish has changed? For example, many, many people don't even know to what parish they belong. Often it's not their fault at all. Nor is it their fault that they hardly know their parish priests except by sight. They might be performing their religious duties perfectly, but perhaps the opportunity for knowing their parish and priests is, for them, very limited. Probably the parish is so large that many people can't know their priest, and their priest can't know many of them well. Maybe their economic and other interests keep them largely outside the parish. At any rate, it has been noticed that for many people the parish church has come to be little more than a religious service station. Just as an automobile driver goes to the gas station to "tank up" when his car needs it, so many a modern parishioner drops in at his parish church simply to fill his parish needs—and that's all. Maybe in many cases that's the way it has to be. But the question is, should the modern parish mean more than that to the modern parishioner?

Much more is being done in Europe today on that question, for we want to know why Catholic life and practice is so poor in some longtime Catholic countries. And a few Catholic social scientists in this country have been turning their attention to the same question. One of the most important elements in finding the answer is the attitude of our Catholic parishioners. What does the parish mean to them? What do they think it should mean? What are the good things in life which the parish does for them?

Of course, parishes differ—as do the parishioners in them. But the only way to make progress in this matter is to start asking. Therefore the Jesuit social scientist who is helping us with the parish census is going to ask one further bit of help. Each one who receives a census form will also receive a page of explanations, and at the bottom of it will be asked this question: "Would you be willing to answer a questionnaire concerning your attitudes on parish life?" If you answer yes, that will of course have no effect on your confidential census report. You simply inform your census taker, who will inform the Jesuit father. Then, depending on how many questionnaires he needs to get a good cross-section estimate, he will get in touch with you. The questionnaire, too, will be confidential—for him only. He will be very grateful for this help, and certainly it will add to the parish's knowledge of itself tremendously.

The Work of the Lay Apostolate

Just about everyone who reads this *Monthly* has received confirmation, the sacrament which made of us public witnesses to Christ—to use our Lord's own word. That means we all have a share, or should share, in the apostolate of Christ's Church: "As the Father has sent me, so also I send you." As St. Paul told the Colossians, that mission of Christ was to reconcile all things to His Father. Primarily that's the work of Christ's vicar, His bishops, His priests. Sharing in their work is what's meant by the lay apostolate.

We saw a few pages back how our holy father told the priests of Rome just this past February that the prime source for help, in the tremendous task which is too great for their slim numbers, is the laity. The sacrament of confirmation gives them the grace to supply that help, if they will.

We see how the pope's words apply to our own parish. In so many parish activities, we know, the help of the laity has been both incalculable and essential. This census project is another example. An important example, too! For even if the priests were numerous enough to do the job themselves, which they aren't, it would still remain true that *some* doors open more readily to a layman than to a priest. Therefore here is an opportunity for a layman to join intimately in the work of introducing Christ and OLM to neighbors who otherwise wouldn't perhaps even be aware of them.

Almost certainly the census will not be merely a matter of ringing bells and writing names. Many a time there will be real opportunity to play the role of the intelligent, apostolic, loving representative of Christ. And if it's true—as in many places it is—that laymen often don't find such an opportunity, certainly OLM parishioners do have that opportunity in this census work.

Just three years ago, in the fall of 1951, in his address to the World Congress of the Lay Apostolate, our holy father said:

"So far as the Church is concerned, she has a threefold mission to perform for all: to raise up fervent believers to the level of present-day needs, to introduce those who hesitate on the threshold to the warm and salutary intimacy of the hearth, and to lead back those who have separated themselves from religion and whom she cannot abandon to their miserable fate.

"An inspiring task for the Church! But it is one rendered more difficult by the fact that, while the Church as a whole has grown greatly, the number of clergy has not increased proportionately. Besides, the clergy must above all keep themselves free for the exercise of the sacred ministry proper to the sacerdotal state, which no one else can do for them.

"For that reason assistance rendered by the laity to the apostolate is an indispensable necessity. . . . Especially in matters of religion there is evidence of the profound and efficacious influence of those who are companions in a profession or condition of life. These factors, and others besides, according to the circumstances of places and persons, have opened wider the doors for the collaboration of the laity in the apostolate of the Church."

In view of the pope's words we are hopeful that a great number of OLM parishioners join this apostolic work. Remember, every team we have above 100 reduces the work load of every team proportionately lower than 85 visits.

Vatican Letter on the Parish

Last summer the Canadian "Social Week" of Catholic social conferences dedicated much of its attention to the parish. As usual the Vatican wrote a letter of greeting, this time written by the then prosecretary of state, Monsignor Montini, recently appointed archbishop of Milan. Since he wrote on the parish, members of OLM will be interested in the following selections.

"Just what is the parish? It is the smallest part of the one and universal flock entrusted to Peter by the Lord. Under the authority of a responsible priest who has received from his bishop the care of souls it is, in the Church of Jesus Christ, the primary community of Christian life, a community of such human size that the shepherd can know his sheep, and the sheep their shepherd. A delimited territory usually traces its contours within the heart of the diocese, and so the parish is bound to an area, intimately linked with local traditions and definite points of view. In the heart of this area, surmounted by its belfry, stands the parish church, with its baptistry, its confessional, its altar, and its tabernacle; the church, symbol of unity, center of the community life.

"It is important to keep this in mind, that the parish is above all the hearth of religious life and of missionary expansion; its true members can be counted at the foot of the altar when the priest distributes the bread of life. The pastor isn't the head of his people in the secular sense of the term (see Matthew 20:25-28), but he is rather the servant of the people of God, having received spiritual authority over his flock only to be for it the 'dispenser of the mysteries of God,' so that it 'may have life, and have it more abundantly' (John 10:10). Jesus known, loved, and served by all: such is, according to the very words of the Holy Father, the purpose of all parish life. And his holiness doesn't hesitate to insist: 'Everything else should be valued insofar as it contributes, and in the extent to which it serves the realization of the purpose which the Church wishes to achieve. . . . Now, it is precisely such a parish, a really living and active cell of the body of Christ, which is called, by its very fidelity to its proper religious mission, to play a role of first rank in the regeneration of modern society.' "

After discussing the impact of the parish beyond itself and its function of sustaining social structure, Monsignor Montini concludes his letter with these remarks on the radiance of the parish:

"The beneficial work of the parish has its impact on many phases of social life. This activity is due, without any doubt, to the courage of its priests, the fashioners of a people's moral and religious life, who, in the modest accomplishments of their priestly ministry, are the soldiers in the vanguard on the front of the general renovation of Christian life, and on the line of defense of moral values . . . for the achievement of social justice and for the reconstruction of the Christian way of life. This activity is due too to the brilliant expansion of the parish's lay apostles of Catholic action, through whom the Church is the life-giving font of human society; they are the Church extended into the world of work or of culture, in the factories and on the hearth, and their presence there is a leaven of Christian regeneration. This beneficial activity of the parish is due finally to the testimony of the parish community itself, gathered together in faith, in prayer, and in charity—a testimony whose striking power elevated society already in apostolic times.

"May every parish once again in today's world be able to be, through its fervor and its unity, the revelation of a social ideal far too little recognized! May it be at the same time a magnetic pole for all men of good will!"

PASTOR'S LETTER TO PARISHIONERS

The following exhibit gives the text of the pastor's letter to the parishioners. A copy was delivered to each family representative by the census worker. The pastor's letter served these two purposes: identification in the people's mind of the census with the parish clergy, not merely with the "visiting priest" who was conducting it; further repeated explanation of some items on the census schedule. Notice the steps taken by the director of the study to identify himself with the pastor in requesting cooperation in a questionnaire and the coordination of this effort with the census.

The pastor also had printed an eight-page booklet containing on pages 4 and 5 a two-page spread showing a census form filled out for an imaginary family. Since it would be impossible to reproduce this booklet here, we have added to the pastor's letter a few instructions found in the booklet but not in the letter.

OUR LADY OF MERCY RECTORY
2496 MARION AVENUE
NEW YORK 58, N. Y.

My dear Parishioners:

With this letter you are receiving your census form, which we ask you to fill out promptly and accurately. By doing your part you will make the parish census a success, which is so important to help us do our Lord's work in the parish. These instructions will be helpful in filling out the census. Please:

Print with pen and ink, or type.

If possible, let one person answer for the whole family. Let this person put an *x* after his own name.

Fill out promptly, put in envelope, seal the envelope yourself.

Use only your last name on the front of the form, use only first names inside.

Married children living at home with their family should fill out their own form (one census form for each family); married children who are absent need simply be listed, with no further information.

Column 5: Use W for white, N for Negro, O for Oriental.

Column 7: Give the highest grade *or* the number of years you went to school.

Columns 8-10: If you went to non-Catholic schools, put P after the proper number or grade; if no one in the family ever attended a Catholic school, scratch out "Catholic" from the title and simply put the proper number in the column.

Column 11: Occupation means the *kind of work* you do.

Column 12: Industry means the *kind of business* in which you do that work.

Column 13: Write S if you are self-employed, H if you work for someone else, W if you are a housewife, Un if you are unemployed.

Column 14: Use C for Catholic, NC for non-Catholic, O for no religion.

Column 15: Use R for rented, O for owned.

Column 16: Mention either actual rent or, if you own your house, how much you think it would rent for.

Columns 17-20: Remember, this means reception of the sacraments in the Catholic Church.

Column 20: Easter duty means receiving Holy Communion since the first Sunday of Lent in 1954 (March 7).

Columns 21-23: These questions are to give the parish priest a good cross-section view of the religious activity of the parish. The answer for one month is only a rough sampling; it does not mean that your year-round activity is the same.

Column 28: If a Catholic priest performed your marriage, the answer is yes; if your marriage was outside the Church, please answer no.

Column 29: If your answer in Column 28 was no and if your marriage has been "straightened out" by a priest (convalidated) since that time, please put the year when it was convalidated; if it hasn't been convalidated, please answer simply no.

The generous volunteer census takers of the parish will be glad to help you answer any questions. To you and to them we express our sincere thanks for the effort and cooperation shown in the parish census project.

Yours in Christ,

Msgr. Patrick A. O'Leary—*Pastor*

(Perforation here)

Dear Parishioner of OLM:

May I add a simple request? The pope has stressed the need of studies of religious life. I am trying to make one small report on the thinking of Catholics about their Catholic and parish life.

If I send you a questionnaire, would you be willing to answer it?

Your name and address will *not* be on the questionnaire, so I'll not know who you are (unless you want me to). Thus your answer will be confidential.

If you are willing to help me in this Catholic research project, would you please put your name and address here so that I can send you the questionnaire, and give it to the census taker?

Thank you very much!

Joseph B. Schuyler, S.J.

Assistant in the OLM Census

Name .... Address ....

QUESTIONNAIRE FOR SELECTED PARISH SOCIETIES

Name of society .... (Specify junior or senior if necessary)
Your age (check one): under 16 ....; 16-20 ....; 21-30 ....;
    31-50 ....; 51-70 ....

Your sex? male ....; female ....
Years of membership in this society? ....
Are you a member of any other parish society? ....; if so, how many?
....

Is the time spent in any or all of these other societies (a) less than,
(b) about the same as, or (c) more than the time spent in this society? Check one: (a) ...., (b) ...., (c) ....

Time spent in the activities of the society each week: time at meeting
.............; time at society's work ....; time spent in coming to and
returning from society's meeting and activity ....

Do you have any social relationship with other members of this society
outside the time spent for society meetings and activities? yes ....,
no .... If yes, please estimate in general the number of hours spent
in these relationships during an average month: .... If yes, please
indicate (a) whether these relationships derived from common membership in this society, or (b) whether membership derived from an
already previously existing relationship, or (c) whether there was no
connection between membership and these relationships. Check one:
(a) ...., (b) ...., (c) ....

Think a moment, then write down your motives for joining and/or remaining in this society. Do not list more than three. Number those which
you do put down according to importance in your own mind. (Please
be frank. Don't answer as you think someone would like to have you
answer, or as you think the answer should be, but as it actually is.)

Are the reasons why you joined (and/or retain membership in this society)
being satisfied? Check one: no ...., partly ...., mostly ....,
yes ....

What do you think is the most important contribution you are making to
the society? (Don't look for a spectacular answer. Presumably the most
obvious one is the true one.) ....

What do you think is the most important gain you receive from your mem-
bership/activity in this society? ....

If there were no such society, would you be trying to do what it does by
yourself? Check one: no ...., I doubt it ...., probably in some
way ...., yes ....

The judgment has been made—and quite validly in some instances—that
often parish societies become more concerned with conserving their
formal organization than achieving their fundamental purpose. Do you
think that is true of your society? Check one: not at all ...., a
little ...., more or less ...., very much ....

Do you have any suggestion whereby the purpose of your society could be
better achieved? ....

ALTAR SERVERS QUESTIONNAIRE

Your age ....

I go to a Catholic ...., a public ...., high school ...., college ...., I work ....

Graduate of Catholic grammar school? yes ...., no ....

The night before you serve early Mass, do you usually go to bed earlier than otherwise? yes ...., no .... If yes, how much earlier? .... When you serve early Mass do you get up earlier than you ordinarily would? yes ...., no .... If yes, how much earlier? ....

Do you usually receive Holy Communion when you serve Mass? yes ...., no ....

Aside from Sundays and holydays do you attend Mass only when you serve? yes ...., no .... How often do you attend Mass when you're not serving? ....

Please check the statement which expresses the *chief* reason why you are an altar server. If you feel that more than one statement should be checked you may do so, but put no. 1 before the clause which you feel is most important. Be honest in your answer; don't check what you think would be the nicest answer, but that which is actually yours. Because I like to serve Mass ...., because, though I don't like to serve, I know it's good to so do ...., because I *both* like it *and* know it's a good thing to do ...., because my parent(s) want me to ...., because the sisters want me to ...., because I learned how to serve and I might as well keep on doing it ...., because the priest(s) want me to ...., because I like the priest(s) ...., because it brings me very close to Christ and the Mass ...., because of some other reason (please name it) ....

Do you know any boys who used to serve Mass but don't any more? yes ...., no .... If yes, please list the reasons why you think they don't serve any more ....

Are any of your friends and closer acquaintances altar servers? yes ...., no .... Do you think these friendships have been strengthened because you're both "on the altar"? yes ...., maybe ...., no ...., don't know ....

Do you think serving on the altar has helped you to understand the Mass better than your comrades who aren't altar servers? yes ...., not especially ...., no ...., don't know ....

Can you use a daily Missal pretty well? yes ...., no ...., a little ....

Do you know the meaning of your Latin responses? yes ...., no ...., a little .... Do you know the meaning of what the priest says to you at Mass in Latin? yes ...., no ...., a little ....

NOCTURNAL ADORATION SOCIETY QUESTIONNAIRE

This brief questionnaire was submitted to a regular Nocturnal Adoration Society attendance of over 800 members. It was taken home and voluntarily answered and mailed to the author by over 140, some 13 per cent of total membership of 1,100, and 18 per cent of those 800 who were present at that particular hour.

Dear Member:

Can you spare a single moment or two? We are preparing a little parish study and we need the help of the members of various societies. Would you be willing to answer a question now on this page?

If you do not wish to do so, it is perfectly all right. If you wish to take it home, answer it there, and send it to me, that is all right too.

Do not sign your name. We are looking for the response of the society, not of particular individuals. You remain anonymous.

Even though the question is very simple and the answer might seem obvious, please do not consider it unimportant. Not many people know why Catholics are active in religious organizations. You might be able to help us help others. Father Brady, your moderator, has given me permission to ask your help in this matter. Many thanks in our Lord.

(Please answer)

How long have you been a member of this society? .... Your age ....
What is your home parish? ....
Why are you a member of the society? ....
(Please be frank. If you wish to write more than one answer, do so. You
    may use the back of this page. Many thanks.)
    (When finished, fold and give to the marshal.)

THE PARISH QUESTIONNAIRE

All families of OLM who received census material were invited to respond to a subsequent questionnaire on religious and parish life. Nearly 1,000 out of less than 2,800 responding families accepted the invitation, and received the following schedule. Nearly 300 actually filled in and returned the schedule, the others probably being discouraged by the questionnaire's unexpected length.

It was implied in Chapter 4 that the questionnaire includes some poorly phrased questions and other errors of judgment and technique. It seems well to call attention to them.

For example, Questions 8 and 9 of Part 2 sought to reveal the respondent's mind not only through asking for his own motivation but for his interpretation of the motives of others. The attempt was not very successful; a more indirect question would have been better. Nor was Question 12 well planned; answers followed the catechism formula, though we intended to see if the respondent understood the formula. Question 29 contained a particularly obscure term for an important concept. Of all the roles of the priest the most important is unquestionably that of leading the community in divine worship—celebrating Mass, administering the sacraments, leading public prayer, and so on. A normal term to express this role would be "liturgical leader," for liturgy means public worship. Pretesting showed no misunderstanding of the expression. Yet, although OLM's parishioners recognized the primacy of this priestly role in other answers, they paid it little attention in Question 29. Our conclusion must be that the term was ill chosen in view of the type of respondent, and that perhaps it was understood as referring more to leadership in the liturgical movement which is striving for certain reforms in liturgical practice.

Question 42 might contain some ambiguity. Father Fichter reported in *Southern Parish* that only 54 per cent of his parish leader interviewees believed in the reality of the devil. To us that percentage seemed extraordinarily small, and we believed it might have been due to the use of the word "person" in Father Fichter's question, "Do you believe that the devil is a real person?" Actually the term person has a technical philosophical meaning; namely, a being which has an intellectual nature. In common speech, however, many people consider the word person to refer to human beings, beings not only possessed of a soul, but of head, arms, legs, and other bodily features. In our questionnaire we eliminated the word "person" and substituted "someone real." Very few of OLM respondents answered in the negative, and even some of them still considered the term "someone real" as referring to a human being, or at least to some bodily being. The question should have been formulated even more clearly. As a matter of fact, a more recent local study did phrase the question more realistically, "Do you believe that the devil really exists?" and received an almost unanimously affirmative response. This probably mirrors the true thinking of the overwhelming majority of practicing Catholics as well as the actual teaching of Christ's Church.

Questions 1 and 2 of Part 3 did not achieve their purpose well, and Question 1 of Part 4 should have used "mostly outside" instead of "all outside."

Despite these errors the questionnaire gave us valuable data on the thinking and attitudes of Catholic parishioners concerning a wide variety of important topics. The questionnaire follows:

Dear Parishioner of OLM:

May I thank you most sincerely for your generous willingness to answer the questionnaire about OLM Parish. It was very encouraging to see how many parishioners signed up to do so—almost one fourth of the parish.

Though the questionnaire is rather long, I think it will interest you. I am counting on your generosity to take the time to do it well.

The information which you give us, as you realize, will be of immense help to the parish, and as Msgr. O'Leary has said, it will help many other parishes also. A big city parish makes it very difficult for priests to know what they should know if they are going to serve you as zealous priests. I know it was your interest in the parish and in the welfare of the Church that prompted you to agree to work with us.

Do not send your name back to me unless for some reason you wish to do so. No one will know who has written the answers. Your pastor, Msgr. O'Leary, has graciously given me permission to ask the questions, and he and the priests of the parish will be interested in the answers. But they will not know who writes them.

The two numbers on the top right corner show (1) the census tract (whether 237, 401, 399, 397, 387, 385, or 383) and (2) the block on which you live (from 1 to 18). They do not identify you.

May I ask you to answer this as promptly as you can. If you wish to ask me any questions, you can reach me at Fo 7-5400. If I am not in, leave your phone number and I can call you back.

Thank you again for your cooperation. Our holy father Pius XII has told us that it is necessary to find out what are the needs of our people; what they think and desire. In answering the questionnaire you will be telling us what you need; what you think and desire. This, together with your prayers, will help us to do God's work more effectively. For that I know God will bless you very much.

Boys of Fordham Prep Sodality have been kind enough to address and deliver these questionnaires. A stamped, self-addressed envelope is enclosed for your convenience.

PART I

Persons of different religious practice and socioeconomic condition often answer even the most obvious questions in different ways. For that reason I am asking these questions about yourself. Presumably you have already answered them on the parish census. Here of course you remain anonymous. To answer, simply put a check mark in the right place, unless another answer is necessary.

1. I was born in New York City ...., elsewhere in U.S. ...., outside the U.S. .... (where? ....).
2. I am male ...., female ....
3. My age is between 20-35 years ...., 36-50 ...., 51-69 ...., over 70 ....
4. I have lived in the parish less than 5 years ...., from 5 to 15 ...., more than 15 ...., from birth ....

5. My highest grade of schooling was ....

6. My highest grade of Catholic schooling was ....

7. The number of persons receiving income in my family is ....

8. The total income in my family is less than $3,000 a year ...., between $3,000 and $4,999 ...., between $5,000 and $9,999 ...., over $10,000 .... My family does .... does not .... have a TV set, does .... does not .... have an automobile.

9. My occupation is professional or managerial ...., clerical or sales ...., operative or skilled craftsman ...., other ....

10. I am .... am not .... a convert. (If so, how long ...., from what religion? ....)

11. I attend Mass (almost) daily ...., weekly ...., monthly ...., a couple of time a year ...., practically never ....

12. I receive Communion (almost) daily ...., weekly ...., monthly ...., a couple of times a year ...., practically never ....

13. I say the rosary daily ...., several times a month ...., occasionally ...., never .... When I do say the rosary I say it usually alone ...., with my family ...., with others ....

14. Have you ever made the series of the nine First Fridays? yes ...., no ....

15. During 1954 among church devotions I attended one or more weekly ...., one or more novenas ...., an occasional service ...., none ....

16. Have you ever made a retreat? yes ...., no ...., how long ago? ....

17. Have you ever read a good life of Christ? yes ...., no .... If yes, whose ...., when ....

18. Have you ever had one of the priests of the parish offer Mass for your intentions? yes ...., no ....

PART II

A few short years ago Cardinal Feltin of Paris wrote to the author of a study on priestly vocation in France: "But above all you have proved, with a multitude of facts to support you, that the number of vocations depends directly on the sociological milieu (environment)." He denies that this statement contradicts the free workings of God's grace. At any rate, there is an important connection between other aspects of people's lives and the religious aspect. Religious sociology maps show that economic, educational, occupational, and social backgrounds influence religious practice. If we know more about these connections and influences, obviously we can work better in our religious duties. That is a major aim of religious sociology—and of this questionnaire.

First, some easy questions: our use of religious facilities. Check or fill in the right answer.

1. The city and diocese are bigger than the parish. Fortunately, downtown churches serve many who have business there, and diocesan activities receive the help of people all over the city. (a) Do you frequently or regularly use downtown churches for hearing Mass, receiving the sacraments, making visits, etc.? yes ...., no .... (If so, how often per month? ....) (b) Are you engaged outside the parish in any diocesewide activity? yes ...., no ....

2. Are you satisfied that your parish church supplies you with all the opportunity for religious worship which you need? yes ...., no .... (If not, what is missing? ....)

3. Counting Mass, visits, devotions, etc., would you please estimate roughly how many hours you spend in your parish church during the average month. Hours ....

4. Are the times of religious services suitable? yes ...., no .... (If not, what change? ....)

5. Some dioceses and parishes have begun to use the privilege of having evening Mass occasionally (for example: First Fridays, holydays, etc.). Some persons think this is not a good idea. Are you in favor .... or against it ....? Would you go to Mass more often if evening Mass were available? yes ...., no ...., don't know .... Do you know others who would go more often if evening Mass were available? yes ...., no ...., don't know ....

6. Our holy father in his encyclical on the liturgy (religious service) has praised various means of having the people join more fully in the Mass. Such means are the dialogue Mass (the people answer the priest), singing hymns suitable to the different parts of the Mass (as they do in many European countries), or the high Mass sung by all the people. On the other hand, the pope also said this should be done only if it satisfied the people's needs and inclinations. Have you ever assisted at a dialogue Mass? yes ...., no .... Have you ever sung at a high Mass? yes ...., no .... Which do you prefer, as now, to hear Mass in silence .... or to join more fully through responses and/or singing ....? If the second, state whether through responses ...., or singing ...., or no preference .... If you prefer the second, would you be willing to do the necessary practice until you learned how? yes ...., no ....

7. Important authorities are trying to work out changes in the preparatory part of the Mass, so that (a) some prayers can be read in English (or other home languages) and (b) the cycle of epistles and gospels will cover 3 or 4 years, to enable us to hear more of the Sacred Word than we do now. Do you favor (a) no change or (b) having such parts of

the Mass in English? Check: (a) ...., (b) ...., no preference .... Concerning the epistle and gospel, would you prefer (a) no change, (b) more selections from the gospel and epistles spread over a three- or four-year cycle? Check: (a) ...., (b) ...., no preference .... What do you do at Mass now? pray the rosary ...., more or less follow along in the Missal ...., use some other prayer book ...., just pray quietly ...., nothing ....

8. Why do you regularly go to Sunday Mass? Because it's a mortal sin if you don't ...., because, even if it weren't a mortal sin to miss, you would want to join in the Holy Sacrifice at least on the Lord's day ...., because it is a habit ...., because people I know always go ...., other .... (please name), I don't go regularly .... Do you think most Catholics whom you know go to Mass because they have to ...., or because they know the Mass is so important ...., or because of habit ...., or because other people go ...., don't know ....

9. Do you know any Catholics who do not attend Mass regularly? yes ...., no ...., how many? .... Do you think it is because (a) they don't understand what's going on? yes ...., no ...., don't know .... (b) they "have nothing to do" at Mass? yes ...., no ...., don't know ....

10. Many good persons go to confession more often than they *have* to go. If you are one of them, what is your main reason for so doing? to receive absolution ...., to receive an increase in grace through the sacrament ...., to ask priestly advice ...., to keep a check on yourself ...., out of habit ...., other .... (please name).

11. What is your main reason for going to Holy Communion more than you have to (if you do)? as a sign of Catholic living ...., to ask favors of God ...., because it increases grace ...., to be more intimately united with Him ...., other .... (please name).

12. Do you know the meaning of confirmation? yes ...., no .... If so, please say briefly why confirmation has been called the sacrament of the lay apostolate. ....

13. OLM Church rings the Angelus bell each day. Do you hear the bell? yes ...., no .... Does it remind you to say the Angelus? yes ...., no ....

14. Let's say a person in your family were seriously ill. Would you prefer (a) to save him from worry and not call a priest until death was almost certain? (b) to call a priest as soon as you see the illness is serious? Check: (a) ...., (b) .... Do you have in your home equipment for a priest's visit to the sick? yes ...., no ....

15. What physical conditions in the parish make it difficult for you or other parishioners to get to church? none ...., crossings ...., hills ...., steps ...., other ....

16. What physical advantages in the parish make it easy for parishioners to get to church? Please name, if any ....

17. About how many persons in your own neighborhood do you know who are born or converted Catholics but who no longer practice their religion? .... How many converts? .... Do they for the most part still consider themselves as Catholic? yes ...., no ...., don't know .... Would you judge that their lack of practice comes from weakness ...., carelessness ...., from "having something against the Church" ...., a marriage difficulty ...., other cause .... (name), don't know .... Is there anything the parish could do for them but hasn't? yes ...., no .... If yes, please name ....

18. I presume that, at least since the work on the parish census, you know the parish boundaries. If so, did you know them before this work started? yes ...., no .... Do you know the names of the priests in the parish? yes ...., no .... Please name them .... Can you name at least five parish organizations or activities? yes ...., no .... Please name them ....

19. Do you usually practice some mortification in Lent? yes ...., no ...., describe ....

20. There are many Jewish people in the parish, especially in the western end. Have you ever heard an explanation of Jewish beliefs and practices? yes ...., no .... Would you like to? yes ...., no .... Would you like to hear about it in OLM Church? yes ...., no ....

21. Preaching is one of the most important parish functions. Do you listen to the sermons? yes ...., no .... Do you ever discuss them outside of church? ...., often ...., rarely ...., never .... In your opinion the sermons at OLM should (a) stay the way they are, (b) have more explanation of the Church's moral and doctrinal teaching, (c) have less explanation and more inspiration and devotion, (d) other. Check: (a) ...., (b) ...., (c) ...., (d) ...., (state what).

22. What religious celebrations have been or are social celebrations in your home? Please name ....

23. Please list, in order of importance to you, the benefits accorded by OLM Parish to you in your life. (Limit your answer to at most five benefits.) ....

24. If any, what benefit could the parish offer which it doesn't offer? ....

25. Are you a member of any parish activity? yes ...., no .... How many hours a month are spent in this or these activities? ....

26. Please give your reasons or motives for belonging to these activities. Do not list more than three reasons. If you put down more than one reason, put the number (1) in front of the most important. ....

27. The role of the priest in the parish is of course a most important one. Changes in our way of living from the small town parish to the large city parish have caused many changes in the life and responsibility of the priest. Archbishop Montini has called the parish the place where the shepherd can know his sheep and the sheep their shepherd. This is no longer so easy. During 1954 did you visit any priest(s) in the rectory? yes ...., no .... Outside of confession itself, have you engaged any priest(s) of the parish in conversation during 1954? no ...., yes ...., seldom ...., off and on ...., often .... As to the priest's time and availability, I believe (a) aside from his day on duty, the priest has little to do, (b) there's always something for the priest to do, but really he never is hard-pressed for time, (c) in so large a parish, with so many activities, it is to be expected that the priest might be otherwise engaged when someone calls. Check: (a) ...., (b) ...., (c) ....

28. In some Catholic lands the priest is not greeted in the street unless he is personally known. In others he is greeted more extensively than here. If you meet a priest do you greet him? usually yes ...., no ...., only if I know him .... Why do you greet him? (a) because I am in the habit of doing this, (b) because he has a respected position in the community, (c) because he represents Christ to me and through him I greet Christ, (d) other. Check: (a) ...., (b) ...., (c) ...., (d) .... The priest usually does ...., doesn't .... return my greeting.

29. The parish priest has many roles to play. They have been named as:

father	educator	mediator
administrator	reformer	liturgical leader
civic leader	preacher and teacher	counselor
recreation leader	of God's word	social leader

Before the names on the above list please place the numbers 1, 2, and 3 to indicate what you think are the priest's most important duties in the parish; and use the letters x, y, and z to show what roles you think are least important.

30. No matter how many priests there are, it would seem there's always a shortage. In some missionary and dechristianized lands this is obvious. In places where the Catholic practice is good and priests are more numerous, there still seems to be more for them to do than they can manage. In some places where there are many practicing Catholics, but many lapsed Catholics and possibly interested non-Catholics, there is this problem: should the priests be used for ministering to and

developing the faith of those who are faithful or should they leave the faithful more to themselves and go out after the others? In other words, just as Christ the great high priest was both prophet (teacher, evangelist) and priest, so is Christ's priest today. As Cardinal Suhard puts it, should today's priest spend his time (a) most in being priest to the faithful, (b) or in being prophet and teacher to those without the faith? Check the one you think most important. (a) ...., (b) .... Do you have any comment in this connection? ....

31. In parish organizations which are not directly religious but in which it is necessary to have the priest as moderator, do you think (a) that all decisions should be left in the hands of the *priest*, (b) that *laymen* should make decisions and that the priest should not interfere unless there is some clear danger to religion, or (c) that decisions should be made by *both* together? Check: (a) ...., (b) ...., (c) ....

One extremely important aspect of parish life is the extent to which the parishioners understand and agree with the Church's teaching. Please answer the next questions according to your present understanding of the Church's teaching.

32. The following Catholic names and events consist of five pairs which are identified with each other:

I	II
1. Incarnation	a. Immaculate Conception
2. Nativity of Christ	b. Our Lord's crucifixion
3. Consecration	c. Virgin birth
4. Preservation from original sin	d. Annunciation
5. Redemption	e. the Mass

Put the letter of the correct word in Column II after each number from Column I: 1 ...., 2 ...., 3 ...., 4 ...., 5 ....

33. Do you think that the Church should make exceptions in difficult cases from its laws on (a) divorce? yes ...., no ...., don't know ...., (b) birth control? yes ...., no ...., don't know ....

34. The Church has spoken often and seriously concerning industrial and economic life. Has the Church ever said definitely that workingmen have the right to form unions? yes ...., no ...., don't know ....

35. The Church has also spoken very strongly concerning the relations between people of different races. Do you think colored people should have the same rights in the Catholic church and school as white people? yes ...., no ...., don't know .... If you lived near Jewish people whose moral life and conduct were as good as your own family's, would you encourage or discourage your children from associating with their children? discourage ...., encourage ...., neither ...., why? .... If near Puerto Rican people? discour-

age ...., encourage ...., neither ...., why? .... If near colored people? discourage ...., encourage ...., neither ...., why? ....

36. Do you think a person should be prevented from having a job or joining in other aspects of social life because he is from a different race or nation? yes ...., no ...., comment ....

37. In the busy city parish of today it is hardly possible to have the same tightly knit social relations and community spirit as in the small rural parish of the past. In view of complex city life do you think the parish should be (a) primarily a religious service station or (b) a community of people bound together by ties of religious agreement and other cooperation? Check: (a) ...., (b) ...., don't know ...., comment ....

38. The parish, as the whole Church, is supposed to influence the world about it. Do you think your parish has an influence on your neighborhood's (a) education? yes ...., no ...., don't know ....; (b) recreation? yes ...., no ...., don't know ....; (c) moral life? yes ...., no ...., don't know .... If yes, much ...., little ...., how? ....

39. Do you agree with the Church's stand on mixed marriages? yes ...., no ...., don't know .... Give two reasons for your answers.
....

40. Some persons are against change, particularly in religious matters, and others believe that some changes are sometimes necessary. Recently the pope changed the law for the Eucharistic fast, making it easier. Do you know about this change? yes ...., no .... Have you taken advantage of this change? yes ...., no .... If there were a reason for so doing, would you take advantage of it? yes ...., no ...., don't know ....

41. If private builders cannot or will not provide it, do you think the government should provide more low-cost housing for poor people? yes ...., no ...., don't know .... If your answer is yes or no, are your reasons mostly political ...., political and religious ...., neither ...., mostly religious ....

42. Do you believe that the devil is someone real? yes ...., no ...., don't know ....

43. If a patient is painfully and incurably sick, do you believe that a doctor should be permitted to give him an overdose of sleeping pills to make him die, thus easing his suffering? yes ...., no ...., don't know ....

44. Do you believe it is better for a family to raise two children in extra comfort or five children in decent but more difficult circumstances? two ...., five ...., don't know ....

PART III

In former rural and smaller parishes social relations and knowledge of everybody else was an important factor in the life of the parish itself. Today, with city parishes so large, we have less of that, but it is still important. This part of the questionnaire concerns the social relationships in the parish.

1. In how many groups, of whatever kind, are you a member? (This can include everything from sewing circles to study clubs, business or professional societies to bowling clubs.) How many? .... How many of these groups are in any direct way connected with OLM Parish? all ...., most ...., a few ...., none .... In how many of these groups are other OLM parishioners also members? all ...., most ...., a few ...., none ....

2. Do any of your relationships come from having gone to OLM parish school? yes .... (many .... few ....), no ...., having children now or recently in OLM parish school? yes .... (many .... few ....), no ....

3. Do your friendships and acquaintances include persons of much different educational background from your own? yes .... (many .... few ....), no ....; a different kind of occupation from your own? yes .... (many .... few ....), no ....; a different religion from your own? yes .... (many .... few ....), no ....; a different financial standing from your own? yes .... (many .... few ....), no ....; a different racial background from your own? yes .... (many .... few ....), no .... (This question includes acquaintances both in the parish and outside of it, if you have them.)

4. If a neighbor were sick, would you think that you should in any way help in his or her duties? yes ...., no ...., or would you think in our day and way of living such charity does not apply and that people should provide for their own help? yes ...., no ....

5. Baptism makes us all members of the mystical body of Christ and Holy Communion causes us to grow in that union. Does that fact influence your attitude toward people of other races, nations, and classes? yes ...., no ...., I haven't thought about that ....

6. Have you been in the parish a long time? yes ...., no .... Are you still a member of any of the groups of friends and acquaintances you belonged to in earlier days? yes .... (most of them .... few of them ....), no ....

7. Please name three qualities that a parish lay leader should have: (1) ...., (2) ...., (3) .... Please name three thoughts that you would suggest teaching young people who might become active in parish work and leadership: (1) ...., (2) ...., (3) ....

8. If a man, are you a member of the Holy Name Society? yes ....,
no .... If a woman, are you a member of the Altar-Rosary Society?
yes ...., no .... If not, why not? ....

PART IV

The cause of much difficulty in the city parish today is, we think, the
great number of distractions and other interests which compete for people's
attention. Of course some of these are good and some are not. This part of
the questionnaire concerns this problem.

1. Work, study (including serious reading), and play (recreation) con-
sume much of the average person's time. Is most of your work, study,
and play time spent inside or outside the parish? Work: mostly in the
parish ...., some in, some outside ...., all outside ....;
study: mostly in the parish ...., some in, some outside ...., all
outside ....; play: mostly in the parish ...., some in, some
outside ...., all outside ....

2. In general, do you think the movies shown in our neighborhood are
good for ...., bad for ...., have no influence on .... parish
life? don't know ...., other answer .... In general, do you
think other kinds of recreation in our neighborhood are good for
............., bad for ...., have no influence on .... parish life?
don't know ...., other answer ....

3. Do you think people who attend church regularly are as much interested in nonchurch matters as those who don't go to church regularly?
yes ...., no ...., don't know ....

4. The members of the Christian Family Movement and of the Cub Scouts
(and their families) are examples of decentralized groups connected
with the parish. Do you wish you could belong to some such group?
yes, ..., no ...., don't understand ....

5. Some studies show that religious practice is least good among people
in their thirties. Do you believe this is true? yes ...., no ....
If yes, why is this so? .... If no, among which age group do you
think religious practice is worst? ....

6. Some studies show that women have a better record of religious practice
than men. We also know that this is not caused by a "more religious
nature or psychology in women." Why do you think it is true? ....,
can't answer ....

PART V

1. Is there any age group or other group of people in the parish for whom
the parish could make better provision? no ...., yes .... Name
the group(s) ....

2. Have you ever tried to interest anyone in becoming a Catholic? no ...., yes .... (often .... a few times ....).

3. Charitable self-criticism can of course be very helpful. Some kinds of criticism are not. Have you ever criticized the Church or parish in front of non-Catholics? no ...., yes .... (very rarely .... several times .... often ....).

4. The parish has a good number of converts. How would you suggest even increasing the number? ....

5. How do you think the parish can get lax or lapsed Catholics back to their faith? ....

6. How do you think we can reduce the number of mixed marriages? ....

7. How many vocations from the parish do you know of? .... How do you think we can help to increase our vocations? .... Would you encourage ...., discourage .... your child's interest in a priestly or religious life? would do neither ...., don't know ....

8. What do you think college graduates should be expected to contribute to the parish? nothing special ...., don't know ...., other ....

CENSUS TAKER'S CARD

OLM 1955 CENSUS	OUR LADY OF MERCY RECTORY 2496 MARION AVENUE NEW YORK 58, N. Y.

The bearer .... is authorized by me to take up information for our parish census.

Thank you for your help!

....

Rt. Rev. Msgr. Patrick A. O'Leary—*Pastor*

(Reverse)

REMINDERS FOR OLM CENSUS TAKERS

---

1. Your aim: to report family-name and religion of every home in your assigned district. 2. Census forms go to: each Catholic family, and each home where there is a Catholic living. 3. Arrange to call back for them. 4. Be ready to help. 5. Remember: you are calling in Christ's name — and that of OLM. 6. No time for argument — only patient understanding. 7. Please ask about the questionnaire. 8. Pray before each call.

Mary Immaculate, Bless the Parish Census.

THE ROYAL McBEE KEYSORT CARD

This very serviceable keysort research card, a product of Royal McBee Company, was developed by the cooperative efforts of the company and Fordham University's Sociological Research Laboratory, especially Mr. John Cwelich of the company and Father Joseph Scheuer, C.PP.S. and Professor Frank Santopolo of the university.

More difficult to describe than to use, the keysort research cards can be quickly sorted by means of the keysorter (a tool resembling an ice pick) so as to make immediately available the cards of all persons of a certain sex, age, national background, schooling, marital status, or religious observance, and so on.

The changes made on the parish census card for the purposes of the OLM census and survey are important and should be noted. Since we expected no use to be made of the family number (bottom left of card) we were able to utilize its sixteen holes for more valuable purposes. We used three of the punches to designate ages 1 to 4, which could not be distinguished under D on the existing card. Under F, schooling, there is no place to indicate Catholic schooling; we therefore used four of the family number holes to show Catholic schooling on the elementary, secondary, collegiate, and graduate levels. Thus we were able to satisfy the parish's first request for the names of Catholic students at non-Catholic schools as reported above in Chapter 4.

Under K, occupation, changes were made to include a coding for skilled workers, the retired, the unemployed, those in military service, and such professional classes as teachers, doctors, and lawyers. Under L, number of children, the no. 3 auxiliary punch (second down from top right) was used to designate 7 children and thus raise to 13 the total number of children who could be enumerated on the card. This was not so important for the present generation of parents, but it was needed for M, the number of children in parents' marriage. For this purpose we changed the H hole to indicate a seventh child in the parents' marriage and shifted non-Catholic designation to a free hole under family number.

Under O, religious observance, we added a hole from family number to indicate the number of times Mass might have been missed in the past month. Under P, marriage status, though mixed marriage could have been ascertained through multiple use of the keysorter, we used one of the two free auxiliary holes (second and third over from top left) to designate mixed marriage indirectly. The other auxiliary hole was used to indicate lack of children on married persons' cards. These changes added significantly to the usefulness of the parish census cards.

Any addition of the cards for future use would contain other changes. Certainly some place should be made for recording membership in parish societies and length of time of residence in the parish. Other changes might be considered desirable because of special conditions prevailing in the parish, although in general a standard card suitable for use everywhere would prove useful and certainly more economical.

OUR LADY OF MERCY FEDERAL CREDIT UNION
Sixteenth Annual Meeting
THURSDAY, JANUARY 16, 1958

Dear Parishioner:

The annual meeting of your parish credit union was held on January 16th. The reports submitted by the treasurer and the chairmen of the credit and supervisory committees reveal that once again the credit union has experienced a very successful year. On the recommendation of the board of directors a dividend of three per cent was declared on shares. This represents an increase of one-half of one per cent over the dividend declared at the end of the previous year.

We should like to take this opportunity to acquaint new members of the parish with the purpose of our credit union. The credit union is a cooperative organization dedicated to the twofold purpose of promoting thrift among its members and providing them with the opportunity to negotiate loans at a low rate of interest. Members are encouraged to save by periodic investments of money in their share accounts. With the approval of the credit committee, members may borrow up to $10,000, repayable in installments over a period not to exceed three years. The limit for unsecured loans is $400 plus the balance in the member's share account. Loans in excess of this amount require security in the form of comakers, stock, bonds, bank assignments, etc. The interest rate charged is one-half of one per cent per month on the unpaid balance of the loan. This rate is lower than that charged by any bank or finance company. Loans are granted for any provident or productive purpose, e.g., medical bills, vacation expenses, education, purchase of automobiles, house repairs, consolidation of existing debts.

The credit union is open for business every Monday evening from 7:30 to 9:30 in the Parish House. Any parishioner may become a member by paying an entrance fee of twenty-five cents and investing at least five dollars in his share account. The latter sum may be paid in installments. Members of the staff will be happy to furnish further information upon request.

We look forward to a year in which more members of the parish will share in the benefits of our credit union. To the loyal members of the staff whose volunteer services make these benefits possible, we convey our sincere thanks. To Monsignor O'Leary, who provided the impetus for the organization of the credit union sixteen years ago, we are immeasurably indebted for the wise counsel and enthusiastic support under which the credit union continues to flourish.

BALANCE SHEET
December 31, 1957

ASSETS

Loans	$ 89,435.00
Cash on hand and in banks	16,254.35
U.S. government bonds	7,000.00
Saving and loan shares	45,000.00
Furniture and fixtures	200.71
Prepaid insurance	374.57
Other assets	561.58
	$ 158,826.21

LIABILITIES

Shares	$ 137,458.28
Regular reserve	9,764.07
Undivided earnings	11,603.86
	$ 158,826.21

STATISTICAL INFORMATION

	Number	Amount
Accounts, December 31, 1957	778	—
Loans made during 1957	255	$ 118,435.00
Loans made since organization	3885	1,204,622.92
Loans charged off since organization	—	1,234.55

BIBLIOGRAPY

Agato, C. D'. *Statistica religiosa*. Milan: Giffre, 1943.

American Catholic Hierarchy. "Religion: Our Most Vital National Asset." *Catholic Mind* 51:56-64, January 1953.

Azevedo, Thales de. "Catholicism in Brazil." *Thought* 28:253-74, Summer 1953.

Aznar, Severino. *La revolucion española y las vocaciones eclesiasticas*. Madrid: Instituto de Estudios Politicos, 1949.

Bertolotti, G. *Statistica ecclesiastica d'Italia*. Savona, 1885.

Bier, William C. *A Comparative Study of a Seminary Group and Four Other Groups on the Minnesota Multiphasic Personality Inventory*. Washington: The Catholic University of America Press, 1948.

———— "Practical Requirements of a Program for Psychological Screening of Candidates." *Review for Religious* 13:13-27, January 1954.

———— "Psychological Testing of Candidates and the Theology of Vocations." *Review for Religious* 12:291-304, November 1953.

Blow, Richard. "The Sociology of Religion in Latin America." *American Catholic Sociological Review* 15:161-75, June 1954.

Boulard, Fernand. *Essor ou declin du clergé français?* Paris: Editions du Cerf, 1950.

———— *Paroisses urbaines, paroisses rurales*. Tournai: Casterman, 1957.

———— "La pratique religieuse dans le diocèse de Rennes." *Connaître une population*. Special issue of *Economie et humanisme*, nos. 2-3.

———— *Premiers itinéraires en sociologie religieuse*. Paris: Editions Ouvrières—Economie et Humanisme, 1954.

———— *Problèmes missionaires de la France rurale*. 2 vols. Paris: Editions du Cerf, 1945.

Brochard, Louis. *Saint-Gervais: histoire de la paroisse*. Paris: Firmin-Didot, 1950.

Brongniart, Marcel. *La paroisse Saint-Médard au Faubourg Saint-Marceau*. Paris: Editions Picard, 1951.

"The Census Debate." *America* 97:498, August 17, 1957.

Le Centre d'Etudes Sociales Godefroid Kurth. *La déchristianisation des masses prolétariennes*. Tournai: Casterman, 1948.

Chairneau, V.-L. *Documentation préalable a l'étude sociologique de la pratique du culte catholique dans le départment de Seine et Marne, 1944-1949*. Meaux, 1950.

Chelini, J. *Génèse et évolution d'une paroisse suburbaine marseillaise*. Marseille: Saint-Léon, 1953.

Ciesluk, Joseph E. *National Parishes in the United States*. Washington: The Catholic University of America Press, 1944.

Clarke, Thomas. *Parish Societies*. Washington: The Catholic University of America Press, 1943.

Conant, James. *Science and Common Sense*. New Haven: Yale University Press, 1951.

Coninck, Léon de. *Problèmes de l'adaptation en apostolat*. Paris: Casterman, 1949.

Coogan, Thomas F. *Catholic Fertility in Florida*. Washington: The Catholic University of America Press, 1946.

Cox, John F. *A Thomistic Analysis of the Social Order*. Washington: The Catholic University of America Press, 1943.

Culver, Dwight W. *Negro Segregation in the Methodist Church*. New Haven: Yale University Press, 1953.

Cushing, Richard Cardinal. "Address to Third Regional Congress." In *The Call of the Popes to the Laity*, pp. 13-18. Paterson: Confraternity Publications, 1948.

Daniel, Yvan. *Aspects de la pratique religieuse à Paris*. Paris: Editions Ouvrières, 1952.

Delaa, Leo and others. "The Changes in Religious Life in Spain during the Last Twenty Years." *Lumen vitae* 6:104-18, January-June 1951.

Delacroix, Simon. "Parish Inquiries in France." *American Catholic Sociological Review* 13:169-73, October 1952.

Deutsch, Morton and Mary Collins. *Interracial Housing*. Minneapolis: The University of Minnesota Press, 1951.

Donovan, John D. "American Catholic Sociologists and the Sociology of Religion." *American Catholic Sociological Review* 15:104-14, June 1954.

———— "The Sociologist Looks at the Parish." *American Catholic Sociological Review* 11:66-73, June 1950.

Droulers, Paul and Antoine Rimoldi. "Religious Sociology in Italy." *Lumen vitae* 6:75-91, January-June 1951.

Drucker, Peter F. *The Future of Industrial Man.* New York: John Day Company, 1942.

Falardeau, Jean. Reviews of *Southern Parish* and *Sociology of the Parish. American Journal of Sociology* 60:308-10, November 1954.

Fesselman, David H. *Transitions in the Development of a Downtown Parish.* Washington: The Catholic University of America Press, 1952.

Fichter, Joseph H. "Catholics in the United States." *America* 82:523-24, February 4, 1950.

———— *Parochial School: A Sociological Study.* Notre Dame: University of Notre Dame Press, 1958.

———— *Social Relations in the Urban Parish.* Chicago: The University of Chicago Press, 1954.

———— *Southern Parish. Volume I: Dynamics of a City Church.* Chicago: The University of Chicago Press, 1951.

———— *Soziologie der Pfarrgruppen: Untersuchungen zur Struktur und Dynamik der Gruppen einer Deutschen Pfarrei.* Münster: Aschendorff, 1958.

———— "Urban Mobility and Religious Observance." *American Catholic Sociological Review* 11:130-39, October 1950.

Fitzpatrick, Joseph P. "Catholic Responsibilities in Sociology." *Thought* 26:384-96, Autumn 1951.

———— "Catholics and Scientific Knowledge of Society." *American Catholic Sociological Review* 15:2-8, March 1954.

Font-Reaulx, Jacques de. *L'église de Crest: Sa construction, cent ans d'histoire paroissiale, 1846-1946.* Crest: Imprimèrie Veziant, 1947.

Furfey, Paul Hanly. "The Missionary Role of the Parish." In C. Joseph Nuesse and Thomas J. Harte, editors, *Sociology of the Parish.* Milwaukee: Bruce Publishing Company, 1951.

Furfey, Paul Hanly. *The Scope and Method of Sociology*. New York: Harper and Brothers, 1953.

Gasquet, Aidan. *Parish Life in Mediaeval England*. London: Methuen, 1906.

George, Gordon. "Some Sociologists out of Bounds." *America* 92:397-98, January 15, 1955.

Gibbons, William, editor. *Basic Ecclesiastical Statistics for Latin America—1954*. Maryknoll: World Horizons Press, 1955.

Godefroy, Jan. *De Toekomst van de Academisch Gegradueerden Opnieuw Beschouwd*. The Hague: Catholic Institute of Socio-Ecclesiastical Research.

Godin, Henri. *La France, pays de mission?* Paris: Editions du Cerf, 1943.

Goguel, François. *Géographie des élections françaises de 1870 à 1951*. Paris: La Fondation des Sciences Politiques, 1951.

Grasso, Pier Giovanni. *Elementi di sociologia religiosa*. Turin: Gili, 1953.

Grond, Linus and others. *Bericht 1, Die Wiener Pfarren von 1932-1952; Bericht 3, Einige vorläufige Ziffern bezüglich der Situation der Weltpriester in einigen oesterreichischen Diözesen;* and *Bericht 10, Zur Wiener Stadt und Kirchenplanung*. Vienna, 1952.

Gros, Lucien. *La pratique religieuse dans le diocèse de Marseille*. Paris: Editions Ouvrières, 1954.

Gurvitch, Georges and Wilbert Moore, editors. *Twentieth Century Sociology*. New York: The Philosophical Library, 1945.

Herberg, Will. *Protestant-Catholic-Jew*. New York: Doubleday and Company, 1955.

Homans, George. *The Human Group*. New York: Harcourt, Brace and Company, 1950.

Houtart, François. "Faut-il abandonner la paroisse dans la ville moderne?" *Nouvelle revue théologique* 77:602-13, June 1955.

———— *The Parishes of Chicago*. (mimeographed) Chicago, 1953.

———— *Les paroisses de Bruxelles, 1803-1951*. Louvain: Institut des Recherches Economiques et Sociales, 1955.

Hughes, Everett C. *French Canada in Transition*. Chicago: The University of Chicago Press, 1943.

Hurtado, Alberto. *Es Chile un pais catolico?* Santiago: Editorial Splendor.

Katholiek Amsterdam: Schets van zijn Kerkelijke en sociale Ontwikkeling. The Hague: Catholic Institute of Socio-Ecclesiastical Research, 1954.

Kelly, George A. *Catholics and Practice of the Faith.* Washington: The Catholic University of America Press, 1946.

Kerkhofs, J. *Godsdienstpraktijk en sociaal Milieu.* Brussels: Lumen Vitae, 1953.

Labbens, Jean. *Les 99 autres . . . ou l'église aussi recensé.* Lyons: Vitte, 1954.

Le Bras, Gabriel. *Collection de sociologie contemporaine.* 2 vols. Paris: Presses Universitaires de France, 1954.

———— *Introduction à l'histoire de la pratique religieuse en France.* 2 vols. Paris: Presses Universitaires de France, 1942, 1945.

Le Bret, L.-J. *Guide pratique de l'enquête sociale.* 2 vols. Paris: Presses Universitaires de France, 1951-1952.

Leclercq, Jacques. "Les problèmes de la sociologie religieuse." *Bulletin de L'Institut des Recherches Economiques et Sociales de L'Université de Louvain* 13:683-93, June 1948.

Leoni, Aldo. *Sociologia e geografia di una diocesi.* Rome: Gregorian University, 1952.

Leplae, Claire. *Pratique religieuse et milieux sociaux.* Louvain: Institut des Recherches Economiques et Sociales, 1949.

Ligier, Simon. *L'adulte des milieux ouvriers. Volume 2, Essai de psychologie pastorale.* Paris: Editions Ouvrières, 1951.

———— *Recherches sociologiques sur la pratique religieuse du Jura.* 4 vols. (mimeographed) Lons-le-Saulnier: Jules-Ferry, 1951.

Ligutti, Luigi G. *A Survey of Catholic Weakness.* Des Moines: National Catholic Rural Life Conference, 1948.

Loomis, Charles P. and J. Allan Beegle. *Rural Social Systems.* New York: Prentice-Hall, 1950.

McCaffrey, Augustine. *Youth in a Catholic Parish.* Washington: The Catholic University of America Press, 1941.

MacIver, Robert M. and Charles H. Page. *Society: An Introductory Analysis.* New York: Rinehart and Company, 1949.

Mensching, G. *Sociologie religieuse: Le rôle de la religion dans les relations communautaires des humains,* translated by Pierre Jundt. Paris: Payot, 1951.

Michonneau, George. *Revolution in a City Parish.* Westminster: Newman Press, 1952.

Michonneau, Georges and H. C. Chery. *Paroisse, communauté missionaire.* Paris: Editions du Cerf, 1945. Published in English by Newman Press (1950) under the title *The Missionary Spirit in Parish Life.*

Miner, Horace. *Saint-Denis, a French Canadian Parish.* Chicago: The University of Chicago Press, 1938.

Mols, R. "Croissance et limites de la sociologie religieuse." *Nouvelle revue théologique* 77:144-62, 263-81, February, March 1955.

Mugrauer, Bertha. "Variations in the Pastoral Role in France." *American Catholic Sociological Review* 11:15-24, March 1950.

Mulvaney, Bernard. "Catholic Population Revealed in Catholic Baptisms." *American Ecclesiastical Review* 133:183-93, September 1955.

Nuesse, C. Joseph and Thomas J. Harte, editors. *Sociology of the Parish.* Milwaukee: Bruce Publishing Company, 1951.

O'Dea, Thomas. "The Sociology of Religion." *American Catholic Sociological Review* 15:73-103, June 1954.

Odell, Clarence B. "The Distribution and Age of the World's Largest Cities." *Annals of the Association of American Geographers* 40: 139-40, June 1950.

Oesterreichs Bevölkerung in Bild und Zahl. Vienna: Oesterreichischen Statistischen Zentralamt, 1953.

La paroisse: cellule sociale. Montreal: Institut Social Populaire, 1953.

Peiro, Francisco. *El apostolado seglar.* Seville, 1933.

——— *El problema religioso-social en España.* Madrid: Razon y Fe, 1936.

Perenna, R. *Innovazione e rinnovamento della Parrochia.* Como, 1950.

Perrot, Jean. *Grenoble: essai de sociologie religieuse.* Grenoble: Centre d'Etudes des Complexes Sociaux, 1954.

Die Pfarre: Gestalt und Sendung. Wien: Herder, 1953.

Pin, Emile. *Pratique religieuse et classes sociales dans une paroisse urbaine Saint-Pothin à Lyon.* Paris: Editions Spes, 1956.

Pius XII. *Christian Worship: Encyclical Letter (Mediator Dei) of His Holiness Pius XII* [1947], translated by G. D. Smith. London: Catholic Truth Society.

———— *The Unity of Human Society (Summi pontificatus)* [1939]. New York: America Press.

Quoist, Michel. *La ville et l'homme.* Paris: Editions Ouvrières, 1952.

Rapport over de binnenstad Rotterdam. The Hague: Catholic Institute of Socio-Ecclesiastical Research.

"Religion in the Census." *Commonweal* 66:438, August 2, 1957.

Ross, Eva. "The Sociology of Religion in France Today." *American Catholic Sociological Review* 11:12-14, March 1950.

Rossi, G. de. "Cio che possono dire i dati statistici di una parrochia." Milan: Vita e Pensiero, 1914-1915.

Roy, Maurice. *The Parish and Democracy in French Canada.* Toronto: University of Toronto Press, 1950.

Ryckmans, A. "Qu'est-ce qu'un catholique pratiquant?" *Nouvelle revue théologique* 76:965-72, November 1954.

Salazar, Maria Cristina. *A Socio-Religious Survey of the Parish of Cristo Rey in Manizales, Colombia.* Washington: The Catholic University of America Press, 1957.

Sarabia, Raymond. *España . . . ; es catolica?* Madrid: El Pepetuo Socorro, 1939.

Schmitt-Eglin, Paul. *Le mécanisme de la déchristianisation.* Paris: Editions Alsatia, 1952.

Schnepp, Gerald J. *Leakage from a Catholic Parish.* Washington: The Catholic University of America Press, 1942.

———— "Nationality and Leakage." *American Catholic Sociological Review* 3:154-63, October 1942.

Schuyler, Joseph B. "Elements of Organization and Disorganization in Northern Parish." *American Catholic Sociological Review* 18:98-112, June 1957.

———— "The Parish Studied as a Social System." *American Catholic Sociological Review* 17:320-37, December 1956.

———— "Religious Behavior in Northern Parish: A Study in Motivating Values." *American Catholic Sociological Review* 19:134-44, June 1958.

Shaughnessy, Gerald. *Has the Immigrant Kept the Faith?* New York: The Macmillan Company, 1929.

Spencer, A. E. C. W.; E. Mellon; and W. N. T. Roberts. *Youth and Religion.* London: Young Catholic Workers, 1958.

Stouffer, Samuel A. and others. *The American Soldier.* Princeton: Princeton University Press, 1949.

Structures sociales et pastorale paroissiale. Paris: Union des Oeuvres Catholiques de France, 1948.

Suhard, Emmanuel Cardinal. *The Church Today: The Collected Writings of Emmanuel Cardinal Suhard.* Chicago: Fides Publishers, 1953.

Swoboda, Heinrich. *Grossstadtseelsorge.* Regensburg: Pustet, 1911.

Thomas, John F. "Family and the Parish." *Social Order,* new series, 1:291-96, September 1951.

Timasheff, Nicholas S. "The Basic Concepts of Sociology." *American Journal of Sociology* 58:176-86, September 1952.

United States Census of Housing 1950, Block Statistics, New York City. Washington: Government Printing Office, 1950.

United States Census of Population 1950, Census Tract Statistics, New York, N. Y. Washington: Government Printing Office, 1950.

Ut vitam habeant. Rome: A. V. E., 1935.

Virton, P. *Enquêtes de sociologie paroissiale.* Paris: Editions Spes, 1953.

Vivere in Christo. Milan: Treviso, 1940.

Wach, Joachim. *Sociology of Religion.* Chicago: The University of Chicago Press, 1944.

———— "Sociology of Religion." In Georges Gurvitch and Wilbert Moore, editors, *Twentieth Century Sociology.* New York: The Philosophical Library, 1945.

Weber, Gerard P. *Chaplain's Manual: Christian Family Movement.* Chicago: Chicago Federation of the Christian Family Movement, 1952.

Wilson, Logan and William Kolb. *Sociological Analysis.* New York: Harcourt, Brace and Company, 1949.

Yinger, J. Milton. *Religion in the Struggle for Power: A Study in the Sociology of Religion.* Durham: The Duke University Press, 1946.

———— *Religion, Society and the Individual.* New York: The Macmillan Company, 1957.

Zeegers, George and Jan Godefroy. *Demographie en Gezinspolitiek*. The
Hague: Catholic Institute of Socio-Ecclesiastical Research.
——— and A. Oldendorff. *Sociografische Aspecten van de Emigratie*.
The Hague: Catholic Institute of Socio-Ecclesiastical Research.
——— and others. *Artsenbehoefte en Artsenvoorziening, 1950-52*. The
Hague: Catholic Institute of Socio-Ecclesiastical Research.